TEACHING FREUD

D1473849

American Academy of Religion
TEACHING RELIGIOUS STUDIES SERIES

SERIES EDITOR
Susan Henking, Hobart and William Smith Colleges

A Publication Series of
the American Academy of Religion
and Oxford University Press

Teaching Lévi-Strauss
Edited by Hans H. Penner

Teaching Islam
Edited by Brannon M. Wheeler

Teaching Freud
Edited by Diane Jonte-Pace

Teaching Freud

EDITED BY DIANE JONTE-PACE

UNIVERSITY PRESS

2003

OXFORD

UNIVERSITY PRESS

Oxford   New York
Auckland   Bangkok   Buenos Aires   Cape Town   Chennai
Dar es Salaam   Delhi   Hong Kong   Istanbul   Karachi   Kolkata
Kuala Lumpur   Madrid   Melbourne   Mexico City   Mumbai   Nairobi
São Paolo   Shanghai   Taipei   Tokyo   Toronto

Copyright © 2003 by The American Academy of Religion

Published by Oxford University Press, Inc.
198 Madison Avenue, New York, New York 10016

www.oup.com

Oxford is a registered trademark of Oxford University Press

All rights reserved. No part of this publication may be reproduced,
stored in a retrieval system, or transmitted, in any form or by any means,
electronic, mechanical, photocopying, recording, or otherwise,
without the prior permission of Oxford University Press.

Library of Congress Cataloging-in-Publication Data
Teaching Freud / edited by Diane Jonte-Pace.
p.   cm. — (AAR teaching religious studies)
Includes bibliographical references and index.
ISBN 0-19-515768-0; ISBN 0-19-515769-9 (pbk.)
   1. Freud, Sigmund, 1856–1939.   2. Psychiatry and religion.   I. Jonte-Pace, Diane E.
(Diane Elizabeth).   II. Series.
BF175.4.R44   T43   2003
150.19'52'0711—dc21   2002071526

9   8   7   6   5   4   3   2   1

Printed in the United States of America
on acid-free paper

To my students and colleagues,
for teaching me new ways to read Freud,
to read culture, and to read myself

Contents

Contributors

KIRK A. BINGAMAN is Adjunct Professor of Pastoral Care and Counseling at San Francisco Theological Seminary. An ordained Presbyterian minister, he also has a clinical practice in pastoral counseling and is the Director of Satellite Offices for the Lloyd Center Pastoral Counseling Service in San Anselmo, California. His book, *Freud and Faith: Living in the Tension*, is forthcoming.

DONALD CAPPS is William Harte Felmeth Professor of Pastoral Theology at Princeton Theological Seminary. His recent books include *Men, Religion, and Melancholia* (1997), *Living Stories* (1998), *Social Phobia* (1999), and *Jesus: A Psychological Biography* (2000). He has served as editor of the *Journal for the Scientific Study of Religion* and as president of the Society for the Scientific Study of Religion. He has also served as a member of the editorial board of the *Religious Studies Review*.

CAROL DELANEY is Associate Professor of Cultural and Social Anthropology at Stanford University. Her publications include *The Seed and the Soil: Gender and Cosmology in Turkish Village Society* (1991), *Naturalizing Power: Essays in Feminist Cultural Analysis*, coedited with Sylvia Yanagisako (1995), and *Abraham on Trial: The Social Legacy of Biblical Myth* (1998). She has served as a member of the editorial board of the *Religious Studies Review*.

JAMES E. DITTES is Professor of Pastoral Theology and Psychology at Yale University, where he has been on the faculty since 1955, appointed jointly to the Divinity school, the Department of Psychology, and the Department of Religious Studies, which he has chaired. He has served as editor of the *Journal for the Scientific Study of Religion* and as executive secretary and president of the Society for the Scientific Study of Religion. His most recent books are *Driven by Hope: Men and Meaning* (1996) and a textbook, *Pastoral Counseling: The Basics*.

SANDRA LEE DIXON is Associate Professor of Psychology of Religion in the Department of Religious Studies at the University of Denver. She teaches a course on religion and psychobiography, as well as core curriculum courses dealing with Freud and Augustine. She is the author of *Augustine: The Scattered and Gathered Self* (1999), a psychological and cultural study of Augustine. She wrote her doctoral dissertation at the University of Chicago on psychological and cultural dimensions of Augustine's moral arguments for coercing the religious practice of the Donatist splinter-group of the Christian church.

VOLNEY GAY is Professor and Chair of Religion, Professor of Psychiatry, and Professor of Anthropology at Vanderbilt University. He is a Training and Supervising Analyst at the St. Louis Psychoanalytic Institute. He serves on the editorial boards of several scholarly journals. He is also vice-chair of the Committee on Research and Special Training, American Psychoanalytic Association. His book *Freud on Sublimation* (1992) won the Heinz Hartmann Award from the New York Psychoanalytic Institute. His book *Joy and the Objects of Psychoanalysis* was published in 2001.

JAY GELLER is Senior Lecturer of Modern Jewish Culture at Vanderbilt University and Fulbright/Sigmund Freud Society Visiting Scholar of Psychoanalysis in Vienna. He has published numerous articles and chapters examining the relationships among gender, sexuality, and representations of Jews (especially Jewish bodies) in Freud's works. He also writes on the construction of Jewish identity since the Enlightenment and on German-Jewish figures, such as Heine, Kafka, and Benjamin.

JANET LIEBMAN JACOBS is Professor of Women's Studies at the University of Colorado at Boulder. She is the author of several books and edited collections, including *Divine Disenchantment: Deconverting from New Religions* (1989), *Religion, Society, and Psychoanalysis* (1997), and *Victimized Daughters: Incest and the Development of the Female* (1994). Her articles have appeared in *Journal for the Scientific Study of Religion*, *Signs*, and *Sociology of Religion*. She has spent the last few years studying modern descendants of the Spanish Crypto-Jews, and her book on the subject is forthcoming.

DIANE JONTE-PACE is Professor of Religious Studies and Associate Vice Provost for Faculty Development at Santa Clara University. She serves as chair of the editorial board of the *Religious Studies Review*. Her publications include *Speaking the Unspeakable: Religion, Misogyny, and the Uncanny Mother in Freud's Cultural Texts* (2001) and *Religion and Psychology: Mapping the Terrain*, coedited with William Parsons (2001).

JEFFREY J. KRIPAL is the Lynette S. Autry Associate Professor of Religious Studies at Rice University. His publications include *Kali's Child: The Mystical and the Erotic in the Life and Teachings of Ramakrishna* (1995), which won the American Academy of Religion's History of Religions Prize; *Vishnu on Freud's Desk: A Reader in Psychoanalysis and Hinduism* (1998), which he coedited with T. G. Vaidyanathan of Bangalore, India; and *Roads of Excess, Palaces of Wisdom: Eroticism and Reflexivity in the Study of Mysticism* (2001).

WILLIAM PARSONS is Associate Professor of Religious Studies and Chair of the Department of Religion at Rice University. He is the author of *The Enigma of the Oceanic Feeling* (1999) and coeditor with Diane Jonte-Pace of *Religion and Psychology: Mapping the Terrain* (2001). His articles have appeared in numerous journals and edited books, including the *Journal of Religion* and *Vishnu on Freud's Desk: A Reader in Psychoanalysis and Hinduism* (1998).

MARY ELLEN ROSS is Associate Professor of Religious Studies at Trinity University. She has published in the fields of ethics, the psychoanalytic study of religion, and feminist theory. She is the coeditor with Paula Cooey and Sharon Farmer of *Embodied Love: Sensuality and Relationship as Feminist Values* (1987). Her essay "The Humanities of the Gods: The Future and Past of Freud's Psychoanalytic Interpretation of Religion" appeared in *Sigmund Freud and His Impact on the Modern World*, edited by Jerome A. Weiner and James William Anderson (2001).

ROBERT A. SEGAL is Professor of Theories of Religion, University of Lancaster, U.K. He previously taught in the United States at Reed College, Stanford University, and Tulane University. He is the author of *The Poimandres as Social Sciences* (1986), *Joseph Campbell* (1990/1997), *Religion and the Social Sciences* (1989), *Explaining and Interpreting Religion* (1992), and *Theorizing about Myth* (1999). He is the editor of *In Quest of the Hero* (1990), *The Gnostic Jung* (1992), *The Allure of Gnosticism* (1995), *The Myth and Ritual Theory* (1998), *Jung on Mythology* (1998), and *Hero Myths* (2000). He is European Editor of *Religion*.

ERNEST WALLWORK is Professor of Ethics at Syracuse University and has a private practice as a psychoanalyst in Washington, D.C. He is the author of *Psychoanalysis and Ethics* (1991) and *Durkheim: Morality and Milieu* (1972), which was nominated for a National Book Award. Wallwork is coeditor of *Critical Issues in Modern Religion* (1990).

TEACHING FREUD

Introduction: Teaching Freud and Religion

Diane Jonte-Pace

Both education and psychoanalysis, Freud warned in "Analysis Terminable and Interminable," are "'impossible' professions" in which "one can be sure beforehand of achieving unsatisfactory results."[1] In spite of his understanding of the unsatisfactory consequences of psychoanalysis, Freud did not turn aside from his own impossible profession. Nor do the authors in this volume turn aside from theirs: all are educators; all teach psychoanalysis in some form; and, compounding the "impossibilities," most teach courses on Freud in departments of religious studies.

The contributors to this volume are both teachers and scholars: all have contributed in significant ways to the literature on psychoanalysis and religion. This volume provides an opportunity for these teaching scholars to articulate something we seldom write about: how we teach Freud and religion; how we integrate our scholarly lives with our pedagogical lives; how we live and work with the impossibilities of our professions.

The contributors to this volume were invited to describe their courses on Freud and religion. They were encouraged to focus on the academic contexts within which they teach; to articulate their pedagogical goals, assumptions, and practices; and to explain their methods of integrating scholarship and pedagogy. The intent was to produce a volume as useful to the new professor constructing a first course on Freud in religious studies as it would be to the more seasoned professor interested in incorporating new ideas and pedagogical methods into a well-established course. The result is a collection that admirably fulfills this intention and, in fact, goes well beyond it: not only are the essays discussions of how we teach Freud but they are also scholarly contributions to the "Freud and religion" literature. In addition, they are written in a style that will be accessible to students.

Each chapter is a thoughtful, informative, and often quite personal account of our courses, our departments, our students, and our universities. The contributors describe, in lively and engaging essays, their scholarly and pedagogical engagements with Freud as a critic and interpreter of religion; as a Jew in an anti-semitic milieu; as an architect of contemporary culture; as a creator of the modern, postmodern, or gendered self; and as a subject, particularly in the last few years, of acrimonious debate.

Why Teach Freud?

There are a number of reasons that scholars in religious studies teach Freud today. First, his influence on our culture is undeniable. He is clearly one of the architects of modernity. His ideas are almost omnipresent in our culture, our ideologies and institutions: our assumptions about self and society, health and pathology, gender and sexuality are infused with Freudian concepts. Freud developed a discourse of emotions, motivations, and instincts that has sculpted our sense of who we are as human beings, both intrapsychically and interpersonally. He developed the therapeutic practice to which most forms of psychotherapy and counseling trace their origins. His ideas are referenced in film, television, advertising, and popular culture. To understand our culture, we need to understand Freud: cultural studies cannot avoid psychoanalytic studies.

Within religious studies, the contributors to this volume argue, it is vitally important to teach Freud. A century ago Freud was one of the central instigators of the debate over secularism and religion in modernity. His critique of religion continues to resonate in contemporary controversies and conversations in culture at large. It is prominent as well in the current discussion of the role of religion—and the history of the study of religion—in the universities.[2] As we "teach the debates" (Graff 1993)[3] shaping culture, the academy, and the field of religious studies, we inevitably turn to Freud, the prototypical critic of religion.

Freud was not only a *critic* of religion, he was also an *analyst* of religion. If the major thinkers in religious studies ask "What is religion and how might we best understand it?" Freud is surely a paradigmatic cartographer of that terrain. He was one of the first theorists to explore the unconscious fantasies, fears, and desires underlying religious ideas and practices. As scholars of religion we cannot ignore him. We read him not merely as an historical or methodological relic of early twentieth-century scholarship—a grandparent of religious studies, as it were—but rather as a theorist who continues to articulate pressing questions about how to understand religion today.

Thus if we teach the debates over religion and secularism, we find ourselves teaching Freud's critique of religion; if we examine the ways we understand religion, we find ourselves teaching Freud's inquiries into the nature of religion. If we raise profound questions about "who we are" as cultural beings, as gendered, embodied beings, and as psychological or spiritual beings, we find ourselves teaching Freud. Indeed, as Peter Gay (1999) has said, "today we all speak Freud."

Although "we all speak Freud" in our self-concepts and social practices, Freud's legacy is deeply contested. His reputation is perhaps at its lowest point since he came to public attention a century ago. *Time* magazine asked in the mid-1990s, "Is Freud Dead?" Freud's current "archrival" Frederick Crews (1997, 1998) issues frequent barrages against psychoanalytic theory and practice. Freud is accused of sloppy scholarship, unethical practices, and pseudo-scientific claims: his critics charge that his Oedipal theory was generated in an attempt to cover up the tragic realities of incest and that his therapeutic methods and theories led to the proliferation of problematic cases of false memory syndrome. Advancements in neuroscience have thrown into question his dream theories; empirical study is unable to demonstrate the superior efficacy of psychoanalysis over other therapeutic practices; and feminists challenge his views of gender. Our students are often aware that Freud is under attack. Whether they are seminary students angry at Freud for his atheism, undergraduate students resistant to new forms of self-knowledge, or psychology majors who have been taught that Freud was wrong or irrelevant, they often come to our classes ready to reject and dismiss his views.

Indeed, how *can* we teach Freud in our religious studies courses when he is so thoroughly rejected by our students and by others? Nearly every contributor to this volume addresses in some way the contemporary critique of Freud and/ or the resistance to Freud among students. Some contributors join in the critique; others express ongoing ambivalence; still others bracket the critique. Many acknowledge that some of the critiques of Freud may be legitimate—yet most maintain the significance of his insights into instincts, drives, and unconscious wishes; into the effects of the family dynamics of early childhood on later personality structure; and into the ways that psyche and culture intersect.

Other contributors defend Freud in specific ways: some suggest, in response to the attack on Freud's scientific credentials, that he is better viewed as a theorist who borrowed the best scientific ideas of his day, rather than as a scientist manqué. Volney Gay argues that the critics who blame Freud for promoting false memory syndrome have misunderstood his notion of psychic reality. Ernest Wallwork responds to the critics concerned with Freud's ethics by demonstrating a larger moral trajectory in his work. Kirk Bingaman articulates (through a discussion of the work of Judith Van Herik) a feminist defense of Freud, showing that his ideas contribute to the feminist project of uncovering structures of misogyny in culture. The words of poet W. H. Auden (1966), written in 1939 as a eulogy for Freud upon his death, characterize the views of many in this collection:

> . . . if often he was wrong and, at times, absurd,
> to us he is no more a person
> now but a whole climate of opinion
> under whom we conduct our different lives.

Freud is "a whole climate of opinion" now. He cannot be dismissed in our classrooms or our culture. We learn more about ourselves and our world when we study Freud—even when we study his mistakes.

Structure and Organization

The essays in this collection are arranged in four broad groupings. Part I, "Institutional and Curricular Contexts," focuses on the undergraduate, graduate, and "multicultural" institutions in which the contributors teach. Part II, "Teaching Freud as Interpreter of Religious Texts and Practices," focuses on psychoanalytic interpretations of religious figures—Ramakrishna, Jesus, and Augustine—and religious phenomena, myth, and mysticism. Part III, "Teaching the Controversies," introduces major debates in the field: two essays address feminism, gender, patriarchy, Judaism, and ethnicity; a third explores Freud's interpretations of ritual, mysticism, and Moses, alongside those of his challengers and successors. Part IV, "Teaching the Teachings, Teaching the Practice," contains essays describing psychoanalysis as a powerful pedagogy of transformation and insight.

Part I. Institutional and Curricular Context

The first group of essays takes as a central focus the institutional and curricular contexts in which we teach. Diane Jonte-Pace situates the discussion of her course in the context of the Jesuit institution primarily for undergraduates, where she has taught for more than fifteen years. She describes the university, its commitment to Catholicism, its core curriculum, the place of religious studies in the core, and its students. She argues that we must ask who our students are, how they reflect or represent our institutions, and how we can speak in their language as we invite them to consider new ways of thinking about something they resist. She describes a course in which Freud's life, ideas, and legacy are examined from four perspectives: the interpretation of religion; the critique of religion; the intersections of life and theory; and the cultural and theological responses—both positive and negative—to psychoanalysis. By speaking the language of the students—and the language of the institution in which she teaches—she initiates a conversation in which students discover not only that they "speak Freud" with some fluency but also that they know several Freuds. They discover that they themselves are participants in the deeply psychoanalytic discourse of modernity.

Jay Geller describes an introductory course in religious studies at Vanderbilt University in which attention to Freud's Jewishness provides a way of inquiring into the multiculturalism of the American university. As a Jewish postcolonial subject of the Austro-Hungarian Empire, Freud constructed a discourse that became part of normative hegemonic Euro-American ideology. At the same time, Freud's discourse was subversive of the authority of that ideology. Geller shows that teaching students how to read *Moses and*

Monotheism and an array of accompanying texts by interrogating the anomalies, repetitions, and omissions in the texts is simultaneously a process of teaching students "how to read Freud" and "how to read culture." He makes visible the complex forces characterizing the multicultural university itself.

Kirk Bingaman describes the resistance to Freud he encountered in a seminary course for ministry students at the Graduate Theological Union in Berkeley, California. Student disinterest, apathy, and anger toward Freud, he suggests, are generated by psychical splitting and fear. Drawing from the methodological strategies of Ana Maria Rizzuto, Paul Ricoeur, and Judith Van Herik, Bingaman shows that Freud has much to offer to seminarians who choose to work through, rather than around, the complexities that arise when faith and Freud are held together in dialectical tension. Students who begin the course with anger over Freud's atheism can sometimes move toward a Ricoeurian toleration of emotional ambivalence—such students are better prepared for ministry in a postmodern world shaped by the gendered dynamics made visible in Van Herik's reading.

Volney Gay describes a graduate course on Freud's ideas and methods for psychiatry residents, graduate students in religious studies, and pastoral counselors at Vanderbilt University, noting the divergent needs and expectations brought to the course by each group. Focusing on Freud's discovery of "psychical reality," he examines the polarizing debates over false memory syndrome emerging from the misunderstanding of the notion of psychical reality. Gay emphasizes the challenges for the teacher embodied in the nearly inevitable fear of contemplating unknown parts of the self. Comparing religious methods of embracing change and self-knowledge with therapeutic methods, he proposes that both are capable of generating a kind of optimism toward an unknown future: Freud, in particular, provided new methods and new vocabularies to carry us beyond the refusal to know. Gay outlines a series of stages in the process of developing expertise, drawing parallels between the experiences of therapist and teacher. Progress can be traced from the stage of "novice," to "advanced beginner," to "competence," to "proficiency," and finally to "expertise." Although his essay might have been located in Part IV, "Teaching the Teachings," I've situated it in Part I because of its provocative reflections on graduate teaching, the diversity of student expectations, and the stages of development in a teacher's career.

Part II. Teaching Freud as Interpreter
of Religious Texts and Practices

Part II contains essays that are interpretive: they apply psychoanalytic insights and methods to religious phenomena. William Parsons, in "'Let Him Rejoice in the Roseate Light!': Teaching Psychoanalysis and Mysticism," describes a course on the psychoanalytic interpretation of mysticism. Parsons deconstructs the received view of Freud's theory of mysticism as a regressive return to pre-Oedipal merger. He offers instead an innovative interpretation of Freud's provocative chapter on mysticism in *Civilization and Its Discontents*, reading *Civilization* alongside Freud's correspondence with Romain Rolland. He shows how the two theorists anticipated each of the major psychoanalytic approaches to mysticism that would be developed more clearly in later years: the reductive approach, the adaptive approach, and the transformational approach. He concludes by presenting to his students a set of psychobiographical studies of the Hindu saint and mystic Ramakrishna, encouraging the students to appreciate the diversity of psychoanalytic readings of mysticism.

With Donald Capps's essay we turn to an imagined course on Jesus and psychoanalysis. Having just completed a book on this topic, Capps describes a course, at Princeton Theological Seminary based on the book. Acknowledging the limitations of our knowledge of the life of the historical Jesus, Capps nevertheless suggests that we can say with certainty that Jesus was "fatherless": he was not embedded in the paternal and patriarchal structures of honor that characterized his society. Capps is sympathetic to the thesis that Mary was an unwed mother and Jesus an illegitimate child. He interprets the biblical episode of the cleansing of the temple as a symbolic cleansing of the mother's body, and he finds significant Jesus' appeal to God as father (Abba) in his role as village healer of psychosomatic illnesses. Capps's psychoanalytic interpretation allows him to uncover very different patterns in Jesus' life from those proffered by scholars without psychological expertise: Jesus, in Capps's analysis, was a peasant-style "utopian melancholic," rather than an apocalyptic prophet or a social reformist. Capps is well aware of the likely resistance to his views from students, theologians, and biblical scholars. He addresses the critics, making a solid case for a psychological and sociopolitical interpretation of Jesus.

Sandra Lee Dixon of Denver University outlines a course on Augustine in which psychoanalytic concepts are applied to *The Confessions*. She introduces Freud with two early texts, *On Dreams* and *Five Lectures on Psycho-Analysis*. Her students make diagrams of Freud's analysis of a dream of his own: they encounter the concepts of free association, condensation, displacement, repression, overdetermination, and infantile sexuality, and they begin to understand the foundational topographical assumptions about the conscious and unconscious. *Five Lectures* provides her students with another central interpretive concept: the Oedipal complex. In a second unit, students read *The Confessions*, encountering Augustine's remarkable account of his life, his mystical encounters of various sorts, and his theological struggles with sin, sexuality, and the nature of God. Dixon leads her students toward a Freudian interpretation of the major episodes in *The Confessions* by focusing on the parental tensions Augustine reveals. Drawing parallels to the techniques of dream interpretation her students encountered in their earlier readings, she helps them uncover repressions, condensations, displacements, and Oedipal themes. A final unit takes psychoanalytic interpretation of *The Confessions* beyond Freud: Dixon introduces a series of psychoanalytic readings, dating from the 1950s to the 1990s, moving from Freud to Kohut and from a narrow psychological approach to an approach integrating culture, rhetoric, and psyche.

Robert Segal is the only contributor to the volume who teaches outside of America: his course on psychoanalysis and myth is offered at the University of Lancaster in Great Britain. Like many other contributors, Segal begins with his students' reactions to Freud: students typically react negatively to what they perceive as a solipsistic psychologizing of myth in psychoanalytic theory. Segal agrees with his students: through the interpretation of myth as a projection of human characteristics onto the world, Freud severs myth from the world. Segal asks his students to struggle with this central question of myth and world: placing Freud in the history of modern theorizing about myth, he traces developments back to Tylor and Frazer and forward to Eliade, Jung, Malinowski, Bultmann, and others. He focuses in particular on the Freudians: Rank, Arlow, Bettelheim, Dundes, and Winnicott. His students discover that Winnicott, thorough his theory of play and the transitional space, brings myth back to the world. A final unit applies these ideas to a particular cultural form: cinema. The stars of film, his students discover, are like the heroes of myth.

Part III. Teaching the Controversies

With Part III we turn directly to debates and controversies over Freud's thought. In "Rethinking Freud: Gender, Ethnicity, and the Production of Scientific Thought," Janet Jacobs, a sociologist of religion at the University of Colorado, Boulder, examines gender and ethnicity as two major social and political forces that shaped Freud's life and theory. Framing her course in terms of feminist pedagogy and critical thinking, she investigates Freud's Jewishness, the anti-Semitism of his world, his theory of circumcision, and his ideas about the female body. Contrasting Freud's texts on men and women, she uncovers a Jewish male fear of female otherness exacerbated by anti-Semitic accusations of Jewish male effeminacy. She challenges her students to understand the role of gender and ethnicity in the production of scientific ideas: Freud displaced his culture's anti-Semitism, projecting it onto women in theories of female genital inferiority. Like Geller, who examines Freud's double-edged role as a contributor to a dominant discourse *and* as a marginalized other excluded from that discourse, Jacobs teaches her students to ask feminist and sociological questions about the intersections of Freud's life and thought.

Anthropologist Carol Delaney describes the first quarter of the CIV (Culture, Ideas, and Values) course offered to first-year students at Stanford University. The course focuses on "Origins: Prehistory, Myth, and Civilization." A central pedagogical concern is to communicate to students that knowledge is shaped by theories: emphasizing the narratives of origin that shaped the West, she asks her students to read Darwin and Freud alongside the biblical text of Genesis, suggesting that Genesis has subtly influenced our ideas about origins, even as those ideas are secularized in Freudian and Darwinian accounts of our prehistory. She constructs a critique of Freud's *Moses and Monotheism*, centering attention on Freud's notion of gender, his ideas about paternity and patricide, and his Oedipal theory. She concludes by suggesting that the theory of the Oedipus complex has more to do with power and authority than with familial relations and sex. Critiquing Freud from anthropological, historical, and feminist positions, she argues that Freud was wrong in claiming that religion, society, and morals are rooted in the Oedipus complex, but that he was correct in suggesting that notions of God and morality are intertwined with gender: Freud accurately perceived that God is a reification of the concept of paternity. Delaney's essay might be used in the classroom alongside Geller's in Part I, Ross's in this part, and Dittes's in part IV: each offers a dramatically different reading of *Moses and Monotheism*.

Mary Ellen Ross "teaches the controversies" in a very different way: she constructs a dialogic course at Trinity University in San Antonio, situating Freud's cultural texts alongside the writings of other classic theorists. She asks her students to read Freud's *Totem and Taboo* alongside Durkheim's *Elementary Forms of Religious Life* in a unit on religion as social fact. She introduces Freud's "Obsessive Acts and Religious Practices" alongside Turner's writings on the ritual process in a section on ritual. She introduces William James in a section on illusion and experience, asking students to read Freud's *Future of an Illusion* along with selections from James's *Varieties of Religious Experience*. A section on mysticism pairs Freud on the oceanic feeling with Winnicott's writings on transitional phenomena, drawing upon feminist psychoanalysis to critique Freud's "repression of the mother." And a unit on Moses introduces Freud's *Moses and Monotheism* alongside Regina Schwartz's *The Curse of Cain: The Violent Legacy of Monotheism*. Thus the controversies structuring Ross's course are methodological controversies of interpretation. Her course in a sense provides a segue into part IV: although it "teaches the controversies" it also "teaches the teachings." She begins and ends the course with an exercise in dream interpretation that links experience and intellect. Having introduced a reading on dream interpretation at the beginning of the term, she asks students to write psychoanalytic interpretations of dreams of their own at the end. Her course might be used in the classroom alongside Diane Jonte-Pace's in part I and Robert Segal's in part II. Jonte-Pace puts Freud in dialogue with Jung, while Ross and Segal create conversations among Freud, Winnicott, and other theorists of myth, belief, and ritual.

Part IV. Teaching the Teachings, Teaching the Practice

Part IV contains a set of chapters examining the wisdom, insights, and transformative potential of teaching Freud in religious studies. Jeffrey Kripal's essay, "Teaching the Hindu Tantra with Freud: Transgression as Critical Theory and Mystical Technique," focuses on the similarly transformative effects of psychoanalysis and tantric Hinduism in the classroom and in scholarship. Kripal, at Rice University, describes correspondence he received— both positive and negative—in response to his controversial book *Kali's Child*, a psychoanalytic interpretation of the Hindu mystic Ramakrishna inquiring into homosexual eroticism in the life and ecstatic religiosity of the saint.

Drawing parallels between scholarship and pedagogy, Kripal emphasizes the way psychoanalysis and Tantra can function transgressively as social critique, sympathetic recovery, personal therapy, and mystical technique. "The discursive practice that is the psychoanalytic study of the Hindu Tantra," he argues, "possesses the potential to awaken powerful forces within the psyches and bodies" of its practitioners, readers, and students. Kripal's essay might be read by students alongside Parsons's: both discuss mysticism, focusing in different ways on the Hindu saint Ramakrishna.

Ernest Wallwork, a practicing psychoanalyst and professor at Syracuse University, begins his class not with theory but with practice: he introduces Freud's therapeutic strategies. Through several "live demonstrations" in the classroom—of, for example, free association—he shows students how psychoanalysis actually works. He articulates his own "audacious ambition" going beyond standard academic goals: he invites students to change themselves. He proposes, in other words, that they engage the course material both intellectually and existentially. Like Dixon and Ross, he draws on Freud's writings on dreams. A unit on dream interpretation explores Freud's famous "Irma Dream" to demonstrate the mechanisms of dream work. Students subsequently write interpretations of their own dreams. Drawing from *Civilization and Its Discontents*, he turns to the "deep ethic that informs Freud's interpretation of religion and morals," an ethic of passion, reflection, and a "special kind of tolerance for self and others." His final unit moves beyond Freud to highlight developments in the evolution of psychoanalytic theory and their implications for the study of religion and morality. Here he includes such thinkers as Jung, Fromm, Horney, Erikson, Kohut, Tillich, and Levinas.

In the final chapter in the volume, James Dittes of Yale Divinity School criticizes the "detours" often taken in teaching Freud in religious studies: we ask unproductively whether Freud was Jewish or not, and whether he was religious or not. We inquire unnecessarily into Freud's social, historical, and cultural contexts. In his view, we engage in a "conspiracy of dishonesty in our religious studies classrooms" with the pretense that students are not drawn to our courses through their own personal religious questioning. Dittes, on the other hand, prefers to explore the legacy Freud wanted to transmit on "how to aspire to an abundant life." He offers insightful readings of two cultural texts written in the last decade of Freud's life: *Civilization and Its Discontents* and *Moses and Monotheism*. Both are "metapsychical homilies struggling to convey Freud's best wisdom about the strategies for living," yet they offer different "takes" on human vulnerability and limitation. *Civilization and Its Discontents* represents, in a sense, a defense against vulnerability while *Moses and Monotheism* embraces vulnerability. Dittes's chapter represents both an affirmation and a critique of this volume itself: he is refreshingly honest about his sense of illegitimate paths and the detours often taken in teaching Freud; he is critical of the assumptions of many of the contributors to this volume. He offers a profoundly existential affirmation of Freud's teachings. It is fitting that the book, which endeavors to "teach the debates," concludes with Dittes's affirmation and critique.

Conclusion

Although the chapters are divided into the four categories described above, their themes and foci transcend their groupings. They overlap at many points. Others besides the three authors in part III, "Teaching the Controversies," address the contemporary debates over Freud's legacy (Bingaman, Jonte-Pace, Gay, and Geller, for example). Many contributors analyze, interpret, or attempt to resolve student resistance to Freud (Kripal, Jonte-Pace, Bingaman, Gay, Segal, and Delaney). Several incorporate feminist perspectives (Jonte-Pace, Jacobs, Delaney, Ross, Bingaman). Several focus, at least in part, on Freud's Jewish background (Jacobs, Geller, Jonte-Pace, and Delaney). Two comment on the use of films in teaching Freud (Jonte-Pace and Segal); and several show how dream interpretation can productively be used in teaching Freud (Ross, Dixon, Wallwork). All integrate teaching and scholarship; all attest to the vibrant state of religious studies in the academy.

The invitation to contribute to this volume was extended to scholars of religion and psychoanalysis teaching at public universities, private non-affiliated institutions, and religiously affiliated schools. Interestingly, most of those who were able to contribute essays to the volume however, teach at institutions with religious affiliations. The courses described in the volume that are taught at universities *without* religious affiliation tend to be taught in departments other than religious studies: Delaney's course at Stanford is in anthropology; and Jacobs's course at the University of Colorado is in sociology and women's studies.

Several questions inevitably arise: Is it the case that more courses on Freud and religion are offered in the context of religiously affiliated universities than elsewhere? Are the tensions between religion and secularism more likely to be discussed in church-related colleges? Is it possible that professors at public institutions and nonaffiliated private universities, in their own attempts to speak the languages of their academies and of their students, are less likely to offer courses on Freud and religion than their colleagues at religiously affiliated institutions? Is religion—or even the serious critique of religion— somehow taboo in public universities? Further inquiry—such as the Lilly Endowment–sponsored study of religious studies departments in North America—has begun to address these questions. What we can say with certitude is that courses on Freud and religion are being taught with interest, passion, and success, especially—although not exclusively—at religiously affiliated universities in America and Great Britain today.

The "godless Jew" is thus studied intensely in religious, and especially Christian, contexts today. How would Freud react to the irony of this phenomenon— and of this volume? Freud objected strenuously to Jung's effort to turn psychoanalysis into a religion. In response to a letter from Jung in 1910 proclaiming, in grandiose and mythic terms, a "far finer and more comprehensive task for psychoanalysis," Freud responded with these cautionary words, which will be discussed again in this volume: "You mustn't regard me as the founder of a religion. My intentions are not so far-reaching. . . . I am not thinking of a substitute for religion; this need must be sublimated."[4] Similarly, he was, at best, amused by Swiss Pastor Oskar Pfister's accolade, "a better Christian there never was!"[5] I suspect that Freud might feel some discomfort at the essays in the final section of this volume, "Teaching the Teachings." Yet I believe he would be delighted to know that his texts are being read and his ideas discussed, even in departments of religious studies.

A final word: as editor of this volume I want to acknowledge my gratitude to the contributors. As I read and edited these essays I found myself wanting to take each class, to apprentice myself to each of my colleagues, to experience the challenges, critiques, wisdom, and transformations offered by each course. I would like to dedicate this volume to the colleagues, contributors, and students who have taught me new ways to read Freud, to read culture, and to read myself.

Notes

1. "Analysis Terminable and Interminable," *SE* 23: 248. The third "impossible profession," according to Freud, is government.

2. See the recent publications by George Marsden, D. G. Hart, and James Burtchael. Stephen Haynes (1997) offers some interesting reflections on this issue as well.

3. Attesting to this new attention to pedagogical questions in our field is the recent proliferation of publications focusing on teaching. Two examples are the special 1997 issue of the *Journal of the American Academy of Religion* devoted to "Teaching and Learning in Religion and Theology," and the new journal *Teaching Theology and Religion*, initiated in the late 1990s.

4. McGuire 1974, 178–179.

5 In Meng and Freud, eds. 1963, 63.

References

Auden, W. H. 1966. *Collected shorter poems: 1927–1957*. New York: Random House.

Burtchael, James. 1998. *The dying of the light: The disengagement of colleges and universities from their Christian churches*. Grand Rapids, Mich.: Eerdmans.

Crews, Frederick. 1997. *The memory wars: Freud's legacy in dispute*. New York: New York Review of Books.

———, ed. 1998. *Unauthorized Freud: Doubters confront a legend*. New York: Penguin.

Freud, Sigmund. 1964. Analysis terminable and interminable. In *The standard edition of the complete psychological works of Sigmund Freud*, translated and edited by James Strachey. Vol. 23, 209–53. London: Hogarth Press.

Gay, Peter. 1999. Psychoanalyst Sigmund Freud: Great minds of the century. *Time*, 29 March, 64–69.

Graff, Gerald. 1993. *Beyond the culture wars: How teaching the conflicts can revitalize American education*. New York: Norton.

Hart, D. G. 1999. *The university gets religion: Religious studies in American higher education since 1870*. Baltimore: Johns Hopkins University Press.

Haynes, Stephen. 1997. Teaching religion at a church-related college: Reflections on professional identity and institutional loyalty. *Religious Studies News*, February, 18–19.

Marsden, George. 1997. *The soul of the American university: From Protestant establishment to established non-belief.* New York: Oxford University Press.

————. 1998. *The outrageous idea of Christian scholarship.* New York: Oxford University Press.

McGuire, William, ed. 1974. *The Freud/Jung letters.* Translated by Ralph Manheim and R. F. C. Hull. Princeton, N.J.: Bollingen/Princeton University Press.

Meng, Heinrich, and Ernst Freud, eds. 1963. *Psychoanalysis and faith: The letters of Sigmund Freud and Oskar Pfister.* Translated by Eric Mosbacher. New York: Basic Books.

I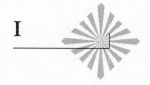

INSTITUTIONAL AND CURRICULAR CONTEXTS

Teaching Freud and Religion in Undergraduate Institutions, Graduate Programs, and Seminaries

Teaching Freud in the Language of Our Students: The Case of a Religiously Affiliated Undergraduate Institution

Diane Jonte-Pace

If the psychoanalyst must speak in the language of the patient, we, the teachers of Freud and religion, surely must teach in the language of our students. Who is Freud—and what is religion—in this language? The answer depends in part on academic context: Freud is taught in religious studies departments at public universities, private unaffiliated colleges, and religiously affiliated seminaries, colleges, and universities. This essay describes a course on "Religion in the Theories of Freud and Jung" at a religiously affiliated West Coast university with approximately four thousand undergraduate students.

Curriculum and Context

The students at Santa Clara University, a Catholic and Jesuit institution in northern California where I have taught for more than fifteen years, are predominantly (nearly two-thirds) Roman Catholic in background and practice. Most of the students come to my course through university requirements rather than pure interest: all students at the University are required to take three religious studies courses during their undergraduate careers, one at each of three levels.

Our first-level courses, such as "Ways of Understanding Religion," "Religion and Modernity," and "Religions of the Book," introduce the study of religion by moving beyond the notion of religion as "belief" to probe the question of what religion reveals about human beings and societies. These first-level courses, primarily for first-year students, attempt to integrate, affirm, challenge, and develop the "big questions" brought by students to their earliest courses at the university. Second-level courses are intended for sophomores and juniors. They focus on a specific and coherent body of material, typically a religious tradition or a methodology. Examples include "Hispanic Theology," "Japanese Religions," and "Psychology of Religion." These courses aim to provide a set of texts, data, and tools, offering a context for sustained efforts at analysis and interpretation. Third-level courses, for juniors and seniors, encourage critical engagement with current issues in religion, focusing on existential, social, or political problems and controversies. The third-level courses model a variety of ways of continuing to think about religion in the contemporary world as students prepare to leave the university. My course "Religion in the Theories of Freud and Jung" is a third-level course for juniors and seniors; other third-level courses include "Ethical Issues in Asian Religions," "Theology of Marriage," and "Biblical Poetry and Ancient Myth."

We have structured our course offerings with this tripartite developmental framework in order to address the kinds of issues, concerns, and questions students have at the beginning, middle, and end of their college years. In addition, we attempt to build on the increasingly complex cognitive and intellectual skills they bring to the classroom at each stage of their college careers (Perry 1970). But this developmental framework is not our only organizing principle: our courses are structured by content and method as well as by level. At each level, courses are offered in three "areas": "Scripture and Tradition"; "Theology, Ethics, and Spirituality"; and "Religion and Society." We constructed these "areas" to ensure breadth in the curriculum of our majors. Religious studies majors take at least three courses, including at least one seminar, in each "area"; nonmajors take courses in any "area" they wish. My course is in Area III, "Religion and Society."

Only a few of my students in this course are majoring in religious studies: their majors are more likely to be finance, biology, or communication. Yet when I teach this course I can assume that all students have some prior familiarity with religion and religious studies through their backgrounds or their required coursework on the first and second levels. Typically, they also have some familiarity with Freud: before the course begins many students already "know" that they dislike, reject, and disagree with Freud. Their distaste for Freud is a point to which I'll return: indeed, it is the point at which I like to begin the course. But there is another source of potential resistance to Freud that must be acknowledged.

Structural and Administrative Resistance to Freud?

While one might imagine that a course on Freud and religion would be viewed with hesitation or suspicion at a Jesuit and Roman Catholic university, I've experienced primarily interest, enthusiasm, and support from the Department of Religious Studies and the university. Never have my courses been challenged as insufficiently Catholic or insufficiently religious. Rather, they have been welcomed as serious attempts to engage the tensions between religious and secular voices in modernity.

Through my course on "Religion in the Theories of Freud and Jung" (and various courses at the first and second levels, such as "Religion and Modernity," and "Psychology of Religion"), I've been drawn into a number of projects at the heart of the university. In the Western Culture Core Program for which Santa Clara University has received high acclaim,[1] I've offered interdisciplinary "common lectures" on "Augustine as the First Psychoanalyst" and on "Freud and Nietzsche as Critics of the Enlightenment Project." In addition, I've organized well-received interdisciplinary "lunch-time conversations" for faculty on psychology and religion. And I've received teaching and research grants to support course development and scholarship in this area.[2] Far from fearing Freud as a demon of unorthodoxy, the faculty and administration of the university have welcomed the course, acknowledging Freud as an important voice in the discourse on religion in modernity.

This welcoming attitude could change in the future. The approval in 1999 of the Vatican document *Ex Corde Ecclesiae* (National Conference of Catholic Bishops 1990) by the American Catholic bishops may seriously undermine courses addressing contemporary thinkers on religion at Catholic universities.[3] The president and provost of the university have assured faculty, students, and trustees that Santa Clara University remains committed to academic freedom, yet it is possible that a day may come when one dare not "speak Freud" in the religious studies departments of Catholic universities. In the meantime, the conversation continues.

Speaking in the Language of the Students

Although the university itself is currently open to Freudian conversations, a number of other questions must be voiced: Are there other forms of resistance at work? What of internal, self-created forms of resistance? Are there subtle techniques of censorship or self-censorship that shape my course? Have I created a course that carefully sidesteps controversial questions in order to avoid the unsettling dimensions of Freud's challenge to religious faith for my students, my colleagues, and my administration? I think not. My sense is that the only censorship at work is the shaping that occurs when one begins a course by speaking in the language of one's students, by addressing the fact that these students feel that they already "know" Freud, and by acknowledging that the Freud they "know" is indeed a foolish and authoritarian figure, an archaic theorist whose outmoded ideas are sexist, reductionistic, and unscientific. My students will come to know many other Freuds before the quarter is over, but I begin my course by inviting a discussion of the Freud whom they know and whom they dismiss. (Such discussions are the norm. Our upper-division classes are usually limited to thirty-five students, a good size for interaction, conversation, and debate.)

One of my goals in inviting students to describe their dismissal of Freud is to demonstrate to the class that in spite of their distaste for him, "we all speak Freud" (Gay 1999, 68). I invite the students to discover that they inhabit a world in which notions of inner life, interpersonal relationship, pathology, and health are shaped by a Freudian vocabulary that permeates institutions and social practices, from therapies to advertising to popular culture. Typically, as the class continues, the language of dismissal will begin to shift into a language of self-recognition: students will become conscious of their near-fluency in the language of everyday psychoanalysis. Our common language gives us a starting point for a set of introductions to other Freuds: the "dissed" and dismissed Freud is not negated (he will be encountered again and again), but he is joined by a Freud who is the creator of a psychological language and worldview, an astute observer of inner life and interpersonal interactions, and a thoughtful and persistent, although critical, interpreter of religion.

Encountering Many Freuds: Interpretation, Critique, Life, and Culture

My course is divided into four units. In each unit, Freud is the primary focus; Jung provides a contrast, establishes a parallel, or becomes a partner in dialogue. We first encounter Freud and Jung as *interpreters* of religion; we then turn to Freud and Jung as *critics* of religion. Our third unit, on the *intersections of life and theory*, introduces Freud the Viennese Jew, child of recent immigrants from Eastern Europe to Vienna, and Jung the son, grandson, and nephew of Swiss Protestant pastors. This unit examines the impact of religious background—and its loss—on the rise of psychological ideas. In the fourth unit, on *psychoanalysis, culture and theology,* we encounter Freud and Jung as products and creators of modernity, exploring their ideas in relation to the perspectives of their contemporary interpreters and critics.

Freud and Jung as Interpreters of Religion

The unit on interpretation introduces our foundational interpretive frameworks, the Freudian Oedipus complex and the Jungian theory of archetypes and individuation. Freud's short essay from 1928, "A Religious Experience," an Oedipal interpretation of an American doctor's crisis of faith, illustrates with clarity Freud's theory of the powerful incestuous and parricidal fantasies influencing us in social relations and religious beliefs. A close reading of this essay also provides an opportunity to encourage both critical thinking and psychoanalytic thinking among students. I ask them to observe gaps and absences in the text, such as Freud's failure to attend to the American doctor's and his own castrative imagery ("removal to a dissecting room of the dead body" [*SE* 21: 170]) even as he theorizes the American doctor's return to faith as a classic Oedipal sublimation ("the outcome of the struggle was displayed once again in the sphere of religion . . . complete submission to the will of God the Father" [171]).

I encourage students to ask why Freud neglected to mention in this text a theme he emphasized so strongly elsewhere: the role of castration anxiety in the renunciation of incestuous and parricidal/deicidal fantasies. Students eagerly discover repressions and evasions in Freud's texts. I suggest that the presence of a dead mother in the text of the American doctor was nearly as unsettling to Freud as it was to the American doctor he analyzed. Freud transformed a dead mother in the text into an erotic mother in the theory, substituting sex for death. Freud was quite comfortable with fantasies of dead and murdered fathers, but he did not easily tolerate images of dead mothers. I use this text for several pedagogical reasons. It introduces the Oedipal theory and illustrates the application of the theory to religion. In addition, it provides an opportunity for students to "think like Freud" at the same time as they "think against Freud." They critique Freud, asking what's absent or problematic in his texts, using, in their critiques, the psychoanalytic tools and methods he developed.

Our discussion of the Oedipal sources of religious belief in "A Religious Experience" is followed by a discussion of the final chapter of *Totem and Taboo* (*SE* 13), where Freud applied the Oedipal theory to the prehistorical origins of culture, morality, and religion. This provides an opportunity to demonstrate Freud's evolutionary assumption of a parallelism between individual psychology (the psychological context of the faith of the American doctor) and cultural psychology (the historical and cultural context of belief, ritual, and morality). Fantasies or enactments of parricide structure both "A Religious Experience" and *Totem and Taboo*. My students tend to dislike Freud's all-encompassing theory of a primal murderous and cannibalistic act at the origins of culture and religion repeated periodically in a ritualized "totem meal." A few, however, have acknowledged that elements of "A Religious Experience" echo their own changing views of God and religion, their crises of faith, or their relations with their own fathers.

I juxtapose Freud's analyses of the parricidal sources of individual and cultural religion with a set of Freudian readings that depart from the incessant Oedipal theorizing of these two texts. Freud's discussion of the origins of "the oceanic feeling" in the first chapter of *Civilization and Its Discontents* (*SE* 21) and his analysis of the mythologies of death and desire in a 1913 essay "The Theme of the Three Caskets" (*SE* 12) provide examples of "another Freud" who abandons, if only briefly, his Oedipal theory. The analysis of the oceanic feeling represents a foray into the pre-Oedipal followed by a return to Oedipus: Freud traces the source of mysticism (religious *experience*) to the earliest experience of the pre-Oedipal child at the mother's breast, yet he reaffirms the Oedipal origins of religious *ideas*. He states, for example, "an infant at the breast does not as yet distinguish his ego from the external world. . . . We are perfectly willing to acknowledge that the 'oceanic' feeling exists in many people and we are inclined to trace it back to an early phase of ego feeling. The further question then arises, what claim this feeling has to be regarded as the source of religious needs. To me the claim does not seem compelling. . . . The derivation of religious needs from the infant's helplessness and the longing for the father aroused by it seems to me incontrovertible" (*SE* 21: 66–67, 72). Students enjoy the opportunity to critique Freud's inconsistencies. Yet, their "dissing" of Freud is contextualized by their experience of reading his texts with care.

The "Theme of the Three Caskets" offers a more sustained non-Oedipal interpretation. Freud constructs a psychoanalytic reading of the mythological and literary theme of the hero whose choice among three women (or three caskets, or three forms of the mother) involves a choice between sex and death. I use this essay to show that Freud is not monolithic in his Oedipal analyses and to engage students in a conversation about contemporary cultural phenomena—films, literature, social practices—that replicate these mythological and literary themes associating women and death. I ask about what kinds of ideas about gender and sexuality are promoted by such patterns. I invite the students to compare this essay from 1913 to the essay "A Religious Experience" from 1928, where we found that Freud was unable to theorize associations of women and death. In anticipation of our third unit on life and theory we speculate on what biographical or social factors might have allowed Freud to dismiss or displace his insights of 1913 about unconscious fears and fantasies associating maternity with mortality when he wrote the 1928 essay in which he turned away from analysis of theme of a dead mother.

I suggest to my students that Freud's interpretation of the theme of the three caskets in myth and literature initiated the sort of analyses of cultural misogyny that contemporary feminist thinkers have now taken up (Mitchell 1974; Buhle 1998; Van Herik 1982; Jonte-Pace 2001a). Students often find contemporary parallels to the myths Freud analyzes in recent films such as *So I Married an Axe Murderer, Basic Instinct,* and *Three Weddings and a Funeral,* where women, sex, and marriage are dangerous and potentially deadly to men.[4] Many students who found Freud's Oedipal theories easy to dismiss now begin to perceive a new Freud, a thoughtful interpreter of myths, legends, and cultural ideologies, a Freud with feminist or protofeminist ideas.

I use these interpretive texts for a number of pedagogical reasons. Most important, they allow me to expose the presence of a number of different "Freuds." First, as noted above, they not only introduce the Oedipal theory in relation to religion but also illustrate the gaps in that theory. In addition, they demonstrate that a non-Oedipal theory occasionally emerges in Freud's writings, a theory that anticipates feminist interpretations of mythic and cultural misogyny. And, as I've suggested, they provide an opportunity for students to "speak Freud" and to "think like Freud."

The Jungian texts I set in dialogue with these differ from year to year; my main concern is to illustrate Jung's concepts of the archetypes and the collective unconscious, and to offer an interpretation of religious experiences or symbols that will contrast clearly with Freud's approach. Max Zeller's brief account of Jung's interpretation of a dream of building a temple provides an example of Jung's notion of the progressive, transformative effect of the collective unconscious on religion (1982); Jung's interpretation, in *Aion,* of Christ as the archetype of the Self (*CW* 9, 2) offers a complex interpretation of Christian symbolism. Alternatively, I've used Jung's description of the archetypes of the collective unconscious in *Two Essays On Analytical Psychology* (*CW* 7).

Particularly successful in the classroom as archetypal interpretations of religion are selected passages from Jung's writings on the hero myth (Segal 1998). On occasion I've shown segments of Bill Moyers's video *The Powers of Myth: Volume 1, The Hero's Journey* (1988) as an illustration of Jungian myth interpretation. Joseph Campbell's discussion of the film *Star Wars* in Moyers's video exemplifies beautifully the archetypal and mythic stages outlined by Jung. The video, with clips from Lucas's film, allows a pedagogy in the "language of the students": these students have grown up on *Star Wars*. Ann Bedford Ulanov's 1971 essay outlining an archetypal analysis of anima/ animus issues in the film *Wizard of Oz* is nearly as effective, although *Oz* is not as deeply embedded as *Star Wars* in the language and experience of our current students.

I conclude this unit on interpretation by asking students to apply their new Freudian and Jungian interpretive skills by writing an interpretation of a film with some connection to religion. We watch the film together, either in class or in an evening outside our class schedule. A viewing of Alfred Hitchcock's *Vertigo* provides an opportunity for a discussion of the themes of mortality and immortality, death and desire, castration anxiety, and the male construction of the female image. Alternatively, I've shown Polish director Krzysztof Kieslowski's *Decalogue 4: Honor Thy Father and Mother,* a powerful narrative involving a young woman whose discovery, on "Easter Monday," that her father may not be her biological parent leads her to consider a sexual relationship with him. Kieslowski's film invites oedipal interpretation, although some of my students have explored the theme of maternal absence and others have found a Jungian "heroic journey toward individuation" below the surface of the text. A different film I sometimes use at this point in the course is Australian director Peter Weir's *Picnic at Hanging Rock* (the 1998 director's cut is superior to the 1974 release), which links death with forbidden desire in a narrative set in a fin-de-siècle school for girls. Juxtaposing the forces of nature and civilization, the film examines the dangerous powers of forbidden erotic fantasies and the numinous qualities of a phallic sacred site. I teach the course often enough that I find it necessary to vary the writing assignments and the films we view. I particularly like Kieslowski's *Decalogue 4* because of its length: at fifty-five minutes, it allows both a viewing and a preliminary discussion on the same day. Students typically write a short interpretive essay over the weekend, returning to class the following week for a more extended discussion of the film.[5]

Freud and Jung as Critics of Religion

With the second unit we turn from an interpretation of religion to a critique of religion. It is important to differentiate interpretation and critique: they are interrelated but separable. I began with interpretation rather than critique because I wanted the students to understand the theories before encountering the critical challenges to religion that are likely to generate defensive reactions. I also began with interpretation because the interpretive material is more specifically psychoanalytic. The critique, especially in *The Future of an Illusion* (*SE* 21) with which we start this second unit, expresses an Enlightenment-based rationalism that is only occasionally "Freudian," psychoanalytic, or Oedipal in the narrow sense.

The Future of an Illusion is our first "critical" text. We read selectively, focusing on three major issues: Freud's definition of illusion as wish-based thoughts that may (or may not) be true; his Enlightenment-based critique of religion as a moral system promoting fearful obedience to an Oedipal authority; and his insistence on the need for a new system of morality based on rationality, self-knowledge, justice, and community, rather than on castrative fears of paternal/divine punishment. I introduce a fourth issue as well, which connects with our previous unit on interpretation: like a psychoanalyst watching for subconscious patterns in the words of a patient, we watch for subtextual patterns in the rhetoric of Freud's writings. I am particularly interested in religious subtexts. A few examples are Freud's use of terminology like "our God Logos" (*SE* 21: 54) with its echoes of the Logos theology of the Gospel of John; his fantasy that, in another era, he would have been martyred as a religious heretic (36–40);[6] and his use of biblical structures and paradigms. We note the way Freud begins *The Future of an Illusion* with a Genesis-like inquiry into our "origins" (*SE* 21: 5) and ends the volume with a utopian and salvific vision in which "life will be tolerable for everyone and civilization no longer oppressive to anyone" (50): he moves from creation to redemption, as it were. Students discover that Freud's rhetoric and vocabulary provide a hint that he harbored grandiose religious fantasies about the future of his own ideas—fantasies he held firmly in check, allowing them expression only in verbal play and metaphor.

I enjoy bringing to class a three-page review by T. S. Eliot of Freud's *The Future of an Illusion*. Eliot, writing in 1928, the year after the publication of the book, found it quite "stupid" (1988, 575). I use this review as a basis for group projects: students work in small groups to discuss what Eliot understood and what he missed (he focuses on the theme of religion as illusion, missing completely Freud's larger concern with morality and community). Students have an opportunity to write a response to Eliot in the voice of Freud on an exam later in the quarter. My pedagogical goal here is to cultivate a kind of critical thinking that invites students to defend Freud against his detractors. They soon realize how far they've come from knowing only one distasteful and easily dismissable Freud.

Civilization and Its Discontents is our next text. Again, we read selectively. Our main focus is Freud's critique of the excessive suffering and guilt caused by a religiously enforced superego. Freud's critique of the "love commandment" as dangerously unrealistic provides a nuanced entrée into the question of the tension between Eros and Thanatos, Love and Death, in the context of morality and civilization (*SE* 21: 109–16). We also read the chapter on individual and cultural responses to suffering, a chapter in which Freud sounds nearly Buddhist in his analysis of the various ways we encounter, resist, or embrace the suffering inevitable in life (74–85). He states, for example, "in the last analysis, all suffering is nothing else than sensation; it only exists insofar as we feel it and we only feel it in consequence of certain ways in which our organism is regulated" (78). Here, as in *The Future of an Illusion*, students observe an implicitly religious subtext in Freud's explicitly antireligious tract.[7]

As in our first unit, we conclude this unit with a set of readings from Jung. Jung is often seen as the friend of religion, a thinker who defends religion against Freud's hostile attacks. I allow Jung, however, to present himself as a more complex figure—sometimes a reformer, sometimes a defender, sometimes a critic. Jung the critic of religion emerges in selected passages in *Memories, Dreams, Reflections* (1963): he presents religion as a rigid and unchanging institution, out of touch with the deeper patterns of the collective unconscious. See, for example, his discussion of his famous childhood fantasy in which God destroys the Basel cathedral with an immense turd (39) and his dream of the underground sacred phallus on a golden throne (12). Jung the reformer of religion, on the other hand, emerges in later chapters, where he states clearly that religion can and must be reinvigorated and transformed: "Our myth has become mute and gives no answers. The fault lies . . . solely in us who have not developed it further" (332). Clips from videos provide a portrait of Jung as supporter and defender of religion. In Aniela Jaffé's near-hagiographic remarks in the film *The Mystery That Heals,* Jung is "the most religious man I ever knew." Similarly, in a BBC interview, an elderly Jung, in response to an interviewer's question "Do you believe in God?" answers "I do not believe, I know." While some students find Jung confusing and contradictory, others are able to tolerate such ambivalence. And some, uncomfortable with Freud's harsh criticism of religion, find Jung's stance(s) deeply reassuring.

At this point in the course, some students typically express anger and resentment because Freud and Jung challenge their previously unquestioned religious and cultural views. I try not to meet their challenges defensively or interpret them as personal attacks. Rather, I invite and encourage their critiques, acknowledging that, indeed, the theories are often bizarre, problematic, and counterintuitive. Their angry responses are sure to initiate class discussion and debate; other students will often come to Freud's or Jung's defense. I've sometimes observed that anger toward the course content can be transformed into critical thinking and insight. Angry students, finding their anger legitimated, often undergo a shift: they become careful critics and analysts of the texts, rather than angry denouncers of the ideas. One of my recent students who entered the class with a strong anti-Freudian animus came to my office at the end of the term to tell me his new "mantra": "the unconscious is real, and everything can be interpreted."

A word about the erotics of pedagogy may be important at this point. More troubling than the angry students are students who fall in love with the professor. The pedagogy of the erotic is often more complex than what might be called the pedagogy of anger. Sometimes this "falling in love" seems to be a result of the open discussions of Freud's ideas about sexuality; at other times it involves students' discoveries that their inner lives are filled with rich new meanings; sometimes it has a religious or spiritual component. I try to communicate to these "loving" students that their love is for the text, not the teacher. Good pedagogy often involves a disentangling of students' attitudes toward teachers from their attitudes toward texts—pedagogy, in other words, utilizes the transference relationship. Freud's insights into the transference (and the dangers of the countertransference) are as applicable to the desk as they are to the couch.

Intersections of Life and Theory

Unit three introduces the complex intersections of life and theory. In this unit we will encounter more secondary literature than we've previously seen. We begin not with the childhood or early years, which we'll read at the end of this unit, but with the Freud-Jung relationship as it is presented in Jung's chapter on Freud in *Memories, Dreams, Reflections* (1963). Jung describes Freud as a brilliant but troubled thinker who, during the early years of their friendship, repressed his religiosity and projected it inappropriately onto his theory of sexuality. Jung describes himself as a calm, reasonable witness to the older man's rantings and obsessions. I pair Jung's account—written decades after the events described—with a set of letters written in 1910, in the midst of the years of intense yet conflicted friendship. These famous letters paint a rather different picture of the relationship: in 1910, Jung was quite evidently an immensely enthusiastic devotee, projecting grandiose religious expectations onto Freud and his theory, and proclaiming prophetically that psychoanalysis would change the world through a Dionysian and liberatory rediscovery of the sacrality of sex: "The ethical problem of sexual freedom really is enormous and worth the sweat of all noble souls. But 2000 years of Christianity can only be replaced by something equivalent. . . . I imagine a far finer and more comprehensive task for psychoanalysis. . . . We must give it time to infiltrate into people from many centres, to revivify among intellectuals a feeling for symbol and myth" (in McGuire 1974, 294–95). A concerned, cautious Freud emerges from these letters, gently chiding Jung for his excesses and warning him not to expect psychoanalysis to become a system of salvation: "You mustn't regard me as the founder of a religion. . . . I am not thinking of a substitute for religion; this need must be sublimated" (295).

Many students experience disorientation as they struggle with the contradictions in these texts. Is Freud the neurotic figure, denying religion and projecting it into a sterile theory? Or is Jung the one who projects religious meanings into psychoanalytic ideas? A historical framework provides a preliminary path out of the contradictions. Students often decide that Jung's view of Freud in 1910 should not be expected to be consistent with his view of Freud in the 1960s when he penned or dictated his autobiographical remarks. A chapter from Peter Homans's *Jung in Context* (1995) provides an additional framework within which these contradictory texts make sense. Through a close reading of the letters and the *Memories, Dreams, Reflections* (Jung 1963) chapter, Homans uncovers elements of a narcissistic transference in the Freud-Jung relationship. Both the religious ideation so evident in the 1910 letters and the sense of betrayal and disillusionment so evident in Jung's chapter on Freud published half a century later are typical of narcissistic transferences, involving idealization and merger, and their dissolution. Homans shows that "the conventional views . . . that Jung resisted Freud's theories or that Freud could not tolerate Jung's innovations address only the surface of their relationship. The letters reveal a far richer, more complex situation . . . [involving] Jung's idealization of Freud and his thoughts about religion" (1995, 55–56). Again, students are invited to think psychoanalytically about psychoanalysis, and the psychoanalytic perspective provides a larger view in which the contradictory texts make sense.

After introducing the notion of the narcissistic transference through Homans's analysis of the Freud-Jung relationship, I ask students to read H.D.'s (Hilda Doolittle's) poem "The Master" (1981), an evocative account of the feminist poet's brief analysis with Freud in the mid-30s. This poem serves several pedagogical and curricular goals: it provides an intimate look at Freud's unconventional analytic style; it is rich with religious images and symbols (Miletus [407], the Stone Sphynx [414], the Lord [416]); and it can be read in terms of the same theme introduced by Homans's essay, the theme of the narcissistic transference. Freud's unconventional style of practicing psychoanalysis is evident throughout the poem: "He was rather casual" (413). References to the sacrality of the "ritual" of psychoanalysis abound: "each vestment had meaning, every gesture is wisdom" (407). Prominent in the poem is a spiritual sense of the therapeutic relationship: "I knew wisdom, I found measureless truth in his words" (407).

H.D.'s poem expresses a complex attitude toward Freud. H.D. is deeply grateful to Freud for the healing she experienced. Her gratitude to Freud contains spiritual and erotic components. Both of these are tempered by anger. She writes, for example,

> His tyranny was absolute, for I had to love him then
> I had to recognize that he was beyond all-men
> nearer to God. (408)

H.D.'s poem also deals with the problem of bisexuality:

> I had two loves separate.
> I asked him to explain the impossible
> which he did. (410)

Students today—far more than students ten or fifteen years ago, when I started using this reading in the course—find this theme an important and moving one.

H.D. raises important questions about whether psychoanalysis has become rigidified into an institutional "religion" ("his pen will be sacred" [413]) or whether it escapes such hardening, remaining a source of psychological and spiritual healing and liberation. She writes:

> They will found temples in his name,
> his fame
> will be so great
> that anyone who has known him
> will also be hailed as master,
> seer,
> interpreter;
> only I
> I will escape. (413)

In H.D.'s portrayal, Freud emerges as a sagacious but sometimes enraging therapist and midwife to the soul who tolerates, or even encourages, a fair amount of religious projection. Avoiding conflict, he accepts her portrayal of his wisdom, stating, "We won't argue about that. . . . You are a poet" (413). An exam question later in the quarter will give students the opportunity to grapple further with the meanings of the poem and its religious, sexual, and narcissistic components. I often ask students to compare Jung's 1910 letter to H.D.'s poem, speculating about why Freud might have brushed aside Jung's religious projections in 1910 but tolerated H.D.'s religious projections in the mid-30s.

We then look into the pasts of both Freud and Jung, focusing on their youths and their religious backgrounds. The first two chapters of Jung's *Memories, Dreams, Reflections* (1963) dramatically portray Jung's struggles with his pastor-father, his boyhood visions, and his increasing alienation from the Calvinist Protestantism of his youth. Freud's religious background is introduced through Dennis Klein's *Jewish Origins of the Psychoanalytic Movement* (1985). Klein's work allows us to examine the complex effects of Jewishness and anti-Semitism on Freud's life and thought.[8] I supplement Klein's text with passages from Freud's highly autobiographical masterwork, *The Interpretation of Dreams* (*SE* 4)—specifically, his account of his father's story of being forced off the pavement with an anti-Semitic taunt. This provides an opportunity for broader discussions of anti-Semitism, of differences among religious, ethnic, and cultural Jewishness, and of Freud's self-identification as a "godless Jew."

We conclude this unit with a short reading from the introductory chapter of Homans's *Jung in Context* (1995), in which both Freud and Jung are presented as paradigmatic modernists. Homans's argument is that both theorists experienced loss of a religious common culture, both withdrew into introspection, and both developed a new vocabulary to articulate their experiences of the inner world. Both "originative psychologists," in other words, developed their depth psychological theories out of personal experiences involving the losses of Jewish and Protestant religious traditions and communities. This reading serves to locate Freud's and Jung's theories within the context of their own lives and within the context of the broader historical forces of modernity. It provides a segue into the next unit.

Psychoanalysis, Culture, and Theology

Our final unit, "Psychoanalysis, Culture, and Theology" introduces reactions from Freud's and Jung's critics, supporters, and interpreters. I show Luis Buñuel's short 1927 film *Un Chien Andalou* as an illustration of the incorporation of psychoanalytic ideas and imagery into surrealist and avant-garde art and culture. I ask students to consider not only how Freud's ideas contribute to the film but also how Freud and Jung might interpret it. We discuss the dreamlike nonchronological narrative structure, the nightmare imagery, the intertwined themes of Eros and Thanatos, and the sense of "discontent" with civilization. Students understand clearly that Buñuel's imagery—for example, a man dragging a piano draped with a dead horse and two helpless priests— evokes Freud's sense of our "discontent" with civilization in general and with religion in particular.

We then move to Paul Ricoeur's question, "Can psychoanalysis purify religion?" A brief reading from Ricoeur's *Freud and Philosophy* (1970) is paired with David Miller's essay "Attack Upon Christendom! The Anti-Christianism of Depth Psychology" (1986). Miller describes the importance and value of the psychoanalytic challenge to religious authoritarianism, infantilism, and literalism. In his view, Freud and Jung, as well as James Hillman and Jacques Lacan, are authentic religious thinkers who avoid the trap of being inauthentically religious.[9] As a companion piece to Miller's article I use a short section of Julia Kristeva's 1991 *Strangers to Ourselves* in which psychoanalysis is described in almost soteriological terms as a new foundation for relational ethics.[10] In contrast to these readings I introduce Martin Buber's critique of Jung in *The Eclipse of God* (1957). In Buber's antimodernist view, Jung's psychology makes God a function of the unconscious rather than a Transcendent Other.[11] I invite students to struggle with Ricoeur's question and with the tension between Buber's and Miller's/Kristeva's interpretations of the relation of depth psychology and religion. These tensions are not new, but these issues remain important in our culture, in our universities (especially, I think, in our religiously affiliated universities), and in the lives of our students.

Our final reading brings us to the heart of current debates over Freud's legacy. I introduce the controversy over the recent show on Freud's life, work, and influence sponsored by the Library of Congress. I ask students to read a packet of magazine articles and newspaper clippings, along with a chapter from *Freud: Conflict and Culture* (Roth 1998), a volume edited by the curator of the controversial exhibit. The intensity and duration of this debate over Freud's scientific, ethical, and professional legacy provide a measure of the importance of Freud's contested place in our culture. I invite students to join in this debate, taking a position on this topic in a short essay at the end of the quarter.

We end the course with a "symbolic feast." Each student brings an item of "symbolic" food to share with the class; each offers a brief Freudian or Jungian interpretation of the food. We've shared Freudian phallic pretzel sticks;

mandala cookies with Jungian themes of *conjunctio oppositorum* illustrated in their chocolate/vanilla patterns; numinous "oceanic" juices (with straws for sucking); gingerbread primal fathers ready to be consumed cannibalistically; and bubblegum cigars. This symbolic feast reiterates in a humorous but embodied way the "totem meal" we encountered during the first unit. It provides a reminder to the students that they now "speak Freud" with some fluency; that they know several Freuds; that these multiple Freuds have complex and interesting relations with religion and modernity; that they themselves are part of a modern world that Freud helped to shape; and that the course has provided them with "tools for thinking" about religion and culture that may be particularly valuable as they leave the university. We thus end the course with a "tasting" of Freud, in direct contrast with the "distaste" with which we began.

Notes

1. Santa Clara University has been ranked second among public and private regional universities in the West for thirteen consecutive years (*U.S. News and World Report* 2002). The core curriculum is an important part of this ranking system.

2. One such grant, the Presidential Research Grant, 1998–2000, has provided support for this very project. A Dialogue and Design grant from the Bannan Institute for Jesuit Education and Christian Values supported the lunchtime conversations on psychology and religion. I am grateful for this support.

3. According to the document produced by the National Conference of Catholic Bishops, *The Ex Corde Ecclesiae: Application to the United States* (2000), this would apply only to professors who are Roman Catholic. Many, however, have suggested that the enforcement of the policy would, at least indirectly, influence all faculty in departments of religious studies and theology at Catholic universities.

4. Occasionally I pair this material with the famous chapter in *Beyond the Pleasure Principle,* in which an infant (Freud's grandson) plays the game of "*fort*" and "*da,*" presence and absence, or life and death. This provides a poetic and touching example of the conflict between the life and death drives, a conflict that takes shape in the experience of the presence and absence of the mother. Some students have pursued this further as a research paper topic. I direct students to other readings on death in Freud's corpus: "Thoughts for the Times on War and Death," "On Transience," "Why War?" and "Medusa's Head." Occasionally I use my own 1996 essay at this point in the course.

5. I make available to the students a number of articles offering psychoanalytic interpretations of religious phenomena: Julia Kristeva's 1987 analysis of the Nicene Creed from *In the Beginning Was Love*; Alan Dundes's 1980 psychoanalytic essay "The Hero Pattern in the Life of Jesus," selected psychological interpretations of Augustine's *Confessions* from Don Capps and Jim Dittes's 1990 edited volume, *The Hunger of the Heart*, etc.

6. He hints that his ideas would have led to his martyrdom: "In former times utterances such as mine brought with them a sure curtailment of one's earthly existence" (*SE* 21: 36). He also draws parallels between those who foolishly fear psychoanalytic ideas and the pagans who, in earlier centuries, feared Christianity: "Everyone is frightened [of psychoanalysis] as though it would expose one to a still greater

danger. When St. Boniface cut down the tree that was venerated as sacred by the Saxons, the bystanders expected some fearful event to follow upon the sacrilege. But nothing happened and the Saxons accepted baptism" (40). He leaves the conclusion unstated: psychoanalysis is parallel to Christianity; the contemporary "bystanders" will eventually accept psychoanalysis.

7. I frequently integrate a short reading from *Moses and Monotheism* to complement *The Future of an Illusion* and *Civilization and Its Discontents*. While *The Future of an Illusion* sets up a contrast between Christian belief and rational morality, and *Civilization and Its Discontents* critiques the "love commandment" central to Christian morality, *Moses and Monotheism* contrasts Christian belief with Jewish morality. My students (mainly Catholics, as noted above) tend to respond defensively to *Moses and Monotheism*. They bristle at Freud's definition of Christian ritual and belief as superstition. I ask them to situate Freud's argument historically, imagining what Viennese Catholicism would have looked like in the 1920s and 1930s, prior to the changes accompanying the *aggiornamento* of Vatican II.

8. Bakan's *Sigmund Freud and the Jewish Mystical Tradition* (1958) offers a complementary perspective. In a semester-long course, I'd include both Klein and Bakan, as well as Boyarin (1997), Geller (1993, 1997), and Gilman (1993), important contemporary theorists of Freud's Jewishness.

9. For students who wish further readings on Freud, Lacan, and religion, I point to my 1992 article and to James DiCenso's 1999 *The Other Freud*.

10. See also Jonte-Pace 1997.

11. Alternatively, I've used Philip Rieff's 1966 volume, *Triumph of the Therapeutic*, a text tinged with nostalgia for an earlier culture of the "religious man," for a discussion of the psychologizing of modernity enacted by both Freud and Jung.

References

Anonymous. December 2002. 2002 Western universities, top schools. *www.usnews.com/usnews/edu/college/rankings*.

Bakan, David. 1958. *Sigmund Freud and the Jewish mystical tradition,* Boston: Beacon.

Boyarin, Daniel. 1997. *Unheroic conduct: The rise of heterosexuality and the invention of the Jewish man.* Berkeley: University of California Press.

Buber, Martin. 1957. *The eclipse of God: Studies in the relation of religion and philosophy.* New York: Harper.

Buhle, Mari Jo. 1998. *Feminism and its discontents: A century of struggle with psychoanalysis.* Cambridge, Mass.: Harvard University Press.

Capps, Donald, and James Dittes, ed. 1990. *The hunger of the heart: Reflections on the Confessions of Augustine.* Society for the Scientific Study of Religion. Monograph Series 8, Princeton Theological Seminary. Princeton, N.J.: Center for Religion, Self, and Society.

DiCenso, James. 1999. *The other Freud: Religion, culture, and psychoanalysis.* New York: Routledge.

Doolittle, Hilda (H.D.). 1981. The master. *Feminist Studies* 7, no. 3: 407–16.

Dundes, Alan. 1980. *Interpreting folklore.* Bloomington: Indiana University Press.

Eliot, T. S. 1928/1988. Review of *The future of an illusion.* In *Freud without hindsight: Reviews of his work 1893–1939,* edited by Norman Kiell. Madison, Conn.: International Universities Press.

Freud, Sigmund. 1953–1974. *The standard edition of the complete psychological works of Sigmund Freud* (hereafter *SE*), *Volumes 1–24*; translated and edited by James Strachey. London: Hogarth Press.

    1900. *The interpretation of dreams. SE* 4–5: 1–627.

    1912–13. *Totem and taboo. SE* 13: 1–163.

    1913. Theme of the three caskets. *SE* 12: 291–301.

    1915. Thoughts for the times on war and death. *SE* 14: 275–301.

    1916. On transience. *SE* 14: 303–307.

    1920. *Beyond the pleasure principle. SE* 18: 3–143.

    1927. *The future of an illusion. SE* 21: 5–58.

    1928. A religious experience. *SE* 21: 167–72.

    1930. *Civilization and its discontents. SE* 21: 64–148.

    1933. Why war? *SE* 22: 195–98.

    1939. *Moses and monotheism. SE* 23: 1–138.

    1940. Medusa's head. *SE* 18: 273–74.

Gay, Peter. 1999. Psychoanalyst Sigmund Freud: Great minds of the century. *Time,* 29 March, 64–69.

Geller, Jay. 1993. A paleontological view of Freud's study of religion: Unearthing the *leitfossil* circumcision. *Modern Judaism* 13: 49–70.

———. 1997. Identifying 'Someone who is himself one of them': Recent studies of Freud's Jewish identity. *Religious Studies Review* 23: 323–31.

Gilman, Sander. 1993. *Freud, race, and gender.* Princeton, N.J.: Princeton University Press.

Homans, Peter. 1995. *Jung in context,* 2nd ed. Chicago: University of Chicago Press.

Jonte-Pace, Diane. 1992. Situating Kristeva differently: Psychoanalytic readings of woman and religion. In *Body/text in Julia Kristeva: Woman, religion, psychoanalysis,* edited by D. Crownfield. Albany: State University of New York Press, 1–22.

———. 1996. At home in the uncanny: Freudian representations of death, mothers, and the afterlife. *Journal of the American Academy of Religion* 64: 61–88.

———. 1997. Julia Kristeva and the psychoanalytic study of religion: Rethinking Freud's cultural texts. In *Religion, society, and psychoanalysis: Readings in contemporary theory.* Edited by J. Jacobs and D. Capps. Boulder, Colo.: Westview Press, 240–68.

———. 2001a. Analysts, critics, and inclusivists: Feminist voices in the psychology of religion. In *Religion and Psychology: Mapping the Terrain,* edited by Diane Jonte-Pace and William Parsons. London: Routledge.

———. 2001b. *Speaking the unspeakable: Religion, misogyny, and the uncanny mother in Freud's cultural texts.* Berkeley: University of California Press.

Jung, Carl. 1963. *Memories, dreams, reflections.* New York: Vintage.

———. 1968. *The Collected Works of C. G. Jung* (hereafter *CW*), edited by Herbert Read, M. Fordham, and G. Adler, translated by R. F. C. Hull. Princeton, N.J.: Princeton University Press.

    1953. *Two essays on analytical psychology. CW* 7, pp. 3–349.

    1959. *Aion. CW* 9, part 2, pp. 3–333.

    1968. *Archetypes of the collective unconscious. CW* 9, part 1, pp. 3–451.

Klein, Dennis. 1985. *Jewish origins of the psychoanalytic movement.* Chicago: University of Chicago Press.

Kristeva, Julia. 1987. *In the beginning was love: Psychoanalysis and faith.* Translated by Arthur Goldhammer. New York: Columbia University Press.

————. 1991. *Strangers to ourselves*. Translated by Leon S. Roudiez. New York: Columbia University Press.

McGuire, William, ed. 1974. *The Freud/Jung letters: The correspondence between Sigmund Freud and C. G. Jung*. Translated by Ralph Mannheim and R. F. C. Hull. Princeton, N.J.: Princeton University Press.

Miller, David. 1986. 'Attack upon Christendom!' The anti-Christianism of depth psychology. *Thought* 61, no. 240: 56–67.

Mitchell, Juliet. 1974. *Psychoanalysis and feminism: Freud, Reich, Laing and women*. New York: Random House.

Moyers, Bill. 1988. *The power of myth, Vol. 1: The hero's journey*. Video. Public Broadcasting System.

National Conference of Catholic Bishops. 2000. *Ex corde ecclesiae: The application to the United States*. Washington, D.C.: US Catholic Conference.

Perry, William. 1970. *Forms of intellectual and ethical development in the college years*. New York: Holt, Rinehart, and Winston.

Ricoeur, Paul. 1970. *Freud and philosophy*. New Haven, Conn.: Yale University Press.

Rieff, Philip. 1966. *Triumph of the therapeutic*. New York: Harpers.

Roth, Michael, ed. 1998. *Freud: Conflict and culture*. New York: Knopf.

Segal, Robert, ed. 1998. *Jung on mythology*. Encountering Jung Series. Princeton, N.J.: Princeton University Press.

Ulanov, Ann Bedford. 1971. *The feminine in Jungian psychology and Christian theology*. Evanston, Ill.: Northwestern University Press.

Van Herik, Judith. 1982. *Freud on femininity and faith*. Berkeley: University of California Press.

Zeller, Max. 1982. Memory of C. G. Jung. In *C.G. Jung, Emma Jung, and Toni Wolff: A collection of remembrances*, edited by Ferne Jensen. San Francisco: Analytical Psychology Club of San Francisco.

2

Freud and/as the Jew in the Multicultural University

Jay Geller

Rarely taught in psychology, occasionally picked up in literature and theory courses, and usually read in order to be condemned in women's and queer studies offerings, the work of the self-proclaimed atheist Sigmund Freud regularly finds its home today in religious studies. One text in particular, *The Future of an Illusion* (*SE* 21; Freud 1961b), one of Freud's least psychoanalytical works, a text which Freud considered both "childish" and a testament to his old age,[1] usually comes to be taken as representative.[2] What does it mean for instructors in religious studies to opt for *Future* rather than *Civilization and Its Discontents* (*SE* 21; Freud 1961a), Freud's pessimistic meditation on the vicissitudes of humanity's instinctual life, the conflict between libido and aggression—between Eros and the death instinct—and the tension, externally, between those instinctual demands and the demands of society and, internally, between the ego and the superego? Students find instead the father of psychoanalysis presented as a rather naive figure of the rationalist Enlightenment with an outrageous optimism about science (and its god Logos), a constructor of arguments against straw men, and a producer of extremely reductive and simplistic explanations who shows little if any respect for religion and the religious. Freud, in effect, has become himself a straw man, and his cultural role has been, at best, relegated to the German-accented caricature that has pervaded popular culture for the past two-thirds of a century.[3]

The current common wisdom further informs us that Freud was a misogynist and a homophobe, who marginalized if not dismissed women's experience (and psychology) and pathologized homosexuality,[4] as well as infantilized non-

Europeans and viewed the working class as a mob at the mercy of group psychology.[5] And not only was he ideologically retrograde but, as his many despisers claim, he falsified evidence, made greater claims than his cases warranted, and showed a complete lack of courage in repudiating the seduction theory (Crews 1998; Masson 1984). Freud's works—thanks in large part to his epigone and simplifiers, but Freud too is not without responsibility—are read as prescriptive rather than descriptive of identity formation in modern Euroamerican life. Hence Freud is understood as not just wrong but also a source of oppression of women and gay people, as well as of non-Europeans and proletarians by making the white male European bourgeois heterosexual (albeit with repeatedly overcome homosexual tendencies)[6] the universal norm. Why bother teaching this retrograde individual, especially now as the perceived role of the university has undergone so many changes in content and composition?

We bother in part because Freud's work is far from univocal on questions of identity, gender, and sexuality, often working against its tendency toward reflecting bourgeois norms, and in part, a rather paradoxical part, because of those very changes. Because, for the American university, which once looked to Germany for its *Wissenschaft* and the WASP elite for its *Mannschaft*, has since the end of World War II begun to diversify demographically and intellectually. First more Jews, women, and working-class students were admitted, then more African American, Asian American, Native American, and Latino students, as well as other immigrant and foreign students, and—a half-generation to a generation later—even the faculty has begun to diversify (cf. Oren 1985). Changes in the world (such as the end of colonial empires) and America's self-image also had its effects: perspectives became both more global and more local. The breakdown of empires (whether French and British colonialism, the Pax Americana, or the Soviet bloc), combined with the self-assertion of the one-time colonials and the growing recognition of the significance of the Holocaust, have fragmented the master narratives that so Eurocentrically explained it all. The progressive faces of once (and still, if less obviously) triumphant hegemonies were unmasked and the histories of oppressions past and present came to the fore. Now the university aims to recognize both global cultures and American subcultures. It endeavors to let in those normally shut out—to promote sensitivity (by members of the dominant group) and to provide a corrective (for the marginalized; Beck 1996).

Further, in and out of the university, American civil culture has experienced a shift from pluralism to multiculturalism. Where once a politics of interest, by which a particular group and its individual members were allowed to pursue its/their objectives as any other group without necessarily becoming like those others,[7] governed (at least in theory) the public sphere, now the politics of identity has come to the fore whereby each group defines itself as victim, oppressed, threatened with cultural loss, and in need of redress. The quest for respect is magnified by a concomitant quest for recognition. Whereas pluralism was in part a response to how the mark of difference marginalized, multiculturalism valorizes the mark—now being unmarked warrants exclusion (Greenberg 1998).

So why read the dead white male talking head called Freud now? Is he of only historical interest or a necessary *rite de passage*: one of the fathers who must be murdered in order for this "post"-generation to move on? Reading as exemplary a text as Freud's *Future of an Illusion*, which at least on the surface does justice to neither his body of work nor his life situation, certainly facilitates, if not justifies, such intellectual parricide. As a consequence, the relevance to the new multicultural university of an examination of Freud's work—in particular the relationship between his social location and the production of that work—is overlooked. However, when we shift focus from Freud the *atheist* jew to Freud the atheist *Jew*, to the individual who wrote "As a Jew I was prepared to join the Opposition and to do without agreement with the 'compact majority'"(*SE* 20), and examine that relationship we encounter the lengths and depths a postcolonial subject goes to survive (and succeed) in the metropole, as well as collide with the one hegemonic discourse occluded by the rush to uncover and subvert hegemonies based on class, gender, race, ethnicity, and sexual orientation: Christianity (cf. Heschel 1998).

Since World War II, as one anthropologist has recently argued, the "Jews became white folks"—that is, they are no longer viewed as belonging to the oppressed, but rather to the oppressors (Biale 1998; Brodkin 1998). At least Jewish men; Jewish women are oppressed by Jewish men and their patriarchal traditions. This allegedly glaring male whiteness sometimes blinds the reader from recognizing that the Jews were, prior to the Shoah, the Europeans' designated other and hence from recognizing Freud the Jew as something more than a dead white guy. This is not to assert that Freud needs to be affirmed (or denounced; cf. Roith 1987) as representative of the Jewish multiculture. Rather, an analysis of Freud the Jew as a postcolonial subject of the Austro-Hungarian Empire allows us to rethink both multicultural curricula and Freud.

Multicultural curricula should not just be affirmative of groups that have historically been marked as marginal and marked for oppression by the dominant unmarked group; rather, these other histories must be seen as part of an unacknowledged (often effaced) but none the less crucial component of the formation of the dominant group. Thus European history cannot be understood outside of the relationship between gentile and Jew—that to omit this relation elides pivotal aspects of European identity formation, not only prior to Jewish civil emancipation but also during its century-long uneven process, as well as after emancipation became enshrined in law. Hence, discussion of Freud in the multicultural university is also not just about Freud's alleged contributions to Euroamerican hegemonic culture. Rather, we must learn to read what has become one of the most normative or exemplary of Euroamerican modes of thinking and knowing (and hence of disciplining and supervising), Freud's psychoanalysis, as itself a hybrid formation that mimics those modes to the point of subverting their authority. "To the extent to which discourse is a form of defensive warfare, mimicry marks those moments of civil disobedience within the discipline of civility: signs of spectacular resistance. The words of the master become the site of hybridity" (Bhabha 1994,

121). And hybridity, Homi Bhabha notes, is "the name for the strategic reversal of the process of domination through disavowal (that is, the production of discriminatory identities that secure the 'pure' and original identity of authority)" (112). In other words, the postcolonial appropriates or repeats the colonizer's discourses by which his or her identity has been constructed as an object of the (stereotypical) disciplinary knowledge that maintains the colonizer's hegemony. However, by virtue of his or her position as both object and subject of discourse—as, in the case of Freud, both Jewish other and Viennese doctor—the postcolonial can displace the products of those discourses and shift their purported referents or unsettle the dominant's claim to sole possession of authority so long as the mimicry is not recognized as such.[8]

Freud as Postcolonial Subject

Born in Freiberg, Moravia, in 1856, Freud together with his family moved to Vienna when he was three. They lived in the district of Leopoldstadt where the vast majority of Jews from the periphery of the Austro-Hungarian Empire had emigrated and where most of the lower-class Viennese Jews such as the Freuds resided; Leopoldstadt figured "the Jewish ghetto in the popular imagination" (Rozenblit 1992, 235). Despite their tenuous financial situation, his parents ensured that young Sigmund acquired a bourgeois *Bildung* at gymnasium and university; he then pursued a bourgeois career path and, after marriage, resided in a bourgeois district. Although he never denied—denial struck him as "not only undignified but outright foolish" (*SE* 20: 273)—and indeed frequently asserted that he was a Jew, Freud realized that he was not in control of the significance of that identification. For many gentiles—and not a few assimilated Jews—"Jew" conveyed the image of the *Ostjuden*, the East European shtetl Jew (Aschheim 1982). This identification was in part sustained because a cultural division of labor between Austro-Germans and Jews remained even though the types of employment in bourgeois Vienna had changed (Verdery 1979, drawing upon Hechter 1975). Also contributing to this identification was the migration of *Ostjuden* to and through Central Europe, especially after the pogroms of the last decades of the nineteenth century and the first decades of the twentieth. Further, the identification was in part generated by a need to make distinctions. Such differentiation helped create, maintain, and confirm identities that could replace those eroded by the forces of modernization, secularization, and commodification. These identities were forged out of the "natural" differences of nation and race, sex and gender. For Freud's German (and Austrian) readers, the space between the inhabitants of the colonizing metropole and those of the colonized periphery created, maintained, and confirmed those essential and hierarchical differences; however, when the colonized enter the metropole and acculturate, the ever precarious identities of the dominant population become even more so. To counter the threat, the colonizers imagine the postcolonial subject is merely mimicking them; underlying differences remain and are forever betrayed (Geller 1994).[9] The Jews perform their difference; for example, their purported disintegrative intellect and particularity correspond to the presumed disintegrative effect of their presence amid the would-be homogeneous and harmonious hegemonic culture of the metropole. Thus, as Freud's works were being consigned to the book-fueled bonfires of May 1933, the speaker called out : "Against the soul-unraveling (*seelenzerfasernde*) overestimation of instinctual life, for the nobility of the human soul, I deliver up the writings of Sigmund Freud to the flames."[10] Six years earlier (1927), Freud's former collaborator and one-time heir apparent, Carl Jung, had already derided the particularity of psychoanalysis: "It is a quite unpardonable mistake to accept the conclusions of a Jewish psychology as generally valid. Nobody would dream of taking Chinese or Indian psychology as binding upon ourselves" (Jung 1953, 149 n. 8).*

Thus, throughout his adult life Freud endeavored to distance psychoanalysis from the label "a Jewish national affair" (letter to Abraham, 3 May 1908; Freud and Abraham 1965); himself from the linguistic, cultural, and religious accouterments of his more traditional forebears; and both from the anti-Semitic representations that littered public—and private—life.[11] Like other black faces, Freud wore the white masks of Austro-German bourgeois sexual, gender, and familial identities (cf. Fanon 1967)[12]—identities that psychoanalytic discourse sustained as much as it provided the narratives and tools to subvert them. And like other postcolonial subjects he internalized the intertwined dominant anti-Semitic, misogynistic, and homophobic discourses that regularly and traumatically bombarded the Jews (and himself as a Jew) with the opposition between the virile masculine norm and the hypervirile cum effeminate other. Freud then reinscribed these images as well as those norms in a hegemonic discourse (the science of psychoanalysis) that in part projected them upon those other Jews (not to be confused with Jewishness per se), as well as upon women, homosexuals, so-called primitives, the masses, and neurotics, and in part transformed these representations into universal characteristics.[13] Freud's repudiation of traditional Jewry climaxed with his depiction of the savage Hebrews in *Moses and Monotheism* (1939). This mass of ex-slaves was unable to renounce its instincts—unlike its later Jewish and bourgeois descendants—and as a consequence murdered its leader Moses. And yet it is this work, perhaps above all others, that allows us to understand and teach the hows (and possible whys) of postcolonial hybridity out of which multiculturalism emerged and to which it should return (albeit differently).

The Pedagogy of Postcoloniality or Multiculturalism *Mon Amour*

How and what does one teach in religious studies in the multicultural university? Teaching demands a number of qualities—engagement, receptivity, and style, let alone a broad background. Engagement arises out of the realization that there is something of value to share and out of the willingness to share values; teaching is an interested profession in which something is at stake. And what is at stake is not only the legitimacy of a discipline, nor is it merely the matter of the authority of teachers' arguments and classroom position. Teachers' interests emerge from their numerous and often contradictory identities and subject positions. Receptivity demands an openness to the questions and answers, the challenges and postures—the diverse interests and identities—presented by the students (and the texts). The line between student and teacher loses its sharpness; they become partners in learning. At the margin between engagement and receptivity lies style. Style is an attitude, a way to read texts, to comport oneself toward the world. Style betrays both the teachers' incompleteness and their demand for more: teachers, like the texts they read and the students with whom they read these texts, always point beyond themselves. All of these qualities combine to indicate that teaching is more than imparting a series of propositions. It is a performance that always threatens to collapse into virtuosity, yet is only successful when it elicits student participation. Teaching eschews passivity. And it never ends.

Religion, too, is recognized as emerging out of concrete practices and not confined to the constraints of theological doctrines. It escapes the ghetto, transgresses the boundaries, into which Protestant modernity would consign it (as well, indeed, as every other seemingly discrete realm of human activity—the economy, politics, art, etc.). The inadequacies of such pigeonholing are pointedly and poignantly clear in students who take courses on the Holocaust to learn about Judaism and more generally in Anglo-American attempts to distinguish the "religion" Judaism from the "people" the Jews; for Jews, the lines between religion, ethnic identity, and community life are very fuzzy. The overlap is better conveyed in the German *Judentum*, which can refer to Judaism, Jewry, or Jewishness. Religion, as *Judentum* exemplifies, inflects life: it is what people do. And among their doings, people religiously engage in tacit as well as explicit acts of interpretation.

So what then does such a teacher teach in an introductory course in religious studies? Not necessarily the "great books" of the Western—or Eastern—tradition. With the multicultural recognition of the nonhierarchical diversity and entanglement of histories, traditions, students, and disciplines the canon has begun to undergo revision (indeed it is always, but perhaps now the perspective from which this reevaluation is going on has shifted; other voices are being raised, and some are being heard) and so are such terms as "tradition" and "canon." Thus, texts are needed that put in question their placement within any tradition—texts on the margin. Actually, all texts are texts on the margin if only so read, but that requires, again, a certain style. Moreover we tradition-trained teachers often do not have the categories in which to confront such marginal texts (to see how they frame a tradition—give it definition even as they are excluded from that definition and even as they subvert that definition).

To help the students achieve that style, as well as to be able to read the texts of the margin, the course should perhaps begin with those marginal texts that offer ready access. One such text is Freud's *Moses and Monotheism*. It reads like a bad novel,[14] and students love to read bad novels. It is a text that continuously rewrites itself, uncovering new facets, providing new interpretations, as we readers should be doing. It describes how texts are formed and thus gives us clues how to read any text, including itself.

> Almost everywhere noticeable gaps, disturbing repetitions, and obvious contradictions have come about [in a text]—indications which reveal things to us which it was not intended to communicate. In its implications the distortion of a text resembles a murder: the difficulty is not in perpetrating the deed, but in getting rid of its traces. . . . In many instances we may nevertheless count upon finding what has been suppressed and disavowed material hidden away somewhere else, though changed and torn from its context. Only it will not always be easy to recognize it. (*SE* 23: 43)

Freud's manifest narrative postulates that Moses was an Egyptian noble and follower of the pharaoh Ikhnaten and his monotheistic cult of Aten. After Ikhnaten's death and the overthrow of his cult, Moses adopted the Hebrews and in turn demanded that they adopt his rigorous ethical monotheism, as well as bound them to the Egyptian practice of circumcision. After having been led out of Egypt, the Hebrews revolted against Moses's stern demands and killed him in the wilderness. Freud continued his story of the Hebrew people as two generations later they joined with the Midianites at Kadesh and adopted their volcano god-demon Yahweh and nonmonotheistic religion. Yahweh was identified with the god of the exodus, and the custom of circumcision was also kept. According to Freud, this "compromise at Kadesh" helped the Hebrews to deal with the trauma of Moses's murder: it aided and abetted the repression of virtually all traces both of the murder and of Moses's Egyptian origins. While the Mosaic tradition was preserved by the Levitical priesthood, it was another six hundred years before monotheism would return with compulsive force. While the historical motif (qua motif) of Moses the Egyptian has recently been explored by Jan Assman (1997), Freud has found few defenders for either his parricidal speculation or his "just-so story" (*SE* 18, citing A. L. Kroeber) of the primal horde that the Sinai saga repeats. Then again, we do not read *Moses and Monotheism* in order to reconstruct the historical origins of Judaism; rather, we engage this work because it raises issues and poses theories and, perhaps above all, because it is a text. It asks all the big questions—and even proffers some answers: What is the nature of text, tradition, scripture, interpretation, religion, divinity, history, community, gender, ethnicity, ethics, identity, and so on? Is the nature of something determined by its origin? What is the relationship between autobiography and writing, between the analyst's situation and the object under analysis? Do we understand history, culture, and change from an individual or supraindividual perspective? Further, *Moses and Monotheism* illustrates the necessity to go beyond the manifest content to seek the latent forces that motivate or condition that content. Reading this work forces the student to ask whether a text that is so apparently wrongheaded and at times so offensive requires that we dismiss it, as well as perhaps its author.

To teach such a multilayered and ambiguous text requires a multilayered and attentive approach—and that leads to its relevance for the multicultural curriculum. First, we engage the manifest level of the text. If this can't be understood, if students don't have some tentative understanding of the work's narrative and arguments, all that follows will be for naught. Nevertheless, as we pursue this preliminary understanding, I call attention to as well as solicit observation of anomalies; for example, to certain figures that repeat (e.g., the references to marks [*Zeichen*], circumcision, doubles, fossils) or shifts in agenda (what question is Freud really pursuing) or aspects of the Moses story that are omitted (e.g., Moses's uncircumcised lips; Exod. 6:12, 30), so that the student will recognize that something else is going on. Drawing warrant from Freud's comment about textual distortions as the traces of suppressed and disavowed material (cited above), together with his own confession in the second of the two embedded prefaces that he was "unable to wipe out the traces of the history of the work's origin" (*SE* 23: 103), we apply Freud to Freud and see if he has let slip the existence of another scene—not Kadesh but Vienna—where Freud, Freud the Jew, substitutes for Moses the non-Jew.

This text-immanent approach is supplemented by outside readings: other Freudian texts (this text is tied into works like *Totem and Taboo,* which address both religious origins and the primal horde; other of his examinations of religion such as *Future*; the role of Jewish representation in texts ranging from *Interpretation of Dreams* to "Fetishism"), as well as biographical (his Jewish background and that of the psychoanalytic movement; the debates over Freud's relationship to that background; the elision of Karl Abraham's work on Ikhnaten that Freud once praised),[15] cultural (anti-Semitism and Jewish "particularity," the role of science and its relationship to religion, representations of gender, body, Jews, etc.) and historical (the changing situation in Austria during Freud's lifetime; his relationship to Father Schmidt and the Austrian Catholic church, etc.) material. While the class will come to certain, perhaps high-falutin', notions about the latent forces and structures of this text, as well as some serious reflection on the kinds of issues of text, tradition, identity, and so on that *Moses and Monotheism* raises, it is hoped a more important lesson will begin to be imparted: how to read. In sum, through this encounter with Freud's *Moses* I want to teach students how to read culture: the often conflicted messages and maneuvers that circulate in the texts we read and lives we lead, the negotiations that take place on the extremely permeable boundaries between cultures. I want students to attend to what is going on, to the anomalies that populate the margins—and middles—of everyday life; how we are all post-colonials and that our hyphenated existences and many subject positions are not merely an aggregate of discrete perspectives, but thoroughly interwoven and often conflicted. And what are the rewards that the study of Freud catalyzes? The articulations of un-thought-through presuppositions and conclusions, the unveiling of questions previously unasked and the mapping of regions previously unexplored, and the development of self-reflective, articulate, dialogue-prone, critically thinking, and vigilant members of the community.

Notes

1. Gay (1988, 524–25) cites Freud's letters to Ferenczi (23 October 1927) and Andreas-Salomé (11 December 1927), as well as the recollection of the French psychoanalyst René Laforgue.

2. Based on an informal survey of religion and psychology and critics of religion courses. According to W. W. Norton, the publisher of the paperback versions of both *Future* and *Civilization and Its Discontents*, the latter is in fact the better seller.

3. This popular caricature was quite evident at the recent (opened October 1998) "Freud: Culture and Conflict" exhibit at the Library of Congress. A comparable case is Charlie Chaplin's portrayal of Adenoid Hynkel in *The Great Dictator,* which forms the image of Hitler for many.

4. The mothers of second-wave feminism, from de Beauvoir and Friedan to Millet and Greer, placed considerable onus for women's continued subjection on Sigmund Freud. While Mitchell (1975) led a number of feminist critics to reconsider the progressive potential of Freud's work, writers such as Roith (1987) still accuse him of an insurmountable bias against women. On the reexamination of Freud's views of homosexuality, Dollimore (1991) and Abelove (1993) address how the moralistic pathologization of homosexuality by the American Psychoanalytic Association has been mistakenly read back to the founding father, Freud.

5. At the "Freud at the Millennium" conference that marked the opening of the Freud exhibit at the Library of Congress (October 1998), several speakers discoursed on racist attitudes in Freud's writings. I felt like Louis in *Casablanca* when informed that gambling was going on at Rick's: "I was shocked." Few European intellectuals of the first third of the twentieth century escaped the bourgeois, racialist cast of their Eurocentrism, especially postcolonial Jewish subjects like Freud who, caught between being a pariah and a parvenu, internalized as much as they may have subverted the dominant ideology. This is not to rationalize his primitivist stereotyping of nonwestern peoples and the proletarian masses (cf. Fuss 1995, 35–36); rather, it is a recognition that often Freud needs to be read against the grain.

6. In a footnote added in 1915 to the first of the *Three Essays on the Theory of Sexuality*, Freud (*SE* 7: 145n) writes: "All human beings are capable of making a homosexual object-choice and have in fact made one in their unconscious. Indeed, libidinal attachments to persons of the same sex play no less a part as factors in normal mental life . . . than do similar attachments to the opposite sex."

7. Of course, group values and objectives were assumed to be compatible with the norm (read the universalization of the values and objectives of the dominant group).

8. In a culture that privileges its own self-identification as the one and only pure, autonomous subject, and that forecloses difference, the postcolonial has really only two choices: either mimic the representation of his or her particular otherness as constructed by the colonizer's discourses or—whether out of narcissistic identification or in order to perform a subversive parody or "to use the master's tools against the master"—create a mimetic approximation. However, from the perspective of the colonizer it can only be an approximation, *"almost the same, but not quite"* (Bhabha 1994, 86; emphasis in original), of the colonizer's identity and therefore both inadequate and proof of the colonized's inferiority. The dominant dictates the terms of identification; cf. "Interior Colonies: Frantz Fanon and the Politics of Identification" in Fuss 1995. Hence, Freud's concern about psychoanalysis being labeled a "Jewish science": the particularity of "Jewish" undercuts the normativity and universality conveyed by "science."

9. Further, the Euroamerican devaluation of mimesis and mimicry threatens the efficacy of hybridity if the subaltern's new clothes are pointed out.

10. "Verbrennung undeutschen Schriftums," *Neuköllner Tageblatt* (12 May 1933); cit. Poliakov and Wulf 1983, 121.

11. Gilman (1993, 201 n.1) provides an extensive list of the literature on Freud's Jewishness; this four-page compendium covers works from 1924 to 1992. For a discussion of more recent works including Gilman's, see Geller 1997.

12. Fanon's analyses of the dilemma of the colonial or postcolonial in the metropole have become a regular counterpoint in studies of Freud's Jewishness; cf. Boyarin 1997, 248; 1998. On the representations of Jews as black, see Gilman 1985, esp. 29–35.

13. Discussions of the postcolonial subject as a negotiator of the interface of local experience and practice with imperial culture, language, and representation can be found in Williams and Chrisman 1994. For the analogous situation in India, see Nandy 1983.

14. I refer to it as "The Off-White Hotel" for those who recall D. M. Thomas's at times kitschy, at times insightful take on the Freud–Sabine Spielrein relationship, *The White Hotel* (1981).

15. Letter of 3 June 1912, Freud and Abraham 1965, 118–19; see Shengold 1972. On Freud's working through many of the other issues surrounding the project that would become *Moses and Monotheism*, see the series of letters beginning 30 September 1934 between Freud and Zweig 1987, 91ff.

References

Abelove, Henry. 1993. Freud, male homosexuality, and the Americans. In *The lesbian and gay studies reader*, edited by Henry Abelove, Michèle Aina Barak, and David M. Halperin. New York: Routledge.

Aschheim, Steven E. 1982. *Brothers and strangers: The East European Jew in German and German Jewish consciousness, 1800–1923*. Madison: University of Wisconsin Press.

Assman, Jan. 1997. *Moses the Egyptian. The memory of Egypt in Western monotheism*. Cambridge, Mass.: Harvard University Press.

Beck, Evelyn Torton. 1996. Jews and the multicultural university curriculum. In *The narrow bridge. Jewish views on multiculturalism*, edited by Marla Brettschneider. New Brunswick, N.J.: Rutgers University Press.

Bhabha, Homi. 1994. *The location of culture*. New York: Routledge.

Biale, David. 1998. The melting pot and beyond: Jews and the politics of multicultural America. In *Insider/outsider: American Jews and Multiculturalism*, edited by Biale, Galchinsky, and Heschel.

———, Michael Galchinsky, and Susannah Heschel, eds. 1998. *Insider/outsider. American Jews and multiculturalism*. Berkeley: University of California Press.

Blüher, Hans. 1926. *Traktate über die Heilkunde, insbesondere die Neurosenlehre*. Jena: Eugen Diederichs.

Boyarin, Daniel. 1997. *Unheroic conduct. The rise of heterosexuality and the invention of the Jewish man*. Berkeley: University of California Press.

———. 1998. What does a Jew want?; or The political meaning of the Phallus. In *The psychoanalysis of race*, edited by Christopher Lane. New York: Columbia University Press.

Brodkin, Karen. 1998. *How Jews became white folks & what that says about race in America*. New Brunswick, N.J.: Rutgers University Press.

Crews, Frederick, ed. 1998. *Unauthorized Freud: Doubters confront a legend*. New York: Viking Penguin.

Dollimore, Jonathan. 1991. *Sexual dissidence. Augustine to Wilde, Freud to Foucault*. Oxford: Oxford University Press.

Fanon, Frantz. 1967. *Black skins, white masks*, translated by Charles Lamm Markmann. New York: Grove Press.

Freud, Sigmond. 1953–1974. *The standard edition of the complete psychological works of Sigmund Freud [SE]*, edited by James Strachey et al. 24 vols. London: Hogarth Press.

    1905. *Three essays on the theory of sexuality. SE* 7: 123–243.

    1921. *Group psychology and the analysis of the ego. SE* 18: 65–143.

    1926. Address to the Society of Bnai Brith. *SE* 20: 273–74.

    1927. *The future of an illusion. SE* 21: 1–56.

    1930. *Civilization and its discontents. SE* 21: 57–145.

    1939. *Moses and Monotheism. SE* 23: 1–137.

———. 1961a. *Civilization and its discontents*. Edited and translated by James Strachey. New York: Norton.

———. 1961b. *The future of an illusion*. Edited and translated by James Strachey. New York: Norton.

———, and Karl Abraham. 1965. *A psychoanalytic dialogue. The letters of Sigmund Freud and Karl Abraham 1907–1926*. Edited by Hilda C. Abraham and Ernst L. Freud, translated by Bernard Marsh and Hilda C. Abraham. New York: Basic Books.

———, and Arnold Zweig. 1987. *Letters of Sigmund Freud and Arnold Zweig*. Edited by Ernst L. Freud, translated by Elaine and William Robson-Scott. New York: New York University Press.

Fuss, Diana. 1995. *Identification papers*. New York: Routledge.

Gay, Peter. 1988. *Freud. A life for our time*. New York: Norton.

Geller, Jay. 1994. Of mice and Mensa: Anti-Semitism and the Jewish genius. *The Centennial Review* 38, no. 2: 361–86.

———. 1997. Identifying "someone who is himself one of them": Recent studies of Freud's Jewish identity. *Religious Studies Review* 23, no. 4: 323–31.

Gilman, Sander. 1985. *Difference and pathology. Stereotypes of sexuality, race, and madness*. Ithaca, N.Y.: Cornell University Press.

———. 1993. *Freud, race, and gender*. Princeton, N.J.: Princeton University Press.

Greenberg, Cheryl. 1998. Pluralism and its discontents. The case of blacks and Jews. In *Insider/outsider: American Jews and multiculturalism*, edited by Biale, Galchinsky, and Heschel. Berkeley: University of California Press.

Hechter, Michael. 1975. *Internal colonialism: The Celtic fringe in British national development, 1536–1966*. Berkeley: University of California Press.

Heschel, Susannah. 1998. Jewish studies as counterhistory. In *Insider/outsider: American Jews and multiculturalism*, edited by Biale, Galchinsky, and Heschel. Berkeley: University of California Press.

Jung, C. G. 1953. The relations between the ego and the unconscious. In *Two essays on analytical psychology*. Vol. 7 of *The collected works of C. G. Jung*, edited by H. Read et al., translated by R. F. C. Hull. New York: Bollingen Foundation.

Masson, Jeffrey Moussaieff. 1984. *The assault on truth: Freud's suppression of the seduction theory*. New York: Farrar, Straus, and Giroux.

Mitchell, Juliet. 1975. *Psychoanalysis and feminism.* Harmondsworth, UK: Penguin.

Nandy, Ashis. 1983. *The intimate enemy: Loss and recovery of self under colonialism.* Delhi: Oxford University Press.

Oren, Dan A. 1985. *Joining the club: A history of Jews and Yale.* New Haven, Conn.: Yale University Press.

Poliakov, Léon, and Joseph Wulf, eds. 1983. *Das Dritte Reich und seine Denker.* Frankfurt/M: Ullstein.

Roith, Estelle. 1987. *The riddle of Freud.* London: Tavistock Publications.

Rozenblit, Marsha L. 1992. Jewish assimilation in Habsburg Vienna. In *Assimilation and community. The Jews in nineteenth-century Europe*, edited by Jonathan Frankel and Steven J. Zipperstein. Cambridge: Cambridge University Press.

Shengold, Leonard. 1972. A parapraxis of Freud's in relation to Karl Abraham. *American Imago* 29: 123–59.

Thomas, D. M. 1981. *The white hotel.* New York: Viking.

Verdery, Katherine. 1979. Internal colonialism in Austria-Hungary. *Ethnic and Racial Studies* 2, no. 3: 378–99.

Williams, Patrick, and Laura Chrisman, eds. 1994. *Colonial discourse and postcolonial theory. A reader.* New York: Columbia University Press.

3

Teaching Freud in the Seminary

Kirk A. Bingaman

Teaching Freud in the seminary! At first glance, it must seem like a supreme act of foolishness; the two hardly go hand in hand. After all, we all know by now that Freud was a reductionist, a positivist, and especially galling to the religious community, an avowed and unapologetic atheist. It was, as Freud himself saw it, his duty to agitate the sleep of humankind, and particularly the slumber of the religious believer. So why devote time, and even an entire semester, to someone who was so misguided, who confused his scientism with science, who was not always completely candid and objective about his clinical data, who posited that religion, more than anything else, is responsible for the intellectual retardation of the human species?

My personal interest in Freud, to the extent of teaching a course and publishing on the subject, began taking shape several years ago, in the context of the seminary classroom. During one class session of the course Religious Conversion, taught at the Graduate Theological Union (GTU), I presented to the students an overview of the classical psychology theorists—Freud and Jung—and their interpretations of religion. At one point, during the lecture on Freud, I noted that the philosopher and theologian Paul Ricoeur had suggested that because of Freud's extraordinary influence in the West, the religious believer is obligated to "converse" with Freud about his theory of religion. I told the class that Ricoeur offers no guarantees, except that the believer will not and cannot, following the encounter, be the same person with the same faith. In other words, an encounter with Freud is risky business. Yet, according to Ricoeur, because of Freud's extraordinarily influential critique of and challenge to religion, the greater risk for the religious believer "lies in avoiding the encounter altogether" (Wulff 1991, 315). Moreover, what religious believers will have to concede, after they have encountered Freud objectively, with a reasonable degree of critical distance from their presuppositional biases, is that Freud not only deserves a no but also a yes: while he did not get *everything* right about religious faith, he still managed to get *some* things right. Therefore, argues Ricoeur, the believer is obligated to keep religious faith *and* Freudian theory in dialectical tension, rather than simply embracing the totality of one while rejecting the totality of the other.

I concluded my presentation to the class by indicating that if we take Ricoeur's words to heart, then this will have major implications not only for our personal religious faith but also for theological education in general and pastoral care and counseling courses in particular. Said another way, if we take Ricoeur as our guide, we will begin making Freud and his theory of religion more of an integral part of theological education. Up to this point, the presentation had gone smoothly, with few interruptions—hardly any questions or comments from members of the class. I suspect that as long as we discussed Freud in a general and detached—that is, safe—sort of way students could acknowledge without too much difficulty that of course the field of psychology and even that of pastoral care and counseling owes something of a debt to Freud. But to up the ante by bringing Ricoeur and his philosophy of "total engagement" with Freud into the discussion was more than some of the students could handle. I remember one student in particular who raised his hand and very angrily proceeded to inform the class that we had no business devoting so much of our time to an atheist like Freud, someone who was "nothing but a false prophet." The implication was that because Freud came down on the "wrong side" of the issue, religious believers are not obligated to take him and his theory of religion seriously.

Indeed, I have witnessed and/or been involved in the teaching of the classical psychology theorists at the GTU, and what I have found is that the ordination-track (M.Div.) seminarian will readily sign up for a class on Jung, the perceived friend of religion, but not one on Freud, the perceived enemy of religion. Several years ago, James Jarrett, professor emeritus of education at the University of California, Berkeley, taught a course on Jung at the GTU. Several dozen seminarians, most of whom were M.Div. students, attended the class. The following year, I taught a course on *Freud and Religion* at the GTU, and had about half as many students as the Jung class; the only M.Div. student was a woman who was not even considering a call to any form of ministry. She, along with the M.A. and Ph.D. students, were all academic-track seminarians. One ordination-track student, who decided to drop the class on Freud, commented, "if only this had been a class on Jung, then I would stay because I'd be learning something relevant to my future ministry.

Methodological Strategies

For the past few years, from that presentation in the classroom to the present, I have been consumed with an interest that is twofold: (1) Freud's theory that religious faith is psychological projection, and (2) the responses Freud and his theory of religion evoke in the religious believer. In a sense, I have been "testing" what Ricoeur puts forward—the religious believer is obligated to hold Freud and religious faith in dialectical tension—in the context of theological education, and I have witnessed a variety of emotional responses: anger, on the part of one student; distancing, on the part of the student who dropped the Freud and Religion class; and apparent mass indifference on the part of the entire student body, which from the beginning keeps Freud at arm's length presumably because he has nothing constructive to offer the candidate for ministry.

Though the emotions and responses differ, there is at least one unifying feature: an aversion to Freud. Rarely do you find students in the context of theological education engaging or reengaging Freud and his theory of religion, let alone acknowledging, with Ricoeur, that Freud did manage to get some things right about the intrapsychic dynamics of religious faith. I find myself wondering if my student in the Religious Conversion class actually deserves more credit than I have given him. He, after all, was willing to engage Freud and Freudian theory for this particular class session, which is more than I can say for many other seminarians. True, he reacted very angrily to Ricoeur's suggestion that religious believers are obligated to listen to and learn from Freud, but then again I suspect that if more of his classmates had been sitting there with him that day and taking Ricoeur's words to heart, they too would have reacted with emotions more potent than indifference. My hypothesis is that anger, indifference, and emotional distancing vis-à-vis Freud, which we frequently encounter in the context of seminary education, are all frontline responses aimed at keeping the Freudian theory of religion far removed from one's religious faith. In keeping Freud at a distance, or in flippantly dismissing him as passé or irrelevant to any discussion on religion, the seminarian is more than likely mounting an intrapsychic defense against a stronger emotional reaction, such as the fear of having one's faith deconstructed. In that sense, the seminarian I encountered in the classroom was being more honest about his genuine feelings toward Freud and about the evocative power of Freud more than sixty years after his death.

It is particularly naive or disingenuous to conclude that Freud's legacy died when he did, or at least died off with the neo-Freudian successors. Nothing, as far as I am concerned, could be further from the truth. The spirit of his work, as Ricoeur has suggested, lives on in the Western world and has been internalized in the Western psyche. So much of the Western "epistemological standpoint" or taken-for-granted reality—especially our views on the human psyche and even the nature of religious faith—can be traced, directly or indirectly, back to Freud. Thus, one can understand why the stakes were so high and the debate so emotionally charged during the Library of Congress exhibit on Freud, "Culture and Conflict," held in 1998 in Washington, D.C. Some, in the interest of good science and/or fairness to religion, denounced the exhibit as too worshipful of one they considered to be an atheist, reductionist, or positivist. Others, though, argued that the shortcomings of Freud as person, scientist, and interpreter of religion do not necessarily preclude a serious discussion of Freudian psychology as a hermeneutical method. I have no doubt that Paul Ricoeur would wholeheartedly support the latter view.

However, as I have been illustrating with examples from the classroom of theological education, what we frequently encounter in communities of religious faith is an attitude toward Freud that is similar to the first of these two views. Seminarians, as I have discovered firsthand, will often point out that since Freud reduced religion to little more than the projection of our own subjectivity onto a perceived cosmic provider and sustainer of the universe, he has nothing to teach believers about religious faith. Lest my "data" be dismissed as mere anecdotal evidence, I offer more conclusive evidence of this attitude toward Freud, as described in the *Dictionary of Pastoral Care and Counseling*: "The full meaning of [recent] developments within psychoanalysis," we read, "has yet to be adequately explored by Christian theology," largely because of Christianity's "distaste for Freudian theory" (Hunter 1990, 988, 1,003). This "distaste for Freudian theory" is manifested in theological education anytime students, when confronted with Freud's challenge to religious faith, move into an either/or position vis-à-vis Freud rather than attempting to live within the tension that is sure to develop after engaging his theory.

The religious believer, to be sure, is presently situated in a particularly complicated postmodern world, which seems to be getting more confusing with each passing day. In an attempt to make this world more manageable and understandable, the believer might be tempted to reduce religious faith to the simplest possible terms, or the lowest common denominator. The world already has more than enough puzzling conundrums, so why add more? And doesn't religion exist to offer the individual a measure of solace and comfort in the midst of the chaos of daily living, a measure of that peace which passes all human understanding? Besides, religion and theology, in and of themselves, have more than enough complexities, as any seminarian can tell you, without adding someone like Freud and his theory of religion to the mix. And yet, religious faith *cannot* be reduced to simple terms, for it is by nature a particularly complex phenomenon. Therefore, it is crucial for students, during the seminary years, to examine the phenomenon of religious faith from the perspective of different fields and disciplines, including those that may reinforce preexisting beliefs—biblical studies, systematic theology, and so on—as well as disciplines that may challenge those beliefs—psychology, the natural sciences, and the like.

But how do we go about holding together, methodologically, Freudian psychology with more traditional interpretations of religion? Several theorists give us important clues. Paul Ricoeur, as I have already pointed out, puts forward the idea that a Freudian hermeneutics of suspicion has both the ca-

pacity to disrupt one's religious faith and the capacity to strengthen and enlarge it. For example, what the religious believer can learn from, to use
Ricoeur's word, the "schooling" of Freud is that an exalted and moralistic
God, who does console and protect but also accuses and punishes, *is* a projection of the Oedipal father of childhood in response to human anxiety and
helplessness. Whether or not Freud's theory of religion finds scientific and
empirical confirmation, Ricoeur is convinced that Freudian psychology, read
hermeneutically, confirms that human beings do at times prefer moral condemnation from a punishing God to an existence that is unprotected and
unconsoled. However, he is not suggesting, like Freud, that ultimate reality
is simply *Ananke*, or harsh necessity, and that human beings, in the face of
this reality, are morally obligated to accept the situation and not pretend it
could be otherwise. Through what Ricoeur calls "the grace of imagination,"
religious believers can move from the Freudian stance of mere resignation in
the face of harsh reality to a more creative mode of dwelling on the earth.

Freud, then, as far as Ricoeur is concerned, is entitled to both a no *and* a
yes from the religious believer. The implication, of course, is that religious
believers cannot sidestep Freud, dismissing him outright because he came to
the "wrong" conclusion about religious faith. Because of the profound and
lasting influence of Freudian theory in the West, believers cannot avoid Freud
and then assume they will have a religious faith credible for today's world.
"[Freud]," writes Ricoeur, "has not only, or even principally introduced a new
kind of therapy, but a global interpretation of the phenomenon of culture and
of religion as an aspect of culture. Our culture analyzes itself through him—
a fact of extreme importance that must be understood and evaluated" (Ricoeur
1966, 61). While seminarians may have some knowledge of Ricoeur and his
theology, they may be in for a big surprise when they discover that he actually spent a good portion of his career conversing with Freud and learning
from psychoanalysis.

Another methodological strategy for applying Freudian theory to the phenomenon of religious faith comes to us from the psychoanalyst Ana-Maria
Rizzuto. Rizzuto is convinced that her years of work in clinical practice have
taught her that our images of God are at least a partial exaltation of parental
or early-caregiver imagoes. This, then, would at least seem to confirm, not so
much the Freud "of science, intellect, and reality, the Freud who said: 'No,
our science is no illusion. But an illusion it would be to suppose that what
science cannot give us we can get elsewhere,'" but another Freud, "the Freud
of object relations, the Oedipus complex, [and] family relations" (Rizzuto
1979, 212). Therefore, dismissing Freud's theory of religion outright before
ever encountering his writings puts clinicians at a disadvantage in their work
with clients. Rizzuto even goes so far as to say that—and this has important
implications for seminarians—our ignorance of God's psychical role in our
lives means that we are "missing an important and relevant piece of information" (1979, x) about the developmental history of those in our care, not to
mention our own. She disagrees with Freud's view that religion is always
neurotic or immature or both, but does find him and his theory of religion

particularly helpful and useful when it comes to the intrapsychic juxtaposition of parental imagoes and images of God. Accordingly, Rizzuto believes that if we can focus our attention on Freud's work with psychical experience, instead of immediately citing and discrediting his conclusion about religious faith and ultimate reality, then he has a great deal to teach religious believers about the origin of their inner representations of God. Rizzuto's work with Freud, to state the obvious, would have major and important implications for the teaching and practice of pastoral care and counseling.

Lastly, the feminist theorist Judith Van Herik gives the seminarian yet another methodological strategy for engaging Freud. For example, Van Herik engages Freudian theory for reasons other than trying to learn what Freud can teach us about the psychical representation of God (Rizzuto) or the human being's willingness to tolerate moral condemnation in exchange for the promise of eternal consolation and protection (Ricoeur). Instead, Van Herik is more interested in the connection between Freud's theory of religion as projection and his asymmetrical theory of gender. The projective, irrationalist faith of the religious believer (male or female), she argues, and the psychology of women are, in the Freudian scheme of things, inextricably linked together through related inner meanings. Religious believers who long for a consoling God to come to them with tender loving care are not very different from women who seem less willing or able than men to fully renounce parental ties. According to Van Herik, the highest form of human development for Freud is that of *ideal* masculinity, a developmental and renunciatory achievement par excellence whereby all reality—psychological and ultimate—becomes depersonalized. While Van Herik does admit that Freud sees God as little more than a mental product, she still urges us to return again and again to his work on religion, as well as to his work on gender, in order to discover important clues about Western religio-cultural attitudes. Because Freudianism, if not Freud, has been so extraordinarily influential in the West, particularly in America, "it is important to continue to return to his writings" (Van Herik 1982, 1). Here, then, is a methodological strategy that approaches Freud with more intellectual neutrality, that is less concerned with the clinical or hermeneutical utility of Freudian theory. Surely, you would think, the methodological framework of Van Herik would at least be acceptable to the majority of seminarians.

Not necessarily. If a seminarian approaches religious faith with an either/or attitude, then the particular individual will not even want to hear what Van Herik has to say. Indeed, I would argue that we are encountering, more and more these days in the context of theological education, an either/or or all-or-nothing way of thinking. When it comes to Freud, this bifurcation is not too difficult to detect: *either*, many seminarians believe, one embraces the totality of one's faith tradition *or* the totality of Freudian psychology. We must, therefore, so the thinking goes, embrace one or the other, but certainly not both. Like oil and water, the two do not mix. And yet, for the seminarian who chooses to work *through*, rather than *around,* the complexities that are sure to develop when religious faith and Freudian theory are held firmly together in dialectical tension, the methodologies of Ricoeur, Rizzuto, and Van Herik can become important road maps. However, for seminarians who steadfastly refuse to take an objective look at the writings of Freud, whether out of devotion to God and/or loyalty to a particular faith tradition, the thought of holding an atheistic theory like Freud's in dialectical tension with one's religious faith will seem repugnant. Seminarians may resort to rationalizing their anxiety away by saying something like, "Freud was an atheist," or "Freud is passé," or "Freud has nothing useful to teach me about religious faith." The first response, at least, is correct: Freud was, if we take him at his word, an atheist. But, as we learn from the methodological strategies of these three theorists, it is simply not true that Freud is passé or that he has nothing important to teach us about religious faith. In any case, out of respect for the purity of religious faith or loyalty to God, seminarians might be tempted to distance themselves from an "all-bad" Freudian theory, keeping it far away from their "all-good" religious faith.

Something Resembling Psychical Splitting?

What can occur, then, internally, when the psyche is beset by conflict between diametrically opposed ideas or images, is that, rather than trying to hold the opposing forces together in dialectical tension, the individual will keep them far apart and will therefore experience a temporary reduction of psychical tension. I use the word "temporary" because the individual, from this point on, must necessarily be on his or her guard since the negative ideas or images have not, as had been hoped, completely disappeared or gone away. Rather, the bad or negative ones have merely gone underground and become unconscious. And if Freud has taught the Western world anything, it is that just because something is removed from consciousness does not mean that it has vanished. It may very well be out of sight, but this is hardly an indication that it is out of mind or completely removed from the psyche. The negative or disturbing idea or image has gone underground, where, even if the individual is not conscious of it, it takes on a life of its own.

Thus, since individuals have only arrived at a *temporary* solution, or a temporary reduction of the psychical tension, they will need to be, from now on, ever vigilant or always on their guard. The negative ideas or images, which have not entirely vanished from the psyche, but have instead become unconscious, will from time to time well up within the individual, demanding expression and equal time with the more positive ones. This, if you will, "splitting" mechanism needs reinforcement; hence, the utilization of subsidiary defensive maneuvers—anger and outrage, distancing, indifference, rationalization, projection and so on. Had the individual been intent on holding diametrically opposed ideas and images together in dialectical tension, or in trying to integrate them into a dynamic whole, the ego would then have been strengthened. Instead, because the individual resorted to splitting off the bad from the good, to keeping the two worlds far apart, the ego has become weak and fragile. As the psychoanalyst Otto Kernberg has pointed out, "splitting, then, is a fundamental cause of ego weakness, and as splitting also requires less countercathexis than repression, a weak ego falls back easily on splitting, and a vicious circle is created by which ego weakness and splitting reinforce each other" (Kernberg 1985, 29).

It would then appear as if there is something akin to the phenomenon of psychical splitting anytime seminarians feel the need to compartmentalize their religious faith, keeping it far away from Freudian theory and, for that matter, any other hermeneutics of suspicion. And what, we may ask, is responsible for this compartmentalization? In a word, *fear*. A weak ego, as Kernberg suggested, falls back on the defensive maneuver of splitting, which is to say that, in the context of theological education, an all-good religious faith is compartmentalized and kept far away from an all-bad Freud. But, and this is extremely important, the failure to hold opposite views in tension can only lead to an erosion of ego strength within the believer. And the believer's ego strength erodes even further when the splitting maneuver has to be reinforced by subsidiary defensive maneuvers—anger, distancing, indifference, and the like. And when in time the secondary defenses need reinforcing, what then? The result can only be an internal state of insecurity, since one's religious faith cannot stay compartmentalized forever. The weak ego, at this point, out of necessity, returns to the familiar mechanism of splitting, and the vicious cycle of mutual reinforcement begins all over again.

It is not my intention to pathologize seminarians who refuse to have anything to do with Freud, implying that there is a psychical fine line between them and clients presenting personality or characterological disturbances. Indeed, there will always be seminarians resistant to Freud who seem nothing at all like, say, a borderline or narcissistic personality. To be sure, the lack of psychical integration on the part of individuals presenting a characterological disturbance, and the lack of psychical integration on the part of seminarians who refuse to integrate any Freudian theory into their belief system, is really apples and oranges. And yet, what I do see anytime seminarians steadfastly refuse to discuss Freud and religion in the same breath is something that does in fact resemble the psychical defense of splitting or compartmentalization. Freud, as seminarians are aware, even if remotely, issued a devastating critique of religion, which, as Ricoeur has pointed out, still deserves a response from the religious community. Moreover, it would certainly do us well to at least keep in mind that Freud's critique of religion will deconstruct, in virtually no time at all, what Ricoeur calls a pre-critical and pre-reflective religious faith of the first naïveté. The religious believer, then, who is in possession of a pre-reflective faith, has every right to be anxious about an engagement with Freud, for the faith of this particular individual, after being subjected to the critique of psychoanalysis, simply will not and cannot stand the test. This will *always* be the fate of a religious faith of the first naïveté anytime it engages Freudian theory, which is why the believer may feel compelled to resort to intrapsychic adjustments of a defensive nature.

Chief among these adjustments is to build and fortify an internal dividing wall that keeps religious faith on one side and psychoanalysis and other hermeneutics of suspicion on the other. God, theology, and the church, then, become a composite all-good object, while Freud, psychoanalysis, and the hermeneutics of suspicion become a composite all-bad object. But this intrapsychic arrangement, while solving one problem—the reduction of psychical tension—creates an even bigger problem—namely, the repetitive weakening of the ego. While seminarians consciously celebrate the fact that they have been able to resist the challenge of Freud by flatly refusing to have anything to do with him and his theory, the ego, at a deeper level, knows full well that an opportunity for emotional and spiritual growth and development has been missed. Put more simply, the ego feels diminished. Therefore, while I am not saying that seminarians who refuse to engage Freud have a personality or characterological disturbance, I do want to say that there is ample evidence to support the theory that individuals who either will not or cannot hold religious faith and Freudian theory in tension, at least for a period of testing, are dividing and compartmentalizing internal objects and figures into all-good and all-bad groups.

Seminarians who decide to begin firmly holding in dialectical tension the truth of Freudian theory and the truth of religious faith must be willing to let go of the innocence and naïveté of times past, and an epistemological framework that heretofore precluded any ambiguity. Paradise, at least in an Edenic sense, will inevitably be lost forever. Seminarians, if they wish to have a religious faith credible for a postmodern world, must be willing to peel away the pre-critical and pre-reflective layers of their faith. Freud, it cannot be emphasized enough, issued a powerful challenge to the religious community, so much so that I would argue that today's seminarians really have no choice but to submit their faith to various hermeneutics of suspicion. Then, and only then, can the seminarian formulate an informed and reflective response to the Freudian critique of religion, instead of falling back on a variety of defensive maneuvers. But, and I know this from personal and professional experience, moving from one level of religious faith to another, especially if the first level has been pre-critical and pre-reflective, involves no shortage of internal dissonance. The fragile ego, if it is asked to hold in dialectical tension religious faith with Freud's theory that religion is psychological projection, may feel like a fish out of the familiar waters of simplicity and certainty. The ego, for the first time, must attempt to live with the ambiguities inherent in religious faith, particularly the ambiguity that while God is transcendently in God's heaven, God is also, as Rizzuto has observed, in the human psyche, juxtaposed with the images of other objects and figures.

The disruption of one's internal world, even if it is a prelude to a more advanced stage of emotional and spiritual development, is never pleasant. In fact, it is downright painful. So what would compel me, a minister and pastoral counselor and theologian, to urge the seminarian to expose his or her faith to the Freudian hermeneutics of suspicion? Might it not be better to leave well enough alone, and let seminarians simply reinforce, during their years of study, the beliefs they already had prior to entering the seminary? This, however, would hardly be adequate preparation and training for those who intend to minister effectively in the future to others working through similar crises of faith and meaning. While I do not wish to minimize the psychical pain that is sure to develop anytime one's faith is cleansed of its primitive naïveté, I do want to point out that there is an even greater pain, one that is considerably more debilitating: the pain of diminishing ego strength, which grows more intense every time we feel we do not have the necessary internal resources needed to engage a hermeneutics of suspicion. Thus, whether seminarians decide to engage Freud and his theory of religion or not, the fact is that there will be psychical pain either way, in one form or another. On the one hand, the pain that results from a direct engagement with Freudian theory will be the *pain of growth*, stemming from, rather paradoxically, the steady strengthening of the ego and the enlargement of one's religious faith. On the other hand, the pain that results from resolutely avoiding Freud and his theory will be the *pain of atrophy*, stemming from the steady decline of ego strength and the diminishment of one's religious faith. It must be remembered that strong psychical defenses—for example, splitting, outrage, distancing, indifference, and rationalization—are not necessarily indicative of genuine ego strength or a strong faith. Rather, it is actually the opposite: strong defenses are most often an indication of a weakened ego and a fragile belief system.

Necessary Modifications

A few years ago I wrote a paper on applying a Freudian hermeneutics of suspicion to the "text" of the religious faith of seminarians. (Bingaman 1999, 91–105). In that paper I argued that it is important for the candidate for ministry, who will one day minister in various ways to other religious believers, to critique his or her faith by way of psychoanalysis. I pointed out that seminarians have little to fear, as Freud peels away the obsessive, neurotic, and naive layers of their religious faith. In fact, I argued, the seminarian's religious faith will ultimately be strengthened by an engagement with Freud. If, in encountering Freud, the seminarian's faith fails the test of authenticity, then surely it was hardly a faith the individual would have wanted to take along with him or her and, following graduation, model to a future congregation. This is not to suggest that I have any illusions about seminarians eagerly getting in line to engage Freud and his theory of religion. With so many seminaries requiring only one pastoral care and counseling course—usually Introduction to Pastoral Care and Counseling—as part of the curriculum, seminarians can get around Freud and the discipline of psychology with little difficulty. In terms of theological education, the only realistic opportunity to engage Freud is when an elective course, like the one I taught on Freud and Religion at the GTU, is offered. Unfortunately, because a class on Freud will necessarily be an elective, students can make up their own minds as to whether or not they will add such a course to their semester schedules.

As I discovered firsthand, seminarians will not sign up for a course on Freud in great numbers. A course on Freud may pique the interest of academic-track students, but ordination-track students, I am afraid, will see little practical value. More than a few seminarians have informed me that they will never, under any circumstances, register for a course on Freud or one on the psychology of religion. I remember overhearing one seminarian, who was in a pastoral care and counseling course I was teaching, telling his classmates that since Freud was an atheist, he wanted nothing to do with him; there was nothing Freud could teach him that would be relevant to his own personal religious faith and the faith of his future congregation. Later, the same seminarian informed me that in avoiding Freud's theory of religion, he was "making certain that I still have my faith when I graduate." Although I did not respond to his comment, I do remember feeling tempted to ask, "*What* religious faith?" Evidently, the faith he has *always* had, a pre-critical and pre-reflective faith of the first naïveté.

I went on to say in that journal article that some of my colleagues have advised me to "go easy" with a Freudian hermeneutics of suspicion, presumably because believers, in general, and seminarians, in particular, have varying degrees of ego strength; some have more than others. I took this to mean that the student with a shortage of ego strength will be less able to tolerate a Freudian critique of his or her belief system. This, at the time, did not sit very well with me. My response was, and I still stand by my earlier remarks, that if seminarians plan to be working, ministerially, in the emotional and spiritual depths of other peoples' lives, then they are obligated to become more familiar with the depths of their own lives. And someone like Freud can offer them a rather descriptive "map" of their interiority, explaining to them why they do the things they do. Moreover, the seminary, I argued, should be a training ground where various theorists, such as Freud, who put forward a hermeneutics of suspicion, can be engaged rigorously and unapologetically. If seminarians are lacking in ego strength, they will then have the remaining seminary years to continue deconstructing their pre-reflective religious faith in order to begin reconstructing one that is more dynamic, one that can withstand the ambiguities and vicissitudes of human living. Nor should seminary faculty, particularly those who teach psychology and pastoral care and counseling courses, feel, in the face of criticism from students, the need to defend the teaching of Freud simply because he came to erroneous conclusions about God and religion. I even went so far as to say, in this paper, that seminary faculty, for the good of the church, the seminary, and their students, cannot back down when it comes to teaching Freud, for they have every right to demand that students deal fairly and objectively with Freud's psychology of religion. To back away from teaching Freudian theory in its totality—weaknesses *and* strengths—reinforces, I suggested, an either/or way of thinking. The alternative would be to hold seminarians accountable for keeping religious faith and Freud's interpretation of religion in dialectical tension, encouraging them not to automatically write Freud off with a premature, broadside attack.

That was then, this is now. I still, for the most part, stand by what I wrote in that paper. For example, I am more convinced than ever that if candidates for ministry want to work in the depths of other peoples' lives, whether as ministers, chaplains, counselors, and so forth, then they are fundamentally obligated to become more familiar with and realistic about the depths of their own lives and their own personal religious faith. And, again, someone like Freud—his conclusions about the efficacy of religious faith notwithstanding—can be an important hermeneutical resource for such an important undertaking. Yes, I still stand by the *spirit* of what I wrote in that article. It is, however, the method of *how* to apply a Freudian hermeneutics of suspicion to the "text" of the seminarian's faith that now stands in need of reassessment. The seminarian who is not yet in possession of the requisite ego strength necessary for holding opposing views together in dialectical tension cannot be expected to engage the totality of Freudian theory all at once. It would seem, then, that because of the evocative power of Freud and his theory, we cannot think in terms of a cookie-cutter application of psychoanalysis to the religious faith of the seminarian. Because of varying degrees of ego strength, we will more than likely need to tailor Freudian theory to the particular seminarian or group of seminarians, depending on the person's individual or the group's collective ego strength.

What I have in mind is helping seminarians prepare themselves emotionally and spiritually for an engagement with Freud. We cannot, as seminary faculty, meet the force of defensive resistance with the unmitigated force of a Freudian hermeneutics of suspicion. For those seminarians who have a modicum of genuine ego strength, who automatically and thus instinctively divide all-good objects and all-bad objects into separate psychical categories, the idea of holding Freudian theory in dialectical tension with religious faith will simply be too threatening. Additionally, if seminarians have never deconstructed and subsequently reconstructed certain aspects of their religious faith, have never felt any need to relinquish their primitive naïveté, then the thought of engaging Freud in a conversation about religion will be more than a little disquieting. At some internal level, the seminarian, or any other believer for that matter, can intuit that a faith of the first naïveté will not stand a chance against Freud. Seminary faculty must therefore be prepared to present Freud and his theory in a variety of different ways, ways that are more cognizant of the varying degrees of ego strength found in their students. Thus, it is similar to a counselor or therapist working with a client: in the early sessions, the therapist and client must work together on the therapeutic relationship, must work to establish trust and rapport. Similarly, there must be, before we can ever expect seminarians to take the plunge into Freudian theory, the establishment of trust between faculty and students. If seminarians can bring themselves to trust their professors, if they can trust that we are introducing them to Freud because we really do have their best interests and the best interests of their religious faith in mind, then our efforts will be more fruitful.

Conclusion

How, then, might we go about introducing psychoanalysis in the seminary, when it is safe to assume that more than a few of our students will feel acutely threatened by Freud's theory that "a personal God is, psychologically, nothing other than an exalted father" (Freud 1964, 73)? For starters, we would do well to adopt a pedagogical strategy that takes into account varying degrees of emotional and spiritual strength, a strategy that is more imaginative than a one-size-fits-all approach. It may also help to keep in mind that the individual who tends to divide internal objects and images into all-good and all-bad categories does so for a reason—namely, to compensate for the lack of genuine ego strength. The individual, then, as Althea Horner puts it, looks for "an object of certain [positive] attributes who responds in such a manner that the good-self identity is maintained" (Horner 1984, 258). In the context of religious faith and theological education, the object of positive or good attributes is most often God, or, more precisely, one's image of God. In this sense, the seminarian maintains a good-self identity by associating exclusively with the image of a perfect God and a pure religious faith. However, to maintain what is in reality a very fragile good-self identity, the individual must be constantly vigilant, guarding against potentially contaminative influences like Freud and psychoanalysis.

When it comes to the clinical setting, and working with clients who resort to the defensive maneuver of completely separating all-good objects from all-bad objects, Horner suggests that "the therapeutic goal becomes that of helping the patient to stay in treatment in order to develop an ambivalent relationship, to tolerate the ambivalence, to accept the reality of imperfection and, in short, to heal the split" (Horner 1984, 258–59). Similarly, when it comes to teaching Freud in the seminary, the pedagogical goal becomes that of helping students stay with Freudian theory long enough to begin to be able to hold the truth of religious faith in dialectical tension with the truth of psychoanalysis, to be able to accept that both theology and psychology have inherent strengths and limitations. This, then, avoids the either/or trap: either we become religious idealists, imaging faith and theology as radically removed and separate from other less perfect dimensions of human life, or we become, like Freud, reductionists, seeing the faith of believers as little more than the insecure projections of the human mind. By exchanging an either/or attitude toward Freud and religious faith for a both/and approach, seminarians will see that it is perfectly legitimate to give Freud *both* a no *and* a yes and still be loyal to God and one's faith tradition. Furthermore, they will be able to see, in the words of Ricoeur, that because "we are henceforth incapable of returning to an order of moral life which would take the form of a simple submission to commandments or to an alien or supreme will, even if this will were represented as divine, we must accept as a positive good the critique of ethics and religion that has been undertaken by the school of suspicion" (Ricoeur 1974, 447).

Note

Portions of this chapter are reprinted by permission. See Bingaman 1999.

References

Bingaman, Kirk A. 1999. Teach your students well: The seminary and a hermeneutics of suspicion. *Pastoral Psychology* 48, no. 2: 91–105.

Freud, Sigmund. 1964. *Leonardo da Vinci and a memory of his childhood.* Edited by James Strachey, translated by Alan Tyson. New York: Norton.

Horner, Althea. 1984. *Object relations and the developing ego in therapy.* Northvale, N.J.: Jason Aronson.

Hunter, Rodney J. gen. ed. *Dictionary of pastoral care and counseling.* Nashville, Tenn.: Abingdon.

Kernberg, Otto. 1985. *Borderline conditions and pathological narcissism.* Northvale, N.J.: Jason Aronson.

Ricoeur, Paul. 1974. *The conflict of interpretations.* Edited by Don Ihde. Evanston, Ill.: Northwestern University Press.

———. 1979. The atheism of Freudian psychoanalysis. *Concilium* 16: 59–72.

Rizzuto, Ana-Maria. 1979. *The birth of the living God.* Chicago: University of Chicago Press.

Van Herik, Judith. 1982. *Freud on femininity and faith.* Berkeley: University of California Press.

Wulff, David M. 1991. *Psychology of religion.* New York: John Wiley.

4

Teaching Freud, Teaching Freud's Values: A Graduate Course

Volney Gay

The happy achievement seems almost a matter of course, and any intelligent student can grasp it without too much trouble. But the years of anxious searching in the dark, with their intense longing, their alterations of confidence and exhaustion and the final emergence into the light—only those who have experienced it can understand it
—Albert Einstein

If hysterics trace back their symptoms to fictitious traumas, this new fact signifies that they create such scenes in phantasy, and psychical reality requires to be taken into account alongside actual reality.
—Sigmund Freud, "On the History of the Psycho-Analytic Movement"

How can we teach Freud after *Time* magazine not long ago asked, "Is Freud Dead?"[1] and many people responded "Yes, and about time, too!" As some wags noted, *Time* asked "Is God dead?" in the late 1970s and the answer to that query is still unclear. While Freud's mortality is assured, the meaning of his work and his intellectual heritage is not. As someone who has written a lot on Freud and is a practicing psychoanalyst, I believe Freud is worth teaching—Freud died, but his values live. Whether this is a good answer for others is the concern of this paper.

What makes Freud worth teaching? Are the twenty-four volumes of the *Standard Edition* sacrosanct, each page full of wisdom? No. Did Freud harbor ideas about women, for example, that many now find wrong? Yes. Did

Freud foresee the numerous ways in which psychotherapy would change after his death in 1939? No. Have not many attacked Freud from the beginning, challenging everything about him and his theories? Yes. Then, is there anything in Freud worth preserving into the next century? Yes. His values are worth preserving because, I will suggest, they stem from his mapping of the inner world[2] and proclaiming it a region worthy of sustained, empathic contemplation. We teach Freud because we believe that he discovered something new about human beings. This new thing, "psychical reality," merits as much attention and respect as that given to "external reality."

While numerous thinkers before Freud understood that the human mind operated in ways outside of conscious control, few were willing to explore these realms with Freud's courage. (Ellenberger 1970). Affirming that "psychical reality" merits our attention and is of a dignity equal to that of external reality seems odd. Yet, a fair reading of Freud's struggles to understand his own mind, and then the minds of his patients, reveals what Einstein describes as "anxious searching in the dark." Indeed, it is difficult to exaggerate the amount of effort it took Freud to conduct his self-analysis and then publicize it in *The Interpretation of Dreams* (*SE* 4–5). For example, in his specimen dream, "Irma's Injection" (107–21), Freud describes feelings of envy, pride, jealousy, narcissistic wounds, male-male eroticism, and more. Given these elements, it is not surprising that Freud's progeny, like Erik Erikson (1954), and Freud's biographers have examined this dream multiple times. It is more surprising that Freud published it and did not hide behind the dreams of his patients.

The ease with which one can overlook Freud's insight and courage appears in the way Ernst Jones (1953) translates Freud's comments, cited above. In the original German text, Freud says that psychical reality (*psychische Realität*) requires to be taken into account alongside "*praktischen Realität*."[3] *Praktischen* does not mean "actual." It means (1) "practical" and (2) "field tested." Translating it as "actual" prejudges the external world as more real than the internal world. This is precisely what Freud is not saying. Indeed, it is a mischievous translation; it inverts Freud's discovery. It also diminishes his courage and ascribes to him a bias in favor of one reality over another. His relentless inquiry led him to reject this materialist bias just as it led him to temper his favorite theories, including the seduction hypothesis.

If Jones, a substantial and field-tested analyst, can get this wrong, then how likely is it that students new to Freud and to psychoanalysis will get it right? They often do not. Recently we have witnessed heated attacks upon Freud for first proposing and then abandoning the "seduction" hypothesis. This hypothesis was that (some) patients suffering from adult hysteria were made ill by early sexual contact with adults. In modern terms, dominated by legal discourse, such forms of contact are now labeled "sexual abuse." Given this label, some complain that, having unearthed the reality of childhood sexual abuse, Freud covered it up. In direct opposition, others have attacked Freud for creating "false memory syndrome" (FMS), in which naive therapists cause patients to fabricate pseudo-memories of abuse. These debates have spawned thousands of articles in dozens of different journals, ranging across the intellectual and scientific spectra. Typically missing from these discussions is reflection upon Freud's extraordinary notion of *psychische Realität*. Because he ascribes to *psychische Realität* ontological status equal to that of practical reality, to say that a belief is based upon psychical reality does not reduce it to a phantom existence, an irrelevancy. On the contrary, fantasies about who one is and who one might be are determining factors in all subsequent behaviors. Fantasies are the source of action, especially if a person is anxious or distressed—in other words, living a normal life. To deny this fact is to engender many injustices. For example, when the FMS debate is politicized one is forced to choose sides in a moralizing drama: you are either against witchcraft trials or you are against sexually violating children. You cannot be against both. Freud rejects this dichotomy since he both affirmed the causal role of fantasy in human motivations and he affirmed that *psychische Realität* is a realm distinct from the realm of field-tested experience, the so-called outside world.

While they differ as to the criminal charge, both sides agree that Freud should be hanged. I suggest that while Freud is responsible for some of the confusion surrounding his various theories, he is not guilty of any offense. For he championed neither form of reductionism. The passage cited above makes it clear that he gave up the seduction hypothesis with much reluctance: it was simple, clear, offered a linear account, and was grounded in the materialism he imbibed in medical school.

When Freud talks about the unconscious, he means a set of internal schematas—that is, ideas linked to feelings, which, when touched upon, evoke feelings that, if expressed, elicit danger. The elaborate set of defense mechanisms Freud elucidated, such as denial, repression, splitting, and projection, are devices that permit one to avoid psychic pain produced when we touch upon such schematas. Why should *these* unconscious thoughts evoke anxiety and thus defense? Because they are about ourselves and when brought to consciousness threaten to "drive" us to act in ways that frighten us. To recognize that one has sexual wishes for a taboo person is dangerous because it threatens to precipitate acting upon those wishes. That imagined event evokes additional scenes of dreadful consequences. To avoid those dreadful consequences, we learn to avoid consciously attending to these antecedent images.

Freud, a physician, focused on those aspects of the unconscious mind that produced suffering. However, the unconscious more generally names the entire set of schemata that derive from psychical reality—what we might call the internal world. Within this realm we find both sexualized contents—the kind that get played out in many forms of clinical presentations—and nonsexualized contents—the kind that do not typically enter into clinical discourse. However, confronting new conceptual boundaries requires effort and induces exhaustion. The first citation at the chapter beginning is Albert Einstein's description of the effort that led to the formulation of the equation $E=mc^2$, announced in a paper he sent to *Annalen der Physik* in June 1905. Of this effort Einstein says, "When the Special Theory of Relativity began to germinate in me, I was visited by all sorts of nervous conflicts. I used to go away for weeks in a state of confusion."[4]

BANCO CENTRAL DE CUBA

1

AÑO 2016

BCC
GM-51

558751
558751

GM-51

PRESIDENTE DEL BANCO

JOSE MARTI

PESO

AÑO 2016

1 PESO

As he notes, looking backward, any intelligent person can grasp the basic logic of the Special Theory. It was looking forward—that is, upwards to an entirely new way of thinking—that required the immense efforts Einstein put into formulating this famous equation.

The task of thinking something radically new evokes anxiety, not neurosis. Einstein's labors evoked this form of anxiety because he felt totally alone in his struggles and unsure of his final destination. It might all have turned to nothing. To face a new hurdle or to cross a new intellectual boundary is precisely what we ask of our students, especially those who take seriously the implications of Freud or any other theoretician who claims to have found new maps to our inner world. Having made such an effort, and having become competent in this new realm with its new language, few of us are willing to forsake our sense of mastery without a struggle. This is one source of the interesting fact that we find so many "schools" of psychotherapy. (Having learned to swim in dangerous water one way, I do not wish to experiment with another method.)

It is not ordinary laziness that drives us to fasten ourselves to a particular school of psychoanalysis, or counseling, or psychotherapy. Rather, to become competent in dealing with emotions in oneself and in one's clients is to have advanced to a new stage, beyond the one with which we entered training. We are reluctant to distance ourselves from the terminology and techniques, grounded in a particular school, that made this new understanding possible. A sophisticated developmental psychologist and psychoanalyst, Fred Pine (1998, 19), has addressed these issues. He cites Donald Kaplan, who "said that the basic analytic situation is always an Oedipal one since there is always a triangle in the office: the patient, the analyst, and the analyst's technique."[5] Kaplan's point seems to me valid and essential to anyone who teaches Freud or any other theoretician of the mind. The analyst's devotion to the analyst's theory of technique may, indeed, impinge upon the patient's experience, but we wonder how easily any of us might forsake our theories entirely.

Analogous to "schools" of psychotherapy are groups of religious believers. Religious teachers also offer theorems about the self or human being that map out our common destiny. If we agree that religious beliefs and practices shape human life—and they do—then they must operate upon their believers the way cherished theories operate upon the clinician, especially upon the clinician who has finally achieved competence. One might use this insight against Freud or against Freudians or against all psychologists: they are just medicine experts like those found in primitive tribes.

If we subtract the hostility from this accusation, it seems to me correct. From a cognitive point of view that owes nothing to Freud, we come back to Freud's admission: there is something in us that resists ascending to the next level of self-understanding. This resistive "something" must operate in behaviorists as well as Freudians, in Republicans as well as Democrats, in rigorous scientific therapists and in rigorous artistic therapists alike. Hence, a typical Freudian conundrum transpires: told about our unconscious mind, we wish to know more about it, but then, on the couch or sitting in a therapist's chair, we suddenly find many reasons to not know. The urge to not know gains strength, increasing as we approach those beliefs and feelings we have tried so hard to keep away from us.

The Unknown Parts of the Self, the Unknown Future

It is frightening to contemplate unknown parts of the self. Because the future names that part of the time line in which they might emerge, we fear it also. In contrast to those who fear the future because it threatens to flood them with dreadful consequences are those who welcome the future because it is secured through the intervention of divine grace. Believing this, they can afford to welcome change since it cannot be other than good. In traditional Christian teaching, for example, this optimism is grounded in the promise that Christ will redeem all who seek him. This teaching animates John Milton's poem "On the Morning of Christ's Nativity," written in 1620:

> No War, or Battails sound
> Was heard the World around,
>   The idle spear and shield were high up hung;
> The hooked Chariot stood
> Unstain'd with hostile blood,
>   The Trumpet spake not to the armed throng,
> And Kings sate still with awfull eye,
>
> But peacefull was the night
> Wherin the Prince of light
>   His raign of peace upon the earth began:
> The Windes with wonder whist,
> Smoothly the waters kist,
>   Whispering new joyes the milde Ocean,
> Who now hath quite forgot to rave,
> While Birds of Calm sit brooding on the charmed wave.

Granting to Christ absolute power over chaotic forces of nature, Milton says that we need not fear any new thing within human history or human experience.

This sense of a secure future need not be confined to religious or transcendental claims. A secularist can also welcome change if he or she aligns it with a benign destiny. To counterpoint Milton we have our own Walt Whitman, who celebrates the "years of the modern" in a poem of the same title. Though writing two and a half centuries after Milton, Whitman resonates with the same fervor about the future. He was vastly optimistic that a new kind of person would emerge from the American experiment:

> YEARS of the modern! years of the unperform'd!
> Your horizon rises, I see it parting away for more august dramas,
> I see not America only, not only Liberty's nation but other nations
>   preparing,
> I see tremendous entrances and exits, new combinations, the solidarity of
>   races,

I see that force advancing with irresistible power on the world's stage,
(Have the old forces, the old wars, played their parts? are the acts suitable to
   them closed?)
I see Freedom, completely arm'd and victorious and very haughty, with
Law on one side and Peace on the other,
Never were such sharp questions ask'd as this day,
Never was average man, his soul, more energetic, more like a God.

By maintaining these forms of trust and security, one can face massive change
without massive anxiety. We can confront "frontiers and boundaries" because
we need not fear the consequences; there are no countries that Americans,
like gods, cannot master.

I cite these grand poems because they evoke emotional extremes: both are
distinctly religious. True, in most classrooms, teacher and students do not touch
upon emotions this deeply. However, our subject matter, both as therapists
and as teachers of psychology of religion, hovers over these questions. Most
of us most of the time skate upon the surface of the terror that animates religious fervor.

Teaching Freud: Four Preliminary Questions

I suggest four preliminary questions one should ask oneself before teaching
a course on Freud. These are:

Who am I talking to?
What am I talking about?
What are my claims?
How could I be wrong?

How we answer the first question conditions how we respond to the second,
and it, in turn, conditions how we respond to the third and fourth questions.
I believe these questions pertain to any course. However, for the purposes of
brevity and clarity, I focus on a specific course with specific students, a graduate course on psychotherapy.

In all courses, our goals are to help students change and to acquire new cognitive skills. Hence, we face difficulties similar to those faced by psychotherapists. True, we are not responsible for the emotional well-being of our students,
and our contact with them and their lived worlds are different. However, their
internal experiences are parallel to those of patients since they also confront
within themselves barriers that make it difficult to move from stage to stage.
Indeed, anyone who struggles to understand new conceptual tasks and subject
matter experiences, in part, what Einstein called "anxious searching in the dark."

Who Am I Talking To?

Like most academics, I speak to different groups about similar topics. I teach
"Freud" in different contexts: an undergraduate department of religion, an

anthropology department, a psychiatry department, a psychoanalytic institute, and a graduate department of religion.

Each context shapes how I teach Freud. For example, psychiatry residents train in a medical setting; graduate students complete courses and prepare to write their dissertations. Psychiatry residents generally have a science undergraduate degree, have done four years of medical school, and find themselves working long hours caring for sick people in a hospital dominated by "the medical model" of illnesses. They feel beleaguered by the amount of clinical work and they feel fixed in a rigid hierarchy where they report to a senior resident, who reports to an attending, who reports to the chair of the department. Their lived world is one of multiple demands upon their time, their patience, and their not-yet-formed abilities to diagnose and respond to severe mental illness. Naturally, they seek help dealing with psychiatric crises, with the hospital's hierarchy, and with their anxiety. Since I am not a physician, but a psychoanalyst, this means suggesting verbal responses to their distressed and volatile patients—or to their distressed and volatile colleagues.

In contrast, graduate students do coursework in a university environment. They generally have humanities degrees, have done divinity or other, post-bachelor studies, and find themselves struggling alone, in darkened libraries or small studies. They feel beleaguered by the amount of intellectual work required of them and by the absence of an exacting hierarchy. This freedom from external authorities has the cost that no one buffers them from their senior professors except a few fellow grad students. Their lived world is one of multiple demands upon their time, their intellectual capacities, and their not-yet-formed abilities to digest and evaluate elusive intellectual structures. They compare themselves against their professors and against great names like Hegel, Freud, Barth, and contemporary masters. These burdens are less obvious than those confronting medical residents—and will not be televised on NBC—but they are just as real.

Differences between these two groups give rise to reciprocal idealizations when they take the same class. Residents are amazed that graduate students can cite Hegel, Freud, Jung, and Michel Foucault—at the drop of a hat. From their vantage point, this erudition is not easily achieved or even visible in medical settings. It strikes them as unattainable and, therefore, ideal. Graduate students are awed by the aura of medicine, its elite status in the United States, and by the hair-raising stories that residents tell about violent patients whom they confronted on locked wards. Differences between these two groups means that teaching Freud evokes different responses: residents ask how he pertains to their cases, graduate students ask how Freud's ideas evolved and how feminists or postmodernists, for example, evaluate them.

Political and social contexts also shape how we teach Freud. For example, it took me three years to realize how many prejudices I brought with me from Chicago when I came to Nashville to teach at Vanderbilt. I was raised on CBS evening news' accounts of the Freedom Riders and others who struggled against southern racism. I imbibed the portrait of the white South as primitive and racist to the core, while ignoring the larger, American share in these institutions. I found it easy to admire Abraham Lincoln and Martin Luther King Jr. and to identify myself with their dislike of slavery and its aftermath. I found it much more difficult to understand northern racism, such as that found in Boston neighborhoods when white parents fumed against busing. The latter seemed to be aberrant. Why did I find it easy to disdain the South and difficult to understand Bostonian racism?

Because it was comfortable. By retaining the illusion of northern superiority I could avoid confronting my deeply embedded racism. It was they, not we, who deserved scrutiny. I did not hear King's larger claims:

> Injustice anywhere is a threat to justice everywhere. We are caught in an inescapable network of mutuality, tied in a single garment of destiny. Whatever affects one directly, affects all indirectly. Never again can we afford to live with the narrow, provincial "outside agitator" idea. Anyone who lives inside the United States can never be considered an outsider anywhere within its bounds.[6]

Why did I miss King's essential message? When I first read his words, I understood them as a defense of his mission to Birmingham, which was in the South. Since I was in the North, and "pro civil rights," I agreed that the South needed to be exposed and reformed. It needed "outside agitators." On reflection, I see that I misunderstood King since his concept of a single America, neither black nor white, required him to deny legitimacy to this claim. There are no "outside" agitators if we are all "inside" the same story and the same American context. Asking what I missed is a Freudian question; it forces me to reflect on automatic judgments that felt correct and seamless. By hating the South I felt aligned with the moral forces King represented. This form of inexpensive solidarity made me feel organized: everything that was progressive belonged to me, everything that resisted progress belonged to others. I did not know this about myself until I taught in the South and my students helped me stumble upon these truths.

What Am I Talking About?

In a course called something like Freud and Religion, or a course called Introduction to Psychotherapy, it might seem easy to answer this question. However, it is not, since both terms designate complex subjects. For example, one can focus on Freud's texts, Freud's models of the mind, Freud's concepts, Freud's theories, or his metaphors, opinions, and literary style. One can also try to teach how Freud thought—that is, to deconstruct the reasoning Freud uses in both his clinical and his applied essays.

"Religion" designates an even larger expanse of human behavior. It ranges from momentary occult events (Gay 1989), to private experiences, to small group behaviors, to vast and complex institutions like the Catholic Church, to apparently universal religious phenomena like myth and ritual (Turner 1969, 1982). Depending on what our students need, one might teach an excellent course on Freud and Religion that used contemporary Freudian theory—say, object relations theory—to talk about New Age Religion. Alternatively, one might use contemporary critical theories of "reading" to evaluate Freud's essays on religion.[7] In the following, I focus on one context and one course, an advanced course in psychotherapy technique for pastoral counselors and psychiatry residents.

What Are My Claims?

Among the hardest questions to ask a Ph.D. candidate is, What, exactly, is your thesis? Many a talented doctoral candidate has written an exposition of Freud and feminism, or Freud and pastoral care, or Freud and Hegel, hoping to finish a proposal only to be stymied by this simple request: what are you claiming? I find this question equally hard to answer when designing a course or writing a book. However, it is worth the struggle since it models for our students the kind of reasoning we wish them to acquire. Eventually, we want them to tell us what their claims are, too.

With regard to cognitive development, I claim there are stages that demarcate beginner to expert. If valid, this point of view gives both teacher and student (or therapist and patient, or coach and athlete) useful guidelines. It also helps decrease students' panic and quells various fantasies that they will never master the tasks at hand. To illustrate these stages, I discuss the steps by which one becomes an expert therapist. These steps are identical, I believe, to the steps by which one becomes an expert teacher of Freud and religion. In both cases our goals are to acquire the capacity to fail properly—that is, to learn what we do not know and to help our students do the same.

How Could I Be Wrong?

In asking this question, it is helpful to stress the third word, "I," since it names the largest barrier to reasoning. (It might serve as an opening, secular prayer to many a course or seminar.) We want students to articulate their claims so that they can ask of themselves the most fundamental question: how can I be wrong?

This question distinguishes academic and scientific discourse from similar discourses, such as journalism and theater. While journalism and theater, like American news stories and TV skits, are often produced by talented people, their central mission is to please. (The central mission of advertising is to persuade.) All North American professors know that students are easily bored and will complain loudly about their distress. However, we serve them best when we help them learn to reason. Of course, there are many forms of reasoning: legal, logical, social scientific, literary critical, historical, and the like. Linking each together is the assumption that we might be wrong; hence, we seek to obey minimal rules of evidence. Binding us together into a given academic or scientific community is the assumption that we might be wrong. The task of reasoning is interpersonal and procedural. It is others who see where I am wrong, and it is established procedures and interpersonal rules that determine what counts as acceptable and unacceptable process.

The assumption of error—that we might be wrong—flies in the face of mob rule and assertions of "truth" generated by passionate proclamations, by narcissistic rage, and by religious zeal, among other forms of human error. Because so much effort goes into becoming competent and aligning oneself with the intellectual channels carved out by our illustrious forebears, to challenge these beliefs and allegiances is to disrupt an important avenue of self-esteem and security.

Cognitive Development and Its Discontents

Among the missions of graduate programs in religion and psychology, as well as psychotherapy institutes, is to train persons to become experts. Given the value therapists ascribe to emotional development, most teachers are attuned to their students' emotional responses. Understanding emotional development and empathic communication substantially enhances the vocabulary and sensibility of teachers. While psychoanalysts can claim some credit for this approach to students' feelings (and their developmental stages), analysts have focused less attention on cognitive development.

To counter this common error, I invoke a general description of the stages of cognitive development not beholden to any school and not age-specific. These range from the mastery of a relatively constrained task, like driving a stick-shift car, to the mastery of more complex tasks, like becoming an expert pianist, or diagnostician, or psychotherapist—or teacher!

In the following I use a stage theory of the development of expertise taken from Dreyfus and Dreyfus (1986, 21–31). I use Dreyfus and Dreyfus's title for each stage, define it briefly, and then describe some therapeutic skills appropriate to this stage. To give a complete list of skills appropriate to each level is the corporate task of a faculty. A complete list of these skills would amount to a complete description of an ideal curriculum.

STAGE 1: NOVICE

The novice, or beginner, learns a new skill by learning explicit rules. These rules are often codified or actually written out, as in intake forms in a psychiatric hospital or lecture notes. At this stage, practitioners can only follow the rules because they lack a larger sense of context. For example, asking point-by-point questions of narcissistic patients alienates them, but the novice therapist charges ahead. The young professor who reads verbatim notes from a graduate seminar to first-year undergraduates alienates all within earshot. Faced with new tasks, the novice demands clear and unambiguous rules, such as "Remain neutral at all times" or "Give Latin derivations for all key terms." This demand for unambiguous rules yields to despair when the novice hears another rule, equally supported by the experts, "Remain natural and friendly at all times" or "Explain key terms, but not too much."

The novice therapist should be able to:

1. Locate, name, and explain defense mechanisms in others.
2. Comprehend the major forms of psychic distress in human lives; e.g., guilt, shame, abandonment anxiety, envy, narcissistic mortification.
3. See symptoms as overdetermined "expressions" of multiple intentions.
4. Comprehend some of the ways in which talking about negative affects relieves psychic pain.
5. Identify major features of one's own emotional response to patient material.

The novice teacher should recognize parallel tasks in teaching a subject matter, Freud and religion, fraught with complex claims and complex feelings. Freud's distaste for religion, for example, evokes anger (or praise) in most students—and most teachers.

STAGE 2: ADVANCED BEGINNER

After sufficient experience, the advanced beginner recognizes similarities between numerous cases. One learns new "rules," such as "Take a history but judge also the patient's response to you." Other "rules" such as those learned by the beginning driver cannot be verbalized, for many of these new rules are context-dependent. We perceive similarities in the gestalt of a situation, even if we cannot identify verbally what those similarities are: "Nobody combines facts or figures to identify the smell of coffee" (Dreyfus and Dreyfus 1986, 23).

The advanced beginner should be able to:

1. Recognize patterns of defense in a patient's behavior.
2. Have a "sense" of the neurotic process.
3. Recognize patterns of resistance to the demands of therapy.
4. See major transference configurations in a patient's response.
5. Locate a particular patient in a diagnostic group.
6. Recognize major countertransference responses; e.g., the urge to quit the process, to promote acting out on the patient's part.
7. Draw upon key features of clinical theory.
8. Have a sense of empathic involvement with the patient's distress.
9. Initiate a supervisory contract.

The advanced beginner teacher follows a similar path: what patterns of insight and resistance does this subject matter evoke in my students (at this particular institution)? How can I forge an alliance with my students?

STAGE 3: COMPETENCE

At this stage one can use both context-free rules and context-dependent rules to meet clearly stated goals. For example, competent surgeons can choose between surgical options by comparing the likely results of each against the goal. The competent therapist can choose between competing models of a patient's presentation. With wisdom and advanced cognitive skills comes increased responsibility:

> The novice and advanced beginner recognize learned components and then apply learned rules and procedures. As a consequence, they feel little responsibility for the outcome of their acts. Assuming that they have made no mistakes, an unfortunate outcome is viewed as the result of inadequately specified elements or rules. The competent person, on the other hand, after wrestling with the question of the choice of plan, feels responsible for, and thus emotionally involved in, the product of his choice. (Dreyfus and Dreyfus 1986, 26)

Much daily work requires this level of achievement. However, it is sufficient only for those tasks that are structured like problems or puzzles, such as those that Sherlock Holmes confronted. Holmes's puzzles, such as what animal killed Lord Baskerville, have complete and well-defined answers. Psychologists, mathematicians, and computer experts often see competence as the height of intelligence, since it is a form of intellectual functioning that one can replicate using computer software. Complex engineering problems can be resolved by reducing them to smaller subproblems. However, psychotherapists, teachers, and religionists rarely enjoy this luxury. The idea of reducing their tasks to simpler tasks arouses fundamental debates about the nature of their expertise.

The competent therapist should be able to:
1. Grasp patterns of drive, defense, and resistance in patient material.
2. Call upon techniques, like dream interpretation, when presented with straightforward material.
3. Feel more able to distinguish between "therapeutic rules" and an appropriate and "natural" response to patients.
4. Recognize subtler countertransference reactions.
5. Be able to rely more upon a self-therapeutic function when confronting countertransference.
6. Initiate a therapeutic pact or contract with a patient and distinguish that from supportive and other forms of psychotherapy.
7. Deepen the supervisory contract.

The competent teacher shows a parallel development, especially with regard to "pet" theories and allegiances with his or her own teachers. Moving beyond one's mentors—a form of growth and loss—emerges here as the central task. It also frees one up to attend to one's students, especially graduate students for whom one is now an idealized mentor.

STAGE 4: PROFICIENCY

At this level one can rely upon "holistic similarity recognition" (Dreyfus and Dreyfus, 1986, 28). That is, proficient persons can do things even if they cannot explain how they accomplish these tasks, such as hit a tennis ball with topspin, cook the roast to the ideal moment, or gauge a classroom's tone before the final exam period. During the split second in which one sees the ball, adjusts the racquet, and tenses one's forearm, there is no time to run through a list of rules about speed, angle, and the like. The proficient player just does it. This form of intuition, or know-how, requires one to have had many previous experiences and to generalize from them a sense of patterns among oneself, one's racket, and the oncoming ball.

A computer program cannot do this—unless someone can sort through the thousands of perceptions, such as "My legs are getting heavy. I probably cannot make a good overhead smash, therefore go to the net now!" and link those perceptions to judgments. These perceptions occur almost instantaneously and cannot be specified by rules stated in ordinary language.

The proficient therapist should be able to:
1. Make use of the scientific literature for daily clinical work.
2. Tolerate and utilize differing supervisory modes and implicit models of "good technique."
3. Establish a working alliance with new patients with increasing ease and confidence.
4. Learn from previous errors with previous patients and be corrected by one's current patients.
5. Decrease one's idealization of "the only way to do therapy" and so decrease one's rigid defenses against "not knowing."
6. Recognize a broader range of countertransference manifestations and have a sense of their location.
7. Tolerate deeper and more archaic levels of a patient's experience, especially more archaic transference impingements.
8. Draw upon a network of associations and previous experience in order to integrate diagnosis and intervention: to "see" a patient's life more holistically than one could previously.
9. Teach basic elements of psychotherapeutic practice.

The proficient teacher must confront the overwhelming pull of "schools" of thought. Each offers comfort and aid by denying the value of other points of views. Here, in the academy, writing becomes a central task.

STAGE 5: EXPERTISE

"When things are proceeding normally, experts don't solve problems and don't make decisions; they do what normally works" (Dreyfus and Dreyfus 1986, 30–31). The novice radiologist sees an X-ray film with dark spots; the advanced beginner sees the spots and recalls (some) of the rules that might obtain; the more advanced radiologist discerns likely diagnoses and compares this film to other films; the expert sees a tumor. The novice therapist sees a frightening person shouting in the waiting room; the advanced beginner sees a patient who merits the label "borderline"; the more advanced therapist recalls diagnostic indicators for borderline ego functioning and recalls his or her supervisor's' voice describing such patients; the expert therapist sees a person suffering intense abandonment anxiety precipitated by an immediate failure on the therapist's part. (That this failure amounts to not controlling something uncontrollable, such as a change in the front-office secretary, does not discharge the expert therapist's sense of his or her causal location in the patient's suffering.)

Experts are not necessarily ideal teachers. Indeed, because expertise is not "deduced" from rules, the expert cannot say how he or she arrived at every solution. To demand such rules on every occasion is either to reduce expertise to a lower form of problem solving or to engender an illusion. The illusion is that some secret "theory," if adhered to religiously, will guarantee success. Going to the other extreme, it is equally an error to conclude that because "expertise is beyond stated rules," the expert cannot and need not demonstrate his or her work.

Expert therapists should be able to:
1. See more clearly the transference-countertransference interface and show how it alters over time.
2. Use multiple frames of therapeutic theory and reference.
3. Grasp more immediately the patterns of resistance and defense that make up "normal character," including one's own.
4. Have a better sense of one's actual character and one's limitations (to distinguish a patient's perception from a patient's transference distortions with more depth).
5. Draw more creatively upon countertransference fantasies.
6. Have increasing empathic comprehension of one's patients and persons in their world.
7. Develop a more flexible understanding of the therapeutic process.
8. Contribute to the scientific literature.
9. Guide the next generation of therapists.
10. Develop the capacity for tragedy, not just irony.

I stress the capacity for tragedy, not just irony, because irony is such an attractive resting place for teachers and therapists (I speak autobiographically). Able to draw upon century-old traditions and cite (if not steal from) Nietzsche and other masters, irony defends one against too closely identifying with failure. To be ironic—in the way Freud was about religion, for example—is to assert that one has risen above those who struggle with concerns the cognoscenti surmounted long ago. Like all humor, irony has a touch of hostility that one can easily ignore, unless one is the target.

To recall our discussion of false memory syndrome, it is noteworthy that when zealots on either side of these debates take the floor they wield moralizing judgments. Black-white reasoning and legalistic terms dominate even as they deny the need for legal process with its exquisitely worked out rules of evidence. "Feeling" justice on their side, they plunge ahead. Those who reject this moralizing stance and defer to expertise share its devotion to process, and to wisdom: "Good evidence for false memories exists, but conversely amnesia and subsequent recall of sexual abuse undoubtedly occur. The principle of *primum non nocere* is particularly important in guiding therapeutic endeavors.". . . (Critchlow 1998, 64–67; Raphling 1994, 65–78). A strict parallel, especially in graduate education, is recognizing that we will meet students whom we cannot teach. This common event, often denied by both parties, issues in many stalemated dissertations.

The Expert Teacher of Freud and Religion?

Experts rarely use a fixed set of well-defined rules to solve complex problems. On the contrary, much evidence suggests that gifted athletes, expert diagnosticians, and expert teachers cannot articulate a complete set of rules with which they solve problems because they do not use rules. Rather, they use rules to teach beginners the rudiments of a field, to advance the curriculum, to codify past successful efforts, and to rationalize their field. The novice and advanced beginner may need to acquire explicit rules, or ask more expert colleagues, when facing a new or especially complex task. But the expert often says something like "In my experience [with three hundred similar cases, or five thousand slides, or fifty seminars] this problem has this kind of outcome." More honest experts will say simply "My intuition tells me so." If pressed to explain in more detail, experts may seek justification in rules or make them up! Or declare ignorance.

Among the rules affirmed by experts are generalizations about rules. These affirmations are "meta-rules" that acknowledge limitations to their mastery of the subject matter. The affirmations typify genuine experts whom we trust because they are willing to affirm that, sometimes, they do not know what they are talking about. They know that they cannot always be right. This kind of Socratic not-knowing appears in *A Little Book of Doctors' Rules*, a delightful book by Clifton Meador, an endocrinologist. He summarizes medical wisdom in the form of 425 rules; for example, number 28: "Learn to distinguish those patients for whom you can be their physician from those for whom you cannot. Refer the latter to another physician. Do it sooner rather than later." Of course, to learn to distinguish between patients you can treat and those you cannot, you must acknowledge that you have failed the latter group. This means admitting that you have been defeated many times. Rule number 64 is one of many lessons in humility:

> The odds of you as a physician
> committing suicide,
> getting addicted,
> getting divorced,
> becoming an alcoholic, or
> going off the deep end are very high.
> Find out why.

One must admire the typography here, for it emphasizes the factual nature of this charge, leveled with good humor and concern, that being a physician is rife with dangers made invisible by ordinary narcissism. To deny these facts and to accept only what feels good narcissistically is to make these afflictions more likely. Indeed, one might argue that this form of denial not only harms many doctors but also it harms many patients. As we learn from rule number 424, "It is usually the second mistake in response to the first mistake that does the patient in."

I return to my original question, Why teach Freud? I suggest two answers. First, Freud discovered a way to investigate psychical reality (*psychische Realität*) without recourse to religion or mysticism. Second, Freud helped set the modernist agenda, the principal organizing themata of this century.[8] Without him and his efforts, we cannot continue to map this inner world. We turn back to ourselves, mere human beings, who are not experts upon ourselves. Freud was not an expert about himself. Nor did he master the inner world. How could he? However, he provided new methods and new vocabularies that take us from the first level of self-understanding, that of raw beginner, up toward the higher levels. These are, I think, sufficient reasons to teach Freud. Without recording his steps and noting his failures, including rules that we now can reject, we cannot graduate to expertise and its freedoms nor can we grasp the optimism in the face of change noted by Whitman and Milton.

Notes

1. *Time*, 29 November, 1993.
2. This map was imperfect and subject to revision. Freud never claimed he exhausted the study of unconscious processes, he never stopped revising his earlier thoughts, and he never wished psychoanalysis to be other than a scientific inquiry, subject to constant revision. On "mapping" see also Gay, (2001).
3. Sigmund Freud, *Gesammelte Werke*. (Frankfurt am Main: S. Fischer, 1952, 1968–1981), Vol. 10, p. 56. Compare the *SE* version of this text, (*SE* 14: 17–18). The *SE* translates the German terms praktischen Realität as "practical reality."
4. http://www.aip.org/history/einstein/great1.htm.
5. Donald Kaplan, personal communication to Pine (1998).
6. Martin Luther King Jr., Letter From Birmingham Jail, April 16, 1963, Part One.
7. (See *SE* 9: 3). Also *SE* 13: 1; *SE* 21: 3, 23: 3.
8. According to Masud Khan (1975, 39), "With the Cubists, Dadaists and Surrealists the narrative becomes utterly suspect. The artists strive to make of the image (in word or plastic idiom) an absolute space and reality from which they do not awaken themselves. Joyce was to claim: 'Since 1922 my book has been a greater reality to me than reality.' Molly Bloom's nocturnal soliloquy, as it ends *Ulysses*, is a critical point in that crisis of consciousness which was to become the fate of Modernism in our times. Most creative effort was to become autotherapeutic and explore the dreamspace. Joyce, in *Finnegan's Wake*, gives the diagnosis and the new therapeutic responsibility in an epiphanic conundrum." See also Yerushalmi 1992, who compares Freud and Arnold Schoenberg as modernists.

References

Critchlow, Stephen. 1998. False memory syndrome: Balancing the evidence for and against. *Irish Journal of Psychological Medicine*, 15, no. 2: 64–67.

Dreyfus, Hubert L., and Stuart E. Dreyfus. 1986. *Mind over machine: The power of human intuition and expertise in the era of the computer*. New York: Free Press.

Ellenberger, Henri F. 1970. *The discovery of the unconscious*. New York: Basic Books.

Erikson, Erik H. 1954. The dream specimen of psychoanalysis. *Journal of the American Psychoanalytic Association,* 2:5–56.

Freud, Sigmund. 1953–1974.

    1900. Interpretation of dreams. *SE* 4–5.

    1907. Obsessive actions and religious practices, *SE* 9:3. *The standard edition of the complete psychological works of Sigmund Freud* (hereafter *SE*), Volumes 1–24, Translated and edited by James Strachey. London: Hogart Press. 9, 3.

    1912–13. *Totem and taboo. SE*, 13: 1.

    1914. On the history of the psycho-analytic movement. *SE* 14: 7.

    1927. *The future of an illusion. SE* 21: 3.

    1939. *Moses and monotheism, SE*, 23: 3.

Gay, Volney P. 1989. *Understanding the occult: Fragmentation and repair of the self.* Minneapolis: Fortress Press.

———.1992. *Freud on sublimation: Reconsiderations*. Albany: State University of New York Press.

———. (2001). Mapping religion and psychologically. In Religion and psychology: Mapping the terrain, edited by Diane Jonte-Pace and William Parsons. London: Routledge, 94–109.

Gedo, John, and Arnold Goldberg. 1973. *Models of the mind: A psychotherapeutic theory*. Chicago: University of Chicago Press.

Jones, Ernest. 1953. *The life and work of Sigmund Freud*. Vol. I, *The formative years and the great discoveries, 1856–1900*. New York: Basic Books.

Khan, Masud. 1975. Freud and the crises of responsibility in modern psychotherapeutics. International Review of Psycho-Analysis, 2: 25–41.

Kernberg, Otto, et al. 1989. *Psychodynamic psychotherapy of borderline patients*. New York: Basic Books.

Langs, Robert. 1984–85. Making interpretations and securing the frame: Sources of danger for psychotherapists. *International Journal of Psychotherapeutic Psychotherapy*, 10: 3–23.

———. 1985. *Workbooks for psychotherapists*. 3 vol. Emerson, N. J.: New Concept Press.

Meador, Clifton, ed. 1992. *A little book of doctors' rules*. Philadelphia: Hanley & Belfus.

Pine, Fred. 1998. Diversity and direction in psychoanalytic technique. New Haven, Conn.: Yale University Press.

Pike, Kenneth. 1954. *Language in relation to a unified theory of the structure of human behavior*. Vol. 1. Glendale, Calif.: Summer Institute of Linguistics.

Raphling, David L. 1994. A patient who was not sexually abused. *Journal of the American Psychoanalytic Association,* 42: 65–78.

Turner, Victor. 1969. *The ritual process: Structure and anti-structure*. Ithaca, N.Y.: Cornell University Press.

———. 1982. *From ritual to theater: The human seriousness of play*. New York: Performing Arts Journal.

Yerushalmi, Yosef Hayim. 1992. The Moses of Freud and the Moses of Schoenberg— on words, idolatry, and psychoanalysis. *Psychoanalytic Study of the Child*, 47: 1–20.

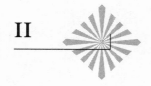

II

TEACHING FREUD
AS INTERPRETER
OF RELIGIOUS TEXTS
AND PRACTICES

5

"Let Him Rejoice in the Roseate Light!": Teaching Psychoanalysis and Mysticism

William Parsons

In the present climate of fascination with mystical experience and spirituality, an informed grasp of the resurgent psychoanalytic theory of mysticism has become a desired end for those invested in teaching religion and psychological studies. Of course, the literature on this topic is rich and complex enough to be packaged for pedagogical purposes in diverse ways. What follows, then, is hardly meant to be an exhaustive or comprehensive survey of the variety of pedagogical options afforded by psychoanalytic studies of mysticism. On the contrary, I concentrate on but one instance of psychoanalytic forays into mysticism: Freud's interpretation of the famous "oceanic feeling." I do so partly because the latter is the *locus classicus* of the psychoanalytic theory of mysticism. But more, this one text also contains the fundamental keys needed to unlock the historical drift of subsequent psychoanalytic theorizing on mysticism.

Fundamental to the pedagogical strategy I have in mind for teaching the psychoanalytic theory of mysticism is the deconstruction of what can be called the "received view" of Freud's psychology of mysticism. Certainly it has generally been assumed that Freud's interpretation of mysticism was both simple and straightforward. To wit: Freud defined mystical experience in terms of the feelings of unity and eternity captured by the phrase "the oceanic feeling." Its psychological etiology is to be found in the pre-Oedipal phase of development where one does not yet distinguish between self and other, between oneself and the Mother. To this is added that Freud evaluated mysticism in classic reductionistic terms: mysticism is essentially regressive, defensive, childish, and escapist.

This "received view" is not without some basis in the text. Certainly it has played a part in forestalling further inquiry into mystical states and experiences. However, if such a view were essentially correct, a sustained analysis of this one chapter could be dispensed with, and any deeper reflection on the pedagogical lessons it could offer would vanish along with it. But taken as a complete characterization of Freud on mysticism, the received view is seriously misleading. To the contrary, then, I assert that a simple regurgitation of the "received view" is a good example of how *not* to "read" (and thus teach) the Freud of *Civilization and Its Discontents*. It assumes a reductionistic, one-dimensional Freud and an equally reductionistic understanding of "mysticism."

A very different reading of both Freud and mysticism accrues if the text is contextualized with respect to Freud's correspondence with Romain Rolland. The latter (which can be found *in toto* in Parsons [1999]) spanned the years 1923–1939 and can be divided into three periods: 1923–27 (the "early" period); 1927–30 (the "middle" period); 1930–36 (the "late" period). The letters of the middle period are central to Freud's analysis of the oceanic feeling, which took place during the year 1929. However, the letters of the early period, which clearly bring into focus the dynamics of the two men's friendship, and the letters of the late period, which catalogue the aftermath of Freud's analysis, are equally integral to a proper understanding of Freud on mysticism.

By asking students to read Freud's analysis of the oceanic feeling against the backdrop of each period of the correspondence (the entirety of which is a readable ten book pages), we are afforded a pedagogical opportunity of surpassing worth. This is true in a general sense, for the challenge to the authority of the "received view" takes place through textual reconstruction and contextualization. Translated into the dynamics of the classroom, this demands not a "lecture" approach but the art of "mediation," by which I mean engaging the student through dialogue in a manner that facilitates the development of those intellectual skills and capacities integral to a broad humanistic education: critical reading and attention to the text, reasoned and judicious judgment, the proper ways to form and reformulate questions, the art of educated and inspired guesses, and the joys of the communal and collegial pursuit of new ideas. This is also true in a more specifically psychoanalytic sense, for Freud's analysis read "in context" also affords us the opportunity to help nurture a psychoanalytically informed humanistic eye for discerning multiple levels of meaning in texts, individuals, and culture.

Certainly the above pedagogical aims can be furthered through various strategies. I have found that one successful strategy proceeds by way of assuming that each individual period of the Freud-Rolland correspondence harbors an inherent "set" of issues and themes that functions as a self-contained pedagogical unit. Each "set" of issues and themes can be linked, and thus elaborated, to corresponding aspects of the text of *Civilization and Its Discontents*. Insofar as this is the case, each period helps to deconstruct the "received view" in various stages, adding nuance of meaning to Freud's psychology of mysticism. Further, the analysis can be linked to subsequent psychoanalytic theorizing about mysticism, to other aspects of Freud's psychology of religion as a whole, and even to general truths germane to the psychoanalytic enterprise.

For example, the major issue that confronts one in the letters of the early period is the dynamics of the Freud-Rolland relationship. These letters reveal the real and symbolic meaning Rolland had for Freud's self-conception as a psychoanalyst, a culture theorist, and a Jew. This meaning evoked events in Freud's biographical past and engaged the social circumstances of his present. The analysis can be made to reveal how Freud's associations to Rolland impacted his understanding and interpretation of the oceanic feeling. Again, by enjoining our students to reflect on these matters we develop in them a specific psychological capacity: that of learning to become "musical" in the art of psychobiography, to apply Freud's archaeological dig to his own works.

The letters of the "middle period," on the other hand, engage the general status of the "interlocutor" in Freud's psychology of religion. They serve to challenge the "received view" directly by examining the letters in relation to the multiple literary references and metaphors, all linked to Rolland and his oceanic feeling, which one finds laced throughout the first chapter of *Civilization and Its Discontents*. Analyzing these references serves a dual function: they thoroughly undermine the "received view" and, when framed as integral parts of Freud's analysis of mysticism, they cast a new light on the deeper, humanistic basis of psychoanalysis. Fleshing out the meaning of these literary texts allows us to formulate a specific "reading" of Freud: the rhetorical, literary genius and Goethe Award winner who linked his theory of the mind to the seminal insights of the great poets and philosophers who preceded him.

Finally, the letters of the "late" period catalogue the aftermath of Freud's analysis, the continued reflections of each man on the relation between psychology and mysticism, and the revelation that the two men entertained not one (the "classic" reductionistic) model but three ("classic," "adaptive," and "transformational") models for the interpretation of mystical states and experiences. These models can then be utilized as the basis for categorizing and comparing subsequent psychoanalytic attempts to interpret mysticism.

In order to make these points and the pedagogical strategies linked to them abundantly clear, I now turn to a more detailed elaboration of each of these periods in turn.

"The Apostle of Love": The Letters of the Early Period

A general psychoanalytic truth that impacts pedagogy is the notion that "ideas" live in the context of interpersonal exchange, and that biographical and social determinants are invariably summoned through contact with the Other. In any act of communication, then, there are multiple layers of meaning, the exegesis of which resembles an archaeological dig. These general truths are illustrated and given specificity in the letters of the "early" period. The latter total seven in number: February 22, March 4, and March 12 of 1923; June 15, 1924; January 29, May 6, and May 13 of 1926. The issue is what meaning, real and symbolic, the figure of Rolland had for Freud and in what ways it impacted his understanding and interpretation of mysticism. With the caveat that teachers always learn something from students, and that one can always be surprised by relevant but unexpected observations and interpretations a student may offer, the following catalogues groups of observations I have found useful in guiding discussion.

First, some brief biographical notes are in order. Renown in his own day, the figure of Romain Rolland (1866–44) is no longer a household name. Born in Clamency, a small French town, the young Romain was spirited off to Paris by his parents as an adolescent, there to attend the prestigious École Normale Supérieure, a move that eventuated in his becoming a professor of musicology at the Sorbonne. Yet these events are not what made Rolland a cultural icon during the early decades of the twentieth century. There are, in fact, four areas of cultural engagement linked with Rolland that are relevant for understanding his relationship with Freud. Most notably, Rolland was a novelist. Known for novels like his *Jean-Christophe*, *The Soul Enchanted*, various plays, his biographies of famous men like Tolstoy and Beethoven, and a series of short essays, Rolland was awarded the Noble Prize for literature. His fame as a writer, however, was second to his international fame as social activist and mediator during the World War I. His *Above the Battle*, a series of essays, letters, and moral diatribes, was praised as a beacon of light in the otherwise irrational night of hostilities between the French and the Germans. The red thread uniting these articles was the reasoned moral appeal to intellectuals, public officials, and governments to create a higher ground of constructive dialogue. Third, Rolland was a pivotal figure in the emerging encounter between East and West. His biographies of Gandhi and the Hindu sages Ramakrishna and Vivekananda did much to help facilitate a bona fide conversation between peoples of diverse nationalities and religions. Finally, Rolland was religious, albeit in a generic way. Brought up Catholic, he renounced Christianity and embraced an unchurched mysticism that he thought could be the subject of rational inquiry, particularly by psychology.[1]

With the above in mind, let us proceed to the text and the letters of the early period. The first "group of observations" mentioned above relates directly to the person of Rolland and begins in the opening paragraph of *Civilization and Its Discontents*. There, Freud refers to a friend of his who he thought to be a "great man," one of the "exceptional few" who eschewed "false standards of measurement" such as wealth and power, knew what was of "true value in life," and whose greatness rested on "attributes and achievements which are completely foreign to the aims and ideals of the multitude." He was, of course, referring to Romain Rolland. The letters of the early period corroborate this view. They reveal that, above all, Freud honored Rolland as a moralist. In line with Freud's idealization of Rolland as a "great man" we see him characterizing Rolland as an "apostle of love" who had "soared to . . . heights of humanity through . . . suffering and hardship" (letter of January 29, 1926). As briefly catalogued above, this is undoubtedly due to Rolland's visible presence as mediator and cultural status as the "conscience of Europe," a title he had earned through his efforts during the war to adjudicate between the Germans and the French on the grounds of enlightened rationality and pacifism. Ernest Jones notes that Freud knew of Rolland's efforts and of the book (i.e., *Above the Battle*) through which he made his appeals (Jones 1957, 97). Freud also links Rolland to the forces of tolerance (the issue of anti-Semitism), inclusivity, and love: "For us your name had been associated with the most precious of beautiful illusions, that of love extended to all mankind" (letter of March 4, 1923) and again: "across all boundaries and bridges, I would like to press your hand" (letter of March 12, 1923). Rolland had been brought up a Catholic, but renounced it in his adolescence. He later married a Jew (Clotilde Breal, the daughter of the French academic Michel Breal, a pro-Dreyfusard) and promoted tolerance and inclusivity in many of his works. This was not lost on Freud, who in a letter to Victor Wittowski once praised Rolland's "courage of conviction, his love of truth and his tolerance" (Freud 1960, 426–27).

The second group of observations consists in linking the above to Freud's two noteworthy associations to the oceanic feeling. The first association occurs when Freud, in noting the unitive element that defined the ideational content of the oceanic feeling, comments: "If I have understood my friend rightly, he means the same thing by it as the consolation offered by an original and somewhat eccentric dramatist to his hero who is facing a self-inflicted death. 'We cannot fall out of this world.' That is to say, it is a feeling of an indissoluble bond, of being one with the external world as a whole." The quote is taken from the end of Christian Dietrich Grabbe's play *Hannibal,* where Hannibal, faced with death at the hands of the Romans, opts for the more noble death of martyrdom. The second association takes the form of an analogy. In attempting to convey a picture of the preservation of psychic contents in the mind, Freud draws an analogy between the development of the mind and the historical development of the Eternal City, Rome. Just as one can see remnants of ancient Rome in the midst of its modern developments, so too is it the case that nothing in the mind, once formed, ever perishes. In this analogy, then, the oceanic feeling corresponds to ancient Rome, the Rome of Jupiter and Minerva.

What are we to make of these associations? Here the pedagogical opportunity arises to become psychobiographical—one that allows us to link the letters of the early period and the text of *Civilization and Its Discontents* with relevant primary texts (notably *The Interpretation of Dreams*) and secondary studies (as listed below). Freud's reference to Grabbe's play can be interpreted as a free association, one that indicates the operation of what has come to be known as his "Hannibal phantasy." We know from Ernest Jones's biography of Freud and more recent historical and sociological forays, particularly those by Carl Schorske and John McGrath, the important role fin-de-siècle Viennese politics played in Freud's life and thought (Schorske 1981; McGrath 1974). During Freud's childhood and student years (1860–80)

Vienna's sociopolitical atmosphere was suffused with the tolerant air of political liberalism and its attempt to actualize the enlightenment ideals of equality, freedom, human rights, and a secular, rational order. These ideals were championed and mediated to Freud by his father and developed in his school years through his association with close friends like Heinrich Braun, later a pivotal figure in European politics. Freud's early desire to study law, his membership in the radical student group Leseverein der deutschen Studenten Wiens, and his inkling to enter politics are all testaments to these early personal and social influences. Like many non-Orthodox, middle-class Jews, he aspired to assimilation and preached the gospel of democracy and nationalism. However, after 1880 any Viennese Jew would survey the political landscape with alarm. The collapse of political liberalism waned in the face of the rise of the anti-Semitic Christian Socialist Party, a trend that reached its apex when, in 1897, Karl Lueger became mayor of Vienna. Freud felt the effects of this movement in many areas of his life, the most important being the continual frustration of his cherished wish to become a professor at the University of Vienna (a fact well illustrated in his dream of the "Uncle with the Yellow Beard"). Doubting the power of a political solution to social injustice, perceiving Catholic complicity in the rise of Lueger, and convinced of the mendacity of religious injunctions to tolerance like the love command, Freud turned away from the outer religio-political realm to that of the inner world, there to seek another arena for the transformation of self and society. Indeed, as Dennis Klein and Peter Homans have pointed out, for Freud psychoanalysis became a new basis on which to construct a social whole. The "cultural texts" were but an extension of the "psychoanalytic movement" and the clearest expressions of Freud's desire to create a social space through which humanity could find its way to increased tolerance and equality (Klein 1981; Homans 1989).

This religio-political reality, then, invariably affected the motivation behind and expression of Freud's "cultural works." Indeed, while ignited in some way by his sociopolitical surround, these motivations can be found rooted in Freud's developmental past. It is here that we come across those famous complexes that have been termed his "Rome Neurosis" and "Hannibal phantasy."[2] As catalogued in *The Interpretation of Dreams*, Freud had a number of dreams during the 1880s and 90s that betrayed the impact of religion and politics on his unconscious, none of which were more significant than the "Rome Dreams." These dreams occurred during a period when Freud developed an irresistible and overwhelming desire to visit Rome, a longing that provoked fear and anxiety and was fulfilled only after a period of successful self-analysis. While seemingly aware of the full import of the latent thoughts and developmental precursors that instigated the dreams, Freud was willing only to divulge that his analysis unearthed his identification with Hannibal. Like Freud, Hannibal had been "fated not to see Rome" and "symbolized the conflict between the tenacity of Jewry and the organization of the Catholic Church" (*SE* 4: 196–97). In addition, Freud related the childhood experience that served to extend the behavioral attitudes associated with his identification with

Hannibal to the religio-political sphere. That experience consisted of a story his father had related to him concerning an encounter with anti-Semitism of his youth, in which he had been obliged to react to a verbal taunt in a compliant and passive fashion. The intent of the father was to affirm to his son how political liberalism had changed things for the better. Unfortunately, this moral entirely bypassed the young Sigismund, who remembered only the "unheroic conduct" of his father. Endeavoring to replace the story with one more befitting his budding sense of masculine narcissism, Freud recalled the scene where Hannibal, promoted by his father, swore an oath to "take vengeance on the Romans." As Schorske comments, Freud's identification with Hannibal's oath was both "pledge and project" and, as project, both "political and filial": "Freud defined his Oedipal stance in such a way as to overcome his father by realizing the liberal creed his father confessed but had failed to defend. Freud-Hannibal as 'Semitic General' would avenge his father against Rome, a Rome that symbolized 'the organization of the Catholic Church' and the Habsburgh régime that supported it" (Schorske, 1981, 191).

The reference to ancient Rome, on the other hand, reveals a wish far removed from Oedipal hostility. Freud's feelings toward Ancient Rome, with all of its maternal connotations, were revealed in a letter to Fliess shortly after his first trip to Rome, a trip made possible by the successful analysis of his Rome Neurosis. Freud wrote that he was unable to enjoy medieval Rome: "I was disturbed by its meaning, and, being incapable of putting out of my mind my own misery and all the other misery which I know to exist, I found almost intolerable the lie of the salvation of mankind which rears its head so proudly to heaven" (Freud, 1954, 335–36). In contrast, Freud said that he "contemplated ancient Rome undisturbed (I could have worshipped the humble and mutilated remnant of the Temple of Minerva near the forum of Nerva)" (335–36). Schorske has pointed out that this Rome was not the Rome of Hannibal, the Rome that engendered Oedipal hostility in Freud. Rather, it was the Rome of the art historian and archeologist Joachim Winckleman, who loved Rome because it was "the mother of European Culture." This was a Rome Freud aspired to assimilate to, the city of culture and love (Schorske, 1981, 190–93).

These seeming contradictory associations are reconciled through the figure of Rolland. As seen in our above analysis of the early letters, Freud referred to Rolland as the "apostle of love for mankind" and portrayed the "oceanic feeling" in terms of maternity and inclusiveness. There was, so to speak, an aura of ancient Rome surrounding the oceanic feeling. Rolland could be counted on to actualize the kind of tolerance and inclusiveness that formed the essence of the love-command. At the same time (in his letter of March 4, 1923), Freud also recalled the horrors of the Middle Ages and the rampant anti-Semitism associated with Christianity and the love-command. So Rolland, the oceanic feeling and the love-command were clearly linked in Freud's mind. From this perspective, its is imperative to note that Rolland's postulation of a connection between the oceanic feeling and religion created intellectual excitement and Oedipal hostility in Freud by providing him with new material that spurred analytic reflections on the love-command. The latter is found in chapter 4 of *Civilization and Its Discontents,* where Freud puts forward the suggestion that the love-command, "Thou Shalt Love Thy Neighbor as Thyself," finds its origin in "the remote regions where the distinction between the ego and objects or between objects themselves is neglected" (*SE* 21: 72). In other words, to the same developmental stage that, when preserved along-side the more narrow adult ego, is subjectively apprehended as the oceanic feeling. One can see how this makes sense, for the love-command simply puts into an ideal and reified form the ethical meaning inherent in an early developmental state in which the self is the Other and the Other the self. It was precisely the privileging of this primitive state, with all of the psychological complications such primitivity implied, that became the basis for Freud's numerous criticisms of the "unbehagen" or unease created by the love-command, not the least of which was its complicity in the "narcissism of minor differences" and anti-Semitic behavior.[3]

In sum, the letters of the early period reveal that the Freud-Rolland friendship revolved around the themes of politics, morality, art, psychoanalysis, and religion. Rolland was a friend of psychoanalysis and a symbol—one that reached deep into Freud's pscho-social past, engaging the themes of assimilation, anti-Semitism, religion, and tolerance. These associations, properly fleshed out with respect to the text and Freud-Rolland correspondence, add nuance, richness, and depth to the enigma known as the oceanic feeling.

Deconstructing the "Received View":
The Letters of the Middle Period

The letters of the "middle" period are but five in number (December 5, 1927; July 14, 17, 20, and 24 of 1929). However, used to contextualize Freud's argument in the first chapter of *Civilization and Its Discontents*, they serve to undermine the received view. In so doing, they also provide opportunities to reflect on: (1) the general role of the "interlocutor" in Freud's psychology of religion; (2) a humanistic "reading" of Freud and psychoanalysis.

The pivotal letter of the group is Rolland's letter to Freud of December 5, 1927. Freud had sent him *The Future of an Illusion* as a gift. Rolland responded by saying he agreed with Freud's analysis, but then went on to make both a claim and a request. The claim was that mysticism (the oceanic feeling) was the true source of religion. The request was for Freud to subject it to analysis. Rolland then directly challenged Freud's project in *The Future of an Illusion*. It is here that the opportunity arises to address the question of the "interlocutor" in Freud's psychology of religion.

We know that Freud was a "decline" theorist, that he thought secularization to be an irreversible historical fact. The argument of *The Future of an Illusion* can be seen as based on this sociohistorical problem. Faced with the inevitable decline of religion and the inability of the "masses" to properly sublimate sexual and aggressive urges, the major problem of *The Future of an Illusion* becomes as follows: "either these dangerous masses must be held down . . . or else the relationship between civilization and religion must undergo a fundamental revision" (SE 21: 39).[4] Freud's solution to the problem was to create a social space for a secular cure of souls (psychoanalysis) that would help "educate" the instincts and promote cultural adaptability. To that end he identified another group in society, the "cultured elite," that would help disseminate psychoanalysis into culture at large. It was to this group that Freud addressed *The Future of an Illusion*. His hope consisted of inserting his psychoanalysis into Western culture as part and parcel of the emerging scientific attitude toward reality, hence helping to avoid the kind of social dislocation that could result from the historical transition from the childhood of mankind to its maturity. It was to this end that Freud employed the rhetorical strategy of creating an interlocutor who embodied the characteristics of the cultured elite and was equally capable of using theological arguments and being swayed by psychoanalysis.

Rolland possessed attributes that made him attractive to Freud as a possible interlocutor and conduit for the dissemination of psychoanalysis. Rolland was a valued member of the intellectual elite, a gentile connected to the reigning Catholic culture in France, a university professor, a Nobel Prize winner, a renowned sociopolitical figure, and a moral exemplar. Discussion can pivot around these qualities of Rolland, proceeding to compare him with the interlocutor of *The Future of an Illusion* and other religious figures who confronted Freud: Oskar Pfister, Ludwig Binswanger, and Carl Jung.

The letters of the middle period also directly undermine the received view. First, a careful reading of Rolland's description of the oceanic feeling in his latter of December 5, 1927, should be compared with the second paragraph of *Civilization and Its Discontents* (where we find Freud summarizing Rolland's description of the oceanic feeling). Rolland refers to the oceanic feeling as a "constant state," a "prolonged sensation" that exists alongside the "critical faculties" without, despite its immediacy and constancy, interfering with their proper function. Freud as well seems to have understood it as such, for in his summary of Rolland's letter in *Civilization and Its Discontents* he characterizes the oceanic feeling as consisting "in a peculiar feeling, which he himself is never without." In other words, the oceanic feeling does not fit the classic portrait of the "marks" of mystical experience (passivity, transiency, ineffability, noesis) as elaborated by William James in his *The Varieties of Religious Experience*. The latter understanding of what constitutes "mysticism," which is central to the "received view," is not germane to Freud's understanding or interpretation of the oceanic feeling. Freud's argument does not emphasize the oceanic feeling as an instance of mystical experience that can and should be understood in terms of regression to the pre-Oedipal stage of development. The oceanic feeling is to be understood as a "constant state" that reveals in some people the "preservation" of an original ego feeling (from the pre-Oedipal stage) that exists alongside the more developed adult ego.[5]

It is true that Freud evaluated the oceanic feeling as being used for defensive purposes, as a way of disclaiming dangers from the outside world and restoring a sense of limitless narcissism. Insofar as that is the case, he championed a "classic" reductive understanding of mysticism. However, at the same time, Freud's analysis in *Civilization and Its Discontents* reveals a more "adaptive" reading of mysticism that has wholly bypassed the proponents of the received view. It is here that a humanistic reading of psychoanalysis can be found.

The analysis centers around the last paragraphs of the first chapter of *Civilization and Its Discontents*. Here, Freud has ended his discussion on the nature of the "oceanic feeling" and its connection with institutionalized religion and turns to a related phenomenon:

> Another friend of mine, whose insatiable craving for knowledge has led him to make the most unusual experiments and has ended by giving him encyclopaedic knowledge, has assured me that through the practices of Yoga, by fixing the attention on bodily functions and by peculiar methods of breathing, one can in fact evoke new sensations and coenaesthesias in oneself, which he regards as regressions to primordial states of mind which have been long ago overlaid. He sees in them a physiological basis, as it were, of much of the wisdom of mysticism. It would not be hard to find connections here with a number of obscure modifications of mental life, such as trances and ecstasies. But I am moved to exclaim in the words of Schiller's Diver: "Let him rejoice who breathes up here in the roseate light!" (*SE* 21: 72)

One cannot help but note the very real difference between this mystical phenomenon and the oceanic feeling. In describing the latter Freud had emphasized the enduring feeling of connection with the outside world. The unitive, statelike character of the oceanic feeling demanded recourse to a pre-Oedipal model of development and the theory of the preservation of psychic contents. In the above passage, Freud speaks of mystical practices (yoga), of ecstasies and trances, and of the regressive descent into "primordial states" for the purpose of achieving a particular kind of wisdom. The description is far more like the transient mystical "experience" elaborated by William James.

In order to properly interpret this passage, students should be offered the opportunity to contextualize it with respect to Schiller's poem "The Diver" as a whole, Rolland's letter of July 17, 1927, and a 1904 document detailing a conversation between Freud and the Swiss poet Bruno Goetz.

To elaborate; the first letter of the middle period was Rolland's letter of December 5, 1927. Then over two years later, on July 14, 1929, Freud responded, telling Rolland of a work, *Civilization and Its Discontents*, that lay "still uncompleted" before him. He had written an introduction to the work consisting of an analysis of "the oceanic feeling" and wondered whether Rolland would give him permission to use his personal remark in a public forum. Three days later, Rolland wrote granting his permission, adding that he was delving into the "ritualistic and multi-secular physiology which is codified in treatises on Yoga." This exchange of letters demonstrates the affinities that abound between the "another friend" Freud mentions (in the above cited passage from *Civilization and Its Discontents*) and Rolland. Both have wide-ranging interests, a love for the truth, and, most significantly, are interested in Yoga, mystical practices, and the physiological basis of mysticism.

The question now concerns the interpretation of this mystical "experience," the regression into the depths of the psyche. In his 1933 work *New Introductory Lectures on Psychoanalysis*, Freud seems to give mystical practices like yoga a place of honor. In a famous passage he states how one could imagine that "certain mystical practices may succeed in upsetting the normal relations between the different regions of the mind, so that, for instance, perception may be able to grasp happenings in the depths of the ego and in the id which were otherwise inaccessible to it," and how " it may be admitted that the therapeutic efforts of psycho-analysis have chosen a similar line of approach. Its intention is, indeed, to strengthen the ego, to make it more independent of the super-ego, to widen its field of perception and enlarge its organization, so that it can appropriate fresh portions of the id. Where id was, there ego shall be. It is a work of culture—not unlike the draining of the Zuider Zee" (*SE* 22: 181). In *Civilization and Its Discontents,* the analysis is similar but decidedly poetic. Freud characterizes it simply with words from Schiller's "The Diver": "Let him rejoice who breathe up here in the roseate light." If one undertakes an analysis of the poem as a whole, something previous commentators have neglected, one finds a curious state of affairs: the condensation of Oedipal with "oceanic" imagery. Briefly summarized, "The Diver" portrays a young man who, on two successive occasions, undertakes the heroic task of grappling with the forces of a feared "whirlpool," portrayed as an "ocean womb" that "boils and hisses . . . a gaping chasm . . . leading down to the depths of hell," in order to retrieve a king's goblet. Motivated by the king's blessing and his crown in return, the page dives into the gloomy depths, miraculously emerging:

> Long life to the King! Let him rejoice
> Who breathe up here in the roseate light!
> For below all is fearful, of moment sad;
> Let not man to tempt the immortals e'er try,
> Let him never desire the things to see
> That with terror and night they veil graciously

Filled with amazement and curiosity, the king asks the page to return to the "purple depths" to bring word to him of the mystery below. With the promise of his daughter's hand in marriage, the idealistic page once again enters the fateful whirlpool, never to return.

This powerful poem can be read as a metaphor for the psychoanalytic task. One "dives" into the "whirlpool" of the unconscious, a whirlpool inhabited by powerful and potentially dangerous powers. Further, the theme of "The Diver" is an Oedipal one: winning the favor of the king, gaining his daughter's hand in marriage only to eventually displace the king himself. Freud's citation of "The Diver" in the passage in question suggests that, far from retreating from psychic reality, the mystic diver goes where few dare to tread.

The conclusions offered here find support in one of Freud's "pre-Rolland" reflections on mysticism. The document in question, which I dub "The Goetz Letters," concern the recollections of a relatively obscure Swiss poet, Bruno Goetz, concerning his encounter with Freud during his days as a student at the University of Vienna.[6] In one such visit, Goetz relayed information about his studies at the university and the enthusiasm that the noted Sanskrit scholar, Leopold von Schroeder, had inspired in him through his lectures on the Bhagavad Gita. At this point, Freud "sprang briskly to his feet" began to pace and responded at length:

> Take care, young man, take care . . . You are quite right to be enthusiastic. For out of the abundance of the heart the mouth speaketh. Your heart will always win the day, but keep that cool head which, fortunately, you still have. Don't be taken off your guard. A clear, sparkling intellect is one of the greatest gifts. The poet of the Bhagavad Gita would be the first to affirm that very thing. Always be on the look-out, always keep your eyes open, always be aware of everything, always be of unswerving courage, but never let yourself be dazzled, never let yourself get tied up in knots. Emotion must not become auto-anaesthesia. Dostoyevsky's principle: "Head first, head over heels into the abyss" is all very fine, but the enthusiasm which it has aroused in Europe is based on a sad misunderstanding. The Bhagavad Gita is a great and profound poem with awful depths. And still it lay beneath me hidden deep in purple darkness there" says Schiller's diver, who never returns from his second brave attempt. If, however, without the aid of a clear intellect you become immersed in the world of the Bhagavad Gita, where nothing seems constant and where everything melts into everything else, then you are suddenly confronted by nothingness. Do you know what it means to be confronted by nothingness? Do you know what that means? And yet this very nothingness is simply a European misconception: The Indian nirvana is not nothingness, it is that which transcends all contradictions. It is not, as Europeans commonly take it to be, a sensual enjoyment, but the ultimate in superhuman understanding, an ice-cold, all-comprehending yet scarcely comprehensible insight. Or, if misunderstood, it is madness. What do these European would-be mystics know about the profundity of the East? They rave on, but they know nothing. And then they are surprised when they lose their heads and are not infrequently driven mad by it—literally driven out of their minds. . . . The most sensible thing to do is to keep on asking questions. At the moment you are interested in the Hindu philosophers. They often went so far as to express their answers in the form of questions. They knew why. (Goetz 1975, 139–43)

The classroom discussion can revolve around how Freud addresses three interrelated aspects of the mystical path: (1) the content of nirvana (the "mystical experience"), (2) the mental and emotional requirements of the seeker, and (3) the role of the sage-therapist. The first engages Schiller's "Diver," the second Dostoyevsky's *The Brothers Karamotzov,* and the third the relation between psychoanalysis and the philosophers.

Concerning the first of these, Freud states: "Nirvana is not nothingness, annihilation, nilhism or sensual enjoyment but that which transcends all contradictions . . . [it is] the ultimate in superhuman understanding, an ice-cold, all-comprehending yet scarcely comprehensible insight" (Goetz, 1975, 142–43). So much, at least, is clear from the text. However, exactly how Freud construed the nature of this insight can be further specified. The realm that transcended all contradictions was, for Freud, not some metaphysical or transcendent reality, but as he indicated as early as 1900 in his *Interpretation of Dreams*, that of the unconscious (*SE* 5: 596). This is given further content in the characterization of the "awful depths" of the Bhagavad Gita in poetic terms: "'and still it lay beneath me hidden in purple darkness there' says Schiller's diver, who never returns from his second brave attempt." Once again, then, we find Freud using the same text, Schiller's "The Diver," to characterize the psychological depths of mystical intuition. However, while the poem has a tragic ending, prefiguring Freud's later, more pessimistic views of interminable analysis, intractable conflict, and guilt, Freud's reference to the "ultimate in superhuman understanding" suggests that the mystic, unlike the page, succeeds in gaining insight into the deepest recesses of his Oedipal distress.

Just as important are Freud's observations concerning the mental and emotional requirements needed to insure a successful outcome to the psychic surgery the mystic undertakes. Given the "awful depths" of the Bhagavad Gita and the possibility of madness, Freud cautions Goetz that the enthusiasm and courage of the mystic diver must be subsumed under the guidance of the intellect. Once again there are literary references—to Matthew 12:34 and Dostoyevsky's *The Brothers Karamotzov*—that reveal a deeper, richer meaning to Freud's admonitions. The latter is of especial interest given that Freud later wrote a short psychoanalytic study of Dostoyevsky that centered around his Oedipal struggles and his creative rendering of them in *The Brothers Karamotzov*. The figure of Dimitri, who Freud calls an "impulsive sensualist" and around whom Dostoyevsky clusters the themes of unbridled passion, parricide, and intellectual and moral weakness, is appropriately singled out for attention. Not so coincidentally, it is also Dimitri who utters "head first, head over heels into the abyss" and who is later brought to trial for the public demonstration of his patricidal urges. Once again, we see Freud conceptualizing the mystic path in terms of his budding metapsychology. Dimitri embodies what can happen to those who enter the abyss "head over heels," who are given to what Freud called "acting out" over remembering and "working through."

Contrasted to the figure of Dimitri is that of the poet-philosopher of the Bhagavad Gita who, as a seeker, knows the value of the intellect and, as therapist, the value of posing answers in the form of questions. Psychoanalytically rendered, Freud intimates that the Indian sages had arrived at the therapeutic wisdom that acknowledges the art of holding the tension between instructive guidance and trusting in the patient's ability to bring to conscious awareness the "answers" that lie buried within him in a time-appropriate, ego-syntonic way. Insight, sublimation, and working through preponderate over acting out. This rendering of mystical therapy recalls another Freud was familiar with and compared favorably with his own—namely, the Socratic. Generally speaking, the fundamental tenets that guide the two systems of thought—the end (self-knowledge), the means (asking questions), the assumptions (the answers are within), and the form (dialogue)—are similar.[7] So, too, did Freud utilize Platonic concepts such as Eros and similes, such as that of the charioteer, to help convey the meaning of his own. Given his classical training and evidence of Freud's awareness of the scholarly debates surrounding the question of the extent of Indian influence on Plato, "The Goetz Letters" suggest that Freud merged the two systems of thought, insofar as they both contained the same germinal element of truth, and then read the more detailed and precise empirical findings of psychoanalysis back into them.

Tracking the Psychoanalytic Theory of Mysticism: The Letters of the Late Period and the Emergence of the Classic, Adaptive, and Transformational Schools

The letters of the "late" period and the texts they implicate allow us to bring in the historical trajectory of the psychoanalytic theory of mysticism since the Freud-Rolland correspondence. The pivotal letter of the late period, Freud's letter to Rolland of January 19, 1930, was precipitated by Rolland's gift to Freud of his biographies of the Hindu saints Ramakrishna and Vivekananda. In his letter of December 5, 1927, Rolland had spoken of the research he was conducting with respect to two Asian mystics. Now, just over two years later, and after having read *The Future of an Illusion* and corresponded with Freud over the matter of the oceanic feeling, Rolland presented Freud with his own views on the nature and origin of mysticism. In the appendix to his biography of Vivekananda, entitled "Concerning Mystic Introversion and its Scientific Value for the Knowledge of the Real, " Rolland took on a paradigmatic study of the psychological approach to mysticism, Ferdinand Morel's *Essai sur l'Introversion Mystique.* Morel, who was a professor of psychiatry at the University of Geneva, eschewed the transcendental epistemological claims of the mystics and applied the central psychological theories and concepts of his day—Janet's hierarchical conception of the mind, Freud's psychosexual developmental theory, Bleuler's study of autism, and Jung's concepts of "introversion" and "extraversion"—to some of the leading mystical texts and authors from various religious and philosophical traditions. While Morel's analysis was complex, he generally framed mystics as regressed and infantile. In playing out their repressed desires, mystics regressed to narcissistic and autoerotic stages of development, spinning out fantasies in various forms—for example, elaborate metaphysical systems and erotically tinged hallucinated encounters with religious archetypes. Deep ecstatic experiences, such as those of a pseudo-Dionysius, were interpreted as a longing for the security and quietude of the intrauterine state. Again, while Rolland's critique of Morel was complex and nuanced, it is fair to state that in general he countered Morel's reductionism with a "transformational" reading of mysticism, one that allowed for a true transcendent, religious dimension to mysticism. Morel had concluded that the unitive experiences of deep mystical introversion signified a return to an intrauterine state. While Rolland agreed that the maternal imagery and symbols pervading mystical texts and the "curious instinct" that gave rise to the worship of the Mother lent strength to Morel's interpretation, he insisted that there lay something beyond the pre-Oedipal, that the kind of awareness the mystic had attained demanded epistemological analysis and a richer view of the unconscious. He then went on to describe the essential characteristic of this layer of the unconscious: unity. Unity was the most archaic dimension of the unconscious, the very foundation of one's Being and the source of the most Real (Rolland 1988, 388).

In his letter of January 19, 1930, Freud thanked Rolland for his biographies and went on to answer Rolland's critique of Morel and psychoanalysis. He admitted that mystical intuition could be "highly valuable for an embryology of the soul when correctly interpreted," but he doubted that it could solve the "riddle of the universe" or lead to ultimate salvation. He closed by saying that he was not "an out-and-out skeptic. Of one thing I am absolutely positive: there are some things we cannot know now."

This exchange between the two men reveals that during the course of their correspondence they entertained three different models for the interpretation of mystical states and experiences: the classic, adaptive, and transformational. The classic model, which can be allied with Freud's pejorative evaluation of the oceanic feeling, views mysticism as defensive and potentially pathological. The adaptive model, which can be linked to Freud's more positive assessment of mysticism as a window into the depths of the unconscious, frames mysticism as a healing enterprise. As Freud stated in his *New Introductory Lectures*, it is here that psychoanalysis and mystical practices adopt a similar line of approach. The transformational model, as advocated by Rolland, allows meta-psychological space for the deeper, transcendent claims of the mystics.

Each of these models has been elaborated through the course of psychoanalytic history. For example, a contemporary illustration of the "classic" approach can be found in Jeffrey Masson's *The Oceanic Feeling* (1980). In line with Freud's view of Eastern religions as promoting states of derealization, depersonalization, and regressive pathology, Masson sees the first noble truth of Buddhism as based on an existential fact: Buddha was profoundly depressed. Searching for a cure to his illness, Buddha engaged in a regressive, introspective activity: meditation. In unearthing the buried traumatic memories that led to his depression, Buddha became so overwhelmed that he sought refuge in a state of manic denial, or nirvana. The adaptive model, on the other hand, has grown in sophistication with the advent of ego-psychology and object-relations theory. A good illustration of developments in Freud's view that mystical practices may be therapeutically effective can be found in the collaboration among Erich Fromm, D. T. Suzuki, and Richard De Martino in their classic *Zen Buddhism and Psychoanalysis* (1960). Fromm observed that while the methods of Zen and psychoanalysis differed, their healing aims could be made to tally if one reformulated Freud's psychoanalytic motto ("where Id was there Ego shall be") around a humanistic framework. Freud's motto indicated that he wanted to make only a localized aspect of the unconscious conscious—that dealing with childhood trauma, the instinctual life, and symptom formation. However, if one enlarged that purview to include the *full* recovery of the unconscious, one would achieve a psychological aim broadly commensurate with Zen, Suzuki's notion of the "art of living," and the ethical aims of the spiritual, humanistic orientation that grounded it.

Finally, developments in the "transformational" model have also taken place since the Freud-Rolland correspondence. Erikson's reference in his book on Luther to the "unborn core of creation" (*ein lauter Nichts*)—a phrase indebted to Angelus Silesius and elaborated in later works in terms of the numinosity of the "I"—certainly suggests a bona fide mystical dimension to the human personality (Erikson 1958; 1981). Again, Wilfred Bion elaborates on the concept of "O," the actualization of which is the ideal aim of the therapeutic encounter, in explicit religo-mystical terms as "the absolute truth, the godhead, the infinite, the thing-in-itself . . . it can 'become,' but it cannot be 'known'" (Bion 1983, 26). Finally, Lacan's notions of jouissance and the Real are similarly mystical. Lacan was influenced by mystics like Plotinus and Teresa, and he objected, in his inimitable way, to Freud's reduction of mysticism "to questions of fucking." He thought mystical utterances were the "best thing you can read," adding that his own work should be regarded as essentially "of the same order" as mysticism (Lacan 1982, 147).

In order to illustrate these approaches in a pedagogically useful manner, I have found it helpful to draw on three recent biographies of Ramakrishna. These biographies are all the more appropriate for they provide continuity with the late period of the Freud-Rolland debate—a debate that, after all, centered around the figure of Ramakrishna and his major disciple, Vivekananda. The three biographies in question are Narasingha Sil's, *Ramakrishna Paramahamsa*, Sudhir Kakar's *The Analyst and the Mystic*, and Jeffrey Kripal's *Kali's Child*. Each clearly represents the orientation of the three schools of psychoanalytic theorizing about mysticism cited above: the classic (Sil), adaptive (Kakar) and transformational (Kripal). As such, they illustrate the diverse psychoanalytic approaches to the transcendent claims of mysticism (in this case being how each treats Ramakrishna's initial vision of Kali). Moreoover, each study has the advantage of treating mysticism as part of the broader question of healing "East and West." That is, each study illustrates differing approaches to the questions surrounding the cross-cultural study of healing, integrating orientations within psychoanalytic anthropology and engaging to various degrees the interdisciplinary resources utilized in the comparative study of mysticism. Specifically, in addition to the issue of the nature of mystical noesis or experience, each study treats the dynamics of mystical desire (eroticism) and the therapeutic effectiveness of mystical sadhanas (practices) as set in their cultural context. The presentation of these studies, then, can be framed around a series of issues pertaining to the cross-cultural study of healing.

To elaborate, Sil explicitly seeks to show the continuities between Ramakrishna's developmental past, his emerging psychosis, and his later theosis (1991, 5). Mystical experience becomes defined in terms of regression, manic denial, reaction formation, and other psychological defense mechanisms. Ramakrishna's famous vision of Kali becomes construed as a hallucination, "possibly the outcome of his depression and aggression towards the most important object [the Mother Goddess] in his life . . . and thus, in Freudian terms . . . a classic case of the shadow of the object falling upon the ego" (Sil 1991, 118). Sil explicitly notes his debt to the psychoanalyst and indologist Jeffrey Masson, approving of his claim that there is "severe pathology" in Ramakrishna and the need to link an analysis of the latter with Freud's case history of Schreber (1991, xi–xii). Sil further concludes that Ramakrishna, owing to developmental trauma, exhibited in his mystical sadhanas, such as his *madhurya bhava* (a form of expressing devotion to Krishna in which one, in an attempt to identify with Krishna's lover Radha, dresses as a woman), moments of gender confusion. However, in so concluding, Sil follows in the steps of those psychoanalytic anthropologists like Géza Róheim and George Devereux, who espouse an unqualified psychoanalytic universalism. In such an understanding of cross-cultural psychology there is no need for ethnographic mediation or Geertzian "thick description" and "native's point of view." Rather, Sil agrees with Masson's stance (1979) that Ramakrishna's transvestitism, which was socially legitimated by his culture, rendered him nothing more than a "happy pervert." Indeed, Sil sees in Ramakrishna's sadhanas R. D. Laing's notion of an ontologically insecure individual, one who acted out infantile, voyeuristic, and autoerotic behavior.

In contrast, Kakar explicitly notes the need to go beyond the classic school's equation of mysticism with pathology (1991, 3). He sees Ramkrishna's many mystical visions, particularly his initial vision of Kali, as motivated in part by loss and separation anxiety and sees represented in them parental figures as well as various aspects (drawing on Mahler) of pre-Oedipal development. But ultimately Kakar, showing he is a member of the adaptive school, draws on Winnicott and his notion of transitional space. Mystical experience (as seen in Ramakrishna's vision of Kali) is interpreted as a transitional form of experiencing, as an adaptive mode of being-in-the-world that is "the preeminent way of uncovering the vein of creativity that runs deep in all of us" (1991, 29). Mysticism is also linked to creativity through Ramakrishna's sadhanas. The essence of each sadhana is seen as constituted by *bhava*, or devotion. The latter is interpreted by Kakar as a culturally specific defense mechanism similar to sublimation. Ramakrishna's *madhurya bhava*, seen by Sil as indicative of perversion, is now understood in terms of Winnicott's "pure female element" and reveals a culture that tolerates males' experiencing their femininity and advocates "being" and "receptive absorption" over "doing" and "active opposition." In so concluding, Kakar adopts a stand on the relation between psychoanalysis and culture that allows for cultural influence in the shaping of "developmental lines" and relativity with regard to evaluating culturally different ways of envisioning reality, gender orientation, sexuality, and individuality (see Kakar 1981, 1982, 1985).

Finally, Kripal's heremeneutical strategy is multidisciplinary. At times he draws on the work of Sil and Kakar and seems to champion their conclusions. But he departs significantly from them in his use of Stanley Kurtz and Ganananth Obeyesekere (his preferred psychoanalytic anthropologists) and Lacan (his psychoanalytic and "transformational" theorist) and the development of a cross-cultural category he calls the "erotic," which conjoins the sexual and emotional basis of mystical experience to its higher ontological expression. In order to compare him with Sil and Kakar, this is best evinced in his analysis of Ramakrishna's first vision of Kali.

Sifting through the multiple versions of this pivotal vision, Kripal isolates two significant psychosocial facts: (1) the culturally shared, tradition-based drama where Kali's sword demands one's severed head in return for mystic vision; and (2) Ramakrishna's personal, idiosyncratic, homoerotic "vocabulary of desire" ("anxious longing," "enkindling," "attraction," "strange sensation," and "wrung like a wet towel"). Exegeting the former with respect to Hindu iconography and rooting the latter in Ramakrishna's developmental past and later homoerotic longing for his boy disciples, Kripal concludes it was the shame Gadadhar felt over illicit homoerotic desires that ignited his first vision of Kali. At the same time, Kripal argues that Ramakrishna's mystical experiences engaged both divine ground and sexual conflict.

In articulating this specifically mystical dimension to the personality, Kripal draws attention to Lacan's reading of Teresa's mystico-eroticism. Noting Lacan's commentary on Bernini's statue, *Teresa in Ecstasy*, Kripal unpacks Lacan's question, "And what is her *jouissance*, her *coming* from?":

> This, it seems to me, is as important a question as any, and I doubt very much that questions of pathology or the dynamics of psycho-social processes, however crucial such issues might be, have anything to do with its answer. It is simply a different type of question. Lacan was clear enough about his own answer to where Teresa was "coming from." He rejected the notion that the mystical can be reduced to sexuality and instead speculated that such ecstatic experiences of a "*jouissance* which goes beyond" issue forth from our own ontological ground. . . . Ramakrishna in *samadhi*, not unlike Bernini's "Teresa in Ecstasy," is obviously "coming." But "what is his *jouissance*, his *coming* from'? . . . I have respected the religious world of Tantra and have chosen to interpret Ramakrishna's mystico-erotic experiences within that universe. I would argue, then, that the saint's experiences were "coming from" the ontological ground of his Tantric world. . . . I would insist, moreover, that such a realization be understood on its own terms, as a genuine religious experience. (Kripal 1995, 326)

In bridging psychoanalytic and Tantric notions of sexuality and vision, Kripal sees in the symbols and acts of Ramakrishna's homoerotic mysticism a progressive (cultural-mystical) as well as regressive (psychoanalytic) meaning. It is Obeyesekere's anthropological take on Ricoeur's dialectic between arche and telos that paves the way for providing a relation between the two:

Sometimes, in exceptional cases, we find genuine two-way "symbols" that function *both* as symptoms, hearkening back to the original crisis, *and* as numinous symbols, pointing to a resolution of the crisis, greater meaning, and what Obeyesekere calls a "radical transformation of one's being." Obeyesekere identifies Ramakrishna as one of those "exceptional cases" in which the symptom became a symbol and turned a crisis into an experience of the sacred: "Ramakrishna's Hinduism permits the progressive development of the personal symbol. . . . Ramakrishna his own mother is mother Kali who is the Mother and the guiding principle of cosmic creativity. Through Kali, Ramakrishna has achieved trance and knowledge of a radically different order from the others, and he can progress tom the heart of a specifically Hindu reality that is essentially salvific." . . .

Here, then, is where I would locate the meaning of Ramakrishna's *eros*— *both* in his obvious infatuation with his boy disciples, an infatuation somehow connected with the archaic "regressive" motivations of his own personal history . . . *and* in a "progressive," essentially mystical, order of rapture and vision . . . what was once a crisis became the secret, not only of his mystical and charismatic success, but of his very divinity. (Kripal 1995, 323–24).

This progressive movement, however, cannot be accounted for by simple sublimation but only through an alchemical transformation of bodily energies that necessitate a move to a specifically tantric worldview, one in which *libido* receives its definition in relation to the erotic-mystical energy known as *shakti*. So, too, must one note the very different view of development inherent in such a worldview. It is the opening of those psycho-physiological structures known as *cakras* and the mystical understanding they bequeath that become the markers of development. From this perspective, libido-based notions of development are relativized and turned on their head. As Kripal points out, from the standpoint of the successful tantric, "Freud only got to the third Cakra" (Kripal 1995, 43).[8]

Concluding Reflections

In the foregoing I have tried to map a plausible pedagogical strategy for teaching Psychoanalysis and Mysticism. Rather than simply mouthing a tired and erroneous "received view" or reiterate attempts to pigeonhole and pathologize mysticism, my pedagogical strategy aims at delineating a historical trajectory that begins with the Freud-Rolland correspondence; fleshes out their debate over the oceanic feeling and their respective advocacy of classic, adaptive, and transformational approaches to mysticism; and ends with an examination of subsequent psychobiographies of Ramakrishna. This map allows for pedagogical aims to be fulfilled above and beyond the desired versing of the student in the origins, development, and increasingly interdisciplinary focus of the psychoanalytic theory of mysticism. It allows the student to practice the art of psychobiography, to spy a humanistic dimension to psychoanalysis, and to become habituated to thinking "in context."

Notes

1. Good biographies of Rolland can be found in March (1971) and Starr (1971).
2. The term "Rome Neurosis" was coined by Schorske (1981), "Hannibal phantasy" by McGrath (1974).
3. David Fisher (1982) has also noted the association of Rolland to the love-command and has attempted to connect Freud's reference to Rome as well as the quote from Grabbe to Rolland. His interpretation of these associations, however, is radically different from my own. According to Fisher, the association of the oceanic feeling to Rome is due to Rolland's first name (Romain) and the association to Grabbe indicates Freud's desire to link the oceanic feeling with narcissistic rage and suicidal feelings (262–63). In this text Fisher also reveals that he thinks the oceanic feeling is a reaction formation against fantasies of world destruction and the "universal hatred of humanity" (267). This link between the love-command and the oceanic feeling can be followed up as desired with respect to Ernst Wallwork's fine study of the love-command (1991).
4. In the discussion that follows I am indebted to the work of Philip Rieff (1979).
5. It should be pointed out that Freud's analysis, which reduces the oceanic feeling to a kind of psychological appendix, was in error. He did not know that Rolland's oceanic feeling was a rather late, mature phase of his mysical life that carried with it the connotation of moral maturity (see Parsons 1999). This point could also be useful for classroom discussion.
6. The German original appeared as "Erinnerungen an Sigmund Freud," in *Neue Schweitzer Rundschau*, 20 (May 1952): 3–11. I have utilized an English translation: "That is all I have to say about Freud: Bruno Goetz's Reminiscences of Sigmund Freud," in *International Review of Psychoanalysis*, 2 (1975): 139–43. Another translation can be found in *Annual of Psychoanalysis,* 10 (1982): 281–91. Ellenberger has cited this document in his *Discovery of the Unconscious* (New York: Basic Books, 1970), 461–62.
7. I would like to thank Robert Kaplan of Harvard University for making this clear to me.
8. For further studies illustrating the classic, adaptive, and transformational schools, see Parsons (1999), chap. 6.

Bibliography

Bion, Wilfred. 1983. *Attention and interpretation*. New York: Jason Aronson.
Erikson, Erik. 1958 *Young man Luther*. New York: Norton.
———. 1981. The Galilean sayings and the sense of 'I'. *Yale Review*, 70:321–62.
Fisher, David. 1982. Reading Freud's *Civilization and Its Discontents*. In *Modern European intellectual history: Reappraisals and new perspectives*, edited by Dominick LaCapra and Stephen L. Kaplan. Ithaca, N.Y.: Cornell University Press.
Freud, Sigmund. 1953–1974. *The standard edition of the complete psychological works of Sigmund Freud (SE)*, Volume 1-24, translated and edited by James Strachey. London: Hogarth Press.
   1900. *The interpretation of dreams*. SE 4 and 5.
   1927. *The future of an illusion*. SE 21: 3–56.
   1930. *Civilization and its discontents*. SE 21: 59–145.
   1933. *New introductory lectures*. SE 22: 3–182.

————. 1954. *The origins of psychoanalysis: Letters to Wilhelm Fleiss, drafts and notes, 1887–1902*. Edited by Marie Bonaparte, Anna Freud, and Ernst Kris. New York: Basic Books.

————. 1960. *Letters of Sigmund Freud*. Edited by Ernst Freud. New York: Basic Books.

Fromm, Erich., D. T. Suzuki, and Richard De Martino, eds. 1960. *Zen Buddhism and psychoanalysis*. New York: Harper Colophon.

Goetz, Bruno. 1925. That is all I have to say about Freud: Bruno Goetz's reminiscences of Sigmund Freud. *International Review of Psychoanalysis*, 139–43.

Homans, Peter. 1989. *The ability to mourn*. Chicago: University of Chicago Press.

Jones, Ernest. 1957. *The life and work of Sigmund Freud*. New York: Basic Books.

Kakar, Sudhir. 1991. *The analyst and the mystic*. Chicago: University of Chicago Press.

————. 1981. *The inner world*. Delhi: Oxford University Press.

————. 1982. *Shamans, mystics, doctors*. New York: Knopf.

————. 1985. Psychoanalysis and non-Western cultures. *International Review of Psychoanalysis*, 12:441–48.

————. 1982. Reflections on psychoanalysis, Indian culture and mysticism. *Journal of Indian Philosophy*, 20:289–97.

Kripal, Jeffrey. 1995. *Kali's child*. Chicago: University of Chicago Press.

Klein, Dennis. 1981. *Jewish origins of the psychoanalytic movement*. New York: Praeger Publishers.

Lacan, Jacques. 1982. God and the jouissance of women. In *Feminine sexuality: Jacques Lacan and the École Freudian*, edited by J. Mitchell and J. Rose. New York: Norton.

March, Harold. 1971. *Romain Rolland*. New York: Twayne Publishers.

Masson, Jeffrey. 1979. Indian psychotherapy? *Journal of Indian Philosophy*, 7:327–32.

————. 1980. *The oceanic feeling*. Dordrecht, Netherlands: D. Reidel.

McGrath, William. 1974. Freud as Hannibal: The politics of the brother band. *Central European History*, 7: 31–57.

Parsons, William. 1999. *The enigma of the oceanic feeling*. New York: Oxford University Press.

————. 1998. The oceanic feeling revisited. *Journal of Religion*, 74, no. 4: 501–23.

Rieff, Philip. 1979. *The mind of the moralist*. Chicago: University of Chicago Press.

Rolland, Romain. 1988. *Life of Vivekananda*. Calcutta: Advaita Ashrama.

————. 1965. *Life of Ramakrishna*. Calcutta: Advaita Ashrama.

Sil, Narasingha. 1991. *Ramakrishna Paramahamsa*. Leiden: Brill.

Schorske, Carl. 1981. *Fin-de Siècle Vienna: Politics and culture*. New York: Vintage.

Starr, William. 1971. *Romain Rolland: One against all*. The Hague: Mouton.

Wallwork, Ernest. 1991. *Psychoanalysis and ethics*. New Haven, Conn.: Yale University Press.

6

Teaching Freud While Interpreting Jesus

Donald Capps

The invitation to write an article on the psychoanalytic interpretation of Jesus for a book on teaching Freud comes at an opportune moment. I have recently completed a book on Jesus that is psychoanalytic in orientation, and am now contemplating teaching a course on the subject in the near future. In an institution like Princeton Theological Seminary, this may require more than the normal justifications for a course of this nature, as the seminary currently boasts a biblical faculty of fifteen, eight of these in New Testament. As I will indicate, however, this is just one of several impediments to such a course. The following discussion, therefore, offers a justification for a course on the psychoanalysis of Jesus—not, however, by engaging in the usual arguments in behalf of interdisciplinary courses, but by demonstrating the intrinsic value of psychoanalytic interpretation of Jesus for the psychology of religion. This requires that I give significant attention to my own Jesus text.

Justifying the Course

That I have not yet taught the course may place me at a certain disadvantage relative to the authors in this book who are reporting on their actual classroom experiences. I would defend this approach, however, on the grounds that I seriously doubt I would have considered teaching a course on this subject had I not already written a book on it. Before writing the book, I would not have thought that there was sufficient justification for a full-semester course on the psychoanalytic interpretation of Jesus. This judgment would have been based on several factors, including the assumption that there is insufficient historical evidence to support a psychoanalytic study of Jesus; the inappropriateness of the use of a theory—psychoanalysis—developed in the modern era to interpret an individual from an ancient culture (though, admittedly, this consideration did not seem so insurmountable in the case of Augustine); the frequent assertion by contemporary biblical scholars that ancient societies did not have a concept of individuality, thus rendering any modern biographical approach, including psychoanalysis, anachronistic; and various other objections arising from the fact that I am not formally trained in biblical studies. That I am now considering teaching a course on Jesus suggests that I do not consider these, either individually or collectively, to be fatal objections to the venture.

Of course, there are other, more contextual causes for hesitation, most notably the fact that psychoanalysis itself is viewed with considerable suspicion by the overwhelming majority of members of theological faculties (witness their vigorous rejection of Erik H. Erikson's *Young Man Luther*), a problem that is compounded by the fact that the subject in this case is Jesus, who, in my own institutional context, is in a separate category from all other religious figures (i.e., *sui generis*). The view of Jesus as one among several *Homo religiosi*, which would not be problematic in a state-supported university, is more suspect in a theological seminary. (In contrast to the seventeen faculty at Princeton Theological Seminary in biblical studies, there is one historian of religions.) Thus, a course on the psychoanalysis of Jesus may be viewed with greater suspicion in my own academic context than is common among academics; they, on the other hand, may be more tolerant of a colleague's idiosyncratic interests than students themselves would be, many of whom might consider a course on the psychoanalysis of Jesus an inappropriate use of the seminary's resources, as well as, perhaps, a not-so-subtle effort to undermine their nascent but fervent faith. So, regardless of the fact that some students would welcome such a course, the fact that others may object to it being offered probably needs to be taken into consideration.

This suspicion of psychoanalysis is part of a larger issue—that is, that theologians tend to have a deep mistrust of anything called psychological, largely on the grounds that it is "reductionistic." I consider the argument against reductionism as something of a red herring, a shibboleth used when more cogent criticisms of psychoanalysis would require greater familiarity with its literature, in that every academic field does—and should—reduce the object of its investigation to the theories and concepts that it employs. Perhaps a more strategic point, however, is my conviction that theologians have nothing to fear in this regard, for my own best efforts to explain Jesus psychoanalytically leave many unanswered questions and also, no doubt, pose new ones that theologians might consider worthy of their own attention. In any case, instead of being cowed by anticipated charges of reductionism, I tried in my book to remain faithful to what Philip Rieff calls Freud's "analytic attitude" (Rieff 1966, 2).

Perhaps the most succinct argument I could make for such a course being offered at my institution is the quotation from T. W. Manson's *The Teaching of Jesus* (1931), which serves as the epigraph for Geza Vermes's chapter in *The Religion of Jesus the Jew* on "Jesus the Religious Man": "We are so accustomed . . . to make Jesus the object of religion that we become apt to forget that in our earliest records he is portrayed not as the object of religion, but as a religious man" (Vermes 1993, 184). This statement might be quoted in a course syllabus not only as justification for the course but also as setting its general parameters (i.e., what it is *not* about).

A more elaborate justification for the course would, however, be very similar to my justification for writing a book on the subject: three decades ago, some biblical scholars began turning to the social sciences (especially sociology and cultural anthropology) to inform New Testament studies. This turn to the social sciences has been enormously illuminating, shedding new light on the social world of early Christianity. It has also, however, produced new disagreements among biblical scholars. One is that increased appreciation for the complexity of first-century Palestine has led to quite different "portraits" of Jesus, depending on whether one emphasizes the larger sociocultural milieu—with its Hellenistic influences—or one focuses on the more circumscribed social milieu of traditional Judaism. Was Jesus more heavily influenced by the larger Hellenistic culture, or was he more embedded in traditional Jewish culture?

A second, related area of disagreement concerns the social roles that were available to Jesus, and his adoption of—or self-identification with—one or more of these roles. Recognizing that Jesus was more than the sum of the activities ascribed to him by the Gospel writers (and also noting that in some cases these attributions were anachronistic), scholars have turned to various sociocultural types of religious authority (e.g., holy man, sage, magician, messiah, itinerant Cynic) in an effort to define his sociocultural identity. In some cases, a scholar will consider one of these identities central, and will view Jesus's activities as the expression of this identity. In other cases, a scholar will attempt to show that Jesus integrated two or more of these sociocultural types. In virtually all cases, scholars have contended that Jesus put his individual stamp on a preexisting sociocultural type, making it distinctively his own. Conversely, if he is not seen to have modified or transformed a sociocultural type, this is virtually tantamount to saying that it was not central to his identity. Each of these types has its proponents, and the very plurality of them—and the plausibility of their applicability to Jesus—has created considerable disagreement as to what Jesus understood his mission to be about and who he understood himself to be.

I do not claim that more explicit use of psychological theories and concepts will resolve all of the issues resulting from the introduction of the social sciences into Jesus studies. I do contend, however, that a psychological point of view—especially a psychoanalytic one—may be very helpful precisely at those points where scholars find themselves at an impasse. When Jesus studies turned to the social sciences, it embarked on a journey that leads to psychology, for the questions that are now being posed about Jesus cannot be answered adequately in terms of sociological theories and categories alone.

Many of the unsolved problems in contemporary Jesus studies center around the issue of Jesus' identity. This is an issue that proved to be elusive and irresolvable on theological grounds, and thus figured significantly in the turn to the social sciences. It is not, however, an issue that can be settled on sociological grounds alone, as it also has a psychological dimension. The questions, "Who was Jesus?" and "What did Jesus understand himself to be about?" are ones that take us inevitably into the psychological realm.

Yet, except for a few notable exceptions, biblical scholars have been reluctant to allow psychological theories and concepts to inform their studies of Jesus. In contrast to their increasingly adept use of theories drawn from the social sciences, they have not made significant or sustained use of the psychological sciences. Since they are attempting to understand an individual—Jesus—their failure to employ psychological theories is both odd and arbitrary. It is true that some scholars make allusions to psychology, as when Marcus Borg invokes William James's discussion in *The Varieties of Religious Experience* of the reality of the unseen world to portray Jesus as one who experienced firsthand the realities of which religion is itself exceptional. More characteristic is the work of John Dominic Crossan, who, according to Mark Allan Powell, has earned considerable praise "through years of devotion to far-ranging scholarship. Archeology, anthropology, sociology, source criticism, literary criticism—if a field has any usefulness for contemporary study of the New Testament, Crossan, it seems, has been there and left his mark" (Powell 1998, 84). While Powell's list of fields where Crossan has been is certainly intended to be illustrative, not exhaustive, psychology is nonetheless not among them, and my own extensive reading of Crossan bears this out. His references to psychological writings are almost exclusively to those who have written from a medical anthropological perspective and occur only in his discussion of Jesus' role as healer; and even these he misreads, failing to note that those authors whom he quotes consider there to be a psychological element in both physical disorders and social illness. He separates the two, contending that Jesus did not cure physical diseases but did heal the social ills resulting from his contemporaries' economic and political exploitation.

In addition, Crossan is typical of Jesus scholars in their almost total neglect of psychoanalytic writings. While Borg does make use of James's *Varieties*, he does not allude to psychoanalysis in general or to Freud in particular. I will comment later on the work of John W. Miller, who appears to be an exception. He is a trained biblical scholar who, in *Jesus at Thirty*, approaches Jesus from a developmental perspective, especially the work of Daniel J. Levinson et al., *The Seasons of a Man's Life* (e.g., their concepts of the age thirty transition and mentoring), and Erik H. Erikson's concepts of identity and generativity. While he employs Freud's "A Seventeenth Century Demonological Possession," however, he overlooks Freud's emphasis on the subject's ambivalence toward his deceased father, as this would presumably counter his highly idealized view of Jesus' relationship to Joseph. There are also biblical scholars whose interpretations of certain aspects of the Jesus tradition are congruent with a psychoanalytic interpretation (at least the one I offer in my book), but who do not draw explicitly on psychoanalytic theory. Those who figure most prominently in my book are Jane Schaberg and Andries G. van Aarde.

Portraits of Jesus

How I got into the Jesus literature is instructive for how one might construct a course on the psychoanalysis of Jesus. To read all, or even most of the voluminous literature on Jesus scholarship would be prohibitive; even the historical Jesus scholars cannot keep up with all of it. What I discovered, however, is that there is a traditional term for the work of individual scholars in the field—namely, that they are said to have offered *portraits* of Jesus. This immediately attracted my attention, both because my own interests in art history began with portraiture as I assumed this would have relevance for my continuing interests in psychobiography, and because I saw that this would enable me to employ the device used by Erikson in *Young Man Luther* of beginning with a select group of scholars whose portraits would reflect, in this case, the range of contemporary Jesus scholarship. Marcus Borg's *Jesus in Contemporary Scholarship* and Mark Allen Powell's *Jesus as a Figure in History* (which he graciously provided me in manuscript form) proved especially valuable in helping me to decide on which portraitists to use. For reasons that I set forth in my book, I selected E. P. Sanders, John P. Meier, John Dominic Crossan, and Marcus Borg. I devote one chapter to Sanders and Meier and one to Crossan and Borg. By focusing on these four, I introduce many of the major issues in contemporary Jesus scholarship.

These portraits of Jesus are valuable for a psychoanalytic interpretation of Jesus for two reasons. First, they constitute the fruit of considerable scholarship carried out by their authors and by many other scholars on whom they draw who, in Powell's apt phrase, offer "snapshots" of Jesus. Therefore, they provide the untrained scholar with a reasonably reliable picture of the current state of Jesus scholarship, including points of general agreement and areas where there are serious disagreements. I will not attempt to summarize these agreements and disagreements here, but only note that I took as my baseline the areas of agreement, as I felt that a psychoanalytic interpretation of Jesus would fail if it were perceived by those trained in the field to be idiosyncratic or largely unrecognizable to them. On the other hand, their disagreements offered a useful wedge, as some of these impressed me as ones that a psychoanalytic interpretation might be able to resolve or reframe. An example would be the disagreement between scholars like Sanders who emphasize Jesus' apocalypticism (i.e., his expectation of God's imminent and direct intervention in human history) and scholars such as Crossan and Borg who stress his this-worldly, social reformist orientation. Which leads to my second point.

On the whole, the most valuable entrée these portraits afforded my interpretation of Jesus were my own disagreements with individual portraitists— disagreements based on the implausibility of their own claims when viewed from a psychological perspective, especially a psychoanalytic one. An example would be John P. Meier's contention that we do not know much about Jesus' early years because they were "insufferably ordinary," though he does acknowledge that Jesus was probably "celibate" (a rather uncommon occurrence among Jewish males). He portrays Jesus as a child and young man who was well adjusted, worked alongside his father and brothers in the family carpentry trade, was probably therefore physically healthy and even muscular, learned the Torah from his devout father, and so forth. For reasons that I set forth in my book, this picture of Jesus is psychologically naive. If the choice is between this reconstruction of Jesus' early years and Crossan's reluctance to comment on them at all, Crossan has certainly chosen the better part. These are not, however, the only options, a third being one that is psychologically astute.

In all four cases, therefore, I identified "concerns" that a psychoanalytic interpreter would raise regarding their portraits, many of which may, to the trained biblical scholar, seem tangential or even picayune, but to psychoanalytic interpreters will prove central to their own portraits of Jesus. These concerns resist easy summary here, but suffice it to say that there were instances in all four cases where, from a psychoanalytic perspective, important issues were either glossed over or entirely overlooked. In general, biblical scholars (not unlike historians) make ad hoc use of informally derived or seemingly commonsensical psychological "theories," or they caricature the psychological in order to justify a decision not to pursue motivational issues. For example, in his discussion of Sanders's emphasis on the temple disturbance as the event that precipitated Jesus' death, Powell says that no serious biblical scholar would claim that Jesus' actions were a "temper tantrum." I suggest that neither would a serious psychologically trained scholar make such a claim, but this does not mean that the psychological reasons for the action are either self-evident or unimportant.

Making a Case for Psychobiography and Psychohistory

The next step in the formulation of the book, which would also become an important segment of a course, was to recognize and answer charges that psychohistory in general—and psychobiography in particular—are spurious enterprises. This is a widely held view among historians, and we may assume that it prevails among biblical scholars, as most identify themselves as historians (even if they also claim to be expert in literary criticism, rhetorical theory, theology, etc.). Many of these criticisms are unthoughtful and uninformed. To address the legitimate concerns of serious critics, however, I addressed them in the first two chapters of a section called "Methodological Considerations." William McKinley Runyan's *Life Histories and Psychobiography: Explorations in Theory and Method* is an invaluable resource, as he summarizes the major criticisms of psychobiography and either offers a rebuttal outright (on the grounds that the criticism reflects a misunderstanding of psychobiography) or proposes a way for the psychobiographer to avoid the mistakes that have prompted legitimate criticism. I will not try to summarize his discussion here, but would note that he recognizes psychoanalysis to be the best theoretical basis for psychobiography among the many psychological theories available, largely because the issues that concern it are also the most important issues any biographer needs to consider. In the first of these two chapters, I highlight the criticisms that are most salient to a psychoanalytic interpretation of Jesus, and then provide an illustration of a psychoanalytic study by Richard L. Bushman of Benjamin Franklin's methods of dealing with conflict and conciliation, a study that is both inherently illuminating of Franklin's personality and immune to all but the most virulent criticisms of this genre. While Bushman's study would seem light years away from Jesus of Nazareth, it actually proves more useful than a mere illustration of psychobiographical method, as it focuses on matters pertaining to disputes over table and food, an especially important issue in Crossan's portrait of Jesus.

The second chapter in this methodological section centers on the psychohistory of groups, with particular emphasis on a group's emotional expression. This chapter turns on Runyan's point that psychobiography is concerned with a person not in isolation but "in a situation." It employs Zevedei Barbu's argument in *Problems of Historical Psychology* that what the psychologist has most to offer in historical studies is an emphasis on and knowledge of human emotions, here viewed as the group's emotionality. I also allude to Bruce Mazlish's point in a 1971 address entitled "What is Psychohistory?" that psychohistorical studies at that time were relatively weak with regard to the study of family life, including the family of the biographical subject. This chapter also gives considerable attention to John Demos's psychoanalytically informed studies of family and village life in seventeenth-century Massachusetts, which serve to draw attention to emotional strains and conflicts that have their counterparts in lower Galilean family and village relationships.

I realize that the analogy between the two societies is imperfect (as all analogies are), but the comparative method has become quite accepted, even commonplace, in Jesus studies since the introduction of sociological and especially anthropological methodologies three decades ago. The two basic points of convergence in this case are that intrafamilial conflict spills out into the village, contributing to interfamilial conflict (while moderating the intrafamilial); and that, emotionally speaking, rather high states of individual and collective anxiety are a fact of village life, with many of these centering around sexual prohibitions and violations, and conflict between parents and their adult children. Psychosomatic illness is also common, as the somatization of anxieties is more socially accepted than outright madness, and these have both intergenerational and gender-related provocations. As belief in demon possession is an important feature of Galilean village life, I discuss the cases of two alleged witches—one male, the other female—from Demos's *Entertaining Satan*, noting that allegations of their social contentiousness in disputes involving property and sexual matters preceded the charge of witchery.

The third chapter in this methodological section provides an overview of the social world of Jesus' day, using what I call a "zoom lens" approach. I begin with the honor-shame ideology that prevailed in Mediterranean societies in general, drawing especially on David Gilmore's observation (cited by Crossan in *The Historical Jesus*) that "Mediterranean honor" is "a 'libidinized' social reputation; and it is this eroticized aspect of honor—albeit unconscious or implicit—that seems to make the Mediterranean variant unique" (Crossan 1991, 10). Needless to say, the psychoanalytically oriented reader cannot but seize on this observation. Also noteworthy is Gilmore's claim that "evil eye belief is widespread" and is "probably one of the few true Mediterranean universals. It is also one of the oldest continuous religious constructs in the Mediterranean area" (Crossan 1991, 7). Other issues discussed in this overview of Mediterranean societies include social stratification (with so many class distinctions made that I later employ Freud's discussion in *Group Psychology and the Analysis of the Ego* and *Civilization and Its Discontents* of the "narcissism of minor differences" to account for some of the anxieties in Galilean village life and related social conflicts); and the patronal system that prevailed in all aspects and all levels of society.

As the chapter moves into the Palestine area, I focus especially on the peasant class (to which Jesus almost certainly belonged) and which Crossan discusses in rich detail in *The Historical Jesus*. Then, I center more particularly on Galilee at the time of Jesus, which was the locus of his own life, with the exception of one and possibly more visits to Jerusalem. This section of the chapter centers on conflicts between city and rural populations, political tensions between rulers and ruled, and the dramatic increase in large landholding and absentee ownership. I note R. Redfield and M. Singer's very useful distinction, cited by Sean Freyne, between *heterogenetic* and *orthogenetic* cities, the former being ones in which relations with villages in surrounding countrysides are pragmatic and based on mutual interests, while in the latter relations are based on loyalty to a shared worldview and acceptance of the past and its myths. The Galilean cities of Tiberias and Sepphoris (which Jesus appears to have avoided) were heterogenetic, while Jerusalem was orthogenetic and especially revered by Galileans, in spite of—or perhaps because of—their geographical distance from it. Discrepancies between the ideal and the real Jerusalem became all-too-apparent—often disillusioning—to Galileans who made the long pilgrimage to Jerusalem (sometimes directly through the hated Samaria, such hatred itself an example of the "narcissism of minor differences").

Another important issue discussed in this section is the high incidence of social banditry in Galilee, which may be viewed against the backdrop of Josephus's description of Galileans as "inured to war from their infancy," and Crossan's account of instances in which Galileans were prone to emotional volatility (i.e., spoiling for a fight). I then turn to the issue of family and kinship in Galilee, giving particular emphasis to marriage customs and regulations concerning sexual relations between betrothed couples (the latter of which depended to a greater extent on their "honor" than in Judaea, which provided more carefully formulated legal remedies for prospective husbands). These are issues that assume considerable importance in my psychoanalytic interpretation of Jesus' childhood and early adult years.

It should be apparent from my discussion thus far that the book does not leap directly into a psychoanalysis of Jesus; nor does it, for that matter, begin with an introduction to earlier psychoanalytic texts in which biblical subjects are addressed. While this may frustrate some readers, I consider this a necessary detour, especially in this case, because the resulting portrait of Jesus depends very heavily on how one views the "situation" in which this particular "person" was located. I believe that John W. Miller's recent psychological portrait suffers for its failure to establish this larger context, assuming that it is sufficient to begin with Jesus' immediate family. While my psychoanalytic study of Jesus is not in the same class with Crossan's *The Historical Jesus* for sheer erudition, it nonetheless has a similar structure, in that his first ten chapters set the larger sociopolitical context for the five chapters and epilogue that focus more centrally on Jesus himself. I would also note, however, that in my text, unlike his, there are two opening chapters that provide portraits of Jesus, so it is not as though the book (or course similarly constructed) holds Jesus in abeyance until its latter half.

The Question of Fatherhood

My portrait of Jesus consists of three chapters and an epilogue. The first chapter centers on what John P. Meier calls "the hidden years" of his life. It specifically addresses the question of his parentage and its implications for his status within his immediate family and in the socioreligious context of Galilee. I take up Miller's argument that Joseph was Jesus' father (he, like Meier, sets the virginal birth concept aside, though Meier more cautiously employs the phrase "putative father" for Joseph); and that he died during Jesus' adolescent years (late enough for four other sons and two or more daughters to be born, but early enough that he did not complete all the obligations of an observant Jewish father, most notably in Jesus' case, arrange for his marriage). Miller's interpretation develops out of Jesus' loss of his beloved father Joseph and his reaffirmation of this relationship in his baptism by John the Baptist through his experience of God as Father ("Abba"). He emphasizes that Jesus abandoned his role as the head of the family in his late twenties when he embarked on his public ministry. This was necessary in order to affirm his independence of his mother but also, and more important, to fulfill his true vocation in life.

Next, I take up Jane Schaberg's controversial argument that Jesus was illegitimate, the son of Mary and of an unnamed father by whom Mary was either seduced (implying perhaps some degree of consent on her part) or forcibly raped. While agreeing that the distinction between seduction and rape employed in first-century Jewish law is itself problematic, and that the answer to this question is ultimately indeterminable, Schaberg considers rape the more likely, as it coheres with Matthew's account of Joseph determining to divorce her quietly. She also agrees that Joseph proceeded with marriage and evidently reared Jesus as his own (though she does not address the latter in any detail). I focus primarily on her careful analysis of the infancy narrative in Matthew's gospel, and her references to extant Jewish literature that portray the fate of the mother and offspring of illicit sexual unions.

Finally, I take up Andries G. van Aarde's argument that Jesus, to all intents and purposes, was "fatherless," a relatively broad category that would include individuals who "grew up without a father or an adopted father and who were thus not embedded within the structures of honor." He emphasizes that such "fatherless" sons (whatever the reasons for their inclusion in this category, illegitimacy being only one of them) were excluded from the temple religion, which was inclusive of not only religious but also legal, political, social, and economic status. He chooses not to speculate on the reasons for Jesus' fatherlessness, but argues that whereas the Mary tradition is undoubtedly authentic, the Joseph tradition is late and unreliable.

I cannot discuss here the evidence these three scholars advance in behalf of their reconstructions, nor is it possible for me to explain in detail how I came to the view presented in the text, which is that Jesus was not fathered by Joseph; that Joseph probably became Mary's husband (in part because his legal protections were not as secure as in the case of Judaean males regarding the question of paternity); and that Joseph did not adopt Jesus (adoption being an early Christian ideal and one of the bases of the Matthean community's deviance, and an important theme in the authentic writings of the apostle Paul; in effect, I invoke here the criterion of dissimilarity used by biblical scholars to differentiate authentic aspects of the Jesus tradition from later Christian additions). In support of the illegitimacy theory itself, I draw attention to Edward Shorter's sociohistorical study of illegitimacy rates in seventeenth- and eighteenth-century Europe, which indicate that illegitimacy increased dramatically with the emergence of large landholdings, as this required that women and girls leave the protection of their families to work in the fields, thus making them more vulnerable to sexual exploitation. Shorter also shows that illegitimacy rates were as high in villages as in cities, but that in villages there was greater social pressure on young men to marry the women they had made pregnant. The identity of the actual father, however, was often a disputed question.

Since a similar development toward large absentee landholders was endemic to Galilee in the time of Jesus, and because Nazareth was a relatively small village, I contend that the situations were comparable, and therefore the illegitimacy theory, and the idea that Joseph proceeded with marriage to Mary, is not at all far-fetched. Where my interpretation differs from Schaberg's is that I believe there is a good reason to doubt whether Joseph adopted Jesus as his own son. Thus, I explore the significance of Jesus' marginality in Joseph's family—for example, attributing his carpenter (or *tekton*) occupation to his marginality (according to Crossan, this was the occupation most available to dispossessed sons), as well as his marriageless and childless status, his residence in Capernaum, his tensions with the family, and the cool reception he received in Nazareth when he returned and spoke in the synagogue. I view James, Joseph's first son, as the de facto first born in the family, a role that he capitalized upon in the early years of the Christian movement in Jerusalem. Thus, against Miller, I argue that Jesus did not give up his position as head of the family because it was not his to begin with. (Birthorder studies support this conclusion, as the Jesus portrayed in the gospels does not act or think like a firstborn.)

Not incidentally, I derived support for my argument from Freud's monograph on Leonardo da Vinci, which is generally credited with being the first psychoanalytic psychobiography. Leonardo was his father's firstborn, but was never formally adopted by him nor included in his will. This was because he was the son of a peasant woman with whom his father, of higher birth and social status, had had sexual relations prior to his marriage to a woman of social status comparable to his own. Bradley I. Collins has recently published a superb critical study of psychoanalytic approaches to Leonard da Vinci that supports the prevailing view that Freud's analysis of Leonardo's childhood memory is flawed, but views much more favorably his reconstruction of Leonardo's parental relationships.

To address the inevitable charge (actually made against Schaberg, whose book has been subject to virulent attack demeaning of biblical studies itself) that one cannot derive "facts" from texts that are silent on the issue in question (the so-called argument from silence), I conclude the chapter with a discussion of David Bakan's essay on the rules that govern the retention and revelation of secrets. He makes twelve propositions in this regard, four of which are especially relevant to the case of Jesus, such as that "persons who associate with one another in the context of a larger group, who have a secret from that larger group, will create a metaphorical or otherwise cryptographical language in which to discuss the secret," and "to conceal a secret, one may tend to reveal a fabricated 'secret,' or a less-secret secret, in order to generate the impression that one is being open and frank" (Bakan 1967, 105). These, I suggest, have applicability to Matthew's infancy narrative. While my book was written prior to the publication of Lawrence J. Friedman's biography of Erik H. Erikson, insights from this book regarding the tortuous language used by the family to conceal the full facts of Erikson's illegitimate conception, and his own observation that "his personal religious concerns were connected heavily to the mystery of his paternity," are relevant to a psychoanalysis of Jesus (Friedman 1999, 439).

The Village Healer

The next chapter focuses on Jesus' social role as village healer, and employs several of Freud's own writings. At the risk of oversimplifying the more complex argument for a psychological element in all physical diseases presented in the book itself, I view the authentic healings of Jesus as psychosomatic (or psychoneurological), triggered in all cases by an underlying anxiety due to familial (especially father-son) or village conflicts. Thus, I make extensive use of Freud's *Inhibitions, Symptoms and Anxiety*, as well as one of his early essays on organic hysterical processes. I have also drawn on the recent writings of Sander L. Gilman, Susan Baur, Karla Cantor, and others who discuss physical disabilities to which Jews are especially susceptible, especially noting those that may be attributed to a genetic trait of flatfootedness (which contributes to lower extremity disorders, particularly among individuals who seek to compensate by altering their gait), and their high levels of hypochrondria (or the somatization of anxiety). Paralysis may be attributed to the former, while various ailments (ranging from digestive disorders to leprosy or skin lesions) are examples of the latter. I also discuss the phenomenon of blindness, connecting it to "evil eye" belief in Mediterranean society and to the eyelid formation of Jews. Because blindness occurs among young males in the authentic healings, it has significant gender implications (as do the authentic paralytic healings, also involving young males, at least at age of onset). In contrast, I view Jairus' thirteen-year-old daughter as afflicted with hysteria, and comment on views then current that hysteria was due to childlessness (Jewish girls being considered marriageable at age twelve, the age most biblical scholars assign Mary at the time of her betrothal to Joseph).

As for why Jesus was able to heal individuals suffering from paralysis, blindness, or hysteria—after all, emotional disorders are often among the most difficult human maladies to cure—I explore his use of the "Abba" formula, noting its importance for his own "cure" relating to his fatherlessness, and its utility as well in what van Aarde calls his "fatherlike performance" (an example of which is his extension of his hand to Jairus' daughter as he gently lifted her from her prone position). Since "Abba" refers to the earliest form of a child's address to father, I discuss his appeal to the power of Abba's name in light of Freud's comment in his defense of the "talking cure" in *Introductory Lectures on Psycho-Analysis* that "words were originally magic" (Freud 1963, 17). This statement has bearing on the controversy in contemporary Jesus studies whether the word "magician" applies to him, and moves this discussion from its exclusively sociological locus to a more psychological one.

I also employ Freud's early article on the antithetical meaning of primary words, noting, for example, that "Abba" has a magical, uncanny quality because it is reversible and also alphabetically precedes Beelzebul, the "father of darkness," and undoubtedly the form in which Jesus and other Galilean villagers referred to the evil one. (Satan is a more universal appelation). Another related text of Freud's that figures significantly in my analysis of Jesus' healing role is his "A Seventeenth Century Demonological Neurosis," in which he discusses the splitting of the father image—thus the ambivalence involved—between God the Father and the Devil (also a father substitute). I relate this to Jesus' own experience of fatherlessness, which he addressed through his association in the desert with John the Baptist. John's baptism offered purification of his sexual pollution owing to his illegitimacy and made him a son of Abba (and symbolic son of Abraham), with Abba especially symbolizing the "namelessness" of his natural father and empowering him to perform his exorcisms and healings. I view Jesus as typical of young men who were attracted to John because he offered a creative alternative to the official temple religion (e.g., baptism in place of circumcision), especially for those who could not—for whatever reason—claim legitimacy on the grounds that they were natural heirs of Abraham, born into the official religion. In light of this analysis of the power of the name Abba, I also discuss father-son conflicts and the sons' tendency to somatize these in the form of demon possession, paralysis, and blindness.

If, in focusing on Jesus' role as village healer, I shortchange his other sociocultural roles and their interrelationships, this is consistent with a growing trend in contemporary Jesus studies to emphasize his healer role, a trend that is part of a movement in New Testament studies generally to stress the importance in ancient Mediterranean societies of the view that a man is known by his deeds, which leads to a parallel tendency to downplay somewhat the earlier emphasis on his parabolic utterances. This emphasis on his healer role is also what a psychoanalytic portrait of Jesus is most disposed to reflect, as psychoanalysis is, after all, a therapeutic endeavor.

While I anticipate objections to my argument that the authentic healing stories lend themselves to a psychosomatic (or psychoneurological) interpretation, and also to my admittedly anachronistic discussion of Galilean Jews' susceptibility to certain illnesses based on studies of nineteenth- and twentieth-century Jews, I would say in defense of the former that I emphasize Jesus' appeal to the name of Abba and thus to the role of faith—Jesus' own and his patient's—in the healing process; and of the latter that interpretations of his healings have generally failed to give adequate attention to the nature of the illnesses, to constitutional susceptibilities (i.e., biological and genetic factors), and to the age and gender of the sufferer. Because there are very few healings judged by Meier (my primary resource in this regard) as authentic, by focusing on these it is possible to take a more microscopic view of the healings and of the possible circumstances (i.e., family and village tensions and conflicts) that gave rise to them.

It is perfectly imaginable in a society that somatizes its anxieties that a paralysis would develop if a young man had an unconscious desire not to comply with his father's or employer's instructions to go work in the fields, or wished to avoid a village conflict involving members of his own family (and where their honor was at stake), or sought to thwart the impulse to stalk and seduce an unattached village girl. Nor is it difficult to imagine that blindness might result from a desire to avoid being the victim of another's "evil eye," or being accused of inflicting the "evil eye" on another, or when one's eyes have become the organ of sexual transgression (viewing mother, sisters, or other women with lust). Sayings attributed to Jesus, such as walking two miles when commanded to go one, have relevance to psychosomatically induced paralysis; while plucking out the eye that offends you has significance in light of psychosomatically induced blindness. Jesus' assurance that Abba will provide a protective circle around the one who believes in him not only activates a primitive childlike trust in what Freud in *The Ego and the Id* calls "the father of personal prehistory" but also becomes a powerful means of disabling anxiety itself.

The Multiple Symbolic Meanings of the Temple Disturbance

The final chapter on Jesus takes a step back and attempts to view him in a more wholistic fashion (from the eight- to fifteen-foot distance that normally prevails between portrait artist and subject). Here I introduce the idea that Jesus may be viewed as a "utopian-melancholic personality," and present my argument that Jesus should be considered neither as an apocalyptic prophet (Sanders) nor as a social reform prophet (Crossan and Borg), but as a peasant-style utopianist. To explain how I understand "utopian," however, I take exception to sociology of religion discussions (cited by Crossan) that view the utopianist as being similar in his transformative goals to the social reformist, but as being to the left of the social reformist in his expectations for creating a kind of heaven on earth. This view, heavily influenced by the history of religious communes, does not cohere very well with the fact that Jesus was a member of the peasant class.

By citing several utopianism theorists, including Krishan Kumar, Ruth Levitas, and Ernst Bloch, I argue that Jesus was not a *social* utopianist in that he fully recognized that a social reform program initiated by a member of the peasant class had little chance of success. On the other hand, his idea of the "kingdom of God" (generally viewed as an authentic piece of the Jesus tradition) suggested a more basic, indeed, childlike utopian outlook that takes notice when unexpected good things happen (to a peasant who only hopes matters will not get worse, such occurrences qualify as "miracles"). Thus, as Kumar points out, the peasant classes contribute the most basic of four elements that constitute utopian thinking, that of *desire* (the others being harmony, hope, and design), and Ruth Levitas argues that desire is the fundamental feature of utopianism, with hope having a distinctly secondary status. I suggest, therefore, that Jesus' "kingdom of God" idea is born of a desire that reflects a sense of lack. As Bloch puts it, utopia begins with the perception that "something is missing." Enter male melancholia.

To make the link between his utopianism and his melancholia, I draw on Robert Burton's *The Anatomy of Melancholy*, the first edition of which appeared in 1621, which makes a connection between melancholia and utopian desires. I use Freud's "Mourning and Melancholia" and "The 'Uncanny'" essays in my analysis of Jesus' (and his male colleagues') melancholia, using my earlier argument in *Men, Religion, and Melancholia* to make the case that the "lost object" to which Freud refers in the former essay (and whose internalization is responsible for the son's excessive self-hatred and utopian aspirations) is the mother, from whom he became estranged in early child-hood. This discussion, which is too detailed to summarize adequately here, enables me to focus on Jesus' relationship to Mary and to cut a path through the subsequent idealizations of this relationship formulated by the early church.

Central to this relationship is the temple disturbance, which virtually all contemporary scholars agree was the immediate cause of Jesus' arrest and execution (Paula Fredriksen, who prefews the entry into Jerusalem, is the rare dissenter.) I view it as the culmination of his career as exorcist-healer. As contemporary Jesus scholars (from Sanders to Crossan) also agree, this ac-tion was a "symbolic destruction" of the existing temple on grounds that it was inhospitable to God (Father Abba), whose abode it was traditionally in-tended to be. I also, however, draw on the now discredited "temple cleans-ing" view, shifting its original emphasis from cleansing the temple of illicit business practices (which Crossan disputes) to the idea, developed by David Halperin in his psychoanalytic study of Ezekiel, that the temple symbolizes the mother's body. Thus, if the "manifest" level of Jesus' symbolic action was to destroy the temple because it was not a fit place for Abba, largely because it excluded persons like himself, the latent meaning of the action was that it "cleansed" the mother's body, thus completing the purification begun with his baptism by purifying his mother of her own sexual pollution due to his illegitimate conception. I argue that only a psychoanalytic interpretation of the temple disturbance takes adequate account of both symbolic levels, the intentional reclaiming of the temple for Abba and his dispossessed sons, and the more deeply (unconscious?) emotional reparative act of purifying his mother, thereby also healing his own self-hatred.

While this is the major argument of the chapter, I discuss related issues regarding Jesus' views on food and table disputes reflective of male melan-cholia (as mother is closely identified with food and its availability); parables where fathers assume the mother's role; and his homelessness (where I differentiate male melancholia involving separation from mother and home, from female agoraphobia entailing confinement to the home in order to pro-tect the woman's honor). I also address psychoanalytic studies of boredom (e.g., Ferenczi) to understand the peasant form of melancholia, and more re-cent studies of impulsivity among young males, the following being espe-cially relevant to Jesus' temple disturbance.

In my view, it is unfortunate that Christianity has centered to such a de-gree on the crucifixion and the resurrection narratives that Jesus' final act—his triumphant reversal of his original fate in life, an exorcism that offers as-surance that such a symbolic reversal is available to others—has not received the attention it deserves. After all, this act was performed under his own agency and therefore had a personal significance that the crucifixion and resurrec-tion stories lack and also obscure. Furthermore, my psychoanalytic reading of the temple disturbance suggests that he was not as deluded as Sanders suggests (owing to the fact that his alleged anticipation of the apocalyptic incursion of God into human history did not occur) nor as ineffective as

Crossan and Borg (with their social reformist view of Jesus) portray him as being. Psychologically, it was an exorcism on a very large scale, as it ended the damage done to himself and his mother when she was seduced/raped by a man whose identity remains a mystery.

This chapter ends where Freud's psychoanalytic career began—that is, with dreams. I argue for a connection between the "appearances" of Jesus and his followers' dreams of him (which may also include visual and auditory hallucinations not uncommon during mourning), and suggest that such dreams may well have had a quasi-therapeutic role in resolving the trauma of his sudden death by crucifixion. Using a distinction between the false and true mother in the Gospel of Thomas, I suggest that if the temple was the body of the false mother, the Dream is the body of the true mother, and thus the locus of the utopian desire which is neither "here" (in the empirical world) or "there" (in a world to come), but in the "no-place" where one dies to the world in the evening in order to rise again in the morning.

A brief epilogue addresses the troublesome question of Jesus' essential identity. I introduce the psychoanalytic idea of "the fictive personality" to shed further light on this issue. This refers to individuals who live in a "fictive world," such as Jay Martin's patient whose life was guided by the novels she read, or Erikson's patient who adopted a Scottish identity because she "needed a past." The most famous example of this in Western literature is Don Quixote. Martin suggests that this "fictive personality" may, for some individuals, be empowering, not debilitating. The issue, however, is not so much whether Jesus was a "fictive personality," but its heuristic value, as it enables us to view Jesus' identity from the perspective of his fatherlike performance (which van Aarde contends on the basis of numerous research studies is common of fatherless sons); and to suggest that the most fatherlike performance of all is to proclaim all the children sons and daughters of the heavenly Father. His refusal to view himself as unique in this regard may thus be the very nucleus of his identity, as well as the point where psychoanalysis concludes and, for those so disposed, theologizing might conceivably begin.

The question any psychoanalytic study of Jesus is likely to raise is whether it merely adds one more portrait to an already cluttered wall, or it might also have such a commanding presence that it casts a shadow on all other portraits. As a realist, I assume that at best, it may be given a small place on the wall, one very much on the periphery, and possibly—as has been the case with Erikson's *Young Man Luther*—so that the establishment "artists" may use it to make invidious comparisons to their own, more celebrated works. Occasionally, however, I allow myself the utopian thought that such a portrait might actually find its way toward the center of the wall, not because of the artist but because the subject of the portrait and the founder of psychoanalysis seem made for one another by virtue of their common ethnicity and religious marginality. Now, just past the end of the second millennium of the Christian Era and the centennial of Freud's *The Interpretation of Dreams*, it would be nothing short of mind-blowing if contemporary Jesus studies "discovered" Freud and adopted him as one of their own.

Is There a Course in This Text?

Having provided an overview of the book in order to make a case for the intrinsic value of psychoanalytic interpretation of Jesus, I now want to discuss the issue of the course itself. If it were offered in a theological seminary or in a master's or doctoral program in religious studies, most of the texts that I have referred to here would be appropriate for adoption, though, of course, one would need to be very selective. My normal procedure is to assign some seven or eight books (usually ones that are brief enough that they are readable in one or two weeks; if not, I assign selected chapters). Then I fill out the course readings with individual book chapters and journal articles that I arrange to have duplicated and distributed to each student. As my reflections on the course itself are at a rather preliminary and exploratory stage, the following lists only the texts that I would expect students to acquire themselves (and the seminary bookstore to stock). This list is of course subject to availability, which in my experience changes from year to year, as even recently published books are suddenly out of print.

Required Texts

Marcus J. Borg, *Jesus: A New Vision*. San Francisco: HarperSanFrancisco, 1987; *or* Marcus J. Borg, *Meeting Jesus Again for the First Time*. San Francisco: HarperSanFrancisco, 1994.

Donald Capps, *Jesus: A Psychological Biography*. St. Louis: Chalice Press, 2000.

John Dominic Crossan, *Jesus: A Revolutionary Biography*. San Francisco: HarperSanFrancisco, 1994.

Richard Q. Ford, *The Parables of Jesus: Recovering the Art of Listening*. Minneapolis: Fortress Press, 1997. Ford is a psychotherapist.

Sigmund Freud, *Inhibitions, Symptoms and Anxiety*. New York: Norton, 1989.

Sigmund Freud, *Leonardo da Vinci and a Memory of His Childhood*. New York: Norton, 1990.

John W. Miller, *Jesus at Thirty*. Minneapolis: Fortress Press, 1997.

E. P. Sanders, *The Historical Figure of Jesus*. New York: Penguin Books, 1995.

Geza Vermes, *The Religion of Jesus the Jew*. Minneapolis: Fortress Press, 1993.

If I were teaching an undergraduate course, the required texts would be reduced (e.g., one of the Freud texts would probably be dropped, as would one or more of the texts on the historical Jesus). Further reductions might be necessary (it has been many years since I taught undergraduate courses in state university settings, so I am relying here on faulty memory), with Borg's *Jesus: A New Vision*, Crossan's *Jesus: A Revolutionary Biography*, and Vermes's *The Religion of Jesus the Jew* being the core texts, whatever other texts remained. While I have obvious problems with the Miller text, it would probably need to be retained, as it illustrates the genre of study the course introduces. A difficult question for me would be the appropriateness of my own book for an undergraduate course (though I think it would be suitable for an upper-level course).

The same question also needs to be raised concerning readings in Freud. As the preceding discussion indicates, I do not rely primarily on books by Freud that are more commonly associated with the psychoanalysis of religion, such as *Totem and Taboo*, *The Future of an Illusion*, *Civilization and Its Discontents*, and *Moses and Monotheism*. Rather, I give considerably more attention to texts that are closer to the center of his psychoanalytic project. For what it may be worth, I view as somewhat unfortunate that students are often introduced to Freud in religious studies courses via *The Future of an Illusion* only (due, in part, to its relative brevity and uncomplicated rhetorical style) as my own experience with this text in the classroom setting is that it typecasts Freud for students as an intolerant opponent of religion and merely inspires them to offer "refutations" of his views based on faith statements or philosophical arguments. I think this gets students' introduction to Freud off on the wrong footing, as they have little idea of the theoretical framework that stands behind the text.

I address this problem through my *Freud, Freudians, and Religion*: *A Reader*, which has excerpts from the writings on religion by Freud, David Bakan, Erik H. Erikson, D. W. Winnicott, Heinz Kohut, and Julia Kristeva. For a course on the psychoanalysis of Jesus, the more obvious choice for a text by Freud would be his monograph on Leonardo da Vinci, which in spite of its problems, has the distinct advantage of being the first psychoanalytic psychobiography (hence, historical value); also, the analysis of the adult da Vinci centers on his painting *Madonna and Child with St. Anne*, thus involving religious themes related to the subject of the course. Given the argument of my own text on Jesus, a second text by Freud would be *Inhibitions, Symptoms and Anxiety*, which should be accessible to upper-level undergraduate students as well as to graduate students. Both are fairly brief, though slightly larger than *The Future of an Illusion*, and available in inexpensive paperback versions.

As for the structure of the course on Jesus, I would probably use much the same organization as my book, first introducing examples of contemporary Jesus studies, then addressing the criticisms against psychobiography and psychohistory, then providing an overview of the social world of Jesus' day, and finally focusing on the psychoanalytic study of Jesus. I need not discuss written assignments here, but I would think that the final product would involve their own efforts to view Jesus psychoanalytically (setting aside other predispositions, if only as an "experiment" they could late disavow), preferably focusing on a rather narrowly defined issue or problem.

Finally, I chose not to clutter this article with publication facts relating to the many texts referred to here, as these are readily accessible from the references listed at the end of my book. Texts directly quoted are indicated below.

Postscript

In the interim between this chapter's writing and its publication, I taught the course and designed it much as described above. It was titled The Psychoanalysis of Jesus and attracted an enrollment of forty students, which was quite impressive given that it was scheduled for 8 A.M. on Monday morning, normally considered the worst possible time to schedule a course at the seminary. I wish I could say that it was an unmitigated success. When a colleague asked me, "How did it go?" I equivocated, "It's too early to tell." As with all courses I have taught for the first time, I learned some things that would influence how I would teach the course the second time around. The following lessons stand out in my mind.

1. I knew that some seminary students harbor great suspicions of historical Jesus studies, but I underestimated the depth and intensity of these suspicions and the fact that students with such suspicions would nevertheless take a course that took the validity of the enterprise of historical Jesus studies for granted. I later learned that such suspicions had been actively encouraged by a biblical professor who openly derided the "Jesus seminar" in the New Testament course required of all entering students.

2. While I was fully aware that psychoanalysis would be problematic for some students (and therefore used the word in the title so that no one would be deceived as to what the course was about), I was less prepared for some students' more general distrust of any scientific paradigm whatsoever. These were not the traditional "fundamentalists" that seminary professors can readily dismiss as benighted and naive, but sophisticated students who, for very diverse reasons, believe that claims made in behalf of science are exaggerated and overblown. These would be the students who might find themselves in the uncomfortable position of appearing to side with the creationists in a course on creationism and evolutionism because they perceive that scientific paradigms bave their own ideological commitments and purposes. Their concerns, which were entirely legitimate, were viewed by some students (and, in less patient moments, myself) as distracting and better reserved for courses taught by our professor of theology and science.

3. While Princeton Theological Seminary is widely known to be a school in which the neo-orthodoxy of Karl Barth reigns supreme, I was insufficiently prepared for students who viewed the Gospels through the lens provided by a neo-orthodox theology and who therefore considered the historical (let alone the *psycho*-historical) questions that were central to the course as subsidiary if not irrelevant to faith claims.

After I became aware that the course had attracted a fair number of dissenters (one of whom reportedly told another student that she had enrolled in the course so that she could develop arguments against everything that it purported to represent or claim about Jesus), I made various appeals and disclaimers in an attempt to set everyone's mind at ease, but a continuing issue throughout the course was some students' negative reaction to the historical Jesus texts assigned (not only Borg and Crossan, which was fairly predictable, but Sanders as well). In that the psychoanalytic material in the course involved my own appropriation of and disagreements with these scholars, I felt I was spending too much time in defending *their* views and methodologies.

A rather unorthodox (at least, for me) "intervention" occurred about halfway through the course, when I devoted half of a class session to an unscheduled personal apologia, as it were, in defense of my commitment to a naturalistic (as opposed to supernaturalistic) epistemology. While I did not expect that this apologia would persuade the students who were unwilling or unable to engage in the enterprise of the course, I hoped at least to disabuse them of the presumption that the profesor, a pastoral theologian, was philosophically naive. For reasons that are unclear to me even now, this intervention seemed to have had its intended effect, and the overwhelming majority of the students subsequently wrote papers that clearly reflected the intentions and spirit of the course.

For many of the students, this intervention was unnecessary, as they were supportive of the course and its intentions from the very beginning. Several of these students indicated to me that the course gave them permission to express their questions and doubts about the historicity of various events portrayed in the canonical Gospels (something they felt that the required New Testament course had not enabled them to do), and, more important, to begin to formulate in their own minds a view or portrait of Jesus that was psychologically credible to them. Thus, as I view the course in retrospect, I think of it as having been, for the majority of the students, an exercise in *reframing*, as it placed the study of Jesus in an unfamiliar and somewhat alien setting or context, and thereby posed a new set of questions and issues that do not typically arise in the courses taught by the biblical faculty. Whether these are the most important questions and issues is, of course, a matter of personal and professional opinion.

As for myself, I frequently took both solace and resolve to "stay the course" from my own mentor's litany (itself derived from psychoanalysis) that resistance is "a sign of vitality" (Dittes 1967, 136–85).

A few weeks after the course ended, James H. Charlesworth, a professor in New Testament at Princeton Theological Seminary and well-known expert in historical Jesus research, published an article titled "The Historical Jesus and Exegetical Theology" in the *Princeton Seminary Bulletin* in which he noted approvingly that the "psychological assessment of Jesus has assumed some prominence after being relatively dormant for over fifty years" and declared that "it is essential to complete what is known from other methodological approaches by adding what one trained in psychology may see. Jesus Research has been converging with psychobiography and psychohistory" (Charlesworth 2001, 55).

This welcome endorsement from a colleague in biblical studies has me thinking—at present—that I should rearouse my own Rocinante and set forth on a second quixotic venture in behalf of my jaded version of Lady Dulcinea. Paraphrasing Freud's observation that "the true masochist always turns his cheek whenever he has a chance of receiving a blow," Andre Green views Don Quixote as "the true moral narcissist," who "always volunteers himself whenever he sees a chance of renouncing a satisfaction" (Green 1980–81, 247). Having the means, motivation, and temperament, the only thing I lack is a faithful companion who doesn't have anything better to do than to accompany an anachronism who holds the odd, apparently discredited belief that you can in fact psychoanalyze a dead man. As we professors are often wont to say, with a note of wary hopefulness in our voices, "Don't all volunteer at once!"

References

Bakan, David. 1967. A reconsideration of the problem of introspection. In *On method: Toward a reconstruction of psychological investigation*, San Francisco: Jossey-Bass.

Capps, Donald. 2001. *Freud and Freudians on religion: A reader*. New Haven, Conn.: Yale University Press.

Charlesworth, James H. 2001. The historical Jesus and exegetical theology. *Princeton Seminary Bulletin* 22: 45–63.

Crossan, John Dominic. 1991. *The historical Jesus*. San Francisco: Harper San Francisco.

Dittes, James E. 1967. *The church in the way*. New York: Charles Scribner's Sons.

Freud, Sigmund. 1963. *Introductory lectures on psycho-analysis*. In *The standard edition of the complete psychological works of Sigmund Freud*, Vol. 15, translated and edited by James Strachey. London: Hogarth Press.

Friedman, Lawrence J. 1999. *Identity's architect: A biography of Erik H. Erikson*. New York: Scribners.

Green, Andre. 1980–81. Moral narcissism. *International Journal of Psychoanalytic Psychology* 8: 243–69.

Powell, Mark Allan. 1998. *Jesus as a figure in history*. Louisville: Westminster John Knox Press.

Rieff, Philip. 1966. *The triumph of the therapeutic*. New York: Harper & Row.

Vermes, Geza. 1993. *The religion of Jesus the Jew*. Minneapolis: Fortress Press.

7

Teaching Freud and Interpreting Augustine's *Confessions*

Sandra Lee Dixon

This chapter will highlight two words of the overall topic, *teaching Freud* and interpreting Augustine's *Confessions*. I emphasize *teaching Freud* because the literature on the psychological study of Augustine, largely psychoanalytical as it is, rarely cites Freud at all.[1] Yet Freudian ideas abound, especially in the articles from the 1960s that launched research on this topic. If we claim to teach Freud, we should, I believe, let students sharpen their minds on the words, at least in translation, of Freud himself. Moreover, self-discipline in the psychological study of Augustine is crucial, as historians and theologians will remind us.[2] If we do not start by disciplining ourselves in our use of theory, I have little hope that we will do so in the interpretation of Augustine's writing.

I proceed both in this essay and in class by thinking of the conclusions of psychoanalytic theory and practice as tools of investigation for understanding a perplexing phenomenon. To employ them deftly, one must, of course, know how they are put together. So we spend time taking them apart and examining the pieces. Then we can reconstruct the tools and test more fully our understanding by using them to produce something different. For those of us who like this sort of project, Freudian theory offers a marvelous means of investigation and Augustine's *Confessions* a wonder of material to reconceive in Freudian terms.

The rest of this chapter will explain more specifically how I try to apply these conceptualizations in class. I will describe the setting and my assumptions about the students and how they learn. Then I will discuss how we examine Freud's conclusions as a prelude to the psychological interpretation of Augustine's *Confessions*. I will remark on the teaching of the *Confessions* itself and give an example of how a class might proceed with the psychoanalytic interpretation of the text. Engaging the students in trying to analyze Freud's own writing and apply it to Augustine's *Confessions* will raise major scholarly questions in the study of Freud and in the contemporary psychological study of the *Confessions*.

The Class and the Teacher

A seminar format best serves my purpose. By "seminar format" I mean that the students are to have read the assignment seriously (increasing their ability to do so during the academic term), that discussion of the text (books open and quoted) predominates; and that the teacher asks questions, coaches the students, and guides them through and back to the text. The demand on the teacher is high in this form of teaching, of course, because one has to be ready to propose contrasting or complementary passages without knowing in advance the issues that will arise.[3] But the texts I suggest from Freud are short, reading notes last from year to year, and so do the diagrams.

I favor drawing diagrams to explicate Freud's theory. My own diagrams deepen my familiarity with the text and give me a framework for fielding suggestions from the floor.[4] I also often give the chalk to the students and ask them to start drawing on the board, usually with suggestions from their classmates. This makes them nervous at first, but after I voice my appreciation of their efforts—even those we improve together as a class—they show more freedom and agency.

If the class is larger than a seminar, similar exercises can work by dividing the class up into small groups, each with a passage to diagram. The teacher decides which order the groups should follow in putting their diagrams on the board. The class discusses the diagrams and suggests modifications, possible connections between them, their relationship to the text, and so forth.[5]

Even teachers who do not feel comfortable with the style outlined above may want to know what texts can work, why, and to what ends. The texts I recommend below can certainly be adapted to other modes of presentation.

Choosing the Early Freud

I use the early Freud in my class on psychobiography. I usually choose *On Dreams*, his condensation of his masterpiece *The Interpretation of Dreams*, and I supplement it with *Five Lectures on Psycho-Analysis*. A practical advantage of these books is that they are short. Using the *Interpretation of Dreams* instead of *On Dreams* would be academically more rigorous, but would require much more of the course's duration just to advance a basic understanding of Freud's ideas.

The theoretical justification for these choices starts with the commonly voiced concern that Freud's ideas are culturally conditioned and cannot apply to other cultures. Concern about culture is one of the major questions in the psychological study of Augustine.[6] While Freud's ideas are culturally conditioned, the concepts in his early works, covering what is known as the "first topography," have been thought to apply more readily across cultures than the ideas of the more familiar "second topography," or id-ego-superego model of the mind.[7] In addition, many of the ideas of the first topography appear in the later schools and offshoots of psychoanalysis. Yet many students have never seen them explicated and these readings urge students to explore this part of Freud's work more fully.

The first topography is so called because Freud himself compared the mind to the layers of the ground. The underground is an image for the unconscious (ucs.)—not readily apparent, full of hidden activity, capable of making variations in the surface. The surface is an image for the conscious (cs.) aspects of mental life—in full view, easily accessed, a source of pressure and material for the area underground (the unconscious processes of the mind). The first layers of the soil are analogous to the "pre-conscious" (pcs.) processes—not readily apparent but not difficult to expose, connecting the visible to the deeply buried, affected by both upper and lower layers. The pre-conscious in Freud's view includes the processes and patterns that could become conscious but often do not, such as the words of a song one knows. The unconscious, on the other hand, is inaccessible without a great deal of work and energy, and it makes its processes felt obliquely or in strange outcroppings on the surface.[8]

The processes that formed this topography, according to Freud, resemble the ones geographers and geologists know: the processes of physics.[9] That is to say, the topographical model includes the idea that pressures could build in the system of the mind, contents could shift, new formations could obtrude into consciousness. These processes will receive further attention below in the discussion of teaching *On Dreams*.

Freud derived the second topography, the id-ego-superego model of the mind, from the first. The second topography depends on further abstraction from the data that Freud interpreted to formulate the first topography. The first topography used concepts that were themselves abstracted from his psychoanalytic practice. With these concepts he described and coordinated an understanding of the processes he believed to underlie the conscious words spoken by patients in analytic sessions. The second topography adds abstractions in order to conceptualize the results of the first topography's processes. These abstractions in turn allow more influence of Freud's own culture on the development of his ideas.[10] Culture would flow through the patients' conscious and pre-conscious to affect the unconscious and the patterns of the id, ego, and superego. As Freud and his followers gave content to these abstract constructs from their work in European culture, they sketched out theoretical constructs, and used the constructs to interpret new data. As they did so, more and more interaction could occur between the theory and the psychoanalysts' own culture.

Even scholars rejecting the universality of Freudian formulations of the id, ego, and superego can still agree that childhood urges can undergo repression in response to cultural pressures. They can agree that the urges remain active, respond to other pressures, and emerge in different forms. They can discuss the interaction of culture and psyche in these terms without having to import the conclusions of the second topography. Proponents of the first topography can emphasize it and downplay the second.

Working in Class with the Early Freud

The pedagogical value of *On Dreams* and *Five Lectures on Psycho-Analysis* is that they allow the students to see Freud's range of concerns and why he thinks we should believe his conclusions. Attending to the context Freud sets for his argument, and to which he returns, enhances its plausibility greatly. In reading *On Dreams* one must linger for a few moments on the indicators of context in order not to forget them. Recognizing them lets students draw together different strands of Freud's theory, especially his emphases on science and meaning.

Regarding context, notice that Freud starts the book: "During the epoch which may be described as pre-scientific, men had no difficulty in finding an explanation of dreams."[11] Here he introduces several important themes of the book: science and what counts as scientific, explanation, and dreams. Then follows a list of the aspects of dreams that might be explained, now that the scientific era has arrived. Before the end of the second paragraph, Freud has the reader crossing from explanation to interpretation of meaning. Such interpretation will occupy our study of Augustine: "What stands in the foreground of our interest is the question of the *significance* of dreams."[12]

Interpreting dreams is not the concern of this paper,[13] but interpreting the text to discover possible indicators of unconscious processes is.[14] We will follow Freud as he "seeks to discover whether dreams can be interpreted, whether the content of individual dreams has a 'meaning,' such as we are accustomed to find in other psychical structures."[15] Here one might ask, "what other psychical structures?" This can serve as a question for the class, because sharp students will have noticed an answer two pages later, at the beginning of chapter two: "I had been led to fresh conclusions on the subject of dreams by applying to them a new method of psychological investigation which had done excellent service in the solution of phobias, obsessions and delusions, etc."[16] "Phobias, obsessions, delusions, etc.," are the other psychical structures, and they, like dreams, appear meaningful to Freud. Here the teacher can underscore an important question in the study of Freud: what are the different conscious phenomena that Freud identifies as coming from similar unconscious processes?

Freud now begins a process of thinking by analogies.[17] He examines dreams as analogous to psychological pathologies. In addition, he implicitly puts the analogy back in the context of what counts as scientific by including words evocative of medical research: "The numerous analogies that exist between dream life and a great variety of conditions of psychical *illness* in waking life have indeed been correctly *observed* by many *medical investigators*."[18]

Freud soon gives a sample of one of his own dreams so he can demonstrate dream interpretation as related to both the function and the meaning of dreams. A diagram, as aesthetically rich or impoverished as you like, can set out the dream's main components in the center of the chalkboard. It should include especially the objects: a dining table (a rectangle), spinach (circle with wavy lines in it), Frau E.L. (whose identity Freud is purposely obscuring), Freud next to Frau E.L. (circles labeled Frau E.L. and SF will do nicely), a pair of eyes or eyeglasses. Then the class can pick out Freud's free associations to the dream.[19] These can be added to the diagram in rays spreading out from the key dream elements in the center. The advantage of this process is that it leads the students to take the work of analysis seriously. The analytic process is more crucial for this part of the exercise than are the conclusions of Freud's dream analysis.

Further theoretical ideas can be mapped onto the diagram as one follows Freud through the text. When the class studies chapter four, where Freud discusses condensation, the diagram will already give a visual image of his points: "the dream work has carried out a work of compression or *condensation* on a large scale. . . . From every element in the dream's content associative threads branch out in two or more directions."[20] The few elements of the dream and the large number of rays of associated material make the dream's condensation evident.

The students may now raise a key question about Freud's ideas: why do the dream elements seem insignificant compared to the amount of material associated with them? Freud's discussion in chapter five of "displacement" answers this question. He says, "What stands out boldly and clearly in the dream as its essential content must, after analysis, be satisfied with playing an extremely subordinate rôle among the dream thoughts."[21] Students grasp his point because they can see on the board that what was important about the dream elements no longer looks important in the whole. Importance, which Freud thinks of as energy (in analogy to physics),[22] has been displaced from its original home in the dream thoughts onto the distorted elements that appear in the dream.

But students may persist in asking the important question of why such rigmarole should take place at all. The answer shows up in chapter eight of *On Dreams*. Freud says that the elaborate process of dream formation happens because of the feature shown by analysis of his dream that pertains to all dreams: "I should eventually arrive at thoughts which would surprise me, whose presence in me I was unaware of, which were not only *alien* but also *disagreeable* to me, and which I should, therefore, feel inclined to dispute energetically."[23] The students, thanks in part to the diagram, are prepared to see the "alien" and "disagreeable" nature of the dream thoughts: Freud's own discomfort about whether he was "selfish" or "unselfish," indebted or forced to pay to highly for whatever he got.[24] In terms of the first topography, the unpleasantness of the dream thoughts lends pressure to push them from the pre-conscious to the unconscious. The pressure, repression, then causes them to take different forms. A result is "overdetermination," the representation of one unconscious thought by many conscious outcroppings, and the relationships of each outcropping to many unconscious thoughts.

Once the processes and the most basic material shaped by them are understood, some students will be ready to consent to Freud's conclusion: "The dream thoughts . . . are not clothed in the prosaic language usually employed by our thoughts, but are on the contrary represented symbolically by means of similes and metaphors, in images resembling those of poetic speech."[25] This sentence links dream interpretation to the interpretation of Augustine's *Confessions*, for it is creative, poetic speech (not the "free association" suggested by Kligerman).[26]

Two key, related thoughts must be borne in mind in the Freudian interpretation of symbolic speech. First is the idea that dreams, with the representations that compose them, are wish fulfilments. That is, they represent the fulfilling of some desire that has not been fulfilled in ordinary waking life. Second, the representation stands not only for the fulfilled wish but also for the desire still awaiting satisfaction. Any fulfilled wish hints at the original longing.[27] Thus, in Freud's own dream, he wished to be seen as "unselfish" and as having paid for whatever he got, but the lingering sense that he was not seen as he wanted is also portrayed in the dream.

Freud treats the famous psychoanalytic ideas of repressed sexuality and infantile sexuality only quite late in the discussions in both *On Dreams* and *Five Lectures on Psycho-Analysis*. In *On Dreams* he notes that the theory of repression does not require that sexual desires be most liable to repression, but allows that they could be. Primarily, he appeals to fact: "No other group of instincts has been submitted to such far-reaching suppression by the demands of cultural education." He adds quite simply that "we have become acquainted with infantile sexuality, which is often so unobtrusive in its manifestations and is always overlooked and misunderstood."[28]

No discussion of the Oedipal conflict follows. Teaching Augustine's *Confessions* will gravitate toward it. For a straightforward presentation we turn to the *Five Lectures on Psycho-Analysis*, a collection of lectures that Freud delivered at Clark University in 1910. In brief, "the child takes both of its parents, and more particularly one of them, as an object of its erotic wishes. In doing so, it usually follows some indication from its parents, whose affection bears the clearest characteristics of a sexual activity, even though of one that is inhibited in its aims." This last sentence indicates Freud's broad understanding of "sexuality," and his emphasis that not all sexuality leads to sexual intercourse.[29] Instead, as the text says, it can be "inhibited in its aims" and manifested as parental affection. Freud's explanation of the Oedipal conflict continues:

> As a rule, a father prefers his daughter, and a mother her son; the child reacts to this by wishing, if he is a son, to take his father's place, and, if she is a daugh-

ter, her mother's. The feelings which are aroused in these relations between parents and children . . . are not only of a positive or affectionate kind but also of a negative or hostile one. The complex which is thus formed is doomed to early repression; but it continues to exercise a great and lasting influence from the unconscious. It is to be suspected that, together with its extensions, it constitutes the *nuclear complex* of every neurosis, and we may expect to find it no less actively at work in other regions of mental life.[30]

These "other regions" include dreams and creative activities, like imagistic writing.

When students are naysayers, as some should be if they are grappling with the material, they are raising the big questions of doubt about Freud's ideas. Returning to the context of Freud's theory can help. Freud as a medical practitioner cared greatly about whether his ideas worked. Evidence for their working comes from *Five Lectures on Psycho-Analysis*. The first lecture includes the description of the very startling medical case that led Freud and his senior collaborator Breuer toward the ideas of psychoanalysis. The famous "Anna O.," described in the lecture, had a strange set of symptoms that were relieved by her talking about them. Like good scientific investigators, Breuer and Freud took seriously the evidence—her feeling better—and tried to understand what might allow such change and how they could more surely produce it.[31] By reading excerpts of Freud's summary of the "talking cure," the teacher can help the students understand why Freud thought the scientific analogy to geology ever made sense and why pursuing it by analogy into a field like dream interpretation might be useful: he was trying to extend a technique that could relieve serious physical and psychological disorders.

Freudian Dreamwork and Augustine's Stories

To use these methods on the study of Augustine and his *Confessions* one must remember that the application of those ideas to the material in the *Confessions* is itself an analogy.[32] This effort may make vivid for the students perennial questions in the appropriation of Freud for religious studies: how analogous is everyday thought to psychological disturbance? How analogous is creative writing to the symptoms of psychological distress or to dreamwork? If we agree with Freud, we will say that the analogies extend very far indeed. Or we may think they do not extend very far at all. Or we may believe that the results vary depending on the material. Raising these issues, interpretation of the *Confessions* proves useful for reflecting on how widely and well Freud's ideas apply.

Application of Freud's ideas to Augustine's *Confessions* can follow a procedure in class similar to the elucidation of Freud's ideas themselves. Based on careful reading of the book, students can begin to diagram relationships between events in Augustine's life or ideas in his text. Then they can create a diagram of Freudian inferences. One student, or even several, will usually raise some psychological problem in understanding Augustine or his text.

Their standard queries include, why does he look at God as he does? What's his relationship to his mother? Why was he so hung up on sex? Good starting points all. A few suggestions on the practicalities of handling the text, then an example, will show how the work can proceed.

The text of the *Confessions* reveals immediately that the book is not primarily designed as a chronological narrative, although it does loosely follow the course of Augustine's life from his birth to his age at writing, roughly his mid-forties. Therefore, consulting the timelines or introductions often included at the front of classroom editions of the *Confessions* can help both students and instructor.[33] One's own notes about locations of specific life events in the text will be crucial. In addition, several short, good introductions to Augustine's life can orient the reader to Augustine's time period and culture.[34]

Other important notes regard translations. Unless the professor can read Latin, the best approach is to have more than one translation at hand. All the recent editions available for classroom use, and many of the older ones, will do. A brief comparison of specific passages will be sufficient to show that leaning heavily on the English words would be ill-advised (e.g., IX.i.1). The class can tune its critical skills by asking what to make of the differences in translations, a question closely related to a major issue in psychoanalysis: what is the importance of specific words compared to major themes, visual images, typical symbols, and behaviors? Students will usually conclude that they should work with what is common to the translations, such as the broad outlines of particular events, invocations of God or the mother church, and laments about Augustine's own sinfulness. The translations can be easily coordinated because the "books" (what we would call chapters) of the *Confessions* are divided and the parts are numbered.[35]

An example of psychological interpretation one could try in class starts with Augustine's illness and near-baptism (*Confessions* I.xi.17), proceeds to the incident of the baths (II.iii.5–8), and relies on the biographical sketch of Monica (IX.ix.19–22) for support. The example combines several advantages: it starts with Augustine's childhood as psychoanalysis would encourage; it raises in good psychoanalytic fashion his relationship with his mother and father; it forces the interpreter to deal seriously with various parts of the book, but does not require knowledge of every aspect of it.

Starting with I.xi.17, I would ask the class what features of the story of the boy Augustine's illness and near-baptism they notice. The answers will recap the story: his mother Monica was a Christian; when Augustine got very ill he asked to be baptized, even though he was just a child; his mother arranged for a baptism, but it did not take place once he quickly recovered; Monica and the rest of the family were Christian, except Patricius, Augustine's father; Patricius did not interfere with Monica's raising Augustine as a Christian; Augustine thinks Monica was better than Patricius, but Monica obeyed Patricius anyway because, according to Augustine, she thought God commanded her to do so; Augustine complains that his family did the wrong thing by not having him baptized in spite of his recovery.

The theme of division between Augustine's parents, one of the issues in published psychological studies, is fairly strong in this passage.[36] Three columns can be set up on the board, one labeled "Monica," one further right labeled "Both," one beyond that labeled "Patricius," with room left for a diagram of the Freudian interpretation. Under "Monica," the class will want words like "Christian (I.xi.17)"; "better than husband (I.xi.17)"; "obeyed husband (I.xi.17)." Under "Patricius," they will place "not Christian (I.xi.17)"; "worse than wife (I.xi.17)"; "accepted wife's obedience (I.xi.17)."

The list will lengthen when one turns to II.iii.5–8. In this incident Augustine's father comes home from the public baths, where he has seen signs of passage through puberty in Augustine's physique, and tells Monica that they may soon have grandchildren. Monica feels much less joy and warns Augustine in private about the dangers of adultery. Augustine scoffs, at least inside himself, at her admonitions. The students might want to put under the column "Monica," ideas like "worry about Augustine's sexuality (II.iii.6)"; "not telling her husband about what she said to Augustine (II.iii.7)"; "thought education might turn Augustine toward God (II.iii.9)." Opposite phrases would belong under "Patricius": "happy about Augustine's sexuality (II.iii.6)"; "telling Monica how he felt about Augustine's sexual maturing (II.iii.6)"; "ambitious *only* for Augustine's worldly success (II.iii.9)"; "catechumen in Catholic Church (II.iii.6)."

The area between the columns can house a list of Monica's and Patricius' points of agreement: "importance of Augustine's education (II.iii.8)"; "hope for Augustine's worldly success (II.iii.8)" (although Augustine insists that their reasons were different, the hope itself was similar). More such points will come out in the examination of the biography of Monica in IX.ix.19–22: no quarrels in marriage (IX.ix.19); both baptized Christians by end of life (IX.ix.22); she was virtuous and gentle (IX.ix.19 and 20) and he was kind (IX.ix.19).

Yet IX.ix.19–22 is also a good place to find further divisions between Monica and Patricius. For instance, she was patient and reasonable in her discussions (IX.ix.19). He was hot-tempered and, when irritated, not susceptible to reason (IX.ix.19).

After setting up such a chart, one can reintroduce the psychoanalytic questions. First, is there anything on the chart that Augustine might find unpleasant enough to have repressed? On a new diagram, the responses can be set out horizontally below a broad, dark horizontal line. This line represents the repression barrier,[37] the power of mental regulation holding back from consciousness the unpleasantness retained in the unconscious. The students might suggest placing below the repression barrier Patricius' variability between anger and kindness, as well as the distress that Augustine might have felt as a child about the division between his parents.

The class can then reflect on that visual presentation of repression and guide their psychoanalytic exploration with following questions. (1) What is the wish associated with each repressed thought or feeling? (2) According to Freud's description of condensation and displacement, what is a plausible series of transformations of the original wish? (3) What is the resulting disguised expression? (4) How does this later expression include both the unfulfilled wish and its desired fulfillment?

If my experience serves as a guide, the students can answer question 1— What is the wish?—if they take a few minutes to discuss it. Question 2 on the unconscious processes of transformation will probably elude them until they try to take an educated guess about what the resulting disguised expression might be—that is, until they answer question 3. Once they make some guesses about the later disguised expressions, they can try to trace a plausible path of condensation and displacement. This analysis resembles what they saw in Freud's analysis of his own dream.

For instance, if the students concentrate on Patricius' variability between anger and kindness, they might identify the unfulfilled wish as a longing for a more reliably kind father. Some student will probably already know that Freud saw God as an exalted father figure.[38] So they can try out some images of God in Augustine's *Confessions* and see if the figurative language shows both the unfulfilled wish for a reliably kind father and its fulfillment. A good passage to suggest that they examine in order to see the disguised portrayal of Augustine's repressed discomfort comes in II.ii.4. In this somewhat startling passage, Augustine claims that God punished him mercifully to bring him back to the only true pleasure, God's own self. He even claims that God kills human beings so that they will die closer to God. In these thoughts we have hints of a father figure's shifts of mood—punishment can be joined to the idea of anger, bitterness affects pleasure, a desire for closeness emerges between the one who threatens and the one who receives the threat. These thoughts represent the repressed elements of thought and feeling about a father both irascible and kind. Below the repression barrier on the board, one could add an arrow from Patricius' variability between anger and kindness so that it points to a newly added word "threat." The arrow could pass thence to the added word "fear," then on to "punishment" (also added). Here the class would be explicating the condensation at work in the images in II.ii.4.

But the powerful figure portrayed in II.ii.4 is not unpredictably variable, as Patricius was. Instead, Augustine assures us that God was always present, always well intentioned, reliable in disciplining people, ever seeking a beneficial outcome. Similar language appears elsewhere in the *Confessions*[39] and provides support for aspects of this interpretation of his conscious representation of God. The arrow in the diagram could turn upward from "punishment" to break through the line of the repression barrier and point to words, written in the diagram's area for consciousness, like "present," "well-intentioned," "reliable." Perhaps a summation of Augustine's idea in II.ii.4, "God's well intentioned punishment" could surmount them all. This part of the diagram would clarify that the elements spelled out from the condensed image have been displaced, as Augustine's feelings related to Patricius have attached themselves to images of God.

Concern with a father's anger, punitiveness, and long-term positive disposition toward his son is, of course, one of the major components of the classic formulation of the Oedipal conflict.[40] Could the students suggest a plausible transformation of such experience, according to Freud's rules of dream interpretation, leading to Augustine's decision to recount Monica's admonitions against his committing adultery? Could his emphasis on her concern serve as a transformed expression of Patricius' interference with Augustine's Oedipal sexual urges toward Monica? That is, if Patricius impeded Augustine's Oedipal advances, and the paternal prohibition was repressed, could it be transformed by being displaced onto Monica in Augustine's portrayal of her admonition to him?

Readers will want to know that the interpretation just proposed is dramatically at odds with any elaborated thus far in psychological studies of Augustine.[41] I advance it because most of those already published have relied heavily on the second topography and thereby introduced many considerations of doubtful relevance to Augustine's life. The Oedipal interpretations to date have not been tied closely to Freud's actual writings, either. Consider the following scenarios, suggested by historians of Augustine's world. While the father in late Roman antiquity could be a very threatening influence,[42] he also would spend a lot of time outside the home. Moreover, the boy near the age Freud indicated for the Oedipal conflict—that is, around five or six—was allowed a lot of freedom to play outdoors. The mother who also wanted a reputation as a good wife, however, was not allowed to spend much time out in the open. This social pattern permitted the boy to loosen the bonds of infantile love for his mother without great risk of threat from his father. Therefore, the pressures at Augustine's time that would have affected the unconscious would not necessarily have led to the patterns of thoughts and feelings explicated through the second topography, specifically not the dynamics of the superego imputed to Augustine.[43]

These considerations could lead to practice with the concept of "overdetermination." One could point out that that each bit of unconscious material should have more than one conscious expression. If any interpretation is to withstand scrutiny, then more representations of a similar concern should be discernible through Freudian interpretation of the text. The class could search the *Confessions* for other clues to Oedipal concerns.

But one need not emphasize the Oedipal line of thought. For the purpose of *teaching Freud*, the object is to study the passage according to the principles of Freudian dream interpretation, and discover how well any hypothesis accounts for the material in the *Confessions*. For instance, the class could turn to the distress that small children can feel about divisiveness in their parents' relationship. Which symbols and images in the text might represent a wish fulfillment about his parents' relationship? What is the wish? What is the fulfillment? Two interesting bits of text related to this problem appear in IX.xiii.36 and 37. In the first, Augustine tells us that his mother asked on her deathbed that she be remembered at Christian worship. In the second passage Augustine asks the reader to remember both her *and* Patricius. Given that he has just finished telling us that Monica had given up her desire to be buried by her husband (IX.xi.28)—that is, was willing to be separated from

him—why does Augustine reintroduce Patricius? How could these little elements of Augustine's story relate to his other representations of divided and
united mother and father figures? What unconscious thoughts might give rise
to them?

Using the Secondary Literature and
Assembling New Conclusions

I have not recommended one definitive Freudian or post-Freudian interpretation of Augustine. The investigative approach outlined above may raise for
students, as well as their teachers, the crucial question of whether there can
be a unitary psychological understanding of a person or a work. A quick look
at the secondary literature will indicate that various psychological interpretations of Augustine have already evolved.

The exercises suggested in this essay prepare the students for insightful
reading of the secondary literature. Graduate students can observe in the secondary literature how an area of investigation may expand and critique itself.
Undergraduates might well be overwhelmed, either by confusion or by the
"rightness" of some specific author's position. They can get their bearings
from Freud's statement, cited above, that the unconscious base for conscious
expression in dreams is something "not only alien but also disagreeable" to
the person's consciousness. Whether this is Oedipal and derivative from a
sexual drive, or pre-Oedipal and drawn from relationships in early childhood,
as later studies using post-Freudian schools of psychoanalysis would say, is
not crucial for undergraduates. The alien nature and disagreeableness, the
ensuing repression, transformation, and disguised expression are the factors
on which they should focus.

Students can follow the changes in viewpoint over time if the secondary
literature is taken chronologically. The study by Kligerman[44] shows Freudian theory and findings adopted as second nature and used largely without
careful reference to Freudian texts. Fredriksen's introduction of psycholo-
gies concentrating on the pre-Oedipal phase of life, its elaborations by Capps,
and Miles's[45] blending of pre-Oedipal concerns with close textual study will
expose students to further critiques, including commentary based on historical and cultural knowledge, considerations of genre, and theological themes.
Laurence J. Daly offers a theoretical shift by relying on Erik Erikson's ideas
to interpret Augustine.[46] William B. Parsons draws out similarities of Erikson's
thought and the object relations perspective of Ana-Maria Rizzuto to propose
that Augustine's psychological conflicts might have been transformed by a
process of maturation, rather than frozen in a largely changeless unconscious.[47]
Volney Gay offers a well argued interpretation from the viewpoint of Kohut's
pre-oedipal self psychology.[48] Browning suggests ways to link Freudian and
pre-Oedipal interpretations.[49] Diane Jonte-Pace's attention to rhetoric and
culture, as well as to the notion of the subject of psychohistory, fosters well-
rounded critique.[50] My own work draws primarily on the theory of Kohut in

combination with theories of culture, and along the way tries to address some of the major problems in earlier studies.[51] Any of these interpretations can be scrutinized rigorously if the basic rules of unconscious psychological transformation are kept in mind as one approaches both the theory of choice and Augustine's text.

The editors of *Hunger of the Heart* tell us that many of the late-twentieth-century psychological studies of Augustine have flowed from Yale Divinity School, where a seminar on the topic was offered by James E. Dittes in 1964.[52] Several authors of chapters in the present volume participated in a similar seminar offered by Don S. Browning at the University of Chicago in the 1980s. Few of us have been "right" about Augustine in more than a passage of our papers or an insight in an essay. But many of us have been inspired, and we have learned our psychological theory by the effort of applying it. Moreover, we encountered a great man—Augustine—even if we cannot specify definitively the vicissitudes of his mind. We have explored Freud's thought and that of his successors and come to recognize how their conclusions are put together and how they work. I encourage you and your students to continue the investigation.

Notes

1. A quick count in Capps and Dittes (1990), yields eight footnote references to Freud's writings in over 350 pages, including many of the widely cited psychological studies of Augustine.

2. Fredriksen 1978, 209–14; O'Donnell 1992, 71; O'Ferrall 1975, 35.

3. See Welty, 1989, 41–49, especially 42.

4. Ibid., 43.

5. One might work this out on computers in technologically advanced classrooms. Certainly one could create Web pages with icons for different parts of the theory and ask the students to arrange them. In such an exercise, giving up the mouse would parallel giving up the chalk. Copies of Web pages could easily be saved for other class periods. They could be left on a server for students to access between classes, transfer to their own computers, revise, and bring back to the next class. I have not yet tried these suggestions, but my point is that visual representation of the text may be quite adaptable to technological advances.

6. Daly 1978, 252–253; Dixon 1999, 9–13, 15, 19–22; Jonte-Pace 1993, 75–78.

7. Obeyesekere, 1990, xx-xxi, 63, 84, 243–44, 250–55.

8. Freud 1915, *SE* 14, 172–173.

9. Freud 1901 *SE* 5, 660 (*GW* 2–3, 222) for metaphorical allusions to geology; see language on opposing forces in Freud, 1910, *SE* 11, 23.

10. Obeyesekere, 1990, 244–45 and 250–54.

11. Freud 1901, *SE* 5, 633 (*GW* 2-3, 189).

12. Ibid., 633. Emphasis in the English, not in the German (*GW* 2-3, 189).

13. Some scholars have chosen to interpret dreams in the *Confessions*, but they neglect the fact that the dreams Augustine reports are his mother's dreams, not his own. We have his ideas associated to them, not hers. Therefore interpreting them is a tricky business, best treated with extraordinary reserve; see Dixon 1999, 98–99.

14. The line between explanation and understanding is hard to draw, but suffice it to say that I am avoiding the idea that psychoanalytic interpretation can fulfill strict

standards of causality implied in the word "explanation." Paul Ricoeur (1970, 65–66, 91–97, 358–63, 375) tries to steer a course through these related but still distinct terms.

15. Freud 1901, *SE* 5, 633. (*GW* 2–3;190).

16. Ibid., 635, (*GW* 2–3,192); see also 671 (*GW* 2–3, 235).

17. For an example later in the book, see ibid., 676-7 (*GW* 2–3, 243).

18. Ibid., 635, (*GW* 2–3,192). My emphasis.

19. Ibid., 636–41 (*GW* 2–3, 194–200).

20. Ibid., 648 (*GW* 2–3, 209). Similarly for his comments on overdetermination on p. 652 (*GW* 2–3 213).

21. Ibid., 654, (*GW* 2–3, 215).

22. Ricoeur 1970, 73–77, 86, 93–94.

23. Ibid., 672 (*GW* 2–3,236).

24. Ibid., 640, (*GW* 2–3,198).

25. Ibid., 659, (*GW* 2–3, 221). The teacher needs to understand that these symbolic representations are not what Freud means when he talks about "fixed" symbols.

26. Kligerman 1957, 471; cf. McMahon 1989. Freud's further comments about "considerations of representability" (Freud 1901, *SE* 5, 659, emphasis omitted) can also be understood to apply to Augustine's use of symbols in the *Confessions*. He was a rhetor by training and needed to consider representability consciously even while his unconscious may have been affecting it without his awareness.

27. Freud 1901, *SE* 5, 674, 679–80 (*GW* 2–3, 238, 247).

28. Ibid., 682, (*GW* 2–3:238, 247).

29. Freud 1910, *SE* 11, 47. Freud is explicit earlier in this text about understanding sexuality broadly (46).

30. Ibid., 47. Emphasis in original.

31. Ibid., 11–16.

32. Ricoeur 1970, 164–65, 172.

33. Augustine 1997; Augustine 1992; Augustine 1961; Augustine 1963.

34. Two good references are Henry Chadwick, *Augustine*, Past Masters, gen. ed. Keith Thomas (Oxford: Oxford University Press, 1986) and James J. O'Donnell, *Augustine*, Twayne World Authors 759 (New York: Macmillan, 1985). See also O'Donnell's marvelous World Wide Web site at http://ccat.sas.upenn.edu/jod/augustine.html. Garry Wills's recent book, *Saint Augustine* (New York: Lipper/Viking, 1999), has received excellent reviews. Peter Brown's *Augustine of Hippo* (Berkeley: University of California Press, 1969) may still be the best read, but it is already influenced by Brown's own understanding of psychoanalysis; statements, especially about Augustine, his father, and mother, should not be read as facts unadorned by interpretation.

35. Unfortunately, two numbering systems have come down through the manuscript traditions. The instructor would do well to have one edition with both systems (e.g., Chadwick's translation) and then coordinate it with other editions that use only one of the systems. In any case, if one avoids using page numbers, then the class can accommodate most of the editions.

36. Kligerman 470.

37. Freud 1901, *SE* 5, 676 (*GW* 2–3, 242–43).

38. Freud, 1930, 74.

39. For example, see also IV.xvi.31, V.ii.2, VI.xvi.26; by extension, God not as punitive but as healing through the use of painful medical techniques (VI.vi.9).

40. Freud 1930, *SE* 19, 30–35; Freud 1961b, *SE* 21, 129–33.

41. Dittes 1965; Kligerman 1957; Woolcott 1966; see Dixon 1999, 69–78.

42. Shaw, 1987,18, 21–22, 31, 40; Hamman 1979, 103.

43. For fuller treatment, see Dixon 1999, 69–78. These complications add to the criticisms of Fredriksen 1978, O'Ferrall 1975, Daly 1981, and Jonte-Pace 1993. The critiques and evidence in sum prevent my recommending the early articles on Augustine (Dittes 1965, Kligerman 1957, Woollcott 1966) as good models of psychoanalytic interpretation. They have an important place, however, in the story of how the psychoanalytic study of Augustine developed.

44. Kligerman 1957.

45. Fredriksen 1978; Capps 1985; Miles 1982.

46. Daly 1981.

47. Parsons 1990.

48. Gay 1986.

49. Browning 1990.

50. Jonte-Pace 1993.

51. Dixon 1999.

52. Capps and Dittes 1990, ix.

References

Browning, Don S. 1990. The psychoanalytic interpretation of St. Augustine's *Confessions*: An assessment and new probe. In *Psychiatry and the Humanities*, Vol. 2, *Psychoanalysis and Religion*, edited by Joseph H. Smith, associate editor Susan A. Handelman. Baltimore: The Johns Hopkins University Press.

Capps, Donald. 1985. Augustine as narcissist: Some comments on Paul Rigby's "Paul Ricoeur, Freudianism and Augustine's *Confessions*." *Journal of the American Academy of Religion* 53: 115–27.

Capps, Donald, and James E. Dittes, eds. 1990. *The hunger of the heart: Reflections on the "Confessions" of Augustine*. Society for the Scientific Study of Religion Monograph Series, no. 8; n.p.: Society for the Scientific Study of Religion.

Daly, Lawrence J. 1978. Psychohistory and Augustine's conversion process: An historiographical critique. *Augustinian Studies* 28: 252–53.

Daly, Laurence J. 1981. St. Augustine's *Confessions* and Erik Erikson's *Young Man Luther*: Conversion as 'identity crisis.'" *Augustiniana* 31: 183–96.

Dittes, James E. 1965. Continuities between the life and thought of Augustine. *Journal for the Scientific Study of Religion* 5: 130–40 (reprinted in Capps and Dittes 1990).

Dixon, Sandra Lee. 1999. *Augustine: The scattered and gathered self*. St. Louis, Mo: Chalice Press.

Fredriksen, Paula. 1978. Augustine and his analysts: The possibility of a psychohistory. *Soundings* 61: 209–14.

Freud, Sigmund. 1953–1974. *The standard edition of the complete psychological works of Sigmund Freud* (hereafter SE), translated and edited by James Strachey. Vol. 5. London: Hogarth Press.

——. 1901. On dreams. *SE* 5, 631–686.

——. 1910. *Five Lectures on psycho-analysis. SE* 11, 1–55.

——. 1915. The unconscious. *SE* 14, 159–215.

——. 1923. *The ego and the id. SE* 19, 1–66.

——. 1930. *Civilization and its discontents. SE* 21, 57–145.

Gay Volney. 1986. Augustine: The reader as selfobject. *Journal for the Scientific Study of Religion* 25: 64–76.

Hamman, A.-G. 1979. *La vie quotidienne en Afrique du Nord au temps de saint Augustin*, nouvelle éd. Paris: Hachette.

Jonte-Pace, Diane. 1993. Augustine on the couch: Psychohistorical (mis)readings of the Confessions. *Religion* 23: 75–78.

Kligerman, Charles. 1957. A psychoanalytic study of the confessions of St. Augustine. *Journal of the American Psychoanalytic Association* 5: 469–484 (reprinted in Capps and Dittes 1990).

McMahon, Robert. 1989. *Augustine's prayerful ascent: An essay on the literary form of the "Confessions"* Athens, Ga.: University of Georgia Press.

Miles, Margaret R. 1982. Infancy, parenting, and nourishment in Augustine's *confessions*. *Journal of the American Academy of Religion* 50: 349–64.

Obeyesekere, Gananath. 1990. *The work of culture: Symbolic transformation in psychoanalysis and anthropology*. Chicago: University of Chicago Press.

O'Donnell, James J. 1992. *Augustine: Confessions, II: Commentary on Books 1–7*. Oxford: Clarendon Press.

O'Ferrall, Margaret More. 1975. Monica, the mother of Augustine: A reconsideration. *Recherches Augustiniennes* 10:35.

Parsons, William B. 1990. St Augustine: 'Common man' or 'intuitive psychologist'? *Journal of Psychohistory* 18: 155–79.

Ricoeur, Paul. 1970. *Freud and philosophy: An essay on interpretation*. Translated by Denis Savage. New Haven, Conn.: Yale University Press.

Saint Augustine. 1961. *Confessions*. Translated with an Introduction by R. S. Pine-Coffin. New York: Dorset Press.

Saint Augustine. 1963. *The Confessions of St. Augustine*. Translated by Rex Warner, with an Introduction by Vernon Bourke. New York: New American Library.

Saint Augustine. 1992. *Confessions*. Translated with an introduction by Henry Chadwick. New York: Oxford University Press.

Saint Augustine. 1997. *Confessions*. In *The works of Saint Augustine: A translation for the 21st century*, translated with an introduction and notes by Maria Boulding, edited by John E. Rotelle, Hyde Park, N.Y.: New City Press.

Shaw, Brent D. 1987. The family in late antiquity: The experience of Augustine. *Past and Present* 115:18, 21–22, 31, 40.

Welty, William M. 1989. Discussion method teaching: How to make it work. *Change*, July/August, 41–49.

Woollcott, Phillip Jr. 1966. Some considerations of creativity and religious experience in St. Augustine of Hippo. *Journal for the Scientific Study of Religion* 5: 273–83.

8

Psychoanalyzing Myth:
From Freud to Winnicott

Robert A. Segal

The central difficulty I find in teaching Freud on myth is connecting myth to religion and therefore to the world. Teaching that Freud severs myth from the world by severing myth from religion merely states rather than solves the problem. Students expect myth to be about the external world. It is not that they fail to grasp that for Freud myth involves the projection of human characteristics onto the world. It is that for them myth thereby ceases to be about the world and consequently ceases to be myth. It is not that students fail to recognize the similarities that Freud draws between dreams and myths. It is that for them the similarities miss the key difference: where dreams are about dreamers, myths are about the world. Put bluntly, Freud seems to have little to say about myth because myth is part of religion and religion is about the world.

I respond to this problem in several ways. First, I place Freud's theory in the history of modern theorizing about myth. Second, I trace the development of the Freudian theory of myth from Freud's day to the present, showing how contemporary psychoanalysis directs myth away from sheer fantasy, as it is for classical psychoanalysis, to acceptance of reality. Third, I apply D. W. Winnicott's notion of play to argue that myth for a Freudian can actually be about the world and not merely take reality into account.

The psychologizing of myth does not begin with Freud or with Jung. The recognition that myth involves the projection of human qualities onto gods goes back to at least the pre-Socratic philosopher Xenophanes, who, writing in the sixth century B.C., observed that Ethiopians imagined their gods to be swarthy and flat-nosed, where Thracians visualized their gods as fair-haired and blue-eyed. Most famously, Xenophanes asserted that if lions, horses, and oxen had gods, their gods would look like them. Jung in particular is eager to trace a psychological understanding of myth all the way back to ancient Gnostics and to medieval alchemists. Going beyond—and against—Xenophanes, he claims that ancient mythmakers themselves often recognized the psychological meaning of their myths.

Nevertheless, for Freud and Jung alike, the key intellectual accomplishment of modernity has been the disentanglement of the psychological from the physical and the metaphysical—the disentanglement of the inner from the outer. Projections onto the outer world, which had taken the form of gods, have largely been withdrawn. The outer world has come to be recognized as a natural rather than a supernatural domain, to be explained by impersonal scientific laws rather than by the decisions of gods. For both Freud and Jung, the rise of science has spelled the fall of religion. Writes Freud:

> Let us consider the unmistakable situation as it is to-day. We have heard the admission that religion no longer has the same influence on people that it used to. . . . Let us admit that the reason—though perhaps not the only reason—for this change is the increase of the scientific spirit in the higher strata of human society. Criticism has whittled away the evidential value of religious documents, natural science has shown up the errors in them. (*SE* 21: 38)

Writes Jung: "Only in the following centuries, with the growth of natural science, was the projection withdrawn from matter and entirely abolished altogether with the psyche. . . . Nobody . . . any longer endows matter with mythological properties. This form of projection has become obsolete" (Jung 1968, 300). Most remaining projections are onto other persons and peoples, not onto animals, plants, and stones. With the fall of religion has come the fall of myth, or at least myth as it had traditionally been taken: as a story about a god acting in the world.[1]

The Surrender of Myth to Science

I teach Freud on myth by presenting the array of responses to the challenge to myth by science. I begin with the most straightforward response to that challenge: surrendering myth to science. I characterize this response as, typically or stereotypically, that of the nineteenth century, and I link the response to the conflict between science and religion commonly assumed by the nineteenth century (see, for example, White 1965). The theorists of myth I select are the pioneering English anthropologist Edward Tylor, whose chief work, *Primitive Culture*, first appeared in 1871, and the Scottish classicist and anthropologist James Frazer, the first edition of whose main opus, *The Golden Bough*, was published in 1890. Both Tylor and Frazer take for granted that myth is part of religion and, as such, serves to explain physical events. The explanation is always a decision by a god. For example, a myth says that it rains because a god decides to send rain, with the myth often explaining how the god became responsible for rain and how the god exercises that responsibility.

For Tylor, myth provides knowledge of the physical world as an end in itself. For Frazer, the knowledge that myth provides is a means to control over the physical world. For both, myth is the "primitive" counterpart to science, which is exclusively modern. "Modern myth" is a self-contradiction. By science is primarily meant natural science, not social science. The events explained by myth are primarily external ones, such as the falling of rain and the rising of the sun, though also human events like birth and death. Myths about customs, laws, institutions, and other social phenomena are considered secondary.

For Tylor, myth and science are identical in function. Both serve to account for all events in the physical world. Yet more than redundant, the two are incompatible. It is not simply that myth is no longer *needed* once science arises. It is that myth is no longer *possible*. For both offer direct accounts of events. According to myth, the rain god, let us suppose, collects rain in buckets and then, for whatever reason, chooses to empty the buckets on some spot below. According to science, meteorological processes cause rain. One cannot reconcile the accounts by stacking a mythological account atop a scientific account, for the rain god acts *in place of* meteorological processes rather than *through* them. Taking for granted that science is true, Tylor unhesitatingly pronounces myth false.

For Frazer, myth is false because it is tied to magic, which stems from the failure to make basic logical distinctions. As epitomized by voodoo, magic fails to distinguish between a symbol and the symbolized: a voodoo doll is assumed by practitioners to be identical with the person of whom it is an image rather than merely symbolic of the person. Otherwise what one did to the image would not affect the person. Voodoo works by imitating on the image what one wants to happen to the person.

For Frazer, magic puts myth into practice in the form of ritual, which is an attempt to gain control over the physical world, especially over crops. Typically, the king plays the role of the key god of the pantheon, that of vegetation, and acts out the key part of the myth, or biography, of the god: his death and rebirth. As with voodoo, so here, imitating the rebirth of the god of vegetation is believed to cause the same to happen to the god. And as the god goes, so go the crops. Strictly, the cause of the rebirth of crops is thus not a decision by the god, as it would be for Tylor, but the physical condition of the god: a revived god automatically spells revived crops. The ritual is performed at the end—the desired end—of winter, presumably when stored-up provisions are running low.[2] Myth still explains the state of the crops, as for Tylor, but for the purpose of reviving them, not just for the purpose of explaining their revival. For Frazer, myth, together with ritual, is the primitive counterpart to *applied* science rather than, as for Tylor, the primitive counterpart to *theoretical* science. Myth is even more blatantly false for Frazer than for Tylor because it fails to deliver the goods.

The Reconciliation of Myth with Science

Having presented nineteenth-century theories, which pit myth against science, I turn to twentieth-century ones, which seek to reconcile myth with science. I present twentieth-century theories not merely as alternatives to their predecessors but also as repudiations of them.[3] Twentieth-century theories, I stress, have almost defiantly sought to preserve myth in the face of science. Yet they have not done so by challenging science as the reigning explanation of the physical world. They have not "relativized" science, "sociologized" science, or made science "mythic." Rather, they have recharacterized *myth* as other than an explanation of the physical world. I divide twentieth-century theories into three groups: those that maintain that myth, while still about the world, is not an explanation, in which case its function runs askew to that of science; those that maintain that myth is not to be read literally, in which case its content does not even refer to the physical world; and, most radically, those that maintain both that myth is not an explanation of the world and that myth is not to be read literally. I place Freud, and also Jung, in this third camp.

I note that the issue has never been whether "primitives" have myth. That they do is taken for granted. The issue is whether moderns, who by definition have science, can also have myth. Twentieth-century theorists have argued that they can and do. Only at the end of the century, with the emergence of postmodernism, has the deference to science, and thereby the assumption that myth must be rendered compatible with it, been questioned.

Insofar as twentieth-century theories have not challenged the supremacy of science, the pressing question to be raised is why one should even seek to reconcile myth with science. Why not simply accept the incompatibility of myth with science and dispense with myth? The answer of twentieth-century theorists is that nineteenth-century theories, by restricting myth to a literal explanation of physical events, fail to account for the array of other functions and meanings that myth harbors. Myth, it is argued, operates as more or other than an explanation of the external world. The telltale evidence is that it survives. If Tylor and Frazer were right, myth would by now long be dead.

Observing that Sophocles' play *Oedipus Rex* still stirs present-day audiences, who do not believe in Fate, Freud argues that the story must therefore be about other than the impact of the supernatural on our lives: "If *Oedipus Rex* moves a modern audience no less than it did the contemporary Greek one, the explanation can only be that its effect does not lie in the contrast between destiny and human [free] will, but is to be looked for in the particular nature of the material on which that contrast is exemplified" (*SE* 4: 262). Were Tylor and Frazer right, moderns, no less than ancients, would be attributing Oedipus' behavior to determinism from without rather than from within, and moderns, no longer believing in Fate, would be unmoved by the myth. That moderns are still moved means for Freud that the myth must be taken as other than a literal, or religious, explanation of Oedipus' behavior.

Among the twentieth-century reinterpreters of the function, not the literal meaning, of myth, two of the most important have been Bronislaw Malinowski and Mircea Eliade. It is not clear whether for Malinowski (1926), the Polish-born, English-resident anthropologist, moderns as well as primitives have myth. If not, then admittedly his theory provides a less than ideal foil to that of Tylor and Frazer. But his theory remains a foil because for him at least primitives have science as well as myth. Therefore myth cannot be the primitive counterpart to modern science, theoretical or applied. According to Malinowski, primitives use science, however rudimentary, to explain and, even more, to control the physical world. They use myth to do the opposite: to reconcile themselves to aspects of the world that cannot be controlled, such as natural catastrophes, illness, old age, and death. Myths root these woes in the irreversible past actions of gods or humans. (Malinowski does not rigidly subsume myth under religion, the way Tylor and Frazer do, and so allows for myths in which mere humans are the agents.) Equally important, myth reconciles humans to *social* unpleasantries—to the restrictions and obligations imposed by laws, customs, and institutions. Far from unalterable, these unpleasantries *can* be cast off. Myth helps ensure that they are not, by rooting them, too, in a hoary past, thereby conferring on them the clout of tradition. If for Malinowski moderns have myth, then, for example, a myth about the British monarchy would trace the origin of the monarchy back as far as possible, so that to tamper with the monarchy would be to tamper with tradition.

Insofar as myth for Malinowski deals with the social world, it turns its back on the physical world. But even when myth deals with the physical world, its connection to that world is limited. Myth may explain how flooding arose—a god or a human brought it about—but science, not myth, explains why flooding occurs whenever it does. And science, not myth, says what to do about it. Indeed, myth says that nothing can be done about it. Whether or not Malinowski succeeds in keeping the mythic and the scientific explanations distinct and therefore compatible, at least he tries to do so.

Eliade (1968), the Romanian-born, ultimately American-resident historian of religions, tries as well. For him, myth explains the origin of both physical and social phenomena, just as for Malinowski. And the explanation, as for Malinowski, is that a god—though never a mere human—brought it about. (For Eliade, in contrast to Malinowski, myth is a part of religion.) But the payoff of myth is not, as for Malinowski, reconciliation to the unpleasantries of life. On the contrary, the payoff is escape from the world and return to the time of the origin of whatever phenomenon is explained. Myth is like a magic carpet. Because all religions, according to Eliade, preach that gods were closer at hand in days of yore than now, to be whisked back in time is to be able to brush up against the god—the ultimate payoff. Myth is a medium for encountering god.

Eliade goes beyond Malinowski and, even more, Tylor and Frazer in proclaiming myth panhuman and not merely primitive. He cites modern plays, novels, and movies with the mythic theme of yearning to leave the everyday world and enter another, often earlier one. If even moderns, who are professedly atheistic, have myths, then myth must be universal. Yet as much as Eliade wants myth to be compatible with science—social science or natural science—he, like Malinowski, never explains how they are. And he certainly never explains how modern myths, in which the agents are humans, can effect an encounter with gods.

Among twentieth-century reinterpreters of not the function but the literal meaning of myth, two of the most prominent have been the German New Testament scholar Rudolf Bultmann and the German-born philosopher Hans Jonas, who eventually settled in the United States. Both offer existentialist readings of myth. While they limit themselves to their specialties, Christianity and Gnosticism, they apply a theory of myth per se.

Bultmann (1953) acknowledges that, read literally, myth is about the physical world, is incompatible with science, and should be rejected as uncompromisingly as Tylor and Frazer reject it. But unlike both Malinowski and Eliade as well as both Tylor and Frazer, Bultmann proposes reading myth symbolically. Taken symbolically, or "demythologized," myth is no longer about the external world. It is now about the place of human beings in the world. Myth no longer explains but describes, and describes not the world itself but humans' *experience* of it. It describes the alienation from the world that humans experience before turning to God and the at-homeness in the world that humans experience upon turning to God. Myth ceases to be primitive and becomes universal. It ceases to be false and becomes true. It presents the human condition. Like Eliade, Bultmann desperately wants moderns to have myth, but unlike Eliade, he actually tries to work out how myth can be compatible with science. Yet even when demythologized, myth still refers to God, albeit of a nonphysical kind. Moderns must therefore still believe in God in order to retain myth.

Like Bultmann, Jonas (1963) seeks to show that ancient myths still have a message for moderns rather than, like Eliade, to show that moderns have myths of their own. For Jonas, as for Bultmann, myth read symbolically describes the alienation of humans from the world prior to their acceptance of God. Because ancient Gnosticism, unlike mainstream Christianity, sets immateriality against matter, humans remain alienated from the material world even after they have found the true God. In fact, the true God can be found only by rejecting the false god of the material world. Gnostics overcome alienation from this world only by transcending the world. Unlike Bultmann, Jonas does not try to sell a whole ancient religion to moderns. He simply isolates the Gnostic description of how the world is experienced before the revelation and parallels it to the secular existentialist description of how the world is experienced permanently. Because he confines himself to Gnostic descriptions of the *experience* of the world and ignores Gnostic descriptions of the world itself, he, like Bultmann, shows one means of making myth and science compatible. Whether moderns would accept the Gnostic depiction of even the experience of the world is a question that Jonas, like Bultmann, leaves unanswered.

Classical Psychoanalytic Theorizing about Myth

At last, I turn to Freud, who, together with Jung, offers the most extreme departure from Tylor and Frazer. For Freud transforms both the literal meaning and the explanatory function of myth. For him, as for Jung, the subject matter of myth is the unconscious, and the function of myth is to provide an encounter with the unconscious.

Just as Tylor and Frazer take their cue to myth from science, so Freud and Jung take their cue from dream. While Freud analyzes myths throughout his writings, it is fitting that his key discussion of his key myth, that of Oedipus, occurs in *The Interpretation of Dreams* (1900). The opening line of that discussion has already been quoted:

> If *Oedipus Rex* moves a modern audience no less than it did the contemporary Greek one, the explanation can only be that its effect does not lie in the contrast between destiny and human [free] will, but is to be looked for in the particular nature of the material on which that contrast is exemplified. There must be something [latent] which makes a voice within us ready to recognize the compelling force of destiny in the *Oedipus*. . . . His [Oedipus'] destiny moves us only because it might have been ours—because the oracle laid the same curse upon us before our birth as upon him. It is the fate of all of us [males], perhaps, to direct our first sexual impulse towards our mother and our first hatred and our first murderous wish against our father. Our dreams convince us that that is so. King Oedipus, who slew his father Laïus and married his mother Jocasta, merely shows us the fulfilment of our own childhood wishes. But, more fortunate than he, we have meanwhile succeeded, in so far as we have not become psychoneurotics, in detaching our sexual impulses from our mothers and in forgetting our jealousy of our fathers. Here is one in whom these primaeval wishes of our childhood have been fulfilled, and we shrink back from him with the whole force of the repression by which those wishes have since that time been held down within us. While the poet . . . brings to light the guilt of Oedipus, he is at the same time compelling us to recognize our own inner minds, in which those same impulses, though suppressed, are still to be found. (*SE* 4: 262–63)

In teaching, I first show how Freud breaks with the literal meaning of myth. On the surface, or manifest, level, the story of Oedipus describes that figure's vain effort to elude the fate that has been imposed on him. Latently, however, Oedipus most wants to do what manifestly he least wants to do. He wants to act out his "Oedipus complex." The manifest, or literal, level of the myth hides the latent, symbolic meaning. On the manifest level Oedipus is the innocent victim of Fate. On the latent level he is the culprit. Rightly understood, the myth is not about Oedipus' failure to circumvent his ineluctable destiny but about his success in fulfilling his fondest desires.

Yet the latent meaning scarcely stops here. For the myth is not really about Oedipus at all. Just as the manifest level, on which Oedipus is the victim, masks a latent one, on which Oedipus is the victimizer, so that level in turn masks an even more latent one, on which the real victimizer is the mythmaker and any reader of the myth smitten with it. Here the myth is about the fulfillment of the Oedipus complex in the male mythmaker or reader, who identifies himself with Oedipus and through Oedipus fulfills his own kindred yearnings. At heart, the myth is about oneself. It is not biography but autobiography.

In whom does the Oedipus complex lie? To a degree it lies in all adult males, none of whom has fully outgrown the desires that first arose in childhood. But the complex lies above all in neurotic adult males who are stuck, or fixated, at their Oedipal stage. For many reasons they cannot fulfill their desires directly. Their parents may no longer be alive or, if alive, may no longer be so intimidating or so alluring. Furthermore, the parents would not readily consent. Anyone who succeeded in the act would surely be caught and punished. And the guilt felt for having killed a father whom one loved as much as hated, and for having forced oneself upon a resisting mother, would be overwhelming. But the biggest obstacle to the enactment of the complex is more fundamental. One does not know that the complex exists. It has been repressed.

Under these circumstances, myth provides the ideal kind of fulfillment. True, the fulfillment is mental rather than physical, vicarious rather than direct, and above all unconscious rather than conscious. But myth still permits some degree of release. If on the one hand the outer layers of the myth hide its true meaning and thereby block fulfillment, on the other hand they reveal that true meaning and thereby provide fulfillment. After all, on even the literal level Oedipus does kill his father and does have sex with his mother. He simply does so unintentionally. If on the next level it is Oedipus rather than the mythmaker or reader who acts intentionally, the action is still intentional. The level above therefore partly reveals, even as it partly hides, the meaning below. The true meaning always lies at the level below but is always conveyed by the level above. By identifying themselves with Oedipus, neurotic adult males secure a partial fulfillment of their own lingering Oedipal desires, but without becoming conscious of those desires. Myth thus constitutes a compromise between the side of oneself that wants the desires satisfied openly and the side that does not even want to know they exist.

When Freud observes that modern audiences, who no longer believe in Fate, are still moved by the play of Oedipus, he takes for granted that the myth is not about the external world. When he claims that modern audiences are moved by the destiny of Oedipus only because "it might have been ours," he takes for granted that the myth is really about us. When he asserts that the "guilt of Oedipus" "compel[s] us to recognize . . . those same impulses" in us, he takes for granted that the myth fulfills our wishes. Like dream, myth is a fantasy.

In teaching, I show how Freud ties the function of myth to the meaning. Myth vents unconscious desires by telling a story in which those desires are fulfilled. The fulfillment comes through identification with the named hero and thereby through the experience of the same emotions felt by that hero as the plot—the disguised plot—unfolds.

In *Dreams in Folklore,* written with D. E. Oppenheim, Freud interprets dreams in folklore, but none of the pieces of folklore considered is a myth (see Freud and Oppenheim 1958). The classical Freudian analyses of myth are Karl Abraham's *Dreams and Myths* (1913) and Otto Rank's *The Myth of the Birth of the Hero* (1914).[4] Both Abraham and Rank follow the master in comparing myths with dreams and in deeming both the disguised, symbolic fulfillment of repressed, overwhelmingly Oedipal wishes lingering in the adult mythmaker or reader. But Rank's work is by far the richer and sprightlier of the two. He considers more myths, analyzes them in more detail, and most of all presents a common plot, or pattern, for one category of myths: those of heroes, specifically male heroes. Rank provides a manifest pattern that he then translates into latent terms. Rank later broke irrevocably with Freud, but at the time he wrote *The Myth of the Birth of the Hero* he was an apostle and soon emerged as Freud's heir apparent.[5]

For Rank, heroism covers what Jungians like to call the first half of life: the period from birth to young adulthood. This period involves the establishment of oneself as an independent person in the external world. The attainment of independence expresses itself concretely in the securing of a job and a mate. The securing of either requires both separation from one's parents and mastery of one's drives. Independence of one's parents means not the rejection of them but self-sufficiency. Similarly, independence of one's drives means not the rejection of them but control over them. It means not the denial of drives but the rerouting of them into socially acceptable outlets. When Freud says that the test of happiness is the capacity to work and love, he is clearly referring to the goals of the first half of life, which for him apply to all of life. Classical Freudian problems involve a lingering attachment either to parents or to drives. Either to depend on one's parents for the fulfillment of desires or to fulfill them in antisocial ways is to be fixated at childhood.

Rank's pattern, which he applies fully to fifteen hero myths, goes from the hero's birth to his attainment of a "career":

> The hero is the child of most distinguished parents; usually the son of a king. His origin is preceded by difficulties, such as continence, or prolonged barrenness, or secret intercourse of the parents, due to external prohibition or obstacles. During the pregnancy, or antedating the same, there is a prophecy, in form of a dream or oracle, cautioning against his birth, and usually threatening danger to the father, or his representative. As a rule, he is surrendered to the water, in a box. He is then saved by animals, or by lowly people (shepherds) and is suckled by a female animal, or by a humble woman. After he has grown up, he finds his distinguished parents, in a highly versatile fashion; takes his revenge on his father, on the one hand, and is acknowledged, on the other, and finally achieves rank and honors. (Rank 1914, 61)

Literally, or consciously, the hero is a historical or legendary figure like Oedipus. The hero is heroic because he rises from obscurity to the throne. Literally, he is the victim of either his parents or, ultimately, Fate. While his parents have longed for a child and abandon him only to save the father, they nevertheless do abandon him. The hero's revenge, if the parricide is even committed knowingly, is, then, understandable: who would not consider killing one's would-be killer?

Symbolically, or unconsciously, the hero is heroic not because he dares to win a throne but because he dares to kill his father. The killing is definitely intentional, and the cause is not revenge but sexual frustration. The father has refused to surrender his wife—the real object of the son's efforts: "as a rule the deepest, generally unconscious root of the dislike of the son for the father, or of two brothers for each other, is referable to the competition for the tender devotion and love of the mother" (Rank 1914, 74). Too awful to face, the true meaning of the myth gets covered up by the concocted story. Rather than the culprit, the hero becomes an innocent victim or, at worst, a justified avenger: "The fictitious romance [i.e., the myth] is the excuse, as it were, for the hostile feelings which the child harbors against his father, and which in this fiction are projected against the father" (Rank 1914, 68–69).[6] What the hero seeks gets masked as power, not incest. Most of all, who the hero is gets masked as some third party rather than as the mythmaker or reader.

Why the literal hero is usually the son of royalty, Rank never explains. Perhaps the manifest clash thereby becomes even more titanic: it is over power as well as revenge. And when, as in Oedipus' case, the hero kills his father unknowingly, the conscious motive can hardly be revenge, so that ambition or something else non-Freudian is needed as an overt spur.

Literally, the myth culminates in the hero's attainment of a throne. Symbolically, the hero gains a mate. One might, then, conclude that the myth expresses the Freudian goal of the first half of life. In actuality, it evinces the opposite. The wish it fulfills is not for detachment from parents and from antisocial impulses but, on the contrary, for the most intense possible relationship to parents and for the most antisocial of urges: parricide and incest, even rape. Taking one's father job and one's mother's hand does not quite spell independence of them.

The mythmaker or reader is an adult, but the wish vented by the myth is that of a boy of three to five: "Myths are, therefore, created by adults, by means of retrograde childhood fantasies, the hero being credited with the myth-maker's personal infantile [i.e., childhood] history" (Rank 1914, 82). The adult mythmaker re-creates his own childhood fantasy of fulfilling his Oedipal desires, attributes that fantasy to the named hero, and then identifies himself with that hero: "In investing the hero with their own infantile history, they [the mythmakers] identify themselves with him, as it were, claiming to have been similar heroes in their own personality" (Rank 1914, 81). The myth thus fulfills the desires never outgrown by the adult who either invents or uses it. That adult is psychologically an eternal child: "There is a certain class of persons, the so-called psychoneurotics, shown by the teachings of Freud to have remained children, in a sense, although otherwise appearing grown up" (Rank 1914, 63). In short, the myth expresses not the Freudian goal of the first half of life but the childhood goal that keeps the neurotic from achieving it.

Contemporary Psychoanalytic Theorizing about Myth

Like any other theory of myth, the psychoanalytic one is the application of a broader theory. There are no theories of myth per se. There are only applications of theories of culture, society, religion, literature, and the mind. But then as the psychoanalytic study of the mind has evolved, so has the psychoanalytic theory of myth. I next teach developments in Freudian theory since Freud.

Led by the development of ego psychology, which has expanded psychoanalysis from a theory of abnormal personality to a theory of normal personality, contemporary Freudians such as Jacob Arlow see myth as contributing to normal development rather than to the perpetuation of neurosis. For them, myth helps one grow up rather than, like Peter Pan, remain a child. Myth abets adjustment to society and to the physical world rather than childish flight from them. Myth may still serve to fulfill id wishes, but even more it serves the ego functions of defense and adaptation and the superego function of renunciation. Myth now offers the psychoanalytic counterpart to Malinowski's anthropological brand of socialization. Furthermore, myth for contemporary Freudians, as for Malinowski, serves everyone, not merely neurotics. Put summarily, contemporary Freudians take myth positively rather than, like classical ones, negatively. As Arlow characterizes the contemporary Freudian approach:

> Psychoanalysis has a greater contribution to make to the study of mythology than [merely] demonstrating, in myths, wishes often encountered in the unconscious thinking of patients. The myth is a particular kind of communal experience. It is a special form of shared fantasy, and it serves to bring the individual into relationship with members of his cultural group on the basis of certain common needs. Accordingly, the myth can be studied from the point of view of its function in psychic integration—how it plays a role in warding off feelings of guilt and anxiety, how it constitutes a form of adaptation to reality and to the group in which the individual lives, and how it influences the crystallization of the individual identity and the formation of the superego. (Arlow 1961, 375)

For classical Freudians, myths are like dreams. Both serve to satisfy repressed wishes. For contemporary Freudians, myths are unlike dreams. Where dreams still serve to satisfy wishes, myths serve to deny or to sublimate them. Writes Mark Kanzer: "Where the dream represents the demands of the instincts, the myth tends to perpetuate and represent the demands of society on the mental apparatus for symbolization and acceptance" (Kanzer 1964, 32). For classical Freudians, myths are simply public dreams: "The manifestation of the intimate relation between dream and myth . . . entirely justifies the interpretation of the myth as a dream of the masses of the people" (Rank 1914, 6). For contemporary Freudians, myths, *because* public, serve to socialize: "Myths are instruments of socialization" (Arlow 1961, 379).

In his book *The Uses of Enchantment* the well-known Freudian Bruno Bettelheim says much the same as Arlow and others, but he says it of fairy

tales *rather than* of myths, which he oddly sets against fairy tales and interprets in a classical Freudian way. Classical Freudians tend to see myths and
fairy tales as akin, just as they do myths and dreams. It is contemporary Freudians who contrast myths to fairy tales, but usually they favor myths over fairy
tales, seeing myths as primarily serving the ego or the superego and seeing
fairy tales as primarily serving the id. Bettelheim does the reverse. To be sure,
he does not consider myths to be wish fulfillments. In fact, he seems to echo
Arlow in maintaining that "myths typically involve superego demands in
conflict with id-motivated action, and with the self-preserving desires of the
ego" (Bettelheim 1977, 37). But for Bettelheim, in contrast to Arlow, the
mythic superego is so unbending that the maturation it espouses is unattainable: "Mythical heroes offer excellent images for the development of the superego, but the demands they embody are so rigorous as to discourage the child
in his fledgling strivings to achieve personality integration" (Bettelheim 1977,
39). For Bettelheim, fairy tales no less than myths preach maturation, but they
do so in gentler ways and thereby succeeed where myths fail: "In the myth
there is only insurmountable difficulty and defeat; in the fairy tale there is
equal peril, but it is successfully overcome. Not death and destruction, but
higher integration . . . is the hero's reward at the end of the fairy tale"
(Bettelheim 1977, 199). In myths the heroes, who are often gods, succeed
because they are exceptional, and everyday mortals can scarcely aspire to
emulate them. In fairy tales the heroes are ordinary persons whose success
inspires emulation. In short, myths for Bettelheim wind up hindering psychological growth, where fairy tales spur it.[7]

The key exception among classical Freudians to the paralleling of myths to
fairy tales is the Hungarian anthropologist and folklorist Géza Róheim, who
contrasts myths to fairy tales, or folktales, in a fashion that presciently anticipates that of Arlow and others. For Róheim, myths provide "a more adult" and
folktales "a more infantile" "form of the same conflict" (Róheim 1941, 279).
Folktales are sheer fantasies: "the child obtains a fulfilment in imagination of
those unconscious wishes which it cannot yet obtain in reality" (Róheim 1922,
181). By contrast, myths "link up phantasy and reality" (Róheim 1941, 275).
Oedipal folktales end in parricide. Oedipal myths end in submission to the res-
urrected, triumphant father, who is the real hero (see Róheim 1941, 277–78). In
"fairy tales and popular legends dealing with the co-operation between mortals
and immortals, the supernatural beings are always deceived; human cunning
wins the day" (Róheim 1974, 252). In myths "the heroes sin against the gods
and must atone for this with an eternal punishment or an eternal task" (Róheim
1974, 251). Where in the tale of Jack and the Beanstalk Jack outsmarts the ogre,
becomes rich, and lives happily ever after (see Róheim 1941, 275), in the myth
of Prometheus the hero "becomes the representative of renunciation; and his
achievement, the great cultural act of the discovery of fire, is performed with
energy, or better libido, that has been diverted from its original aim" (Róheim
1974, 260). Moreover, Prometheus is punished by Zeus for stealing fire: "The
desire [id] continually returns (the liver) and is continually eaten by the eagle
(superego)" (Róheim 1974, 261).[8]

Much like Róheim, who is cited only in passing, Arlow takes fairy tales as serving to fulfill wishes and takes myths as serving to renounce or sublimate them. Just like Róheim, Arlow contrasts Jack to Prometheus, and then adds the case of Moses at Mt. Sinai. Manifestly, all three stories describe a hero's ascent to the domain of an "omnipotent figure resident in the heavens" and a return "with some token of power, wealth, or knowledge" (Arlow 1961, 381). Latently, the three stories express Arlow's favorite theme: "the practically universal fantasy wish to acquire the father's phallus by devouring it and using the omnipotent organ in keeping with the child's notions about its functioning" (Arlow 1961, 381). Where Jack brashly steals whatever he wants from the ogre, Prometheus fears Zeus and is punished by Zeus. But like Jack, he still steals. In contrast to both, Moses ascends Mt. Sinai as the servant, not the antagonist, of God and relays God's laws to the Israelites below:

> The fairy-tale version of this problem [i.e., Jack and the Beanstalk] belong[s] to the wish-fulfilling tendency of childhood in which contribution of the superego is minimal and unformed and the fear of retaliation is disposed of omnipotently. . . . What is epitomized in this variation [i.e., the myth of Prometheus] is the stage beyond the untroubled wish fulfillment of the simple fairy tale, the overwhelming impact of the fear of retaliation. . . . What was originally [i.e., in Prometheus] a crime of defiance and aggression against the gods is, in this later version [i.e., the myth of Moses], represented as carrying out the wishes of God Himself. (Arlow 1961, 382–83)

Where Prometheus is put in his place for daring to challenge god, Moses is elevated to godlike status for deferring to god. Moses thus fulfills his wish to become the father, but not by toppling him.

As for Rank, so for Arlow, the presumably male mythmaker or reader identifies himself with Moses and thereby vicariously becomes the real hero of the myth, but now as law giver rather than as rebel: "The mythology of religion fosters social adaptation of the individual and integration with the community and its values by virtue of the fact that the individual unconsciously identifies with the idealized qualities of the mythological hero" (Arlow 1982, 188). For Arlow, as for Freud and Rank, myth represents a compromise, but not between the open fulfillment of wishes and the sheer repression of them. Rather, myth combines fulfillment with sublimation and renunciation. It satisfies at once id, ego, and superego.

In contrast to classical Freudians—with the exception of Róheim—contemporary Freudians not only distinguish myths from fairy tales but also distinguish one mythic scenario from another. Where Rank deciphers a common plot to all male hero myths, Arlow spots variations on any common plot: "It is not sufficient for us to be able to demonstrate, with monotonous regularity, evidence of the same id wishes in the text of the myth. By applying our knowledge of ego psychology we obtain insight into the differences between myths, even when these myths deal with the same theme" (Arlow 1961, 379). For Arlow, the differences among Jack, Prometheus, and Moses are more significant than the similarities. By granting variations in plot and in meaning, a contemporary psychoanalytic approach makes the theory applicable to a much larger spectrum of myths.[9]

The term "contemporary," or "modern," Freudian does not mean that all present-day Freudians have spurned the classical approach. One of the pre-eminent Freudians on myth, the American folklorist Alan Dundes (1975, 1980, 1987, 1989, 1997), is defiantly old-fashioned. For him, myth expresses repressed wishes rather than renounces or sublimates them. Declares Dundes: "The content of folklore, I would maintain, is largely unconscious. Hence it represents id, not ego, for the most part. From this perspective, ego psychology cannot possibly illuminate much of the content of folklore" (Dundes 1987, xii). Unlike the sober, dour, didactic readings of myth given by "modern" Freudians, Dundes delights in demonstrating the hidden, antisocial wishes vented by myths. Those wishes are as often anal as Oedipal, and as often homosexual as heterosexual. Dundes goes beyond most professional analysts in using myth as a key to understanding culture and not merely to understanding the mind. At the same time he brings the strictures of folkloristic methods to bear on the interpretations of analysts, oblivious as analysts invariably are to the initially oral nature of folklore, to the existence of multiple versions of any myth, and to the distinctiveness of myth among the genres of folklore. Indeed, for folklorists the story of Oedipus is a tale *rather than* a myth.[10]

Psychoanalysis and the World

The telling phrase that applies to all Freudians is, to quote the first long excerpt from Arlow, "adaptation to reality." For contemporary Freudians, no less than for classical ones, myth presupposes a divide between the individual's wishes and reality. Where myth for classical Freudians functions to satisfy in the mind what cannot be satisfied in reality, myth for contemporary Freudians functions to help one accept the inability to be satisfied in reality. Still, for both varieties of Freudians, myth is not about reality—that is, the external world. It is about the individual, who comes smack up against reality. It is about the clash between the pleasure principle and the reality principle. Myth either shields the individual from reality (the classical view) or foments acceptance of reality (the contemporary view). Rather than explaining reality, myth takes reality for granted and responds to it, either negatively (classical view) or positively (contemporary view). To explain reality, one turns to natural science. Myth taken literally is incompatible with science, in the same way that it is for Tylor and Frazer. Myth psychologized is compatible with science because it is no longer about reality.[11]

Tylor and Frazer have a psychology of their own, and it is incorporated in their theory of myth. But for them myth does not arise from any confrontation between the individual and reality. It arises from the experience of reality, which one wants either to explain (Tylor) or to manipulate (Frazer). Whatever role the individual plays in creating myth, the subject matter of myth is still the world, not the individual. Even though for Tylor, especially, mythic explanations stem from the analogy that "primitives" draw between the behavior of humans and that of the world, myth is still about the world, not about humans. Tylor is not even fazed by the subsequent kinship between humans and a deified world—an issue for those who, like Bultmann and Jonas, are concerned with the experience of the world. Frazer, for his part, does attribute myth, as part of religion, to the experience of the failure to control the world through magic—an experience which leads to the assumption that the world operates instead at the behest of gods. But myth is still not about how the world is experienced. It is about the world itself.

For Freudians, myths project human nature onto the world in the form of gods—for Freud himself, largely fatherlike gods. To understand the world is to withdraw those projections. The world really operates according to mechanical laws rather than according to the wills of a divine family. There is no symmetry between humans and the world. There is a disjunction. Even myths about heroes, who can be either human or divine, involve projection: the plot of hero myths is the fantasized expression of family relations, with the named hero playing the role of the idealized mythmaker or reader. Heroism itself is more fantasy than reality. There are no comic-book heroes in the real world. There are only human beings, some better than others.

For Jungians as well as for Freudians, myths project human nature onto the world in the form of gods and of heroes, who, similarly, can be either human or divine.[12] To understand the world is, similarly, to withdraw those projections and to recognize the world as it really is. Jungian projections are more elusive than Freudian ones because they cover a far wider range of the personality. There are an endless number of sides of the personality, or archetypes. Almost anything in the world can be archetypal—that is, can provide a hook for the projection of an archetype.

Unlike Freudians, Jungians have taken myth positively from the outset. For them, the unconscious expressed in myth is not a repository of repressed, antisocial drives but a storehouse of innately unconscious archetypes that have simply never had an opportunity at realization. Myth is one means of encountering this unconscious. The function of myth is less that of release, as for classical Freudians, than that of growth, as for contemporary ones. But where even contemporary Freudians see myth as a means of adjustment to the demands of the outer world, Jungians see myth as a means of the cultivation of the inner world. The payoff is not adjustment but self-realization. Myth is a circuitous, if still useful, means of self-realization exactly because it involves projection: one encounters oneself *through* the world. Ordinarily, projections are recognized and thereby withdrawn only in the course of analysis—a point that holds for Freudians as much as for Jungians. If for either Freudians or Jungians myth can still be employed once the projection has been recognized, then the middle man—the world—has conveniently been eliminated.

Both Freudians and Jungians bypass the power of myth at the conscious, usually literal, level. While both appreciate the need to be moved by the life of the named hero or protagonist, that figure can be fictional. One does not have to accept the historicity of Oedipus to be moved by his saga. Moreover, the named figure is a mere peg onto which to hang the autobiography. The story of Oedipus is moving only because, to repeat Freud, "it might have been ours." A story that can never be imagined as happening to oneself will not work. In short, myth for Freudians and Jungians alike never takes one outside oneself. No theory of myth is more solipsistic than theirs.[13]

Winnicott

Does psychoanalysis offer any way of bringing myth back to the world and thereby meeting the understandable expectation of students that a theory of myth link myth to the world? I think that it does, through the approach of the English child psychiatrist D. W. Winnicott (1982, 1987), who, formally, belonged to the Independent School of British psychoanalysts. Winnicott himself does not analyze myth, but his analysis of play and of its continuation in adult make-believe provides one road back to the world. Among others who have written on the significance of play, Jean Piaget confines play to childhood, however indispensable childhood play is for establishing lifelong cognitive capacities. Johan Huizinga, author of *Homo Ludens*, so emphasizes the dependence of adult culture on the "play element" as to efface the line between play and reality. As he writes of myth itself, "Now in myth and ritual the great instinctive forces of civilized life have their origin: law and order, commerce and profit, craft and art, poetry, wisdom, and science. All are rooted in the primeval soil of play" (Huizinga 1970, 23). By contrast, Winnicott makes play other than reality. Play constitutes its own reality. It does not merely feed ordinary reality.

For Winnicott, play is *acknowledged* as other than reality: children grant that they are just playing. But play is no mere escapism. It involves the appropriation of reality for oneself. It involves the construction of a reality that has personal meaning. To pretend that a spoon is a train is to take a spoon and to turn it into a train. Far from projecting oneself onto the world, as for Freud and Jung, play is the construction of a world. As Winnicott continually declares, play is "creative." Far from confusing itself with reality, play demarcates the difference. Play grants itself the right to treat a spoon as a train, and a parent is barred from asking whether the spoon really is a train. Once play is over, the train is again a mere spoon.

To use Winnicott's famous term, play is a "transitional" activity. It provides a transition not merely from childhood to adulthood but also from the inner world of fantasy to outer reality: "Play can easily be seen to link the individual's relation to inner reality with the same individual's relation to external or shared reality" (Winnicott 1987, 145). Play links the realms by taking items from the external world and constructing a reality to fit the fantasy: play takes a spoon and transforms it into a train. Yet play does not deny the difference between the inner and the outer worlds, for only during play is the spoon a train. On the one hand, play is recognized as make-believe: outside of play the spoon is conceded to be only a spoon. On the other hand, the make-believe is taken seriously: within play the spoon really is a train.

As adult extensions of play, Winnicott, in stereotypically English fashion, names gardening and cooking, in both of which one creates a world with personal meaning out of elements from the external world. Winnicott also names art and religion, in both of which as well one constructs a world, though with a far deeper meaning to it:

> It is assumed here that the task of reality-acceptance is never completed, that no human being is free from the strain of relating inner and outer reality, and that relief from this strain is provided by an intermediate area of experience which is not challenged (arts, religion, etc.). This intermediate area is in direct continuity with the play area of the small child who is "lost" in play. (Winnicott 1982, 13)

Winnicott is not, like Huizinga, asserting that art and religion and other aspects of culture *are* play. Rather, he is asserting that culture is akin to play in the creation of a world to which one has a comforting relationship. Just as the infant ideally has a positive, secure relationship with its mother, so through play the child creates a world that offers the same kind of relationship, and so through culture the adult creates a world that offers the same kind of cosy relationship on a vaster scale. Culture does not merely parallel the security provided by the infant's mother and by the child's play but also presupposes them. Without good mothering there can be no play, and without play there can be no culture. Following Peter Berger, one might say that religion in particular creates a "sacred canopy," but for Winnicott that canopy is *recognized* as a creation, as make-believe. While Winnicott, like Bultmann and Jonas, is indisputably concerned with the individual's relationship to the world, he, unlike them, is also concerned with the world itself.[14]

A transitional activity or object provides a transition from the known world to the unknown one. The activity or object acts as a guide, offering the security needed to dare to explore the unknown world. Just as a child clings to a physical object—a teddy bear—to create a safe world that then enables the child to explore with confidence the world beyond the mother,[15] so an adult clings to a hobby, an interest, a creed, a value, or, so I propose, a myth that then enables the adult to deal with a much wider world.[16] Just as the child knows that the teddy bear is not Mommy yet clutches it as if it were, so the adult recognizes that the myth is not reality yet adheres to it as if it were. Transitional activities and objects do not confuse the symbol with the symbolized, the way, by contrast, magic does for Frazer.[17] On the one hand, transitional activities and objects are themselves created out of elements from the world. On the other hand, they provide reassurance in exploring the world.

In teaching, I do not worry about the persuasiveness of Winnicott's characterization of religion, which doubtless is rarely embraced with the lightness of make-believe. I worry only about the persuasiveness of my characterization of myth as a case of adult make-believe. Undeniably, not all myths are entertained as make-believe. Doubtless there is a spectrum. Some myths are taken and perhaps can only be taken as unassailable truths—for example, myths about the coming end of the world. Other myths, as I will illustrate, are taken and perhaps can only be taken as make-believe—most obviously, hagiographical biographies of heroes. In between would fall myths that can be taken either way—for example, the belief in progress, ideologies, and worldviews such as Marxism. Taken as make-believe, these kinds of myths serve as *guides* to the world rather than as *depictions* of the world.

The "rags-to-riches" myth, which claims that America is a land of boundless opportunity, would fall here. Ironically, the myth is vaunted at least as effusively around the world as in America itself. Undeniably, the credo can be held as an unassailable truth, and can lead to frustration and recrimination when it does not pan out. But it can also be held as "make-believe," which means held not as a false characterization of American life but as a hoped-for one. Here America is seen as if it were a haven of opportunity. Contentions that race, class, gender, or religion impedes opportunity are recognized but fended off, rationalized away as excuses for personal failure. In the wake of the civil rights movement, the feminist movement, and multiculturalism, these "excuses," far from being acknowledged as legitimate, are dismissed even more than before: whether or not in generations past, at least by now America offers equal opportunity to all. The present-day epitome of this myth is Anthony Robbins, salesman par excellence for success. What, according to Robbins, keeps persons from succeeding? Not trying. Where there is a will, there is always a way. Taking the rags-to-riches myth as make-believe means trusting Tony Robbins, not because he must be right but because one wants him to be right.

To view a myth as make-believe is not to dismiss it as a delusion. To do so would be to revert to the present either/or option, according to which myth, to be acceptable, either must be true about the external world or, if false about the external world, must concern instead the mind or to society in order still to be true.[18] To view myth as make-believe is to allow for a third way. The choice is not just delusion or reality—or, in Winnicott's terms, illusion or disillusionment.[19] Taken as make-believe, myth can still be true about the world, once it is demarcated as make-believe.

Hollywood Stars as Gods

In expecting myth to be linked to the world, students expect it to be linked to religion and thereby to gods. To clinch the application of Winnicott to myth, I look for the presence of gods in the modern, seemingly secular, avowedly scientific world. Where are gods to be found? They are to be found in the "world" of celebrities, above all of Hollywood stars.

Unlike other kinds of celebrities, such as sports stars and rock stars, Hollywood stars, like gods, are rarely seen in person. Also, unlike other kinds of celebrities, they, like gods, take on disguises—their roles. In film, they, like gods, can do all kinds of things that celebrities who perform in person cannot. And in a movie theater they are gargantuan in size. In all of these ways film stars fit the popular conception of gods, a conception found not only in, say, Homer but also, when read with open eyes, in the Bible. The difference for sophisticated theologians between humans and God may be one of kind—for example, God's having no body. But the popular difference between humans and gods is one of degree: a god's body is bigger. Certainly the biblical God has a body. Otherwise, to cite a single instance, Moses at the burning bush would not have to look away to avoid seeing God and would not have to stop at the perimeter to avoid stepping on the ground where God has walked. On screen, stars are not only bigger than ordinary humans but also stronger and sexier. Like gods, they are greater than ordinary folks in degree, not kind.

It is a cliché that contemporary film stars, like contemporary heroes generally, are drawn from a far wider array of types and that contemporary stars are as much antiheroes as heroes. But the biggest box office draws, male and female alike, still look the part on screen, and it is looks, not acting ability, that put them there. On screen, merely human virtues get magnified into superhuman ones: bravery becomes fearlessness, kindliness becomes saintliness, strength becomes omnipotence, wisdom becomes omniscience. Humans becomes gods.

It is commonly assumed that there is at least one difference of kind, not merely of degree, between humans and gods: gods live forever. But so do film stars—in their films. Here, too, film stars are more godlike than sports stars and rock stars. There may be films of the performances of sports stars and rock stars, and with MTV the make-or-break performances of some rock stars are ever more done on the "small screen." But TV, film, and video are still copies of live performances. The "live" performances of film stars are on film. At the same time some gods, like humans, do die. The difference is that gods are reborn. But then so are some humans. The difference is that gods are reborn again and again. Here, too, film stars are like gods, born anew with each film. New roles amount to reincarnation.

Should one ever encounter a god in person, it would be a once-in-a-lifetime experience. The same holds for encountering film stars. Fans want to get as close as possible to stars. Fans want to touch stars. Getting a piece of clothing is like holding the Shroud of Turin. A fan fortunate enough to shake the hand of a film star will think twice before washing away the contact. Tours of stars' homes are standard fare in Hollywood. The terms used of fans' admiration for their heroes say it all: Hollywood stars are "idolized" and "worshiped." And the greatest are called "gods." As "stars," they shine brightly in a heaven far above us.

It might be said that where gods are born, film stars are made. And it is well known how capricious becoming a star can be. But surely most fans believe that stars are born, not made. When Lana Turner was spotted innocently drinking a milkshake at Schwab's drug store on Hollywood Boulevard, she was discovered, not invented.

It might well be said that where gods are gods in private as well as in public, film stars are stars only onscreen and offscreen are mere mortals. But surely most fans make no distinction. The onscreen qualities are expected to be the offscreen ones as well. Film stars are assumed to be playing themselves on screen, and it is not the ability to act but ironically the opportunity to, apparently, be oneself that is mesmerizing. Thus it comes as a shock to learn that in person Mel Gibson is not very tall. Thus it is considered unseemly for Kirk Douglas, a frail old man battling cancer of the larnyx, to make TV appearances. Garbo was right to become a recluse. Robert Mitchum had to caution his fans against expecting military strategy from him. Few gay Hollywood actors dare come out, lest they be barred from playing straight roles. The cases of Rupert Everett and Ann Heche confirm the point. Tom Cruise is compelled to sue anybody who calls him gay.

Just as gods can, typically, do as they please, so, it is assumed, can film stars. Fans are shocked to discovered that stars are subject to arrest and even imprisonment for drug abuse or other offenses to which the rest of us would not be immune. "But I am a star" has, in effect, been the defense of Robert Downey Jr.

It might understandably be argued that even if film stars are godlike in their attributes, the worship of them still does not restore divinity to the physical world. After all, film stars cannot quite cause the rain to fall, as even the most prima donnish of them would concede. Still, is it only coincidental that, ever more, it is film, if also rock, stars who presume to take responsibility for accomplishing things in the social and even the physical world that whole nations have failed to achieve: ending pollution, saving species, eliminating poverty, canceling Third World debt? A year ago Michael Douglas came to Britain to get things going on nuclear disarmament. Film stars and other celebrities are assumed to have power greater than that of heads of states or of traditional religious leaders. The Pope can pray for an end to misery, but stars can actually do something about it.

Against my argument that film stars are the modern, secular version of gods, it might sensibly be observed that these days nobody believes the hype. No one believes that Hollywood stars are really different from you and me. They may have more disposable income, but they face the same obstacles and tribulations as the rest of us. What sells better than an "unauthorized" biography of a star—a biography that brings a *star* down to *earth*? What is juicier than an exposé? If nothing else, the revelation of the disparity, put mildly, between the onscreen Rock Hudson, the quintessential heterosexual hunk, and the offscreen Rock Hudson, withering away from AIDS, surely drove home the difference between onscreen persona and offscreen reality. It even proved that Rock was a better actor than had been assumed.

But this hard-nosed view of present-day fans is the naive one. Fans continue to "idolize" and "worship" stars not in ignorance of their flaws but in defiance of them. The flaws are either denied or discounted. It is not that fans don't know. It is that they don't want to know, or else don't care. But the devotion of fans is not mindless. It is done knowingly. It is, following Winnicott, make-believe, not credulity. The cult of heroes in every walk of life, not just in films, demands make-believe. Treating Princess Diana as a

wholly selfless, almost saintly person does not require the refusal to acknowledge any evidence to the contrary. It requires the refusal to let the evidence
get in the way. It requires, to use a mildly quaint phrase, the voluntary sus-
pension of disbelief. The myths of movie stars are their authorized, idealized
biographies. Taking those biographies as make-believe reconnects myths to
gods, therefore to religion, and therefore to the world. It offers a way of meeting
rather than conceding the common charge of students that psychoanalysis has
nothing to say about myth, for myth is about the world.

Notes

1. Unlike Freud, Jung laments that the loss of religion as an explanation of the
world has simultaneously meant the loss of an effective means of tending to the unconscious, but Jung no less than Freud praises the triumph of the scientific explanation over the religious one.

2. Frazer also offers an alternative scenario, according to which the king, now
himself divine, is actually killed at the first sign of weakening and is immediately
replaced, thereby ensuring that the god of vegetation residing within the incumbent
regains his health. As the king goes, so goes the god and so in turn go the crops. On
Frazer's dual scenarios, see Segal 1998a, 3–5.

3. To be sure, some recent theorizing about myth has been a variation on either
Tylor or Frazer. Led by the French anthropologist Pascal Boyer (1994), "cognitivists"
follow Tylor in deeming myth a primitive explanation of the world, but they focus on
how the mind constrains mythic explanations rather than, like Tylor, on the explanations themselves. Similarly, the German classicist Walter Burkert (1996) and the French
literary critic René Girard (1972) have given new twists to Frazer's myth-ritualism.
Where in Frazer's alternative scenario, myth is the script for the ritualistic killing of the
king, whose death and replacement ensure the rebirth of crops, for Burkert myth reinforces the ritual that commemorates the past killing of animals for food. The function
of myth is not physical but psychological and social: to cope with the guilt and anxiety
that members of society feel toward their own aggression. Where in the same alternative scenario of Frazer's, the king is willing to die for the sake of his subjects, for Girard
the king (or someone else) is selected as a scapegoat to blame for the violence in society. Rather than directing the ritualistic killing, as for Frazer, myth for Girard arises
afterwards to cover up the deed by turning the victim into a criminal and then into a
hero. The function of myth is social: to preserve the ethos of sociability by hiding not
only the killing but also the violence endemic to society. While Boyer, Burkert, and
Girard do revive the theories of Tylor and Frazer, the variations they introduce do not
bring myth back to the external world. Myth for all three is about human nature, not
about the nature of the world. The three therefore exemplify the twentieth-century rejoinder to Tylor and Frazer rather than any departure from it.

4. For superb overviews of Freudian approaches to myth as well as to other genres
of folklore, see Dundes 1987, chap. 1; 1997, chap. 1. See also the excellent earlier
surveys of LaBarre 1948; 1958, 294–95; Boyer 1979, chap. 2. Still valuable are two
of the earliest surveys: Silberer 1910; Karlson 1914.

5. In fact, Freud himself wrote the section of the work on the "family romance"
(Rank 1914, 63–68). The romance fulfills a non-Oedipal, nonsexual wish: the wish to
replace one's present, ordinary parents with the strongest man and the most beautiful
woman in the world. Rank never recognizes the incompatibility of these contrary

wishes. Like Freud, he takes for granted that the wishes work in tandem, since both get rid of the father. But the Oedipal aim is to get rid of the real, royal father; the non-Oedipal aim is to get rid of the lowly, foster father. Arlow, too, takes the wishes to be compatible and to work in sync: see Arlow 1956, 82. Despite the title of Rank's book, the emphasis is on the hero's Oedipal conflict with his father, not on his birth and so on the relationship with his mother. But the title is prescient because Rank came to regard birth rather than the Oedipus complex as the key trauma and as the key source of neurosis. The book that led to the break with Freud is properly entitled *The Trauma of Birth* (1929). For the fullest presentation of Rank's changing views, see Lieberman 1993.

6. What Rank, like other Freudians, simply calls projection, Alan Dundes renames "projective inversion" to capture the reversal involved: the hero's wish to kill his father becomes the father's wish to kill his son. See Dundes 1996, 152–57.

7. On Bettelheim's contrast of myths to fairy tales, see Segal 1999, chap. 5.

8. Róheim comes to see socialization less as an end and more as a means to the overcoming of the trauma of the separation from the mother at birth. Society becomes a substitute for the mother, giving members a second womb. See Róheim 1943. Far from contrasting myths to dreams, the way he does myths to fairy tales, Róheim (1952) derives myths from dreams—a more extreme position than that of Freud and Rank, who merely parallel them. But then myths can serve to stymie or sublimate wishes rather than to vent them only if dreams can. For an appreciation of Róheim's contribution to the psychoanalysis of myth, see Dundes's introduction to Róheim 1992, ix–xxvi.

9. For an appreciation of Arlow's contribution to the psychoanalysis of myth, see Kramer 1988. On the contemporary psychoanalysis of myth, see not only Arlow (1961, 1964, 1982) but also Tarachow 1964; Kanzer 1964; Stern 1964; Muensterberger 1964; Bergmann 1966.

10. For an appreciation of Dundes's contribution to the psychoanalysis of myth, see Carroll 1993.

11. Rank is especially disdainful of those theorists who turn myths about family life into symbols of natural processes—turning the story of Oedipus, for example, into a symbol of the triumph of light over darkness: "As given by a representative of the natural mythological mode of interpretation, Oedipus, who kills his father, marries his mother, and dies old and blind, is the solar hero who murders his procreator, the darkness; shares his couch with the mother, the gloaming, from whose lap, the dawn, he has been born, and dies blinded, as the setting sun" (Rank 1914, 9–10). Rather than originating in the experience of the physical world, myth for Rank originates in the experience of the family and is then projected onto the world.

12. Hero myths are the favorite kinds of myths for both Freudians and Jungians, and other kinds of myths are often turned into hero myths. For example, the act of creation becomes a supremely heroic feat. See Segal 1998b, 85.

13. Jung does bring myth back to the world with the concept of synchronicity, developed with the physicist Wolfgang Pauli. Synchronicity restores a link between humanity and the world that the withdrawal of projections still insisted upon by Jung removes. Synchronicity refers to the coincidence between our thoughts and the behavior of the world, between what is inner and what is outer. As Jung writes of his favorite example of synchronicity, that of a resistant patient who was describing a dream about a golden scarab when a scarab beetle appeared, "at the moment my patient was telling me her dream a real 'scarab' tried to get into the room, as if it had understood that it must play its mythological role as a symbol of rebirth" (Jung 1973–74, 2: 541). Here the world apparently responds to the patient's dream, but under-

stood synchronistically, the world merely, if most fortuitously, *parallels* the patient's dream rather than is *effected* by it. The patient's conscious attitude, which dismisses the notion of an unconscious, is "out of sync" with the world. Synchronicity is not itself myth, which would be an account of a synchronistic experience.

14. For an appreciation of Winnicott's psychology, see Phillips 1988.

15. Where for Freud it is the father who, in the Oedipal stage, comes between son and mother, for Winnicott the child's separation from the mother is pre-Oedipal and does not involve the father, whom Winnicott ignores. Certainly the father does not fill the void created by the child's separation from the mother.

16. Strictly, interests, creeds, values, and myths are not transitional objects insofar as they are wholly mental and not physical. They are ideas, though they can express themselves concretely. They are closer to internal objects for Klein. See Winnicott 1982, 9.

17. Similarly, a transitional object is not a fetish. For Freud, a fetish is a substitute by a child for his mother's missing penis. The fetish alleviates a son's castration anxiety by restoring the mother's penis. The boy thereby preserves the delusion that his mother has a penis. A transitional object embued with the same associations as the mother—for example, those of touch and smell—enables the child to fend off the anxiety of annihilation and disintegration and, later, of separation and castration by likewise providing a substitute for the mother. But the transitional object is not taken *as* the mother and therefore constitutes no delusion. It is taken as a *symbol* of the mother. It is treated *as if* it were the mother. Rather than a defense against reality, a transitional object occupies the space between fantasy and reality. It bridges the divide between the wish for the mother and her actual absence. While a transitional object can become a fetish, it need not. See Winnicott 1992, 241–42; Bronstein 1992.

18. The issue of the truth of myth arises not just over myths that are purportedly about the external world but also over myths that are purportedly historical, such as biographies of heroes.

19. Winnicott seems to use "illusion" for both the initial, pretransitional phase, in which the infant deems itself the creator of the breast and deems the breast part of itself, and the subsequent, intermediate, transitional phase, in which the infant deems a toy or a piece of cloth identical with the breast yet separate from it. I am here using the term "illusion" in the first sense only, according to which illusion is interchangeable with delusion. To compound the confusion, Freud's distinction between delusion and illusion corresponds, at least roughly, to that between illusion in Winnicott's first sense and illusion in Winnicott's second sense. See *SE* 21: 30–31. Yet also see Winnicott's own kindred use of the terms in Winnicott 1992, 241—a portion of the original 1951 essay not included in the revised version in Winnicott 1982.

References

Abraham, Karl. 1913. *Dreams and myths*. Translated by William A. White. Nervous and Mental Disease Monograph Series, no. 15. New York: Journal of Nervous and Mental Disease Publishing. Rev. translation in Abraham, *Clinical papers and essays on psycho-analysis*, edited by Hilda C. Abraham, translated by Hilda C. Abraham, D. R. Ellison, et al. (London: Hogarth Press and Institute of Psycho-Analysis, 1955), 151–209.

Arlow, Jacob A. 1956. *The legacy of Sigmund Freud*. New York: International Universities Press.

————. 1961. Ego psychology and the study of mythology. *Journal of the American Psychoanalytic Association* 9: 371–93.

————. 1964. The madonna's conception through the eyes. *Psychoanalytic Study of Society* 3: 13–25.

————. 1982. Scientific cosmogony, mythology, and immortality. *Psychoanalytic Quarterly* 51: 177–95.

Bergman, Martin S. 1966. The impact of ego psychology on the study of the myth. *American Imago* 23: 257–64.

Bettelheim, Bruno. 1977 [1976]. *The uses of enchantment*. New York: Vintage Books.

Boyer, L. Bryce. 1979. *Childhood and folklore*. New York: Library of Psychological Anthropology.

Boyer, Pascal. 1994. *The naturalness of religious ideas*. Berkeley: University of California Press.

Bronstein, Abbot A. 1992. The fetish, transitional objects, and illusions. *Psychoanalytic Review* 79: 239–60.

Bultmann, Rudolf. 1953. New Testament and mythology (1944). In *Kerygma and Myth*, edited by Hans-Werner Bartsch, translated by Reginald H. Fuller (London: SPCK), 1: 1–44.

Burkert, Walter. 1996. *Creation of the sacred*. Cambridge, Mass.: Harvard University Press.

Carroll, Michael P. 1993. Alan Dundes: An introduction. In *Psychoanalytic Study of Society*, vol. 18 (*Essays in Honor of Alan Dundes*), edited by L. Bryce Boyer, Ruth M. Boyer, and Stephen M. Sonnenberg (Hillsdale, N.J.: Academic Press), chap. 1.

Dundes, Alan. 1975. *Analytic essays in folklore*. The Hague: Mouton.

————. 1980. *Interpreting folklore*. Bloomington: Indiana University Press.

————. 1987. *Parsing through customs*. Madison: University of Wisconsin Press.

————. 1989. *Folklore matters*. Knoxville: University of Tennessee Press.

————. 1996. Madness in method plus a plea for projective inversion in myth. In *Myth and method*, edited by Laurie L. Patton and Wendy Doniger (Charlottesville: University Press of Virginia), 147–59.

————. 1997. *From game to war and other psychonalytic essays on folklore*. Lexington: University Press of Kentucky.

Eliade, Mircea. 1968 [1959]. *The sacred and the profane*. Translated by Willard R. Trask. New York: Harvest Books.

Frazer, James George. 1890. *The golden bough*. 2 vols. London: Macmillan.

Freud, Sigmund. 1953–74. *The standard edition of the complete psychological works of Sigmund Freud (SE)*, volume 1–24, translated and edited by James Strachey. London: Hogarth Press.

　1900. *SE* 4–5: 1–627. *The interpretation of dreams*.

　1927. *The future of an illusion. SE* 21. 3–56.

————, and D. E. Oppenheim. 1958. *Dreams in folklore*. Translated by A. M. O. Richards. New York: International Universities Press.

Girard, René. 1972. *Violence and the sacred*. Translated by Peter Gregory. London: Athlone Press; Baltimore: Johns Hopkins University Press.

Huizinga, Johan. 1970 [1949]. *Homo ludens*. London: Paladin.

Jonas, Hans. 1963. Gnosticism, existentialism, and nihilism (1952), in his *The Gnostic religion*. 2nd ed. Boston: Beacon Press [1st ed. 1958], 320–40.

Jung, C. G. 1968. *Alchemical studies*. In *Collected works of C. G. Jung*, edited by Sir Herbert Read et al, translated by R. F. C. Hull et al., vol. 13. Princeton, N.J.: Princeton University Press.

———. 1973–74. *Letters*. Edited by Gerhard Adler and Aniela Jaffé, translated by R. F. C. Hull. Princeton, N.J.: Princeton University Press.

Kanzer, Mark. 1964. On interpreting the Oedipus plays. *Psychoanalytic Study of Society* 3: 26–38.

Karlson, Karl Johan. 1914. Psychoanalysis and mythology. *Journal of Religious Psychology* 7: 137–213.

Kramer, Yale. 1988. In the visions of the night: Perspectives on the work of Jacob A. Arlow. In *Fantasy, myth, and reality: Essays in honor of Jacob A. Arlow*, edited by Harold P. Blum et al. (Madison, Conn.: International Universities Press), chap. 2.

LaBarre, Weston. 1948. Folklore and psychology. *Journal of American Folklore* 61: 382–90.

———. 1958. The influence of Freud on anthropology. *American Imago* 15: 275–328.

Lieberman, E. James. 1993 [1985]. *Acts of will*. Amherst: University of Massachusetts Press.

Malinowski, Bronislaw. 1926. *Myth in primitive psychology*. London: Kegan Paul; New York: Norton.

Muensterberger, Warner. 1964. Remarks on the function of mythology. *Psychoanalytic Study of Society* 3: 94–97.

Phillips, Adam. 1988. *Winnicott*. Modern Masters Series. London: Fontana Press.

Rank, Otto. 1914. *The myth of the birth of the hero*. Translated by F. Robbins and Smith Ely Jelliffe. Nervous and Mental Disease Monograph Series, no. 18. New York: Journal of Nervous and Mental Disease Publishing. Reprinted in Rank et al., *In quest of the hero* (Princeton, N.J.: Princeton University Press, 1990), 3–86.

Róheim, Géza. 1922. Psycho-analysis and the folk-tale. *International Journal of Psycho-Analysis* 3: 180–86.

———. 1941. Myth and folk-tale. *American Imago* 2: 266–79.

———. 1943. *The origin and function of culture*. Nervous and Mental Disease Monograph Series, no. 69. New York: Journal of Nervous and Mental Disease Publishing.

———. 1952. *The gates of the dream*. New York: International Universities Press.

———. 1974 [1934]. *The riddle of the sphinx*. Translated by R. Money-Kyrle. New York: Harper Torchbooks.

———. 1992. *Fire in the dragon and other psychoanalytic essays on folklore*. Edited by Alan Dundes. Princeton, N.J.: Princeton University Press.

Segal, Robert A., ed. 1998a. *The myth and ritual theory*. Oxford and Malden, Mass.: Blackwell.

———. 1998b. *Jung on mythology*. Princeton, N.J.: Princeton University Press; London: Routledge.

———. 1999. *Theorizing about myth*. Amherst: University of Massachusetts Press.

Silberer, Herbert. 1910. Phantasie und mythos. *Jahrbuch für psychoanalytische und psychologische Foschungen* 2: 541–652.

Stern, Max M. 1964. Ego psychology, myth and rite: Remarks about the relationship of the individual and the group. *Psychoanalytic Study of Society* 3: 71–93.

Tarachow, Sidney. 1964. Introductory remarks: Mythology and ego psychology. *Psychoanalytic Study of Society* 3: 9–12.

Tylor, Edward Burnett. 1871. *Primitive culture*. 2 vols. London: Murray.

White, Andrew Dickson. 1965 [1896]. *A history of the warfare of science with theology in Christendom*. Abridged edition, edited by Bruce Mazlish. New York: Free Press.

Winnicott, D. W. 1982 [1971]. Transitional objects and transitional phenomena. In his *Playing and reality* (London and New York: Routledge), chap. 1. Original version (1951) in Winnicott, *Through paediatrics to psychoanalysis* (London: Karnac Books, 1992 [1958]), chap. 18.

———. 1987 [1964]. *The child, the family, and the outside world*. Reading, Mass.: Addison-Wesley.

III

TEACHING THE CONTROVERSIES

9

Rethinking Freud: Gender, Ethnicity, and the Production of Scientific Thought

Janet Liebman Jacobs

Teaching Freud poses a number of challenges to those of us who view the academy as a site of intellectual resistance. Each year as I introduce the study of Freud and psychoanalytic theory in my courses, I tell my students that at best I have an ambivalent relationship to Freud, whose work embodies a particular kind of genius that is representative of the misogynistic thinking of the late nineteenth and early twentieth centuries. As I seek to legitimate my own fascination with Freud and the necessity for understanding the psychoanalytic mind, I remind my students that as a clinician working in Vienna, Freud was often a "healer" of last resort for women who were deeply troubled by fears, anxiety, and painful emotional memories. In reading Freud's case studies, one is left with the impression that, as an analyst, Freud had a certain empathy for the women in his care and that the "talking cure" created an atmosphere of trust at a time when psychosis in women was rarely taken seriously. That being said, it is also painfully clear that Freud used the most intimate details of his female patients' lives to construct theories of development and personality that reinforced notions of female inferiority and weakness within a gendered understanding of human psychology.

How then are we to understand, interpret, and explain both the genius and the misogyny of Freudian theory for a future generation of students who rightfully may question the theoretical value of a psychoanalytic paradigm so laden with sexism? Feminist theorists have grappled with these issues for almost a century, as scholars such as Jane Flax reminds us:

For all its shortcomings, psychoanalysis presents the best and most promising theories of how a self that is simultaneously embodied, social, "fictional," and real comes to be, changes and persists over time. Psychoanalysis has much to teach us about the nature, constitution and limits of knowledge. . . . Freud's work also reveals some of the external and internal sources of relations of domination, especially those rooted in the "family romance"—sexuality, gender and the tensions between men and women, desire, cultural conventions, and the demands of the social order. . . . Without full knowledge and investigation of Freud's own antimonies and ambivalence, we risk entering into and replicating the series of displacements, contradictions, and repressions that characterize his work as much as a radical break with the past. (Flax 1990, 16–17)

It is the power of Freud to define and characterize psychosexual development that draws contemporary feminist theorists, including myself, to his work and that compels me to teach psychoanalytic theory year after year. Precisely because Freudian theory has been so significant for the construction of modern scientific thought, the study of Freud provides a wonderful teaching tool for those of us who are interested in interrogating the relationship between the production of scientific theory and the social forces that inform the intellectual and emotional development of the scientist. The extensive writings on Freud, his life and his cultural background, have provided contemporary scholars such as Daniel Boyarin, Jay Geller, Sander Gilman, and Estelle Roith with the rare opportunity to turn Freudian theory back on itself by offering a critical perspective that in effect psychoanalyzes the "father" of psychoanalysis. By examining the social and political forces that helped to shape Freud's identity, we are better able to understand the fears, shame, and marginalization that influenced Freud as he sought to establish himself within the anti-semitic and patriarchal world of Viennese science and medicine. Freud's particular social location, as a Jew and as a male scientist, helps to demonstrate for students the intersection of gender and ethnicity in the formation of the intellectual self.

The feminist approach to teaching that will be outlined here challenges traditional notions of scientific truth as defined by a positivist model of scientific research and problem solving (Harding and O'Barr 1987; Reinhharz 1992). Since the 1970s, a body of feminist literature has emerged that identifies "the ways in which the development of science has been shaped by its particular social and political context " (Keller 1987, 237). This area of feminist scholarship illuminates the relations of power that inform the production of knowledge as male dominance, racial privilege, and social class have historically influenced the definition of scientific problems, the methods of research employed by the scientist, and the interpretation of human behavior for the construction of theory. As such, feminist scholars argue that androcentric models of scientific endeavor assume a false universalism that fails to take into account the social, political, and psychological factors that influence those who are at the center of scientific development. Thus, what traditional male theorists define as objectivity, the developmental psychologist Piaget describes as an "anthropocentric illusion," a misconception that has shaped the history of science by "ignoring the existence of the self and thence regarding one's own perspective as immediately objective and absolute" (Piaget 1972, 212). In its failure to identify and explore the role that the self plays in the production of knowledge, male-centered science has thus created the illusion of objectivity.

To counter this trend in the sciences, Piaget called for a self-examination on the part of the scientist. Such a critical self-evaluation would help to acknowledge the social and personal biases that have influenced the parameters of scientific knowledge and the theoretical premises on which scientific theory is based. Although Freud did not engage in the type of self reflection that Piaget suggests, feminist and postmodern critiques of psychoanalysis allow us to retrospectively interrogate the social and political attributes of Freud's world that informed his own psychic life and thus his understanding of the human condition. In deconstructing Freud in this way, students are better able to see the complex nature of scientific inquiry and the biases that underlie male-centered theories of female behavior and development. In taking this approach, the study of Freud can be taught from two interrelated perspectives. The first perspective analyzes Freud's positionality as a male scientist within European culture. This analysis can then be contextualized for the students through an examination of his status as a Jew within the Christian-centered world of Viennese society.

Feminists Reevaluate Freud

Within the feminist discourse on Freudian theory, a number of critiques situate Freud within a male scientific culture that privileged male perceptions of reality. Simon de Beauvoir, in her groundbreaking work *The Second Sex* (1952), suggested that Freud's emphasis on penis envy among women could be meaningful only within a scientific world that defined the male body and male experience as the standard against which all human development is measured:

> He [man] thinks of his body as a direct and normal connection with the world, which he believes he apprehends objectively, whereas he regards the body of woman as a hindrance, a prison, weighed down by everything peculiar to it. . . . Thus, humanity is male and man defines woman not in herself but as relative to him; she is not regarded as an autonomous being. . . . She is defined and differentiated with reference to man and not he with reference to her. . . . He is the Subject, he is the Absolute—she is the Other. (De Beauvoir 1952, xvii–xix)

It is within this realm of masculinist science that Freud's theory of anatomical deprivation is given meaning, as the position of woman as other and man as the absolute creates the underlying assumptions that led Freud to elaborate the terrible misfortunes that are the fate of the female psyche:

> The psychical consequences of envy for the penis, in so far as it does not become absorbed in the reaction-formation of the masculinity complex, are varying and far-reaching. After a woman has become aware of the wound to her

narcissism, she develops, like a scar, a sense of her inferiority. When she has passed beyond her first attempt at explaining her lack of a penis as being a punishment personal to herself and has realized that that sexual character is a universal one, she begins to share the contempt felt by men for a sex which is so lesser in so important a respect. . . .

There is yet another surprising effect of penis envy, of the discovery of the inferiority of the clitoris, which is undoubtedly the most important of all. (*SE* 19: 253–54)

Freud further explains that the girl child's deep humiliation over the inadequacy of her genitalia leads her to give up pleasure in the form of masturbation, "after all this is a point on which she cannot compete with boys" (255), forcing her away from masculinity and toward femininity. This psychological response establishes the primacy of the phallus in the female psyche, a critical psychic event that dooms women to contend with the devastating effects of having been born female. Such a theory of development, argues de Beauvoir, could become dominant only in a scientific world that assumed male superiority in both body and mind.

De Beauvoir's critical insight is closely tied to the analytic work of Karen Horney. Horney's work on Freudian theory, which emerged in the early part of the twentieth century, contributed greatly to the developing science of psychoanalysis. Writing in the 1920s, Horney provides a window into Freud's psychic life through an analysis of the boy child's perceptions of the body as it relates to the patriarchal power structures of European society. Horney's characterization of the developing male psyche suggests that boys hold the naive assumption that girls are anatomically similar to boys and therefore possess a penis. When the boy child becomes aware of the absence of the male genital on the female body, he is saddened by her loss even as he imagines that the little girl has been punished with castration. Horney thus presents an image of the male psyche in which fear of castration is tied to the young boy's identification with his genitals, a developmental stage that leads to his conviction that the girl child will always suffer from anatomical loss and envy of male physiology. While Horney does not contest this interpretation of male psychosexual development, she does call into question the assumptions about female development that are derived from a masculine psychological orientation. In particular, Horney posits an alternative hypothesis to the biological origins of penis envy in which she emphasizes the social relations of power that create feelings of inferiority in girls and women. In this regard Horney writes:

We might follow Georg Simmel's train of thought and reflect whether it is likely that female adaptation to the male structure should take place at so early a period and in so high degree that the specific nature of a little girl is overwhelmed by it. . . .

Georg Simmel says in this connection that "the greater importance attaching to the male sociologically is probably due to his position of superior strength," and that historically the relation of the sexes may be crudely described as that of master and slave. Here, as always, it is "one of the privileges of the master that he has not constantly to think he is master, while the position of the slave is such that he can never forget it." . . . In actual fact a girl is exposed from birth onward to the suggestion—inevitable, whether conveyed brutally or delicately—of her inferiority. (Horney 1967, 58–69)

Horney's feminist analysis provides a starting point from which to teach Freud from the perspective of gender and power relations. In providing a social explanation for the girl child's envy of the male, and perhaps even the penis, which is symbolic of masculine power and privilege, her point of view allows for a more discerning and nuanced understanding of Freudian theory. Through the study of Horney, the effects of internalized sexism can be illuminated within the context of Freud's observations on the sense of loss and inadequacy that characterized the psychological narratives of his female patients. The lessons from Horney are therefore many. First, her theoretical insights allow us to explore the effects of gender on the construction of knowledge, with particular attention to the way in which female psychology has been understood and defined from a male scientific point of view that privileged biological origins of female inferiority. Second, as it is Freud who is revered, remembered, and traditionally taught within the academy, the inclusion of Horneyian theory contributes to the establishment of a successor science within the university. In this regard, the classroom can become a site of intellectual resistance, as the study of Freud interrogates the effects of male bias on developmental theories of personality formation. In this way, the study of Freud helps us to understand the complex and subtle forms of sexism that permeate the canons of Western scientific thought. If we stop here, however, and interpret Freud solely through the lens of male privilege and scientific hegemony, we fail to recognize the importance of other cultural forces in the creation of Freudian psychoanalytic theory, most important that of the impact of Jewish ethnicity and religion on Freud's understanding and perceptions of the male and female psyche.

In expanding our successor science to include an analysis of the intersection of gender, race, and religion, the teaching of Freud moves into a postmodern framework where knowledge and theory cannot be understood apart from the social location of the theorist and the cultural factors that informed his or her own perceptions of reality and social behavior. The value in this pedagogical approach is in revealing the relationship between structural forces of domination and the production of knowledge, ideas, and values in Western society. There are, however, certain risks in assuming this postmodern stance. The danger of this approach is in contextualizing a body of thought to the point of reductionism such that, in the case of psychoanalysis, Freudian theory is labeled and therefore dismissed as a purely "Jewish science."

As a Jewish feminist scholar, I am only too aware of this dilemma. Because I share the views of other feminist theorists that psychoanalysis, despite its limitations, offers significant and meaningful possibilities for the study of the self, I do not wish to promote a kind of ethnocentric critique that locates Freud exclusively within a "Jewish" mindset, thus reinforcing ethnic stereotypes that may contribute to the promulgation of anti-Semitism. At the same time, I also believe, as do many other scholars, that Freud, and especially his construction of the female personality, cannot be understood without reference to his Jewish identity and the effects of anti-Semitism on the development of the Jewish masculine self in European society. Therefore, despite a tendency toward reductionism, I think it is essential that we push the study of Freud beyond the boundaries of gender and into the area of racial and ethnic analysis.

Jewishness, Circumcision, and the Female Body: A Postmodern Critique of Freud's Gender Theory

The phallocentric aspects of Freudian theory have been of particular interest to those of us who seek to explain and teach Freud from the perspective of a racialized male identity. The value of this type of analysis is that it engages students in an application of psychoanalysis through an examination of Freud's inner psychic life from a historical and cultural perspective. In order to elaborate this point, it is first necessary to consider the nature and character of anti-Semitism within Austrian society at the turn of the century. This historicizing of the scientific period helps to illuminate the cultural constructs of the Jew that were pervasive throughout Europe and that undoubtedly informed Freud's psychological development as he came of age in a Gentile world where the Jew was clearly identified as the racialized other (Gilman 1993). This racialization, manifested in depictions of Jewish difference and inferiority, was tied to biological theories of blood and kinship. In both the scientific and popular literature of the time, Jews were portrayed as physically dark and somehow diseased. While such notions of racial impurity would find their most extreme expressions in the proliferation of Nazi ideology, the culture of nineteenth-century Vienna provided the foreground for Aryan racism through the promulgation of images of the Jewish male as deviant, weak, and effeminate (Boyarin 1994; Gilman 1993).

The racialization of the Jew (and therefore of Freud) was compounded by what Franz Fanon (1967) describes as the Jew's association with evil, an identification that arises out of the roots of anti-Semitism in Christian theology. Within this theological framework, the Jews were held accountable for deicide and were characterized as avaricious, immoral, and unclean (Jaher 1994). In this Christian-centric depiction of Jewish culture and religion, rituals were often designated as the site of Jewish deviance. The celebration of Passover and the baking of matzoh thus became identified with fears surrounding ritual murder, while circumcision was reviled as a barbaric practice of the Jews, as the writings of the Italian physician Paolo Mantegazza demonstrates:

> Circumcision is a shame and infamy: and I, who am not in the least anti-Semitic, who indeed have much esteem for the Israelites, I who demand of no living soul a profession of religious faith, insisting only upon the brotherhood of soap and water and of honesty, I shout and shall continue to shout at the Hebrews, until my last breath: Cease mutilating yourselves: cease imprinting upon your

flesh an odious brand to distinguish you from other men; until you do this, you cannot pretend to be our equal. (As cited in Gilman 1993, 57)

Given the anti-Semitic environment in which psychoanalysis was developing, how might these race and religious ideologies have affected Freud as he came to intellectual consciousness in a racist society? The research on racism and stigma suggests that the effects on the marginalized individual are indeed significant and psychologically powerful. Fanon makes this point especially clear in *Black Skin: White Masks* (1967), a revolutionary text that elucidates the complicated relations of gender, race, and self-identity. In this work Fanon poignantly describes that crucial moment in his own life when the cultural representations of the African in European consciousness penetrated his psyche, transforming forever his understanding and definition of himself as a racialized body. Of this experience, Fanon wrote:

> I was responsible at the same time for my race, for my body, for my ancestors. I subjected myself to an objective examination, I discovered my blackness, my ethnic characteristics; and I was battered down by tom-toms, cannibalism, intellectual deficiency, fetishism, racial defects, slave ships. . . . I move slowly in the world, accustomed now to seek no longer for upheaval. I progress by crawling. And already I am being dissected under white eyes, the only real eyes. I am fixed. . . . They objectively cut away slices of my reality. I am laid bare. (1967, 112–116)

Because it is impossible to avoid the hegemonic influence of the dominant culture, herein described by Fanon, the marginalized individual has no choice but to reject those parts of the self that lend truth to the stereotypes and stigmatized representations of otherness. For the European Jewish male, this meant assimilation and the attending rejection of the ethnic/religious self, a strategy of survival that offered the promise of social equality. Such accommodationist strategies were especially important at the turn of the century, when anti-Jewish sentiment began to emerge within the European scientific community. During the time that Freud attended medical school in Vienna, anti-Semitism within the academy was rampant, with the greatest prejudice being directed against the Jews of Eastern European extraction. The writings of Theodor Billroth, a faculty member at the Vienna Medical School, reinforced the notion for Freud and other Viennese Jews that any identification with Eastern European Jewry would jeopardize their ability to succeed. In what became an inflammatory report on the German universities, Billroth maintained that Eastern European Jews were "for the most part lacking in the talent for the natural sciences, and . . . absolutely unsuitable to become physicians" (Klein 1985, 50).

As the discrimination against Eastern European Jews grew more pervasive, the gap between the assimilated "Western" Jews of Freud's generation and the nonassimilated Eastern Jewish populations widened. In comparison with the German educated and nominally religious accultured Western Jew, the Eastern Jew represented the separate and mysterious Jewish culture that Gentile Europe feared. Living in isolated enclaves in rural Eastern European communities, the nonurban Jews frequently spoke only Yiddish, wore the clothes of the strictly observant Jew, and continued to construct their lives around rituals that were misunderstood and denigrated. The bibliographic data on Freud's early life suggests that, like other assimilated Jews of Austria, he began to see the Eastern Jewish community through the lens of anti-Semitism that characterized the dominant culture. As a young man, Freud reacted with disdain when confronted by the shtetl society of his parents and grandparents. After a visit to his parents' birthplace in Moravia at the age of seventeen, Freud documented his deep disregard for Eastern European Jewry in a letter he wrote to Emil Fluss. Having encountered a provincial Jewish father and son on his return trip to Vienna, Freud wrote:

> Now this Jew talked the same way as I had heard thousands of others talk before, even in Freiberg. His face seemed familiar—he was typical. So was the boy with whom he discussed religion. He was cut from the cloth from which fate makes swindlers when the time is ripe: cunning, mendacious, kept by his adoring relatives in the belief that he is a great talent, but unprincipled and without character. I have had enough of this rabble. (Klein 1985, 46)

The harsh language of Freud's description makes explicit his contempt for his Eastern Jewish roots. In this letter Freud repeats the accusations that were so often held against the Jews: immorality, cunningness, and dishonesty. Such a response is illustrative of the effects of internalized anti-Semitism, as Sander Gilman explains in his work on Jewish self-hatred:

> One of the most successful ways to distance the alienation produced by self doubt was negative projection. By creating the image of the Jew existing somewhere in the world who embodied all the negative qualities feared within oneself, one could distance the specter of self hatred, at least for the moment. (Gilman 1986, 270)

The intense Jewish self-criticism that is evident in Freud's youthful reaction to the Eastern European Jewish family is especially revealing in that his mother, Amalia, was known to be a "typical Galician woman" whose language, mannerisms, and dress were not unlike the family that Freud had encountered on the train (Roith 1987, 110). It was therefore Freud's mother who came to represent the vilified Jewish other. In the anti-Semitic world of Freud's Vienna boyhood, Amalia's apparent ethnicity might certainly have led the young Freud to distance himself from the primacy of the maternal bond, as her Jewishness, both cultural and religious, was a threat to the developing "German" child. This ethnic turning away from the mother may help to explain the comparatively insignificant role that Freud accorded the mother in psychosexual development. Although Freud acknowledged the significance of the mother as the first object of gratification, his work deemphasized the pre-Oedipal stages, focusing instead on the importance of the Oedipal crisis, the father, and the phallus as the signifiers of psychological maturation. In minimizing the role of the mother, Freud minimized his identification with Amalia and thus with the Jewish other that she represented, both in the dominant culture and in Freud's unconscious fears. The resolution of the Oedipal crisis, the turning away from the mother (female body) and toward the father (phallus), might then be understood as the turning away from the Jew and toward assimilationism.

The internalized anti-Semitism that Freud expressed in his youth, although rarely communicated so openly in his later years, nonetheless reemerged in his theories of castration anxiety and female genital inferiority. As the assimilated Jew, Freud was self-consciously European, speaking only German, eschewing the religion of his ancestors, and claiming little knowledge of tradition or belief. Yet Freud's fascination with the unconscious belied the inner fears, self-doubt, and ethnic anxiety that was inextricably tied to his status and experience as a Jewish male within dominant Christian society. Daniel Boyarin described this inner psychic reality as the "internalized self-contempt that the colonized male comes to feel for his disempowered situation" (1994, 36). Freud's inner psychic life, to which he gave voice in the theories of the unconscious, thus bore traces of the self-hatred and internalized anti-Semitism that was symptomatic of Jewish experience in prewar European culture. I would therefore argue that Freud's ethnic self-contempt ultimately found expression in the Oedipal drama of castration and the representation of the female body as the mutilated male. That such imagery was pervasive in Freud's work has been attributed to his own unconscious feelings of denigration that arose out of his position as the circumcised Jewish male whose body signified both physical and political emasculation. In *Freud, Race and Gender,* Gilman discusses how the use of language, and especially slang terms in Viennese culture, associated the circumcised penis with a woman's clitoris, thus stigmatizing the Jewish male as effeminate both in character and body:

> This is reflected in the popular fin de siècle Viennese view of the relationship between the body of the male Jew and the body of the woman. The clitoris was known in Viennese slang of the time simply as the "Jew" (Jud). The phrase for female masturbation was "playing with the Jew." The "small organ" of the woman became the *pars pro toto* for the Jew with his circumcised organ. This pejorative synthesis of both bodies because of their "defensive" sexual organs reflected the fin de siècle Viennese definition of the essential male as the antithesis of the female and the Jewish male. (1993, 39)

As misogynistic imagery informed the popular perceptions of female genitalia as inadequate and deformed, the attribution of a shared physiology between Jewish males and women reinforced the notion that ritual circumcision, in its "feminization" of the phallus, represented the continued marginalization and powerlessness of the Jewish male in European culture. As such, Jewish ritual perpetuated a tradition that reinscribed the physiological manifestation of Jewish otherness. In this regard, the ritual itself would seem to be important for Freud's construction of the Oedipal crisis, as it is the father who brings the infant son to the male-centered rite of Jewish circumcision.[1] The patriarchal figure thus becomes identified with this ritualized ceremony that physically as well as symbolically signifies the Jewish male's convenant with God.

If we consider the underlying cultural referents and beliefs that informed Freud's developing consciousness and ultimately his scientific stance, it is possible to read his theories of female inferiority and fear of castration as narratives of danger that haunted the unconscious of the assimilated Jewish male, particularly as the phallus became the primary site of Jewishness in a culture where the Jew might have "passed" had his body not betrayed him. In reading Freud's texts on castration, one cannot help but be struck by the language of disdain and repulsion that Freud invokes when describing the boy child's reaction to the sight of female genitalia:

> It is not until later, when some threat of castration has obtained a hold upon him, that the observation becomes important to him: if he then recollects or repeats it, it arouses a terrible storm of emotion in him and forces him to believe in the reality of the threat which he has hitherto laughed at. This combination of circumstances leads to two reactions, which may become fixed and will in that case, whether separately or together or in conjunction with other factors, permanently determine the boy's relations to women: horror of the mutilated creature or triumphant contempt for her. (*SE*: 19: 252)

As Freud describes this pivotal unconscious transformation, the boy child's reaction to the female body takes on the quality of a nightmarish-like experience, as the image of the female genitals creates a sense of horror and fear in the male child, who envisions the female as a "mutilated creature." From the perspective of internalized anti-Semitism, Freud's fear of castration might then be better understood as fear of mutilation, a deep-seated fear that for Freud would be grounded not in an acultural or ahistorical primal fantasy of castration but in the reality of ritual circumcision that had left his own genitals "mutilated" and feminized.

Freud elaborates the theory of castration anxiety in the case of Little Hans, explaining that the female body represents a threatening possibility for the Jewish male child whose penis has already been scarred. As the illustrative case study of castration anxiety, Little Hans has been the subject of numerous analyses of the relationship between Freud's Jewish identity and the development of his psychoanalytic theory (Geller 1992, 1999; Gilman 1993). As Jay Geller (1999) significantly points out, Little Hans was in fact Herbert Graf, the son of Max Graf, a Jewish colleague of Freud's. Hans (Herbert), was therefore a Jewish child whose own genitals had been "wounded" prior to that frightening moment when he became aware of the scarred female body that brought to consciousness the fear that he might be "made into a woman" (*SE* 10: 36). Although Freud does not identify Little Hans as a circumcised Jewish male, scholars have made much of the footnote to this case study in which Freud locates the shared roots of misogyny and anti-Semitism in the unconscious fear of castration that informed the psychosexual development of Christian masculinity:

> The castration complex is the deepest root of anti-Semitism, for even in the nursery little boys hear that a Jew has something cut off his penis—a piece of his penis, they think—and this gives them the right to despise Jews. And there is no stronger unconscious root for the sense of superiority over women. (*SE* 10: 36)

In reality, Little Hans, like Freud, was a Jew who had "something cut off his penis." Thus, while he may not yet have been made into the despised female, he already understands that his circumcised genitals are a source of danger in an anti-Semitic and male-centered world.

Freud's analysis of anti-Semitism, male dominance, and the castration complex brings him closer to an appreciation of the significance of race and gender for the developing self. Yet he fails to take this analysis far enough. Rather than interrogating the effects of internalized racism and sexism on the developing male psyche, Freud put forward a theory that, according to Roith (1987), projected his own fears of Jewish otherness on to women. The result of this unconscious process was the creation of a scientific approach that underscored his identification with the aggressor (the anti-Semitic Christian world), thereby assuring his acceptance in a male scientific community where biological theories of female inferiority prevailed. In locating "the problem of femininity" in the deformed female genitalia, Freud provided an additional and pivotal link between female bodily inferiority and female moral, intellectual, and social deficiency. Maintaining that the absence of castration anxiety leads to the formation of a weak superego in women, Freud provided a rationale for male dominance that reinforced and gave legitimacy to sexist scientific and social ideologies:

> I cannot evade the notion (though I hesitate to give it expression) that for women the level of what is ethically normal is different from what it is in men. Their super-ego is never so inexorable, so impersonal, so independent of its emotional origins as we require it to be in men. Character traits which critics of every epoch have brought against women—they show less sense of justice than men, that they are less ready to submit to the great exigencies of life, that they are more influenced in their judgments by feelings of affection or hostility—all these would amply be accounted for by the modification in the formation of their super-ego which we have inferred above. (*SE* 19: 257–58)

If Freud's texts on men can be read as narratives of genital danger, then Freud's texts on women may be read as narratives of genital hatred borne out of the Jewish male's fear of otherness. This aspect of Freudian psychoanalysis is perhaps most evident in his writings on women and shame that formed the basis for a 1932 essay:

> Shame, which is considered to be a feminine characteristic *par excellence* but is far more a matter of convention that night be supposed, has as its purpose, we believe, concealment of genital deficiency. We are not forgetting that at a later time shame takes on other functions. It seems that women have made few contributions to the discoveries and inventions in the history of civilization; there is, however, one technique which they may have invented—that of plaiting and weaving. If that is so, we should be tempted to guess the unconscious motive the achievement. Nature herself would seem to have given the model which this achievement imitates by causing the growth at maturity of the pubic hair that conceals the genitals. (*SE* 22: 132)

By implication, Freud suggests that men have no such unconscious motive, that their genitalia, rather than a source of shame, are a source of pride and perhaps even prestige. Yet such claims to wholeness and physical integrity could not be made by Freud (or other Jewish men) whose circumcised body occupied a transitional psychic space between female and male, Jew and non-Jew, powerless and powerful. Referring once again to Mantegazza's description of circumcision as "shame and infamy," it is clear that the Jewish male body was associated with the shamefulness that Freud so strongly attributed to female physiology.

If we accept that the case of Little Hans is, in fact, a window into Freud's unconscious, then Freud's greatest fear would also be his greatest shame, as he saw the reflection of his own mutilation in the "horrific" image of the inferior female body. To defend against such fears and the attending deep wound to the ego that this anxiety would arouse, Freud "cut off" an intrapsychic part of himself, that which was Jewish and feminized, casting these fears and emotions onto the universal woman over whom he could remain dominant and superior. It is perhaps more than coincidence that Freud once used the terms "horror" and "shame" to describe a group of Jewish mourners who had humiliated him in front of his Christian colleagues (Klein 1985) . If language is indeed a key to the unconscious, then Freud's description of the Jewish mourners reveals that both the Jew and the female invoked a sense of horror and shame within the psyche of the colonized Jewish male.

Conclusion

The goal of this essay has to been to encourage the teaching of Freud from a feminist perspective that problematizes the role that race and ethnicity play in the construction of male-centered scientific theory. This approach helps to elucidate the ways in which gender intersects with race in the developing persona and intellectualism of the marginalized male scientist. Teaching Freud from this standpoint helps students to understand the biases inherent in the production of knowledge and the role that domination plays in the creation of scientific paradigms. In order to explore the ways in which social and political forces inform the development of scientific thought, I have suggested that scholars engage students in a speculative psychologizing of Freud, making his inner psychic life the subject of critical examination. Situating Freud's unconscious within the historical and cultural realities of turn-of-the-century Europe allows us to imagine and recognize the effects of prejudice and privilege on the developing scientific mind. As we seek to create a classroom environment where multiple truths are considered, studying the controversial and challenging aspects of Freud offers exciting possibilities for establishing a climate of critical thinking and intellectual resistance in the academy.

Notes

1. The traditional religious ceremony in which circumcision takes place is performed eight days after the birth of a male. The rite is typically performed by a trained

male ritualist who circumcises the child in the presence of the father. In biblical times, it was the father's obligation to circumcise his son.

References

Boyarin, Daniel. 1994. Epater l'embourgeoisement: Freud, gender and the decolonized psyche. *Diacritics* 24: 17–41.
De Beauvoir, Simone. 1952. *The second sex.* New York: Vintage Books.
Fanon, Frantz. 1967. *Black skin: White masks.* New York: Grove Weidenfeld.
Flax, Jane. 1990. *Thinking fragments: Psychoanalysis, feminism and postmodernism in the contemporary west.* Berkeley: University of California Press.
Freud, Sigmund. 1953–1974. The standard edition of the complete psychological works of Sigmund Freud (*SE*), Volumes 1–24, translated and edited by James Strachey. London: Hogarth Press.
    1909. *SE*:10. Analysis of a phobia in a five year old boy: 5–149.
    1925. *SE* 19. Some psychical consequences of the anatomical distinchion between the sexes. 243–58.
    1932. *SE*: 22. Femininity. 112–35.
Geller, Jay. 1992 "A glance at the nose": Freud's inscription of Jewish difference. *American imago* 49, no. 4: 427–444.
Geller, Jay. 1999. The godfather of psychoanalysis: Circumcision, antisemitism, homosexuality, and Freud's "fighting jew." *Journal of the American Academy of Religion* 67, no. 2: 355–85.
Gilman, Sander. 1986. *Jewish self-hatred: Anti-Semitism and the hidden language of the Jews.* Baltimore: Johns Hopkins University Press.
———. 1993. *Freud, race and gender.* Princeton: Princeton University Press.
Harding, Sandra, and Jean F. O'Barr, eds. 1987. *Sex and scientific inquiry.* Chicago: University of Chicago Press.
Harding, Sandra. 1987. The instability of the analytical categories of feminist theory. In *Sex and Scientific Inquiry,* edited by Sandra Harding and Jean F. O'Barr. Chicago: University of Chicago Press.
Horney, Karen. 1967. [1926] The flight from womanhood: The masculinity complex in women as viewed by men and by women. In *Feminine psychology,* edited by Harold Kelman. New York: Norton.
Jaher, Frederic. 1994. *A scapegoat in the new wilderness: The origins and rise of anti-Semitism in America.* Cambridge, Mass.: Harvard University Press.
Keller, Evelyn Fox. 1987. Feminism and science. In *Sex and scientific inquiry,* edited by Sandra Harding and Jean F. O'Barr. Chicago: University of Chicago Press.
Klein, Dennis. 1985. *Jewish origins of the psychoanalytic movement.* Chicago: University of Chicago Press.
Piaget, Jean. 1972. *The child's conception of the world.* Totowa, N.J.: Littlefield, Adams.
Reinharz, Shulamit. 1992. *Feminist methods in social science research.* New York: Oxford University Press.
Roith, Estelle. 1987. *The riddle of Freud: Jewish influences on his theory of female sexuality.* London: Tavistock Publications.

10

Why Do We Have to Read Freud?

Carol Delaney

"Why do we have to read Freud?" my students at Stanford groan when they notice an assignment on Freud. The question is asked in a tone reminiscent of children's "Do I *have* to eat my spinach?" The assignment is seen as a chore to be gotten through rather than an intellectual adventure. This is a far cry from my own first reading of Freud in an academic context. Then it seemed almost clandestine, as reading Nietzsche was, and evoked a feeling of excitement, as if, finally, we were about to taste the forbidden fruit. Nothing of that aura remains. By a process of social osmosis students today seem to have absorbed a fairly pervasive view that Freud's theories are either wrong or outdated and of no practical use in their world. The first task, therefore, is to convince them both of the importance of reading Freud and of his continuing relevance.

Even though students resist reading Freud, they unselfconsciously use many of his concepts—the notion of the unconscious and repression, the Oedipus complex, the Freudian slip, the superego, to name only a few. In discussion sections, the students also respond to a number of cartoons and jokes that demand some knowledge of Freudian theory. At least some of his concepts and theory have clearly entered the cultural mainstream. Indeed, I suggest that it would be difficult to understand twentieth-century Western notions of self and society without knowing something about Freud.

Although I teach Freud in a number of courses, both undergraduate and graduate, in this paper I will focus primarily on both the pedagogy and experience of teaching Freud, specifically *Moses and Monotheism*, in the fall quarter of the Anthropology track of Stanford's much-debated CIV (Cultures, Ideas, and Values) program.[1]

I also teach Freud in a course called Symbolic Anthropology. In the graduate version of that course, I teach his theory of the "interpretation of dreams" using his book by that title, and in the undergraduate version of the course I use his shorter book *On Dreams*, along with his work on the origins of jokes and what have become known as "Freudian slips." The section on Freud in the Symbolic Anthropology courses follows a section on surrealism and precedes one on Saussure's theory of language and the origins of structuralism—all imagined as important contributions to the development of the symbolic turn in anthropology that flowered in the 1970s and 1980s.

The Anthropology CIV track at Stanford

In the early 1990s the fall-quarter segment of the Anthropology CIV track was called Origins: Prehistory, Myth, and Civilization; it was followed by Encounters (winter quarter) and Identities (spring quarter). There were approximately 150 students and two lectures every week; these were followed each time by a discussion section, each consisting of fifteen students, lasting an hour and three-quarters. In the fall we considered the origins of humans, of writing, of agriculture, and of civilization.[2] When I taught the course, I focused on the ancient Near East, but another professor focused instead on the New World. My intention, arrived at in collaboration with the discussion group leaders, was to present these origins not so much as positive knowledge accumulated fact by fact over time but as the precipitates of changing debates and theories.

The most important pedagogical point, we felt, was to introduce freshmen to the idea that facts, and thus our knowledge, are intimately related to *theory*—in this case theory about origins. To this end, we ranged a number of different narratives about origins that had been influential in the West. Students read Genesis alongside Darwin's *Origin of Species* and Freud's *Moses and Monotheism*. Darwin discussed the natural origin of species from simple to more complex, as well as the differentiation into different species. But he did not have much to say about society, about its social institutions, and especially about specific cultures and their differences. Freud's birth in 1856 preceded the publication of *Origin of Species* (1859) by only a couple of years. Like many nineteenth-century theorists, he, too, was interested in origins, specifically the origins of human society. Expanding upon his work with individuals, he constructed a theory about the origin of society, human psychology, and religion that has its foundation in the Oedipus complex. Neither Freud's origin myth nor Darwin's theory of origins recapitulates Genesis, the predominant origin myth in the West. At the same time, because Genesis has had such an enormous impact on the Western worldview, I believe it has subtly influenced notions of origins even as they are secularized. In our study of Genesis, I was not concerned about whether it accurately portrays the real true origins of ancient Near Eastern culture. Rather, as a cultural anthropologist, I was concerned with the way in which these origins are *represented*. Representations of origins affect our notions of who we are and how we got to be who we are. The link with the quarter on Identities is obvious. The question of origins, however, also prefigures the encounter with other peoples. That is, how do we in the West, whose primary origin myth was Genesis, encounter peoples whose origin stories were significantly different? I stressed that when I speak of myth I do not mean a "just so" story, a kind of fairy tale or false tale. Nor do I believe myths are relegated to, and part of, a particular period in human history: the notion that myth was followed by religion and finally by science is part of the evolutionary viewpoint that Freud and many nineteenth-century theorists subscribed to. I suggest, instead, that we live by myths, that they ground and orient us in the world.

By juxtaposing such unlikely texts, students noticed some of the shared assumptions and concepts; they also noticed more clearly the points of divergence and difference. Although all peoples have myths of origin, not all of them are myths of "creation." For example, some stories of origin recount emergence from underground without specifying where the ground came from; others imagine a continual oscillation between coming-into-being and going-out-of-being. These other forms of origins bring several questions into focus: How does a myth of creation affect notions of time and history? Does it automatically imply a creator?

In addition to the primary texts, we included work by nineteenth-century archeologists, travelers, and social evolutionists, and more critical work by twentieth-century linguists, biologists, and anthropologists. Freud's *Moses and Monotheism* was situated between a reading of Genesis and a study of nineteenth-century theorists of human cultural origins such as Morgan, Bachofen, and Tylor—men who are generally taken as the ancestors of modern anthropology. Freud shared many of the assumptions of these theorists. His cultural works, although published in the twentieth century, have much more affinity with nineteenth-century thought about the origins of society and culture than they do with twentieth-century anthropology. This briefly outlines the structure of the course and some of its underlying premises.

Freud in the Anthropology CIV Track

Moses and Monotheism may seem like an odd text to chose to introduce students, particularly freshmen, to Freud. However, in the design and context of the course, it makes a great deal of sense. I do not subscribe to the view that *Moses and Monotheism* is a rather pitiable text of Freud's waning years, as it has often been described. Nor do I think its primary relevance has to do with his relation either to his Jewishness or to his father, as several scholars have recently argued (e.g., Balmary 1982; Robert 1976; Yerushalmi 1991).

Instead, I find it to be key to his entire corpus (see Delaney 1998) and, thus, extremely useful for alluding to his other work. Although it recapitulates his theory of the origins of society and religion discussed at greater length in *Totem and Taboo*, the story of Moses is much more familiar to most undergraduates than theories of totemism and primitive society. Freud's attempt to construct a theory about the origin of society, religion, and gender is important and worthy of consideration. Afterall, it is not as if these issues have been resolved. However, in order to understand Freud's attempt, it is necessary to situate the writing of *Moses and Monotheism* in its cultural and historical context. In the course I briefly describe fin de siècle Vienna, where Freud grew up and practiced. It was an extremely patriarchal place where theories of gender were hotly debated and caricatured (e.g., by Otto Weininger [1903]; and by Karl Kraus, editor of *Die Fackel*). Debates were comon, for example, over whether genius is by its very nature masculine in character and thus whether the only role for women in the creative process is as muse, inspiration, or nurturing support. Gender was also used metaphorically to characterize race or, as we would say today, ethnicity. In Vienna, the "Aryan" symbolically was male, while the Jew was figured as female. No doubt, these sentiments affected Freud's desire to reinstate the patriarchal character and tough-mindedness of Judaism that is so evident in *Moses and Monotheism*. The period was, also, obviously, one of increasing anti-Semitism.

Freud was writing *Moses and Monotheism*, his last major work, during the years of Hitler's rise to power in Germany and was still at it when the Germans took over Austria. During that time his daughter Anna was taken by the Gestapo and held for questioning; his bank accounts and publishing endeavors were confiscated and his office closed. He remained until the last possible moment and finally, with the help of friends, left for London on June 4, 1938. He died there in 1939, thus missing some of the worst horrors of the war and the deaths of three of his sisters in concentration camps. Would the specific horrors of that war have changed his views about the effect of the advance of civilization on the renunciation of aggressive behavior?

He kept *Moses and Monotheism* a secret because he knew it would make many people—Christians and Jews alike—angry. He finished it in exile in London and lived just long enough to see it published and to hear some of the criticism, an example of which came from an anonymous Bostonian:

> I read in the local press your statement that Moses was not a Jew. It is to be regretted that you could not go to your grave without disgracing yourself, you old nitwit. We have renegades like you by the thousands, we are glad we are rid of them and we hope soon to be rid of you. It is to be regretted that the Gangsters in Germany did not put you into a concentration camp, that's where you belong. (Cited in Gay, 1988, 647)

Many people, including his circle of colleagues and strongest supporters, were embarrassed by *Moses and Monotheism* when it first came out. Some considered it the musings of an old man who was losing his grip. Others have seen it as Freud's way to deal with his relation to his father or to his Jewishness (see above). His own reason—or one of his reasons—as stated in the book was to answer for himself why the Jews were so hated. I think we need to take the book quite seriously (as Freud did). It is the microcosm of his work; in it he recapitulated themes that had been important throughout: (1) the Oedipus complex, (2) the transmission of cultural memory, (3) the correlation between individual and cultural development, (4) the relation of a leader to his followers, and (5) the neurotic element in all religion.

Origins and Patricide

The major thesis of *Moses and Monotheism* is that Judaism repeated, in historical times, the primeval deed (the murder of the primal father) that ushered in society and religion. The foundational power of the original deed was discussed in the earlier book, *Totem and Taboo,* published in 1913. That was his first major foray into cultural analysis; in it he attempted to apply the theory and lessons of individual psychoanalysis to culture and society, arguing that "religious phenomena are to be understood *only* on the model of the neurotic symptoms of the individual" (*SE* 23:58, emphasis mine); in other words, that society is psychology writ large. This is, once again, evidence of his unilineal, evolutionary view of human society. Not only does it assume a universal human psychology, but it also assumes that differences in religion were to be explained, not in relation to differences in culture but in relation to the locations of each culture on the evolutionary ladder. Not unlike Durkheim in his *Elementary Forms of the Religious Life,* Freud also seems to assume that there is some kernel or essence of religion that has persisted throughout time and that it is ultimately psychological in nature. Even today, while it is quite common to believe that there is something almost *sui generis* about religion, this is not the position taken by most cultural anthropologists. While I think most would agree that there is a religious part or aspect to the human person and to human society, the notion of religion as a separate sphere or domain of society (along with economics, politics, family, or kinship) focused on specific things such as "the supernatural," hedged around by specific personnel, rituals, and beliefs, and set apart from everyday life à la Durkheim has become more problematic. Instead, I suggest that this notion about religion is itself a product of a particular kind of society. It did not emerge until the late nineteenth century, and it is still not applicable to many societies (cf. also Smith 1962). Rather than representing different rungs on the evolutionary ladder, different religions or religious beliefs and practices may be relevant to the different cultures and the different myths that each holds up for its people to live by. As Mary Douglas said: "Psychological explanations cannot of their nature account for what is culturally distinctive" (1966, 121).

For Freud there was really only one myth—the Oedipus myth—and he assumed that it was foundational at both individual and social levels: "It is the fate of all of us, perhaps, to direct our first sexual impulse towards our mother and our first hatred and our first murderous wish against our father" (*SE* 4:262). When Freud used the word "us," it is clear he meant males. The theory is developed from the standpoint of the male ego. He continues this bias in his theory of social origins: "The beginnings of religion, ethics, society and art converge in the Oedipus complex. . . . these and the problems of social psychology are soluble on the basis of one single concrete point . . . a man's relation to his father" (*SE* 13:156–57).

Here it is extremely important, pedagogically as well as theoretically, to ask why the "beginnings of religion, society, and ethics and art" might not also be related to a man's relation to his son (or daughter) or to his mother, or to his wife? Beyond that, why should it be *men's* relations not women's that are foundational for the social world—especially since it is women who have done most of the socialization? These are simple questions, they do not demand esoteric knowledge—indeed, they are commonsense. Yet Freud didn't raise them, nor did most of his followers. Freud was not stupid, nor were they; pointing out their neglect, however, can alert students to the way cultural assumptions are simply taken for granted and become embedded in theory. We are not exempt.

Although Freud abandoned the notion of an originary patricidal deed when analyzing individuals, he reverted to it in his theory of society and culture.[3] The origin of Oedipal conflicts at the cultural level were situated not in fantasies, as in individual psychology, but in real, historical events. The origin story Freud tells, first in *Totem and Taboo* and then recapitulates several times in *Moses and Monotheism*, is as follows: Once upon a time there was "a violent and jealous father who keeps all the females for himself and drives away his sons as they grow up. . . . One day the brothers who had been driven out came together, killed and devoured their father, and so made an end of the patriarchal horde." (*SE* 13:141 and repeated *SE* 23:81). In order that the sons not have the same thing repeated on themselves, they formed what Freud considered *the* social contract: (1) they renounced their rights to all of the women hoarded by their father, (2) they began the first communal society based on laws, (3) they set up a taboo on murder, and (4) they began to worship the totem surrogate for the father. "In this way the dead father became stronger than the living one had been. . . . They could attempt in their relation to this surrogate father to allay their burning sense of guilt, to bring about a kind of reconciliation with their father" (*SE* 13:143–4). That, in essence, is Freud's view of the origins of religion, society, and morals. It was a good story and a clever one but it cannot be, and is not, taken seriously by anthropologists (see Malinowski 1927; Wallace 1983). I will briefly outline some problematic assumptions before I turn to what I consider the most serious flaw.

Some Problematic Assumptions

Freud's first assumption is that violence among males is a primary instinct, tied to sexual jealousy, and is heterosexual (the desire to possess all the women). Aggression, however, can be evoked by any number of causes (for example, a threat to one's life or family, fear, jealousy, and at the command of others, as in war and torture). He also seems to have forgotten his insight that polymorphous sexuality was natural, primitive, and universal, and that heterosexuality was a later "achievement." If this is so, why would these primeval men have desired *only* women, and if denied access to them, why wouldn't they have engaged in homosexual acts?

A second assumption is that one primary male could have kept all the women to himself and kept his sons at bay. What would have prevented them from fleeing? Or, if he had helpers, who were they? The sons could also have banded together and joined with the women and overpowered this male. That scenario exists in other Greek myths with which Freud was familiar. Of course, if the father was so threatened by sons, he could simply have killed them at birth, and this too occurs in other Greek myths.

Third, Freud says that the murder of the primal father is the deed that ushered in the origin of society and culture. Regardless of whether it happened only once or innumerable times as Freud later believed (*SE* 23:81), it still marks the transition from savage to fully human. Yet he ignores that getting together for a common purpose, namely the murder, *presupposes* some kind of sociality and language—that is, a *human* society.

Not unlike biblical commentators who assume that ancient peoples practiced child sacrifice, Freud believed that "Cannibal savages that they were, it goes without saying that they devoured their victim as well as killing him" (*SE* 13:142). He simply assumed that primeval people were cannibals. While it is true that a few contemporary primitives have practiced cannibalism, not all have; and it is extremely problematic to argue from a few contemporary examples back to the dawn of civilization.

Most anthropologists also question the notion of a primal patriarchal horde, a notion Freud took from Darwin and Atkinson. Not only is it purely *hypothetical* but it also assumes a facile transfer of animal behavior in explanations of human behavior. Instead, as Marx was first to notice, theory about animals is first taken from observations of humans and then transferred to animals. Isn't it curious, he said, how "Darwin recognized among beasts and plants his English society with its divisions of labor, competition, opening of new markets, 'inventions,' and the Malthusian 'struggle for existence'" (cited in Sahlins 1976, 53)? More important, primatologists have shown that the structure and behavior of primate groups depend on which primate one is talking about.[4]

The Major Flaw: Ignorance of Paternity

The most important question, however, has never even been raised. *How can there be a patriarchal horde without a notion of "father"?* The entire story depends on the assumption of paternity, the ignorance of which is most often attributed to supposedly primitive peoples such as the Trobriand Islanders, Australian aborigines, and a few others. Yet Freud and most other theorists are, also, ignorant of the *meaning* of paternity. Fatherhood is not as self-evident as Freud assumed. Indeed, elsewhere, he says it is the very *discovery* of paternity that marked an advance in civilization:

> A great advance was made in civilization when men decided to put their inferences upon a level with the testimony of the senses and to make the step from matriarchy to patriarchy . . . A witness who testifies to something before a court of law is still called "Zeuge" (literally "begetter") in German, *after the part played by the male in procreation.* (*SE* 10:233, n.1, emphasis mine)

But if the *discovery* of paternity was supposedly the inspiration for the transformation of society and culture, how could such a notion have been present *ab origine*, at the very origins? Therein lies a palpable and very serious contradiction in Freud's thinking.

Without a concept of father there could only have been a primal male in the primal horde, and it is highly unlikely that would have the same emotional resonance. Without the notion of father (i.e., "begetter"), the story and the deed would not make the sense Freud derives from it. Without the notion of father as the one who engendered the sons, the killing of the male head of the horde could not possibly have had the power and meaning Freud attributed to it. The murder would only have been homicide. It might only tell us about male aggression, but it could not have been a patricide—a crime that Freud felt was much more weighty.

Without a notion of father, could the meaning of *son* carry the same valence? If only men are the "begetters," then sons, too, would have that power when they grow up. This could be imagined as a threat to the father's power. But the sons would not have felt a burning sense of guilt about a man they hardly knew and who had treated them so cruelly and then banished them. Yet it is the remorse these sons are supposed to have felt that was so profound that it left a generalized feeling of guilt bequeathed to all subsequent generations. Moreover, the guilt and the totem substitute for the father, after passing through a series of transformations and sublimations, eventually became the great Father God that Freud deals with in *Moses and Monotheism*.

Freud is right, I think, that monotheism is all about fatherhood. In Judaism, with which he is primarily concerned, but also in Christianity and Islam, the *notion* of paternity—its significance for men and the patriarchal order—is extremely important. Yet this is rarely the focus of religious investigation or discussion. In Genesis, for example, one need only recall the recitation of the patrilineages with all the "begats" to realize that the issue of paternity is important. Moreover, the story of Abraham that is foundational for all three "Abrahamic" religions revolves around a male-imaged God, a father and a son. The name Abram meant "exalted father," and Abraham, "father of nations." The shift in his name was also marked on his flesh, not on just any part of the body, but on the very organ thought to be *the* generative organ, namely the penis. The notion of paternity, as we shall see shortly, involved notions of generativity or creativity, notions that symbolically allied men with God. In other words, gender is intimately related to theology and religion, and that is what I try to indicate to students. The primary issue, for me, is not how a religious tradition deals with women and men—what kinds of rules and regulations apply—but rather with how gender is symbolically configured and the ways it is employed theologically.

The Meaning of Paternity

An anthropological perspective on kinship and gender can be extremely useful here. In my lectures I go to some length to explain that paternity is not something *discovered* but a cultural construction. This is extremely difficult for most people to realize, for they assume it is a fact of nature; furthermore, they assume that the word "father" merely reflects that natural fact. It is even more difficult to point out that "mother," too, is a cultural construction. Both are relative to a particular *theory* of procreation—a theory that is neither universal nor even the one most of us subscribe to today. The very notion of paternity construes the male as the "begetter"—that is, the male was (and still is in most contexts) imagined as being the primary procreator, the one who transmits the life and identity and soul of each person. The understanding of paternity was (and is) symbolized by the notion of *seed*. The male "sows" the seed (which carries the life, identity, and soul of each person) into the woman who nurtures it and brings it forth. The word "seed" is used more times in Genesis than elsewhere in the Bible, another indication that generativity is conceptualized as masculine in nature whether by God or by human males. In this view of procreation, the woman is construed as "soil"—the nurturing medium in which the seed can grow but is not imagined as identity giving. This becomes immediately apparent when one thinks about the images evoked by the words "paternity" vs. "maternity" or the phrases "to father something" vs. "to mother something." What it means to be a mother is conditioned by what it means to be a father. It is hardly that "mother" simply represents a natural fact and that paternity and fatherhood were "discovered" when men "put their inferences upon a level with the testimony of the senses." What is "natural" is that babies come out of the bodies of women.[5] How the baby got there, what it is composed of, and how it is related to that woman, let alone anyone else, are all matters of cultural construction. Since I have dealt with this at great length elsewhere I will not belabor it here (see Delaney 1986, 1991, 1998).

The main point here is that this understanding of procreation has for millennia bestowed power and authority on men. Found not just in Genesis but also in Aristotle, in Aquinas, and other religious thinkers, it also seems to have been in Freud's mind despite scientific knowledge that was becoming available to him, namely genetic theory. Genetic theory posits that both male and female contribute the *same* kind of things (genes) via sperm and ovum. The woman, of course, contributes much more by nurturing the fetus to term, by giving birth, and frequently by nursing it and generally being the primary caregiver, but these aspects are usually *the* definition of the woman's role.

Freud, by assuming the male as begetter, as primary parent, simply amplifies the cultural myth rather than analyzing it.

Moses and Monotheism

Freud projected the origin story from *Totem and Taboo* onto a biblical canvas. He thought he could pierce through the accumulated accretions and distortions—"the striking omissions, disturbing repetitions, palpable contradictions" (*SE* 23:43)—and ultimately find traces of the original deed, or rather its repetition. The book reads somewhat like a detective novel, and he notes that "the distortion of a text is not unlike a murder. The difficulty lies not in the execution of the deed but in doing away with the traces" (43). Ironically, *Moses and Monotheism* is, itself, full of "striking omissions, disturbing repetitions, palpable contradictions," and Freud did not cover his tracks well. By using the same technique on him, we can get a glimpse of what he was, perhaps unconsciously, trying to cover up.

Freud felt that the ancient murder was a deed so horrible that it left a powerful impression on the perpetrators—so powerful, in fact, that it left a permanent mark. It became an acquired characteristic of the human race as it passed from barbarity to society. (One might recall that Freud was a Lamarckian.) In *Moses and Monotheism,* he goes on: "The mental residue of those primeval times has become a heritage which, with each new generation, needs only to be awakened." But by actually repeating the primal crime on the person of Moses, the emotional fervor attaching to the original murder was not just reawakened, it was reacquired and reinforced. That is what gives Mosaic monotheism its power, according to Freud.

It is extremely important to remind students, many of whom are not familiar with the biblical story of Moses, that *there is no story in the Bible* that resembles Freud's version. In the Bible, Moses is not murdered, and certainly not by his sons. Because of Freud's prior belief that there is some eternal kernel in all religions and that ultimately they all derive from the Oedipus complex, he constructed a myth on analogy with his version of the Oedipus myth. His interpretation of the Moses story was over-determined. The striking omissions in his version of the Oedipus myth are also worth pointing out. Although Oedipus did kill his father, he didn't know it was his father; although he married his mother, he didn't know, at first, that she was his mother. If there were latent wishes, we do not hear of them. Furthermore, he was an adult, not a child, when he committed these acts. More to the point, however, is the fact that the first murderous wish *in the myth* was the father's (see also Bakan 1979; Devereux 1953); indeed, the wish became the deed. Laius tried to do away with his son Oedipus by piercing his foot with a nail (crucifixion?) and leaving him to die on the hilltop. The paternal deed, not the son's desires, provides, surely, plenty of reason for that particular son to want to get rid of his father. But Freud ignores this potential motivation and instead situates the impetus within the son and from Oedipus to all sons.

In *Moses and Monotheism,* Freud doesn't even claim that it is Moses' sons who do the deed but his symbolic sons, namely his followers. But there again slips one of Freud's main points for the motivation—that the sons want to get rid of the father because of incestuous wishes toward the mother. In the Bible there is no mention of anything remotely like this, nor does Freud even try to make a case for such incestuous wishes, however veiled. But his clever sleight of hand blinded him to the implications for his theory. The theory depends on real, true kinship ties between father and son(s), son(s) and mother. But if the murderous desires can be aroused between symbolic relations, perhaps the Oedipus complex has as much, if not more, to do with power and authority as it has with familial relations and sex. Conceding that would have required Freud to reconsider his entire corpus. While Lacan and some feminists influenced by him have focused on the symbolic, authoritative aspects of fatherhood—"the law of the father"—they have not, in my opinion, resolved the issue. They assert that the phallus symbolizes the law and authority of the father, but they deny that the meanings of the phallus are derived from the physical penis. In contrast, I argue that it is precisely because of the supposed generative role of the penis in the theory of procreation just discussed that the phallus can symbolize the law and *authority* of the father.

Freud's Moses[6]

Freud's basic argument is that Moses was Egyptian and a follower of the Aton monotheistic religion installed by Ikhnaton and that he had hopes of rising in the Egyptian hierarchy. With the early death of Ikhnaton and the destruction of the Aton cult, these dreams were dashed. Freud imagined that Moses had been put in charge of the Jewish people, but with the return to power of Ikhnaton's enemies, he and they were persecuted. This, according to Freud, provided the motive for the exodus. Moses chose them as his people, successfully led them out of Egypt, and tried to reinstitute the Aton religion. While wandering hungry in the desert, these people began to "murmur" and one day rose up against him and killed him. Freud believes the murder was repressed, but as with the murder of the primal father recounted in *Totem and Taboo,* the guilt or remorse after this terrible deed led them to reify, if not deify, Moses and made them adhere even more strictly to his rules. This is the power and the austerity behind Jewish monotheism. It is a good story, but it is rife with "striking omissions, disturbing repetitions, palpable contradictions," just as Freud thought the biblical Moses story was.

Omissions and Distortions

In this section, I will not go over the entire argument but lift out the points that I find problematic with his interpretation. My counterarguments are in italics. Freud's first argument is that Moses was an Egyptian because of his name, which *is* Egyptian. *But just because the name is Egyptian doesn't mean he was Egyptian. If the second Moses (among the Midianites) borrowed his name, as Freud claims, why couldn't Moses in Egypt also have borrowed his name?*

Another feature that makes Freud think of the Egyptian origin of Moses was circumcision, which was practiced by the ancient Egyptians. *However, in the Bible, circumcision is instituted by Abraham, not Moses, and Abraham went down into Egyptian hundreds of years before Moses was born and thus could have introduced the practice to the Egyptians. Freud never even contemplates that. Instead, he blithely discounts the story of Abraham as being too far in the mists of time. This seems very odd, given his use of another myth (the Oedipus myth) to discuss human psychology.*

Because the Moses story contravenes the standard version of the "birth of the hero" myth, Freud takes this as a clue pointing to the distortion of the real story in the biblical text. In the "birth of the hero" myth, as described by Otto Rank, the hero typically is born to nobility but brought up by humble parents and then through various trials resumes his original position. That *is* the Oedipus story. But the biblical Moses is born to humble Levite parents and is brought up in the king's palace and then becomes the savior and leader of the Jewish people. Freud thinks this obscures the "real" picture, which is that rather than coming from the Jewish Levites, he chose them as his people, "his nearest adherents, his scribes, his servants." *Even if that is true, there is a deeper problem. How could Freud have assumed there was a Jewish people or Levites without Judaism? If Moses is the father of Judaism, the one who instituted the religion of Judaism, as Freud claims, then what could being Jewish or Levite have meant prior to the Exodus?*

Why should Freud concentrate on a story about the murder of Moses, *which is not in the text,* and ignore the command of Moses to murder three thousand of his *own* people because of their disobedience? "Thus saith the Lord God of Israel, Put every man his sword by his side, and go in and out from gate to gate throughout the camp, and slay every man his brother, and every man his companion, and every man his neighbor. And the children of Levi did according to the word of Moses; and there fell of the people that day about three thousand men" (Exodus 32:27–28). Why should the murder of Moses be more horrific than their slaughter, so much so that his murder is repressed and distorted, but the murder of thousands at his command remains in the biblical text? The reason seems to be that they had killed their "symbolic" father, the reincarnation of the primal father, and thus the deed was a reenactment of the primal, originary deed. *However, and this is very important: in biblical tradition, Moses is referred to as* rabeynu *(teacher) but never father* (avinu). *That title is reserved for Abraham, whose very name includes the word for "father" and means "the father is exalted" or "exalted father." Second, Moses is not considered to be the one who introduced monotheism. That, too, is attributed to Abraham, which is why all three monotheistic religious traditions return to that foundational story, why they are called the Abrahamic religions.*

Why, indeed, did Freud choose Moses and not Abraham? Why does he fabricate a story of the murder of the "symbolic" father and ignore the story *in* the biblical text of the father who is willing to sacrifice his son?[7] Perhaps Abraham did actually murder his son, as some commentators have asserted, and perhaps *that* is the murder that was repressed. Freud never considers that possibility. Had he done so, he might also have made more sense of Christianity than he did. Not only did he dismiss and distort Jewish tradition, he also did violence to Christian tradition.

Christianity

The murder of Jesus became for Freud not the completion of the suspended sacrifice of Isaac or its repetition (possibilities he easily could have made a case for and which would have accorded more with some forms of traditional exegesis), but instead the expiation of the original crime, namely the murder of the Father.

Freud assumed that among Jews at the time there had been "a growing feeling of guiltiness," both because of their steadfast refusal to admit that they had killed the father God and also because they had become more lax in fulfillment of the law. Their guilt was "a precursor or the return of the repressed material" (*SE* 23:86]. He claimed that Paul rightly traced it to its primeval source and "this he called original sin; it was a crime against God that could be expiated only through death" (86). Original sin was thereby transformed by Freud into murder (of God the Father); he ignored both Jewish and Christian religious tradition, which interpreted it as disobedience. He also failed to take into account a traditional Jewish interpretation of Abraham's deed—that his obedience to God made up for, atoned for, Adam's disobedience. It was, after all, disobedience that caused Moses to call for the murder of his followers. If Freud had asked why obedience was so important, he might have considered its requirement as potential motive for murder. Had he followed the traces of authority and power, he might have been led down a different path.

What I find so surprising in this account is that he ignored tradition altogether and substituted his own psychoanalytic explanation of events. At least in the individual case studies he describes the patient's story; had he employed a similar method in his cultural studies, he would have presented the traditional story and then (psycho)analyzed it, but instead he simply dispensed with it. In his terms, Jesus' death, as an expiation for the original murder, liberates Christians from guilt because his death amounts to their admission that they have killed God (the Father). Christian doctrine, on the contrary, teaches that through Christ's death Christians are liberated from *sin*—his death atones for their sin. Freud has changed the terms from sin to guilt and reduces the significance and meaning Christ's death has for Christians. No wonder they were outraged.

He also blames Jesus for what happened. "That the Redeemer sacrifice himself as an innocent man was an obvious tendentious distortion. . . . [He] could be no one else but the one who was most guilty, the leader of the brother horde who had overpowered the Father" (*SE* 23:87). Freud goes on to say that Christ was either "the heir of an unfulfilled wish-phantasy [or] his successor and his reincarnation" [87]. In other words, he was the son who had usurped the father's place "just as in those dark times every son had longed to do" (88). Christianity, in his view, is the triumph of the sons, the brother-band; it is, according to Freud, a son-religion, whereas Judaism remained a father religion.

Jews could not or would not join the brother-band; they obdurately refused to acknowledge the murder of the father and, instead, compensated ever more persistently by their adherence to the strict regime required by the father. This is Freud's torturous way to explain one of the terrible accusations Christians throughout the centuries have hurled at the Jews—namely that they are "Christ killers." No doubt such accusations were being heard again in Freud's Austria. When Christians say to Jews: "You have killed our God," Freud interprets this to mean not Christ the son but the "archetype of God, the primeval Father and his reincarnations" (90).

Freud's contorted explanation ignored other possibilities that resonate much better with both historical and theological traditions, especially the idea embedded in the Creed—that it was God the Father who sacrificed his only begotten son. He might then have easily interpreted the Crucifixion as a repetition and coming to consciousness of the original repressed murder—that of Abraham's son. If that were too strong, he might have interpreted it as the fulfillment of an original repressed wish. In a very general sense Christians believe that their religion is the culmination of the law and the prophets, the fulfillment of Judaism; more specifically, it is the fulfillment of the promises given to Abraham. He would have been closer to tradition and to the psychological complexes it has bequeathed. The fact that Freud repeatedly and steadfastly avoids the story and figure of Abraham, and any allusion to possible murderous wishes on the part of the Father or fathers, is, I believe, a "striking omission" that deserves considerable attention.

In my own work (1998) I suggest that his "avoidance reaction" is an attempt to protect his notion of the "Great Man"—the one who "can stamp (a) people with its definite character and determine its fate for millennia to come" (*SE* 23:107), as Moses was for Freud. The imago works two ways: projected onto a cosmic frame, it becomes the image of God; constricted to smaller canvas, he is, for each child, his father. He must be obeyed, he arouses jealousy and murderous wishes in the "sons," but his own suppressed violent desires are never scrutinized. For Freud, the Father is beyond question, like God.

Freud and Religion

Moses and Monotheism is, for me, an excellent text to use to illustrate some major points of Freudian theory and expose some of its flaws. But there is another way in which I find the book extremely useful and important. Although not in the way he intended, I believe Freud did actually expose the ligaments of the God concept of the monotheistic religions. The concept is all about the father—not any real fathers, nor anything natural in male nature, but about the reification of the *concept* of paternity. The concept of God is, in my opinion, a denaturalized concept of paternity (pure creativity); conversely, the notion of father is a naturalized divinity. As one Christian theologian has noted: "There is something divine in the father, seeing as there is something fatherly in God" (Quell 1967, 5:965). This also seems pretty close to what Freud said. A major difference between them is that the theologian believes in the reality behind the symbol, whereas Freud believes that if we could but pierce the veil of our projections we would be emancipated from these illusions and live in the bright light of reality.

Because Freud held human psychology to be universal and therefore separate from the cultures that form it, he was prevented, or prevented himself, from perceiving and analyzing different kinship structures and meanings and their interrelation to the cultures in which their significance was/is realized. Thus, he assumes that the concept of God is universal (because he also assumes the Oedipus complex is) and is at the foundation of all religions. He does not imagine that it is neither universal nor necessary for religious beliefs. More important but also springing from the assumptions of universality, he does not analyze the concept of "father" or paternity. For him it is a natural fact, although one *discovered* at a particular point in time, and one that carries with it a natural *author*ity. Had he analyzed the meaning of "father," he might have realized that the concept of paternity or fatherhood is relative to a particular theory of procreation, one that we no longer hold true even as we perpetuate it in nonscientific contexts. At the very least, however, he might have realized that the meaning of "son" is relative to "father" and that there is an interpersonal dynamic that demands as much focus on the father's motives as of the son's, and the way that authority and obedience figure in this dynamic.

I think there were also personal, maybe even unconscious, reasons that he did not investigate the meaning of paternity: perhaps he wanted to shore up, uphold, affirm the power and authority of the father, of all fathers, perhaps out of his own guilt for his father or out of fear of losing his "symbolic" position as "father" of the new intellectual movement so hard fought for and threatened from many sides.

My concern, however, is not to psychoanalyze Freud but to demonstrate what an anthropological and gendered perspective can contribute to analysis of his work and, perhaps most important, to whet students' appetites for this kind of detective work. It would be inaccurate to claim that my analysis of Freud and his view of religion is *the* anthropological perspective (as if there is just one); it is my own position influenced by the study of religion at divinity school, anthropological study at the doctoral level, and by a feminist perspective on gender.

While society, religion, and morals may not be rooted in the Oedipus complex, Freud helps us to realize that they are inextricably intwined with gender, and for this reason alone, the study of Freud is valuable in the university.

Notes

1. The CIV program, a transformation of the Western Civilization course for freshmen, was instituted, over much debate on campus and in the national press, in 1988. There were about ten tracks organized by different departments with different agendas and syllabi; however, there was also a list of texts from which each track was required to select a certain number. The CIV courses were replaced by the I-Hum (Introduction to the Humanities) program in 1997, although a couple of CIV tracks ran through 1998. In the I-Hum program the second two quarters are pretty much the same as in CIV, but the first quarter is devoted to a close reading of only three or four texts. If I teach in one of the new tracks, I might still teach *Moses and Monotheism,* and for the same reasons.

2. The actual course description: This course explores how human culture, language, and civilization have arisen, interact with, and complement our biological selves; how peoples have understood and preserved insights from their past; how they have interacted in the contexts of imperial and colonial expansion; and how they have understood humankind and their place, individually and collectively within the cosmos.

3. The "originary deed" in his theory of individual neurosis was most often father-daughter incest—that is, he had at first assumed there was an actual event that triggered the neurosis. Later, he abandoned this belief and proposed instead that the incestuous desires were part of the daughter's psychology. This part of Freud's theory has received a great deal of attention from feminist scholars who have shown that there seems to be evidence that there were actual acts of incest and further that the psychological explanation made many analysts ignore the incidence of such sexual abuse (e.g., Herman and Hirschman 1981; McKinnon 1995).

4. Anthropologist Alfred Kroeber first critiqued Freud's assumption: "It is a mere guess that the earliest organization of man resembles that of the gorilla rather than that of trooping monkeys" (1952, 302]. The work of Dian Fossey (1983) on gorilla behavior and more recent studies of the Bonobo chimpanzees raise series challenges to that assumption, as does Donna Haraway's (1989) critique of primatology.

5. It is also interesting to point out how, in the story of Adam and Eve, the woman is taken out of the male body—an obvious reversal of the empirical facts open to observation. Was this perhaps a way to express their belief that the male was *the* primary parent?

6. This is, of course, a reference to Yerushalmi's 1991 book by the same title.

7. Freud first got the idea that Moses had been murdered from biblical scholar Ernst Sellin but elaborated it to fit the Oedipal schema, only this time it is symbolic sons and a symbolic father. Still, the kinship definitions are necessary from Freud's interpretation; otherwise it would simply be men killing a man.

References

Bakan, David. 1979. *And they took themselves wives: The emergence of patriarchy in western civilization.* San Francisco: Harper& Row.

Balmary, Marie. 1982. *Psychoanalyzing psychoanalysis: Freud and the the hidden fault of the father.* Translated by Ned Lukacher. Baltimore: Johns Hopkins University Press.

Delaney, Carol. 1986. The meaning of paternity and the virgin birth debate. *Man: Journal of the Royal Anthropological Institute of Ireland and Great Britain* 21, no. 3: 494–513.

———. 1991. *The seed and the soil: Gender and cosmology in Turkish village society.* Berkeley: University of California Press.

———. 1998. *Abraham on trial: The social legacy of biblical myth.* Princeton, N.J.: Princeton University Press.

Devereux, Georges. 1953. Why Oedipus killed Laius. *International Journal of Psychoanalysis* 34:134–141.

Douglas, Mary. 1966. *Purity and danger.* London: Routledge and Kegan Paul.

Fossey, Dian. 1983. *Gorillas in the mist.* Boston: Houghton Mifflin.

Freud, Sigmund. 1953–1974. *The standard edition of the complete psychological works of Sigmund Freud (SE).* Edited by James Strachey. 24 vols. London: Hogarth Press.

   1900. Interpretation of dreams. *SE* 4–5: 1–627.

   1909. Notes upon a case of obsessive neurosis. *SE* 10. pps. 5–249.

   1913. *Totem and taboo. SE* 13. Pps. 1–161.

   1939. *Moses and monotheism. SE* 23. Pps. 7–137.

Gay, Peter. 1988. *Freud: A life for our time.* New York: Norton.

Haraway, Donna. 1989 *Primate visions: Gender, race, and nature in the world of modern science.* New York: Routledge.

Herman, Judith, with Lisa Hirschman. 1981. *Father-daughter incest.* Cambridge, Mass.: Harvard University Press.

Krober, Alfred L. 1920. Totem and taboo: An ethnologic psychoanlaysis. 1920. In *The nature of culture.* Berkeley: University of California Press.

———. 1939 [1952]. Totem and taboo in retrospect. In *The nature of culture.* Berkeley: University of California Press.

Lacan, Jacques. 1985. *Feminine sexuality.* Edited by Juliet Mitchell and Jacqueline Rose. New York: Norton and Pantheon Books.

Malinowski, Bronislaw. 1927. *Sex and repression in savage society.* Chicago: University of Chicago Press.

McKinnon, Susan 1995. American kinship/American incest: Asymmetries in a scientific discourse. *Naturalizing power: Essays in feminist cultural analysis.* Edited by Sylvia Yanagisako and Carol Delaney. New York: Routledge.

Quell, G. 1967. Entry on "pater" in the Old Testament. In *Theological dictionary of the New Testament.* Edited by Geoffrey W. Bromiley. Grand Rapids: William B. Eerdmans Publishers.

Robert, Marthe. 1976. *From Oedipus to Moses.* Garden City, N.Y.: Anchor Books.

Sahlins, Marshall. 1976. *Culture and practical reason.* Chicago: University of Chicago Press.

Smith, Wilfred Cantwell (1962) *The Meaning and End of Religion.* NY: Mentor Books.

Wallace, Edwin R. 1983. *Freud and anthropology: A history and reappraisal.* New York: International Universities Press.

Weininger, Otto. [1903] 1906. *Sex and character.* New York: Putnam.

Yerushalmi, Yosef. 1991. *Freud's Moses: Judaism terminable and interminable.* New Haven, Conn.: Yale University Press.

Teaching Freud in Religion and Culture Courses: A Dialogical Approach

Mary Ellen Ross

Those of us who teach undergraduate classes on religion are engaged in an exceedingly complex enterprise, and the introduction of psychoanalytic frameworks into our courses does little to diminish the complexity. How, after all, are we to do justice to the depth and richness of religious phenomena—symbols, rituals, languages—while at the same time introducing students in a rigorous fashion to psychoanalysis and the ways in which we might draw on and develop this tradition to help explain or clarify religious beliefs and practices? The task is made no easier by the fact that students bring with them many misperceptions about religion and equally fuzzy notions (often quite negative ones) about psychoanalysis. But we needn't despair. My own strategy at a liberal arts institution has been to approach the materials in a largely conversational manner, one that allows upper-division undergraduates (even those who are at first quite resistant) an important role in a discovery of the richness of both the religious and the psychoanalytic materials. Though I begin the class with an introduction to Freud's hermeneutics and his notion of the unconscious, the majority of the assignments are designed to have students approach the psychoanalytic study of religion through Freud's cultural texts.

Freud's Cultural Texts

Freud was an interpreter of culture as much as he was of the individual; indeed, he saw the two as radically interdependent. Freud's *Civilization and Its*

Discontents, first published in 1930, is merely the best known of a series of works that Freud devoted to the psychoanalytic investigation of culture and, as we shall see, of religion in relation to both society and the individual. The other major texts in this tradition were his *Totem and Taboo* (1912–13), *The Future of an Illusion* (1927), and *Moses and Monotheism* (1939). These works make three things clear: (1) Freud viewed culture as a necessary bulwark against nature—a bulwark that demanded immense sacrifice (especially the renunciation of desires) on the part of individuals; (2) Freud viewed the critique of religion as central to his analysis of culture as a whole; and (3) Freud turned to unconscious forces and mechanisms of repression to explain many facets of human behavior, including religion. Peter Gay's magisterial biography *Freud: A Life for Our Time* illuminates these essays by Freud in the context of his life and work as a whole. In addition, several recent studies have focused with particular emphasis on Freud's interpretation of culture. Both Paul Roazen's *Sigmund Freud: Political and Social Thought* (1968) and William J. McGrath's *Freud's Discovery of Psychoanalysis* (1986) offer useful introductions to Freud's social and cultural thought, as does Robert A. Paul's "Freud's Anthropology: A Reading of the Cultural Books" (1991). However, from the vantage point of religious studies, the best short introductions remain J. Samuel Preus's chapter on Freud in his *Explaining Religion: Criticism and Theory from Bodin to Freud* (1987) and the pertinent sections in David M. Wulff's excellent *Psychology of Religion: Classic and Contemporary* (1997). Peter Homans provides a compelling argument that Freud's project was fundamentally a social scientific interpretation of culture in his *The Ability to Mourn: Disillusionment and the Social Origins of Psychoanalysis* (1989); James J. DiCenso offers a fresh reading of Freud's cultural texts and theories of religion from a postmodern context, with particular attention to Jacques Lacan and Julia Kristeva, in his *The Other Freud: Religion, Culture, and Psychoanalysis* (1999); while William Meissner, *Psychoanalysis and Religious Experience* (1984), remains an important introduction to the field. Teachers of courses on Freud's theories of religion will find Homans and DiCenso especially valuable, since both develop rigorous analyses of Freud's enduring fascination with religion as a salient part of human culture.

Teaching Freud's cultural texts also requires some discussion early in the semester to frame the concept of culture itself. As a starting point, students might explore Clifford Geertz's essays: "The Impact of the Concept of Culture on the Concept of Man" and "Religion as a Cultural System," both in his *The Interpretation of Cultures* (1973). Although Geertz himself tended to assume culture as a unity or as something that is shared without contestation, his essays nonetheless open up a series of insights about the power of cultural symbols and beliefs to shape individual and collective behavior. For more recent approaches to culture, instructors will find much of value in James Clifford and George E. Marcus, eds., *Writing Culture: The Poetics and Politics of Ethnography* (1986), in which the contributors stress elements of tension, disagreement, and political practices that make it difficult to view any culture as a uniform set of beliefs and values. Finally, while Freud's own work can now be read as itself guilty of overgeneralized notions of culture, in general students come to see that the psychoanalytic method fits well with the recent emphasis on contestation, since it enables analyses that mediate between collective and individual experience.

Framing the Course: Freud's Hermeneutics

Since a basic understanding of the Freudian hermeneutics is essential to the understanding of psychoanalytic interpretations of cultural formations, and particularly important in the analysis of religion, it is useful to begin the class with a consideration of Freud's interpretative strategies. The primary text here is *The Interpretation of Dreams* (*SE* 4, 5). While individual teachers will each have their favorite passages, it is useful to assign part II, "The Method of Interpreting Dreams: An Analysis of a Specimen Dream"; part II, "A Dream Is the Fulfilment of a Wish"; and part VI, "The Dream-Work," on Freud's method in addition to assigning specific dreams, such as the Count Thun dream or the Rome dreams, the careful study of which enables students to see dream symbols as symptoms of hidden psychical structures. At the very least the class needs to be introduced to Freud's theory that every dream "is the fulfillment of a wish," and at the same time, understand his view that such wishes are usually masked or distorted by the dream work itself (either through condensation or displacement).

I begin with Freud's theories of dreams and their relation to the unconscious because this argument is relatively familiar. This discussion, therefore, offers students a first opportunity to explore Freud's theory of the unconscious, and eventually helps them extend Freud's insights about the importance of latent forces and tensions for both individuals and cultures, with the goal of clarifying Freud's perspective that religious beliefs and practices—much like dreams—also have a content, even if this content or meaning is (generally) unknown to believers. To deepen an appreciation of these ideas, students may find it useful to read Freud's own discussion of the notion of the unconscious in such works as his *The Ego and the Id* (*SE* 19) or to examine the concept indirectly under the entry "The Unconscious" in Laplanche and Pontilis, *The Language of Psycho-Analysis* (1983). That there is a collective unconscious operating in culture as a whole is, of course, a difficult step in Freud's psychoanalytic theory of culture, though this is a topic on which Preus's *Explaining Religion* is especially lucid.

Nonetheless, Paul Ricoeur's *Freud and Philosophy* (1974) remains the best single introduction to Freudian hermeneutics, with undergraduate students benefiting in particular from the distinction Ricoeur developed between a "hermeneutics of suspicion" and a "hermeneutics of retrieval." Yet the status of Freud's method is much contested. On the one hand, several scholars have emphasized the interpretative power of Freud's method; see especially Erik Erikson's "The Dream Specimen of Psychoanalysis" (1954) and Eva M. Rosenfeld, "Dream and Vision: Some Remarks on Freud's Egyptian Bird

Dream" (1956). On the other, there is a growing body of literature that has called Freud's dream interpretation and his method in general into question, on both philosophical and epistemological grounds; see especially Frank J. Sulloway, *Freud, Biologist of the Mind: Beyond the Psychoanalytic Legend* (1979), and the collection of essays edited by Frederick Crews in his *Unauthorized Freud: Doubters Confront a Legend* (1998). For a far more balanced critique, see Jonathan Lear, *Open Minded: Working Out the Logic of the Soul* (1998).

But there is an additional pedagogical benefit to introducing Freudian hermeneutics and the study of dreams at this stage. I have found it beneficial to have students keep a dream journal while taking this class. I return to the exact nature of this assignment below, but it is quite clear that making the analysis of dreams a component of the student's work can only deepen his or her sense both of the richness of symbols and the explanatory force of the unconscious—a kind of sixth sense that is desirable in the religious interpretation of culture.

Approaching Freud and Religion Dialogically

The defining feature of my approach is the dialogical structure of the course—that is, I set each of Freud's cultural texts alongside other important works that interpret religious phenomena from decidedly different perspectives. This tactic has several advantages. After all, many forces in American popular culture make the teaching of Freud a difficult challenge. The cinema and novels have reduced many of Freud's better-known ideas to clichés; the press frequently assails his theories as either demonstrably false or somehow quaintly outmoded; academic trends, both inside and outside of psychoanalysis, have found new gurus; perhaps most damning of all, contemporary university culture has made it easy for students, as Mark Edmundson has recently written, to view even some of Freud's most critical ideas as "interesting," even "entertaining," but ultimately irrelevant. Those of us who love to read Freud and who take his ideas seriously, therefore, must keep in mind that, at the undergraduate level especially, we confront an array of cultural misunderstandings of the very subject we teach.

The dialogical approach helps overcome many of these misperceptions. First, it roots Freud's texts in a larger cultural dialogue about the nature of culture and religion. Students learn, that is, that while Freud's own approach had many distinctive elements, it was and remains part of a larger discussion in the humanities and social sciences about the nature of the religious life. Second, the pairings make it possible for students to develop a language that can help them evaluate Freud intelligently—to see, that is, both the limits and the advantages of his and other psychoanalytic or social-scientific approaches. Finally, this approach invites, even encourages students to become active participants in the ongoing conversation about religion and culture. As Richard Miller, Laurie Patton, and Stephen Webb have recently emphasized, a rhetorical approach (what I here call a "dialogical approach") "provide[s] a space for practicing critical skills and reflective inquiry about matters of personal and public importance" (1994, 820).

Religion as a Social Fact: Freud and Durkheim

Totem and Taboo (*SE* 13) was Freud's first major cultural interpretation of religion—a work that, at its core, was a highly imaginative narrative of the passage from barbarism to civilization. As I have discovered, the narrative Freud develops in this work—beginning with the primal crime: the sons' killing of the father of the primal horde and their eventual "resurrecting" the father in the form of the clan totemic animal—at first strikes most undergraduate students as patently absurd. Yet it is hardly surprising that Freud was attracted to the study of totemism. From the late 1800s on, especially in the field of anthropology, the phenomenon had struck many students of human culture as an essential element in the quest to understand the origins of civilization. The totem (usually a sacred animal or plant around which tribal life was organized) was widespread, as the noted anthropologist Andrew Lang emphasized in his learned entry on this subject in the 1911 edition of the *Encyclopaedia Brittanica*. Freud's own interest in this subject was peaked by his reading of Sir James Frazer's *Totemism and Exogamy* (1910), a work that was to offer Freud much of the evidence he needed for the arguments he developed in *Totem and Taboo*. Teachers will find an excellent analysis of the context in which Freud developed his ideas in Edwin R. Wallace, *Freud and Anthropology: A History and Reappraisal* (1983). By contrast, James J. DiCenso's article "*Totem and Taboo* and the Constitutive Function of Symbolic Forms" (1996) highlights strategies for reading Freud's essay in relation to the psychocultural function of symbols.

Students should approach *Totem and Taboo* in tandem with some study of Freud's theory of the Oedipus complex, which must be introduced early in the course in any case. As is well known, Freud believed every boy wishes to kill his father and sleep with his mother—an idea that was implicit in his *The Interpretation of Dreams* but that he first elaborated in later texts, especially *The Ego and the Id*. *Totem and Taboo* offers an important parallel to this—one which Freud himself saw—for, in primitive societies, according to Freud, the son's awe before the totem served to repress his desire to kill his father, while the elaboration of an incest taboo effectively repressed his desire to sleep with his mother. The literature on the Oedipus complex is itself extensive, but for pragmatic purposes, it is useful to begin with Weinstein and Platt's *The Wish to Be Free: Society, Psyche, and Value Change* (1969), which offers a useful historical contextualization of the theory, arguing that the Oedipus complex developed within the framework of the Western family as it evolved after the industrial revolution. For a competing historical perspective, Carl E. Schorske's "Politics and Patricide in Freud's Interpretation of Dreams" (1981) remains provocative. There are also several excellent discussions of Freud's theory of the Oedipus complex; see, in particular, A.

Parsons, "Is the Oedipus Complex Universal?" (1964); Bennett Simons and Rachel B. Blass, "The Development and Vicissitudes of Freud's Ideas on the Oedipus Complex (1991); and Marie Balmary, *Psychoanalyzing Psychoanalysis: Freud and the Hidden Fault of the Father* (1979). The more ambitious might wish to turn to Gilles Deleuze and Felix Guattari, *Anti-Oedipus: Capitalism and Schizophrenia* (1972).

Above all, however, I have found it useful to pair *Totem and Taboo* with Emile Durkheim's *Elementary Forms of the Religious Life* (1912), which Freud himself had read in his research for *Totem and Taboo*. Although Freud and Durkheim addressed the subject of religion from within the same cultural milieu, their initial presuppositions led them in quite opposite directions. For unlike the suspicious Freud, who searched for the origins of religion and civilization, Durkheim's emphasis was not on origins but rather on the ways in which societies maintain themselves, how they achieve stability, and how social institutions interact to create a coherent order. Within this scheme, God is not the "father" in either the historical or psychoanalytic sense; rather, God is the symbol of society itself. According to Durkheim, therefore, the social order is not merely legitimated but is actually worshiped. In a famous passage, he discusses the ways in which members of a particular society experience "collective effervescence"—a kind of mystical union with one another and society as a whole. Above all, however, this pairing of *Totem and Taboo* with *Elementary Forms* helps students appreciate the social or anthropological dimensions of Freud's project, while casting various aspects of the psychoanalytic approach into sharper relief. The best single introduction to Durkheim remains Steven Lukes's *Emile Durkheim: His Life and Work* (1972). More specifically, Preus's chapters on Durkheim and Freud in his *Explaining Religion* (1987) underscore the similarities as well as the differences in their approaches. Another work that offers a useful contrast between Freud and Durkheim—along with a consideration of Max Müller—is Tomoko Masuzawa, *In Search of Dreamtime: The Quest for the Origins of Religion* (1993).

Ritual: Freud and Turner

"Obsessive Acts and Religious Practices" (1907) was Freud's first essay devoted entirely to the subject of religion in general and ritual in particular; and it achieves a directness, simplicity, and clarity that makes it ideal for presentation to undergraduates. In this essay, Freud focused on the formality, repetitiousness, and symbolism of ritual, arguing that these attributes of ceremony are analogous to the ceremonies of obsessive neurotics. In both cases, fear and guilt arise when the action is not regularly performed, a point eloquently clarified in Judith Rapoport's *The Boy Who Couldn't Stop Washing* (1989), a text I have found useful to introduce to students who are skeptical of the damaging reality of obsessional neuroses. The dynamics underlying obsessive behavior and religious rites are, Freud argues, identical—an instinctual impulse is repressed, but the repression is tenuous, and the impulse threatens to break into consciousness. This causes anxiety, guilt, and the effort to divert the energy of the impulse through displacement. Generally, the displacement takes the form of a compromise between the instincts that threaten to erupt and forces of the psyche that try to suppress them. The symptoms "reproduce something of the pleasure which they are designed to prevent; they serve the repressed instinct no less than the agencies which are repressing it." In the case of obsessional neurosis, the instinct repressed is sexual; in the case of religious rites, the instinct is basically aggressive; this is the primary distinction between the two phenomena. In obsessional neurosis, therefore, the compromise consists of a symptom with sexual significance; in religious rites, the compromise has an aggressive orientation—a sacrificial ritual, for example, allows devotees to commit certain limited acts of violence under the guise of offering a gift to God. Nonetheless, as Volney Gay has argued, ritual need not be seen as pathological, as Freud's analogy to obsessive acts may seem to imply ("Obsessive Actions and Religious Practices" [1975] and *Freud on Ritual* [1979]).

In contrast to Freud's analysis of ritual, which involves looking at ritual in terms of repression and displacement, Victor Turner's depiction of ritual explores its communal and creative aspects. For Turner, ritual is less the expression of the neurotic symptoms of the individual transferred onto the ritual-performing group than a society's expression of itself in an ideal form. In *The Ritual Process*, Turner explores a number of mutually reinforcing qualities that characterize the more positive and constructive aspects of religious rites. First, ritual temporarily reverses ordinary social distinctions and hierarchies. Examples of this leveling appear in the sexlessness and anonymity of ritual participants. Related to this, Turner claims, is the resolution of tensions and polarities within ritual space. A third unifying quality of ritual is the creation of what Turner calls *communitas*, his term for the special nature of the relationship of ritual participants. To define communitas, Turner drew on Martin Buber's ideas on the characteristics of the I-Thou relationship (Buber, 1937). Turner contends that ritual participants relate to each other as full, complex, and unique; thus their interactions differ radically from those that they have in the nonritual sphere, where their relationships are governed by situations of role and status, based on their occupancy of certain social positions. Last, Turner claims that, during ritual time, participants create and experience a perfected version of their own society: they create an ideal world. The value of this utopian vision consists in its function as an inspiration for the initiation and preservation of values such as creativity and egalitarianism in ordinary time. For a sympathetic reading of Turner, see see J. Randall Nichols 41 1985, while Caroline Walker Bynum, by contrast, offers an important feminist corrective to his work in her "Women's Stories, Women's Symbols: A Critique of Victor Turner's Theory of Liminality" (1984). It is also beneficial to read Turner and Freud in light of recent developments in the study of ritual—see especially Catherine Bell, *Ritual Theory, Ritual Practice* (1992), and Jonathan Z. Smith, *To Take Place: Toward Theory in Ritual* (1987).

Illusion and Experience: Freud and James

The pairing of *The Future of an Illusion* (*SE* 21)—Freud's best-known critique of religious belief—and the *Varieties of Religious Experience* (1985),
William James's classic, encyclopedic discussion of belief, serves to broaden
the students' comprehension of religion by contrasting a classic psychoanalytic deconstruction of religion with a pragmatic defense of belief. Such a
pairing seems particularly relevant to our own culture, in which critiques (and
even defenses) of religion presume the victory of science over religion as far
as explanations of natural phenomena go, but that has also witnessed the rise
of neo-pragmatism in the work of Richard Rorty and other successors of James
and Dewey—see especially Rorty, *Contingency, Irony, and Solidarity* (1989).

Freud's essay, of course, presumes an early-twentieth-century scientific
world-view when it dismisses religious belief as unverifiable and, therefore,
implausible. Even more important, however, Freud developed in this essay the
idea of religion as a form of alienation. According to Freud, that is, we distance
ourselves from our own very real human capacities—as limited as these might
be—by projecting all power and authority onto the father-god. We thereby
abdicate our responsibility for slowly improving the suffering entailed in the
human condition through scientific endeavor and passively wait for an illusory
God to save us. This emphasis on the alienating effects of religious belief is
also central to the work of the other "masters of suspicion" Karl Marx and
Friedrich Nietzsche, and at the undergraduate level some consideration of their
writings proves to be useful in developing a fuller appreciation of Freud's
project. Especially productive are Marx's "Theses on Feuerbach," which along
with *Future of an Illusion* compels students to confront the issue of whether
religious belief always lead to alienation and passivity. This latter question leads
naturally to the exploration of the work of William James.

William James's sympathetic and inclusive intellect, as well as his prag-
matist worldview, led him—although he was also a scientist and Freud's
contemporary—to a different conclusion. Like Freud, Nietzsche, and Marx,
James abandoned the attempt to determine whether religious belief is "true"
or untrue in a metaphysical sense. Again, like these three thinkers, he focused
on the effect religious belief has on the lives of believers and their communities. And yet in an exhaustive examination of a multitude of testimonies of
believers—famous and obscure—he concludes that passionate religious belief tends not to encourage alienation but rather to give rise to the living of
what he calls "the strenuous life." For James, who battled depression, immo-
bility, and exhaustion all his life, the strenuous life came to serve as a moral
ideal. He defined this as the life of vigor and enthusiasm devoted to the fur-
thering of the greater social good—a good he understood in utilitarian terms,
as maximizing happiness. For James, the people most likely to embody the
strenuous life were the saints—those who, drawing on the resources of intense religious faith, remained engaged in an energetic effort to improve the

human condition. Thus when William James asserts that "the true is what works," he offers a radically different understanding of truth from Freud. On James, in addition to the superb biography by Gerald E. Myers (1986), see Henry Samuel Levison, *The Religious Investigations of William James* (1981) and Richard R. Niebuhr, "William James on Religious Experience" (1997).

Oceanic Feeling: Freud and Winnicott

In the opening chapter of *Civilization and Its Discontents*, Freud responded to the claim of his friend Romain Rolland that it would be possible to base a theory of religion on what Rolland, in private correspondence with Freud, had earlier identified as an "oceanic feeling," the universal sense of connectedness to the world or to the transcendent. For the most part, recent scholarship has connected this passage with Freudian ideas on narcissism (Masson 1980) or with mysticism (Parsons 1998).

I have found it extremely useful to highlight this passage in *Civilization and Its Discontents* as a starting point for a feminist psychoanalytic critique of Freud's theory of religion in general. As Peter Homans has made clear, Freud believed the "pre-Oedipal, narcissistic features of the oceanic feeling . . . were simply not analyzable" (Homans 1989, 91), and Marion Sprengnether's *The Spectral Mother: Freud, Feminism, and Psychoanalysis* (1990) excavates Freud's avoidance of any sustained consideration of the maternal—what we might call "the repression of the mother"—in his writings. As a counterpoint, therefore, I draw on psychoanalytic thinkers who have turned once again to the mother. Here, several possible strategies are open for juxtaposition with Freud's perspectives. My own emphasis is to introduce pre-Oedipal perspectives, primarily through the writings of D. W. Winnicott. Especially useful in this respect are Winnicott's essays "Transitional Objects and Transitional Phenomena" and "The Location of Cultural Experience" (1980). While Winnicott himself said little about religion, several scholars have drawn on his ideas to develop psychoanalytic models of religious beliefs and practices. For early efforts, see John McDargh, *Psychoanalytic Object Relations: Theory and the Study of Religion: On Faith and the Imagining of God* (1983) and Ross and Ross, "Mothers, Infants, and the Psychoanalytic Study of Ritual" (1983). Other scholars, most notably James Jones (1991) and Diane Jonte-Pace (1987, 1996), have continued to develop these perspectives. But there are other possible pairings from psychoanalysts who, working from within a pre-Oedipal, object relations framework, have developed explicit analysis of religion. Here see especially Marion Milner's creative essay on Blake's *Illustrations for the Book of Job* (1956) and Wilfred Bion's essays on ritual and magic (published posthumously in his *Cogitations* 1992). The Milner is an especially powerful counterpoint to Freud's theory, since she explicitly connects Christian symbolism and beliefs (in particular the incarnation, the crucifixion, and the resurrection) with pre-Oedipal experience.

Reading Moses: Freud and Schwartz

No single Freudian cultural text has received as much attention in recent years as *Moses and Monotheism* (1939), Freud's last work and one that picks up on many of the themes of *Totem and Taboo*. Essentially, Freud develops his famous argument of the princely origins of Moses, an Egyptian, who turned to the Jews after he was disappointed by his own people. But this Moses was a harsh ruler who was murdered by the Jews—an act not unlike the sons' killing of the father of the primal horde in *Totem and Taboo*. Eventually the Jews' guilt or remorse led them to invest Moses with the role of their founder, even claiming that Yahweh had long been his God—a claim that was itself foundational to the invention of monotheism. For this text, teachers have the opportunity to draw on a rich array of interpretations as they develop their discussion of this work which was Freud's final exploration of religion. Yerushalmi's *Freud's Moses: Judaism Terminable and Interminable* (1991) offers a scholarly interpretation of this text in relation to Freud's Jewish identity, while Paul's *Moses and Civilization: The Meaning Behind Freud's Myth* (1996) effectively reintegrates Freud's *Moses and Monotheism* with Freud's other cultural texts, especially his *Totem and Taboo*.

A recent work by Regina Schwartz, *The Curse of Cain: The Violent Legacy of Monotheism* (1997), provides a superb counterpoint to Freud's idealization of Moses, and, indeed, sections of her text grapple directly with Freud. Schwartz's sympathetic understanding of psychoanalysis, as well as her harsh critique of Freud, enables students to see, now at the end of the course, how enormous Freud's influence on religious studies has been. Moreover, since these last two works directly confront the Hebrew Bible and Jewish and Christian traditions, it becomes opportune to ask students to respond to both Freud and other nonreligious readings—whether anthropological or psychoanalytic—of the Scriptures. Given the groundwork laid earlier in the course, discussion can be rigorous as the class seeks to negotiate the multivalent qualities of religious traditions in light of methods that at times illuminate, at times fail to grasp the traditions themselves. Another possible counterpoint to Freud's reading of the Hebrew Bible—and one that has several affinities to Schwartz's method—is Carol Delaney's *Abraham on Trial: The Social Legacy of Monotheism* (1998), especially part IV, where the author subjects Freud to an interesting critique, given his failure to deal with the Abraham story.

The Interpretation of Student Dreams

As noted above, having students keep a dream journal is aimed above all at encouraging them to delve more deeply into Freudian hermeneutics and his theory of the unconscious, but it also—as I shall make clear—does a great deal to help students open themselves up to both the richness of religious symbols and the psychoanalytic method itself—the two primary goals of my class. Indeed, from my experience, the component of the class that best connects the psychoanalytic study of religion with the students' own experience is the dream journal assignment.

The successful use of a dream journal requires preparation and structure. Students are to keep a notebook on a bedside table and describe their dreams as soon as they awake. While some students in the class will protest that they do not remember their dreams, or even that they do not dream at all, in my experience this technique has always worked to make recollection possible. By the end of the semester, all students are able to remember at least some of their dreams. Once students become proficient at recording their dreams, I ask students to pick three dreams for self-analysis. It is useful to specify that they are to use *The Interpretation of Dreams* as a model, with particular emphasis on how manifest dream symbols might conceal an underlying unacceptable wish. At the very least, this process provides not only an exercise in the interpretation of symbols but also experience with the introspection and interpretation involved in the psychoanalytic process itself. At its best, this assignment allows students to enrich their understanding of the multivalent nature of religious symbols and their complex relation to the lives of individuals in culture.

Conclusion

There is clearly no one way of teaching Freud on religion and culture, but it is extremely useful at the undergraduate level—as I have tried to suggest— to approach the material dialogically. There is, of course, no reason to follow the particular pairings of texts I have suggested; individual teachers will have their own preferences and interests. But the dialogical approach is helpful. Above all, such a strategy makes it possible for students to avoid the ahistorical and simplistic types of psychoanalytic readings of religious beliefs and practices that are still among us, as for example in Michael P. Carroll's tendentiously reductive *The Cult of the Virgin Mary: Psychological Origins* (1986). From my teaching of text against text, I have found that students are more than willing to recognize something of the complexity of symbols in human culture and to develop relatively sophisticated analyses of religion. By using a dialogical model, that is, students are enabled not only to master Freud's own hermeneutics but also to develop analyses of religious symbols, beliefs, and practices that are nonreductive, that capture something of the ambiguity of the symbolic in cultural life, while attending to the interplay of psychological, sociological, and anthropological insights into the variety of religious beliefs and practices. Such an approach is nonreductive because it does not establish a one-to-one relation between infant struggles and adult beliefs, but views the religious self as suspended in a constant if unconscious negotiation between maternal and paternal influences, a theme explored eloquently by James W. Jones in his essay "The Relational Self: Contemporary Psychoanalysis Reconsiders Religion" (1991).

In *Civilization and Its Discontents*, Freud wrote that religious beliefs are "so patently infantile, so foreign to reality, that to anyone with a friendly attitude to humanity, it is painful to think that the great majority of mortals will never be able to rise above this view of life" (*SE* 21: 74). In a profound sense Freud knew that psychoanalysis itself would never free men and women from their illusions. But I doubt he could have anticipated the rich array of approaches either within psychoanalysis or in conversation with psychoanalysis that his own seminal explorations made possible.

References

Balmary, Marie. 1979. *Psychoanalyzing psychoanalysis: Freud and the hidden fault of the father*. Translated by Ned Luckacker. Baltimore: Johns Hopkins University Press.

Bell, Catherine. 1992. *Ritual theory, ritual practice*. New York: Oxford University Press.

Bion, Wilfred. 1992. *Cogitations*. London: Karnac Books.

Buber, Martin. 1937. *I and thou*. Translated by Walter Kaufman New York: Scribner's.

Bynum, Caroline Walker. 1984. Women's stories, women's symbols: A critique of Victor Turner's theory of liminality. In *Anthropology and the Study of Religion*, edited by Frank Reynolds and Robert Moore. Chicago: Center for the Scientific Study of Religion.

Carroll, Michael P. 1986. *The cult of the Virgin Mary: Psychological origins*. Princeton, N.J.: Princeton University Press.

Clifford, James, and George E. Marcus, eds. 1986. *Writing culture: The poetics and politics of ethnography*. Berkeley: University of California Press.

Crews, Frederick C., ed. 1998. *Unauthorized Freud: Doubters confront a legend*. New York: Viking.

Cuddihy, J. M. 1974. *The ordeal of civility*. New York: Basic Books.

Delaney, Carol Lowery. 1998. *Abraham on trial: The social legacy of biblical myth*. Princeton, N.J.: Princeton University Press.

Deleuze, Giles, and Felix Guattari. 1977. Anti-Oedipus: Capitalism and schizophrenia. Translated by Robert Hurley, Mark Seem, and Helen R. Luce. New York: Viking.

DiCenso, James. 1996. *Totem and Taboo* and the constitutive function of symbolic forms. *Journal of the American Academy of Religion* 64: 557–74.

———. 1999. *The other Freud: Religion, culture, and psychoanalysis*. New York: Routledge.

Durkheim, Emile. 1912. *The elementary forms of religious life*. Translated and with an introduction by Karen E. Fields. New York: Free Press, 1995.

Edmundson, Mark. 1997. On the uses of a liberal education as lite entertainment for bored college students. *Harper's Magazine* (September), 39–59.

Erikson, Erik. 1954. The dream specimen of psychoanalyisis. In *Psychoanalytic psychiatry and psychology*. Edited by Robert Knight and Cyrus Friedman. New York: International Universities Press.

Frazer, James. 1910 *Totemism and Exogamy*. London: Dawsons Press.

Freud, Sigmund. 1953–1974. *The standard edition of the complete psychological works of Sigmund Freud (SE)*, Volumes 1–24, translated and edited by James Strachey. London: Hogarth Press.

1900. *The interpretation of dreams. SE* 4–5. 1–627.

1907. Obsessive actions and religious practices. *SE* 9: 115–27.

1912–13. *Totem and taboo. SE* 13: 1–161.

1914. The Moses of Michelangelo. *SE* 13: 211–38.

1919. The uncanny. *SE* 17: 217–56.

1923. *The ego and the id. SE* 19: 1–66.

1927. *The future of an illusion. SE* 21: 5–56.

1930. *Civilization and its discontents. SE* 21: 64–145.

1939. *Moses and monotheism. SE* 23: 7–137.

Gay, Peter. 1987. *A godless Jew: Freud, atheism, and the making of psychoanalysis.* New Haven, Conn.: Yale University Press.

———. 1988. *Freud: A life for our time.* New York: Norton.

Gay, Volney Patrick. 1975. Psychopathology and ritual: Freud's essay, "Obsessive actions and religious practices." *Psychoanalytic Review* 62: 493–507.

———. 1979. *Freud on ritual. Reconstruction and critique.* Missoula, Mont.: Scholars Press.

———. 1983. *Reading Freud: Psychology, neurosis, and religion.* Chico, Calif.: Scholars Press.

Geertz, Clifford. 1973. *The interpretation of culture.* New York: Basic Books.

Homans, Peter. 1989. *The ability to mourn: Disillusionment and the social origins of psychoanalysis.* Chicago: University of Chicago Press.

James, William. 1985. *The varieties of religious experience: A study in human nature.* Cambridge, Mass.: Harvard University Press.

Jones, James W. 1991. The relational self: Contemporary psychoanalysis reconsiders religion. *Journal of the American Academy of Religion* 59: 119–135.

Jonte-Pace, Diane. 1987. Object relations theory, mothering, and religion: Toward a feminist psychology of religion. *Horizons* 14: 310–327.

———. 1996. At home in the uncanny: Freudian representations of death, mothers, and the afterlife. *Journal of the American Academy of Religion* 64: 61–88.

Lang, Andrew. 1911. Totemism. *Encyclopaedia Britannica* 27: 79–91. Cambridge: Cambridge University Press.

Laplanche, Jean, and J.-B. Pontalis. 1983. *The language of psycho-analysis.* Translated by Donald Nicolson-Smith. London: Hogarth Press.

Lear, Jonathan. 1998. *Open minded: Working out the logic of the soul.* Cambridge, Mass.: Harvard University Press.

Levison, Henry Samuel. 1981. *The religious investigations of William James.* Chapel Hill: University of North Carolina Press.

Lévi-Strauss, Claude. 1962. *Totemism.* Translated by Rodney Needham. Boston: Beacon Press.

Lukes, Steven. 1972. D*urkheim: His life and work, A historical and critical study.* New York: Harper & Row.

Masson, Jeffrey Moussaieff. 1980. *The oceanic feeling. The origins of the religious sentiment in ancient India.* Dordrecht: D. Reidel.

Marx, Karl. 1998. *The German ideology.* New York: Prometheus Books.

Masuzawa, Tomoko. 1993. *In search of dreamtime: The quest for the origins of religion.* Chicago: University of Chicago Press.

McDargh, John. 1983. *Psychoanalytic object relations theory and the study of religion: On faith and the imagining of god.* Lanham, Md.: University Press of America.

McCutcheon, Russell T. 1998. Methods and theories in the classroom: Teaching the study of myths and rituals. *Journal of the American Academy of Religion* 66: 147–64.

McGrath, William J. 1986. *Freud's discovery of psychoanalysis*. Ithaca, N.Y.: Cornell University Press.

Meissner, W. W. 1984. *Psychoanalysis and religious experience*. New Haven, Conn.: Yale University Press.

Miller, Richard B, Laurie L. Patton, and Stephen H. Webb. 1994. Rhetoric, pedagogy, and the study of religions. *Journal of the American Academy of Religion* 62: 819–50.

Milner, Marion. [1956] 1987. *The suppressed madness of sane men: Forty-four years of exploring psychoanalysis*. London: Tavistock Publications.

Myers, Gerald E. 1986. *William James: His life and thought*. New Haven, Conn.: Yale University Press.

Nichols, J. Randall. 1985. Worship and anti-structure: The contribution of Victor Turner. Theology Today 41: 401–409.

Niebuhr, Richard R. 1997. William James on religious experience. In *The Cambridge Companion to William James*, edited by Ruth Anna Parsons. Cambridge: Cambridge University Press.

Parsons, Anne. 1964. Is the Oedipus complex universal?: The Jones-Malinowski debate revisted, and a South Italian Nuclear Complex. *Psychoanalytic Study of Society* 3: 278–328.

Parsons, William Barclay. 1998. *The enigma of the oceanic feeling*. New York: Oxford University Press.

Paul, Robert A. 1991. Freud's anthropology: A reading of the cultural books. In *The Cambridge companion to Freud*, edited by J. Neu. Cambridge: Cambridge University Press.

————. 1996. *Moses and civilization: The meaning behind Freud's myth*. New Haven, Conn.: Yale University Press.

Philp, Howard Littleton. 1974. *Freud and religious belief*. Westport, Conn.: Greenwood Press.

Preus, James S. 1987. *Explaining religion: Criticism and theory from Bodin to Freud*. New Haven, Conn.: Yale University Press.

Rapoport, Judith L. 1989. *The boy who couldn't stop washing: The experience and treatment of obsessive compulsive disorder*. New York: Dutton.

Rice, Emanuel. 1990. *Freud and Moses: The long journey home*. Albany: State University of New York Press.

Ricoeur, Paul. 1974. *Freud and philosophy*. New Haven, Conn.: Yale University Press.

Rieff, Philip. 1966. *Freud: The mind of the moralist*. New York: Viking.

Roazen, Paul. 1968. *Sigmund Freud: Politics and social thought*. New York: Knopf.

Rorty, Richard. 1989. *Contingency, irony, and solidarity*. Cambridge: Cambridge University Press.

Rosenfeld, Eva M. 1956. Dream and vision: Some remarks on Freud's Egyptian bird dream. International Journal of Psycho-Analysis 38: 97–105.

Ross, Mary Ellen and Cheryl Lynn Ross. 1983. Mothers, infants, and the psychoanalytic study of ritual. *Signs: Journal of Women in Culture and Society* 9: 26–39.

Schorske, Carl E. 1981. Politics and patricide in Freud's *Interpretation of Dreams. 1973*. In *Fin-de-siècle Vienna: Politics and Culture*, edited by Carl Schorske, New York: Random House.

Schwartz, Regina. 1997. *The curse of Cain: The violent legacy of monotheism*, Chicago: University of Chicago Press.

Simons, Bennett, and Rachel E. Blass. 1981. The development and vicissitudes of

Freud's ideas on the Oedipus complex. In *The Cambridge Companion to Freud*, edited by Jerome Neu. Cambridge: Cambridge University Press.

Smith, Jonathan Z. 1987. *To take place: Toward theory in ritual*. Chicago: University of Chicago Press.

Sprengnether, Madelon. 1990. *The spectral mother: Freud, feminism, and psychoanalysis*. Ithaca, N.Y.: Cornell University Press.

Sulloway, Frank J. 1979. *Freud, biologist of the mind: Beyond the psychoanalytic legend*. New York: Basic Books.

Turner, Victor. 1969. *The ritual process*. New York: DeGruyter

Van Herik, Judith. 1982. *Freud on femininity and faith*. Berkeley: University of California Press.

Wallace, Edwin R. 1983. *Freud and anthropology: A history and reappraisal*. New York: International Universities Press.

Weinstein, Gerald, and Fred Platt. 1969. *The wish to be free: Society, psyche, and value change*. Berkeley: University of California Press.

Winnicott, D. W. 1980. Transitional objects and transitional phenomena. In *Playing and Reality*, edited by D.W. Winnicott. Harmondsworth: Penguin.

———. 1980. The location of cultural experience. In *Playing and Reality*, edited by D.W. Winnicott. Harmondsworth: Penguin.

Wright, Jack. 1994. *Freud's war with God: Psychoanalysis versus religion*. Lafayette, La.: Huntington House Publishers.

Wulff, David M. 1997. *Psychology of religion: Classic and contemporary*. New York: John Wiley.

Yerushalmi, Yosef Hayim. 1991. *Freud's Moses: Judaism terminable and interminable*. New Haven, Conn.: Yale University Press.

IV

TEACHING THE TEACHINGS, TEACHING THE PRACTICE

12

Teaching the Hindu Tantra with Freud: Transgression as Critical Theory and Mystical Technique

Jeffrey J. Kripal

Since the appearance of my "Oceanic" works, letters have come forth from all corners of the earth . . . like a gushing of waters that had been suppressed. I have amassed a complete file of these letters. And that is why I think that, in history and in action, one must always take into account these invisible forces that act in secret when they are not made manifest by explosions in broad daylight.
—Romain Rolland to Sigmund Freud, May 3, 1931

The "oceanic" works of which Rolland writes here were his famous biographies of Ramakrishna and Vivekananda, that "twin-headed, three-volume work" as Freud called them (Parsons 1999, 176), which played an especially important role in the historical genesis of the psychoanalytic theory of mysticism. Indeed, as Parsons has recently taught us, it was the unfinished correspondence between these two men that generated the parameters and general trajectories of the psychoanalytic study of mysticism itself. In 1927, the French savant wrote to Freud about the biographies of Ramakrishna and Vivekananda that he was working on, and he proposed to Freud that he analyze the "oceanic" mystical experience (*une sentiment océanique*) of the saints and of Rolland himself—the latter had read the saints' experiences "in correspondance"[1] with the phenomenology of his own (Parsons 1999, 104)—as something qualitatively different from the illusions that Freud had shown constitute "the common-man's religion."[2] Freud responded to the friendly request with just such an analysis, psychoanalyzing Rolland's "oceanic feeling" as a psychic regression to the primary narcissistic state of the infant and suggesting that further inquiry might uncover "connections here with a number of obscure modifications of mental life, such as trances and ecstasies" (SE 21: 73). Not an "out and out skeptic" by his own admission, Freud even eventually admitted that "certain mystical practices" share a "similar line of approach" to psychoanalysis in that both seek to peer into and appropriate the inner depths of the psyche by "upsetting the normal relations between the different regions of the mind" (Freud 1933, 79–80) even as he openly doubted whether such states could reveal anything but the unconscious workings of the psyche, an "embryology of the soul" perhaps, but certainly nothing useful for adjusting one's inner life to the inevitability of the external objective world (Parsons 1999, 176–77).[3] Thus began the psychoanalytic study of mysticism, discursively poised between the French mystical writer, the Viennese Master, and the Hindu saints Ramakrishna and Vivekananda.

I must confess that I feel a special affinity with Rolland, the friend of Sigmund Freud. His Catholic religious roots; his pre-Oedipal psychic disposition so powerfully oriented toward the feminine, the maternal, and the mystical; his unflinching skepticism and criticism of traditional religious claims (Rolland denied both the existence of a personal God and the immortality of the soul); his humanistic social vision that knew no cultural boundaries (Freud called him the "apostle of love for mankind"); his remarkable insider/outsider assertion that his constant awareness of the oceanic feeling ("like a sheet of water which I feel flushing under the bark") in no way affected his critical faculties and freedom to use them (Parsons 1999, 174); his desire to create a dialectical "mystical psychoanalysis" that might be true to both the critical deconstructive powers of psychoanalysis and the inherent beauty of the mystical; his call to "live irony"—that is, to affirm both the sacrality of the individual human being and its grounding (and ultimate dissolution) in the ocean of being, what I would call a "mystical humanism" (Parsons 1999, 99)—and, of course, his biographies of Ramakrishna and Vivekananda—all this I can relate to, idealize, and identify with on the most personal and intimate of psychological, religious, and intellectual levels.

We even share a similarly thick and global file of letters in response to our respective Ramakrishna books. Since the appearance of my *Kali's Child* six years ago, I have corresponded, often at great length, with hundreds of individuals from a wide range of social, religious, and professional backgrounds, among them professional Indologists and Buddhologists; Indian intellectuals, historians, and literary critics; Indian and American devotees of different global gurus (Osho, Ammachi, Muktananda, Ramakrishna, and Vivekananda); swamis; an eroticist; playwrights; Sufis; independent mystics; a prominent contemporary American guru; psychoanalysts, psychologists, and psychiatrists; graduate students, philosophers, novelists, theologians, and social activists. Many of these souls I now happily count as personal friends. And yet how different were the Indian receptions of Rolland's text and my own. His became a devotional classic and played an important role in the Western construction and image of the Ramakrishna tradition; to this day it is sold in the tradition's many bookstores around the world. Mine was viciously attacked[4]— and passionately defended (Vaidyanathan 1997)—in the national Indian press and was the object of no less than three heavily advertised protest movements in India, two of them ban movements that ended with the CBI (India's FBI) and the Lower House of the Parliament, respectively. Rolland's file, it seems, was rather different from my own.

Or was it? Rolland poetically describes his own letters as "gushing" waters (rivers, oceans, and subterranean streams all carry explicit mystical connotations for Rolland) "bursting forth" after a period of suppression (a term with clear psychoanalytic resonances), and suggests to Freud that they revealed "invisible forces that act in secret when they are not made manifest by explosions in broad daylight." In what follows I will claim the same for my own letters, imaginatively inserting myself and my work between Freud the ambivalent reductionist and Rolland the psychological mystic in an attempt to extend, deepen, and develop their dialogue about mysticism, particularly in its Hindu Tantric forms. I have always understood my own text as both a psychoanalytic and a mystical document; in Parsons's apt phrase, I practice a "transformational" psychoanalytic hermeneutic, engaging both the critical, deconstructive powers of psychoanalysis and the positive *Grund* of mystical forms of subjectivity (Parsons 1999, 123–39). Indeed, I have recently written at considerable length about the mystical grounding of my scholarship in a series of visionary and mystico-erotic experiences I underwent as a young man in a Catholic monastic seminary and, later, in Calcutta as a graduate student (Kripal 2001). Taken as a whole, the negative and positive receptions of *Kali's Child* as revealed in my own correspondence file dramatically confirm this dual self-understanding. Since I have dealt at some length elsewhere with the negative receptions (Kripal 1998a, 1998b, 2001a), I want to turn here to the positive side and explore its patterns. Without denying either side, I want to affirm here the critical, healing, and even mystical potential of a psychoanalytic transformational hermeneutics.

I will approach this correspondence not as an exercise in self-aggrandizement but as a kind of deeply personal and, I hope, theoretically rich entry into some of the most pressing hermeneutical and pedagogical issues that Indologists routinely struggle with, to varying degrees, in their writing and teaching and thinking: the powers of Western critical theory and their relationship to the often pre-critical self-understandings of students and readers; the Western origins and epistemological structure of the modern study of religion; the porous interface between "insider" and "outsider" subjectivities; the liminal and potentially transformative nature of the hermeneutical circle wherein both the interpreter and the interpreted can and often do change places; and the politics and ethics of cross-cultural scholarship in an age of postcolonialism, postmodern relativism, and aggressive Hindu nationalism.

It is my own conviction that each of these issues is rendered especially acute and problematic when psychoanalytic methods are used, and that my particular experiences can be used fruitfully as a kind of magnifying glass through which individual readers can focus their own theoretical visions and pedagogical practices. It is for this and in this sense of "pedagogy" as the practice of public scholarship that I write here. The reception issues surrounding *Kali's Child*, I will argue, are precisely those of the Indological classroom, rendered here in an especially dramatic—and so especially instructive—form.

I write primarily for my correspondents and my critics, who have asked me the same question over and over again: "What about the book's religious reception?" Indeed, I have been struck many times by the fact that people are far more interested in how the book has been received (i.e., how others—who have usually never read the book—react to it) than what the book actually says. At first I was rather annoyed by this, operating, as I was, with a naive apolitical vision of scholarship, and this despite the fact that my work's sympathetic treatment of homoeroticism and Tantric antinomianism were enfolded with some potentially radical sociopolitical, ethical, and even ontological implications. Now, after six years of thinking, corresponding, and public speaking, I take such questions as roundabout ways of asking basic pedagogical and political questions: How do we present truths to our audiences that many do not and perhaps cannot hear? What do we do with socially subversive (but potentially liberating) truths? And how do our cultural, religious, and economic positions affect—negatively or positively—the way our scholarship is received by communities that do not share these positionings? Put baldly, why should a Bengali-speaking devotee of Ramakrishna living in Calcutta (or Atlanta, for that matter) listen to a white American male of Czech-German descent talk about Ramakrishna's mystical homoeroticism?

Transgression: Psychoanalytic and Tantric

My own answer to this question can be summarized in one word: *transgression*. Here, theoretical method meets mystical discipline, and the two—in true mystical fashion—become one. In less oblique and playful terms, to take seriously Hindu Tantric forms of spirituality—as we find, for example, in the case of Ramakrishna—is to engage, at least imaginatively, in a theoretical and religious discipline of transgression on multiple levels (intellectual, cultural, sexual, political, emotional). Such imaginative transgression, now embodied in one's scholarship and writing, in turn has the power to elicit from one's readers and listeners unusual and dramatic responses (both positive and negative)—contemporary versions, no doubt, of those "invisible forces that act in secret" about which Rolland wrote to Freud. Like a traditional Tantric *cakra* (a secret ritual "circle" of practitioners within which antinomian substances and acts are ingested and performed), the hermeneutical circle into which the psychoanalytic interpreter and his or her readers enter through a ritualized and disciplined engagement with the texts is liminal and dangerous but also potentially soteriological, performing, as it does, a type of "transgression in the service of transcendence," if I may borrow (and completely change) an expression from Ernst Kris (1952). Once such a circle is entered vis-a-vis Tantric textual materials, many of one's assumed dualisms (sexual/spiritual, insider/outsider, past/present, East/West) are capable of deconstruction and temporary dissolution. Such an experience of emptiness, however fleeting, inevitably leaves traces of itself in one's scholarship, rendering it, like Tantra and psychoanalysis themselves, something of a categorical and social scandal.

Such scandalous transgression, of course, is hardly foreign to Hinduism. Indeed, many of the loosely related subcultures and local traditions that constitute the grand sweep of the Hindu tradition grant a remarkably central place to the soteriological and gnoseological value of transgression—that is, the act of stepping out of the social system through a ritual or image to perceive some basic ontological truth about the human being and its socially constructed, and so ultimately illusory, worlds. In David Kinsley's always eloquent terms:

> There is an insistence in Hinduism that the world as it appears to us is a show, that there remains hidden from our normal view an aspect of reality that is different, perhaps shockingly different, from our ego-centered way of apprehending it. The world is not the way we like to think it is, and the sooner we realize that, the quicker we will make progress in acquiring spiritual maturity. (Kinsley 1997, 7)

Tantrism, with its antinomian rituals and techniques, is a particularly acute form of this general Hindu spirituality of transgression. And the goddess Kali (who iconographically and hermeneutically focused my study as the mythological embodiment of my theoretical thinking), perhaps better than any other Hindu symbol, embodies this transgressive mysticism. With her sword raised to decapitate her next (always male) victim, her open, often wild sexuality, her extended tongue and gory garb (she wears a garland of decapitated heads and a skirt of human arms, at times even dead fetuses for earrings), she inverts and offends every possible social value: "Kali insults, subverts, and mocks the social status quo, particularly as it defines proper behavior for women" (Kinsley 1997, 7). And herein lies the explanation for both the mystical and offended receptions of my work: *both were responding to the very same thing—that is, a type of mystical-methodological transgression.* Whereas one group of respondents read this positively, seeing in my work on Ramakrishna reflections of their own theoretical insights or mystical experiences (usually of a socially marginal, psychologically extreme, or philosophically deconstructive nature), the other group, conditioned by a whole host of neo-Vedantic and neo-Hindu assumptions about the body, Hinduism, *brahman,* and sexuality, could see only blasphemy and insult.

Such is my basic thesis for this essay. It now remains for me to demonstrate or flesh it out. But first it is perhaps necessary to understand, however briefly, what it was that the letters were responding to so positively and negatively. What was it I wrote that created such a stir? *Kali's Child* focused on a large corpus of nineteenth- and early-twentieth-century Bengali texts on the life and teachings of Ramakrishna and concluded that the saint's visions, mystical states, and ecstatic flights were driven by mystico-erotic energies that he neither fully accepted nor understood. More specifically, I argued that the saint's visions and ecstasies could be properly understood only by positing some type of homosexual orientation in the saint;[5] only then could we make sense of the saint's fear of and rejection of (hetero)sexuality, his effusive responses to his young male disciples, and his tendency to go into trances or ecstatic states in two very different situations for two very different reasons: before sexualized women (trance here functioning as a negative defensive mechanism) and before young male disciples (trance here functioning as a positive sublimating mechanism). Moreover, to encompass the full range of mystical, pathological, ontological, and emotional dimensions that I saw expressed in these texts, I developed a dialectical category I called "the erotic," which I defined as "a dimension of human experience that is simultaneously related both to the physical and emotional experience of sexuality and to the deepest ontological levels of religious experience" (Kripal 1998a, 23). Building on the categories of Ricoeur's *Freud and Philosophy* (1970) and Gananath Obeyesekere's *The Work of Culture* (1990), I argued that the erotic functions in these texts as an essentially dialectical process that manifests both "regressive" returns back to childhood and early traumatic experiences and "progressive" leaps forward into vision and religious ecstasy. Such a dialectical understanding of the erotic enabled me to make some sense of both the graphic sexual nature of Ramakrishna's visions, many of which seemed to hark back to the pain and trauma of his childhood, adolescence, and early adulthood, and the essentially mystical nature of his ecstasies, which seemed to point forward to some degree of personal healing and the theological speculations and doctrines that would eventually deify him as a modern *avatara* or "incarnation" of God. The erotic here was rooted in a painful pathological past and yet branched out into a more hopeful theological, even mythological, future.

Extending the Secret Talk into the Present

While presenting such ideas over the past ten years to various academic and lay audiences, I have often found myself caught between two critics: the offended devotee, who seems only to notice (and passionately reject) the regressive side of the dialectic, and the critical scholar, who has little trouble with the regressive side but is often suspicious of the progressive dimension. Both the book's psychoanalytic method and its sexually explicit content, for example, have offended many Hindus, despite the fact that I eschew any simplistically reductionistic conclusions concerning the saint's erotic mysticism, insist on the progressive dimensions of his later ecstasies and deification, and support my arguments with extensive references to a three-thousand-page

Bengali corpus that is, for the most part, widely available to any Bengali reader who cares to wade through it. Consider, for example, the very first paper I delivered on the subject, a rather technical piece on the textual distribution of Ramakrishna's *guhya katha* or "secret talk" (Kripal 1991). At some point in the paper I used the word "erotic" a single time to describe the content of these passages (I was not yet brave enough to tell people what the passages actually said). A Bengali man, a medical doctor I believe, came up to me afterward, quite offended by that single adjective, and assured me that there was absolutely nothing about the saint that could be described with such an offensive word. There was little I could say or do in such a situation except smile and thank him for his comment. I have also heard, mostly from scholars, the opposite charge—namely, that I have not been reductionistic enough: "Why *do* you take the saint's religious experiences so seriously when they are so obviously rooted in his sexuality," they seem to say, as if it were obvious to everyone what the terms "sexuality" and "religious" actually refer to. Neither of these audiences, I would suggest, really "gets" what I am trying to get at, for each wants to collapse the dialectic of the erotic in some, well, nondialectical way. For the offended devotee, it is all "spirituality." For the reductionistic scholar, it is all "sex." Both have failed to transgress. Both are still caught in their own dualistic assumptions about "spirituality" and "sex."

But others clearly do get it and are able to engage psychoanalytic discussions of sexual orientation, gender identity construction, and maternal mysticism on their own terms, even as they challenge, develop, and take them in new, often fascinating directions. Two analytical processes have catalyzed and made possible such dialogue and development: (1) the psychoanalytic focus on revealing secrets, which seems to have the uncanny ability of calling forth the secrets of others; and (2) transference and countertransference phenomena between myself and my readers, which effectively open up a trusting and creative discursive space for us to explore together the themes of the book. A word about each of these processes is in order before I proceed to a discussion of the different types of responses.

Kali's Child presented itself as a study of secrets. Beginning with the assertion that the English translation (Nikhilananda's *The Gospel of Sri Ramakrishna*) of the central text of the tradition (Mahendranatha Gupta's *Kathamrita*) bowdlerized and even completely omitted aspects of Ramakrishna's "secret talk" (*guhya katha*) and a demonstration of how even the five volumes of the Bengali text are structured cyclically around an ambivalent attempt both to reveal and to conceal these Tantrically coded mystico-erotic secrets, I proceeded in the body of the book to translate, interpret, and contextualize in considerable detail Ramakrishna's secrets. The further facts that Ramakrishna's Sakta Tantric culture was itself coded in esoteric terms and practiced within secret antinomian rituals made such an approach more than appropriate. Indeed, Ramakrishna himself spoke in excited, revelatory terms and so invited his listeners (and now readers) to enter this esoteric discourse, "Listen! Now I'm telling you something very secret." Interestingly, the Ramakrishna of the texts also often asks his listeners to help him interpret his visions, explain his ecstatic states, and even tell him who he is; it is as if he does not know and needs the interpretations of others—listeners and now readers—to come into meaning. The hermeneutical patterns of the text are thus "open-ended," dialectical, still in process, and extend into the present of the text before the reader, who has become Ramakrishna's audience through the magical acts of reading and interpretation.

What I attempted to do in my own text is re-create and extend these esoteric and hermeneutical processes, imaginatively enter them (as the Ramakrishna of the texts invites us to do), and understand them anew. To do so, however, I had to deal with some very intimate details of the saint's life (that is, after all, why the passages were secret). The rhetorical result was a kind of intellectual transgression that participated in the esoteric structure of the Bengali texts and, by so doing, imaginatively relived the Tantric revelations and occultations of Ramakrishna's life and teachings, sexual details and all. There is a certain excitement, a hint of danger, a note of awe in any such enterprise, and indeed all these emotional states are richly represented in the Bengali texts. Typical are the following lines from an early biography of Ramakrishna: "This Tantra is a powerful branch of the Vedas [the ancient and most sacred Scriptures]. It is a very secret scripture. Its mystical practice is also very secret. . . . The path of the Tantras is very quick, but it is as terrifying as it is quick; there is the fear of demons on this path. . . . One can become mad" (Mitra 1897, 53–54). Who does not want to hear such powerful, dangerous, efficient, and potentially pathological secrets? Is not this the very logic of secrecy, a seductive telling that one is not telling everything and thus an invitation to listen for more? Within such a rhetoric, every concealing implies, indeed *demands,* a revealing, and every revealing promises to be concealed again. Such is the psychology and dialectic of esotericism.

Still within this same discursive field, readers and hearers of such secrets are naturally inspired to speak their own secrets. Hence one of the most encouraging and serendipitous aspects of the book's reception for me was the consistent pattern, repeated over and over again in the letters, of readers spontaneously sharing their own secrets with me. Having read the book as a sympathetic treatment of Ramakrishna's secrets, they assumed, and not unreasonably so, that I was open to such things, that I was sympathetic, that I would try to understand. And so they re-created and extended Ramakrishna's "secret talk" in their own. I thus read, among other things, of powerfully erotic, if emotionally conflicted visions of Kali, of parental sexual abuse linked to trance states, of the emotional sufferings of those with culturally vilified sexualities, of transsexual experiments with the goddess, and of ecstatic and dream experiences induced by the reading of *Kali's Child.* The rhetorical patterns and emotional tone of such contemporary "secret talk" quite accurately echo and extend, if in a distinctively modern or postmodern voice, the "secret talk" of both the Bengali texts and *Kali's Child.* A kind of "hermeneutical union" has thus been realized between the subject of the study (Ramakrishna), the author of the study (myself), and the readers of the study (the correspondents) within a single esoteric discourse shared orally and now textually across cultures and times.

Scholarship and (Counter)Transference

Psychologically speaking, such "secret talk" was made possible by what psychoanalysts call transference phenomena—that is, the transference of emotional associations and reactions originally connected to some figure of one's past onto an analogously perceived figure of one's present. Any scholar of religion who has ever stepped into a classroom to teach a course about religion knows this process well, even if he or she cannot give it a psychoanalytic name. In an American, largely Christian context, on that first day of class, most of the students have already framed the course as a reenactment of some previous (and too often dreaded) Sunday school class or church service. The professor of religion thus becomes a preacher, the classroom a church, and the message a threat to be enforced with promises of punishment or damnation, or at least a modicum of healthy guilt. Even if none of this is in fact true, that is precisely what many of the students expect, for they have transferred the emotional memories of their previous experiences of a professional dealing with religion onto this one. This is hardly the students' fault, as American culture, like most cultures, provides precious little exposure to the academic study of religion before the college experience; indeed, in most cases, that exposure can be precisely measured as nil. Little wonder, then, that students routinely transfer their childhood or adolescent experiences of religion onto the professor of religion and enter that first classroom "in fear and trembling." Regardless, nothing of intellectual significance can be accomplished until this transference is worked through, challenged, and effectively dissolved. The students have to be convinced that the professor is a fellow questioner and not a preacher, that the classroom is an open discursive space for thinking about religion and not a church or temple, and that the message is about the powers of critical thinking and not the fires of some threatened hell or angry elder. In my own pedagogical experience, once this is all apparent to the students, the class atmosphere changes almost immediately to one of open dialogue, humor, and intellectual honesty; there is something deeply human and liberating about speaking one's mind, especially when it is such at odds with the surrounding public religious culture.

Similar but significantly darker transference phenomena showed themselves in the negative reception of *Kali's Child*. This process was encouraged somewhat by the fact that my surname (of Czech origins) also happens to be a popular surname in northern India, where it is usually associated with individuals of the Sikh tradition. "Jeffrey J. Kripal," then, strikes the Indian eye as an unusual amalgamation of Western-Christian (Jeffrey) and Indian-Sikh (Kripal) traditions. (In a recent twist on the story, relatives at a family union informed me that local tradition in Eastern Europe traces the family's origins back to Gypsies who had migrated from India.) Accordingly, I was vilified in one American-Hindu cartoon as a secular, liberal Sikh (complete with turban) teaching in a godless American university. In other contexts—for example, in the letters to the editor of a major Calcutta newspaper or in personal correspondence—I have been portrayed as a sinister gay man, as an NRI (Non Resident Indian—that is, an Indian living in a foreign country), or as an ill-trained pseudo-scholar who just made it all up, as it were. Now none of this is true. I am not gay. I am not a Sikh. I am not an Indian living abroad. (Although I fail utterly to see what is wrong with any of these identities.) Nor am I a mud-slinging dilettante. I am a heterosexual American of Czech-German descent with a Ph.D. in the history of religions who is interested in the question of sexual orientation and its relationship to mystical forms of religious experience, and I published an anonymously peer-reviewed manuscript with a major academic press on the topic. All of this name-calling, then, is an unfortunate collection of emotionally charged transferences, personal and cultural hatreds projected onto the blank slate that was "Jeffrey J. Kripal."

Certainly common Indian perceptions of "the West" as materialistic, morally dissolute, and anti-religious, and "the East" as spiritual, moral, and religious—that is, the typical orientalist constructions—also played into such transferences. They too will have to be deconstructed and dissolved before any genuine dialogue can take place. Our contemporary global culture, the hermeneutical powers of critical theory, and the philosophical realities of the postmodern world may promise to reduce all such binarisms to virtual nonsense. Still, because of the colonial legacy, any perceived encroachment on the part of a Westerner, however well-intentioned or appropriately trained, is almost immediately coded—and so effectively fended off—as yet another example of Western colonialism (the dualism returns). In such an atmosphere, knowledge of any kind can easily and facilely be reduced to a form of intellectual imperialism. A hermeneutical method like psychoanalysis that wants to critically examine universal themes across cultures and times, and this through an open discussion of the intimacies of sexuality, becomes particularly problematic, even when its history is defined by a fantastically rich literature, a radically critical approach to *all* religion, including and especially Western religion, genuine cross-cultural dialogue, and the constant adjustment of its categories (Vaidyanathan and Kripal 1998). Certainly this postcolonial demonization of theoretical knowledge itself is the greatest single obstacle to the future practice and teaching of psychoanalytic Indology.

I believe that such criticisms have seriously misread both the intentions and the trajectories of religious studies scholars in the West. Among other things, what such criticisms fail to take into account is the fact that often such scholars, far from taking up the psychoanalytic, anthropological, or historical-critical pen to "imperialize" another culture do so, in effect, to understand and interpret their own now postmodern "colonized souls." In some genuine sense, *they* are the converted ones, if not in a religious sense, then at least in an aesthetic or intellectual sense. Certainly this was so in my own case. I grew up in an American society that was post-Christian, radically pluralistic, and increasingly global in worldview. Within such a cultural context, religious forms migrate with great ease across national boundaries through books, higher education, and now the Internet. The stunningly plural complex of Hindu practices and belief systems, so strikingly different from anything I had seen in my own, seemed a particularly rich resource to draw from. That I chose as a topic of study the tradition that had had the most impact on my own American culture—the Ramakrishna tradition—was certainly no accident. I was simply trying to make sense of something that had permanently altered the religious, philosophical, and even ontological landscapes of my own psyche and soul. In Clooney's apt phrase, I was struggling with "theology after Vedanta" (Clooney 1993)—that is, I was asking serious questions about the cogency and legitimacy of my own "Christianity after Hinduism." To frame such a willingness to step out, if not actually leave, one's own indigenous religious tradition in order to sympathetically understand another's as an act of colonial oppression or intellectual imperialism is hardly fair; in psychoanalytic terms, it is a false and ultimately dysfunctional transference of a past cultural event (colonialism) onto a present one (the practice of religious studies within a global culture) whose dynamics must be made conscious and worked through. Certainly there are features and patterns of the latter that are analogous to those of the former (for both globalism and religious studies are driven largely by Western intellectual forces), but to collapse the two into a single process seems simplistic at best.[6] Such a move, it seems to me, too often functions as an unconvincing defense mechanism, as a strategy not to think critically about one's own religious world. In essence, it is a failure to transgress.

Despite such formidable ideological obstacles, however, there is good reason to hope that not everyone is convinced of the impossibility of genuinely cross-cultural humanistic, psychological, and comparative scholarship. Psychoanalytically informed studies of Hinduism, for example, continue to be published at an impressive rate by major academic presses, with Oxford University Press (New Delhi) possessing one of the longest and most distinguished lists (the dualism collapses again). On a personal pedagogical note, I would also point out that many, if not most, of my religiously inclined correspondents—and even many of my scholarly ones—responded positively to *Kali's Child* precisely because of its ability to speak to their own spiritually colonized (read: converted) psyches. In effect, they saw their own struggles reflected in my own. Here, because the transferences were completely different, the tones were positive and trusting instead of negative and hateful. More specifically, these readers assumed that since I had written a warmly appreciative book about a Hindu saint's mystico-erotic experiences, I must be myself open to such experiences and capable of helping them decipher their own. They thus transferred their expectations of what a therapist or mystically inclined scholar might be onto me and spoke their own secrets. Now I am certainly not a therapist, but I do have mystical inclinations (I suspect many, if not most, scholars of mysticism do and have written a book about this thesis [Kripal 2001]). Consequently, this transference was much closer to my own self-understanding, even if I had to tell my correspondents on more than one occasion that I did not understand and could not help them with this or that state or vision—omniscience and infallibility are not among my traits. Because of this "transference match" or "therapeutic alliance," if I may borrow a term from the realm of therapy, and the trusting, personal tones of the transference, the result of these exchanges were radically different. Instead of a ban movement and a hate campaign, a "gushing" flood of letters ensued, sparkling and bubbling with the intimate religious lives, personal lives, and mystical experiences of their writers. I was and still am honored to be the object of such a happy and personally syntonic transference, even if I must often and repeatedly confess my own baffled ignorance before the power, suffering, and beauty of my readers' rich religious lives.

Both these positive and negative transferences and my own reactions to them, however, raise another crucial pedagogical issue; the reality of countertransference—that is, the emotional responses of a writer or teacher to the reactions of his or her readers and students. These must be constantly and self-reflexively monitored in a fashion analogous to the therapeutic art. Significantly, in a therapeutic situation, the analyst is not necessarily looking for positive transferences. *Any* transferences—idealizing, hateful, loving, ambivalent—are potent opportunities for further insight and analysis. And indeed, I have suggested elsewhere that the negative reactions to *Kali's Child* are especially fruitful places to reflect on the political nature of religious studies, the reality of censorship, the theoretical powers of a psychoanalytic method (Kripal 1998a), the potentially liberating function of scholarship on human sexuality, and the truth of my historical thesis (Kripal 1998b). The writer or teacher should thus not measure success by the presence or absence of positive transferences. Quite the contrary, it could be argued that the mark of a genuinely powerful pedagogical event is the presence of dramatically negative reactions, as these, and perhaps only these, are a clear sign that one has precisely located and effectively challenged some core belief or assumption,[7] hence the folk belief in the importance and eminently positive value of a "controversial" work. Of course, negative reactions in and of themselves prove nothing, for it is entirely possible for a writer or teacher to simply be offensive, crude, and mean, but this is far less likely in a published context, where numerous peer review processes and other professional checks and balances usually preclude such a possibility. "Controversy," after all, implies both positive and negative reactions from the reception community. Simple ignorance or prejudice are an entirely different matter.[8]

Psychoanalysis as Critical Theory

Flipping through these letters again, I would isolate at least two major discursive patterns: psychoanalysis as critical theory and psychoanalysis as mystical technique. The former I would further subdivide into psychoanaly-

sis as social criticism, sympathetic recovery, and personal therapy. A few
words about each of these are in order.

Psychoanalysis as Social Criticism

The Buddhologist José Cabezón has pointed out that academic "work that
lacks scholarly rigor is ultimately ineffective politically, and . . . truly scholarly work is creative in such a way that it must of necessity have implications
in a political sphere" (Stemmeler and Cabezón 1992, 7). I think that this is
particularly true for psychoanalytically informed scholarship. Often criticized
for its lack of attention to sociological realities, psychoanalysis can just as
easily function as a laserlike focus on these same realities, this time manifested in the emotional-sexual lives of the subjects under study (Herdt 1999).
After all, to study gender and sexuality is to study society embodied and performed in the most intimate details of a social actor's life. Moreover, to study
something like homosexuality in a sympathetic fashion in the age of AIDS,
reactionary fundamentalism, and hate crimes is to call into question any and
all blanket cultural condemnations of these sexualities and the social visions
that the condemnations crystallize. When one carries such a study through
from outside the culture, the political and social implications become even
more profound and complicated. Add to this the fairly recent colonial history
of South Asia, which renders any outside perspective on the culture suspicious at best in the eyes of Indians, and the iconic or canonical, almost unquestioned status of a famous saint, and the stage is set for some fairly profound encounters, misunderstandings, and cross-cultural possibilities. It has
thus always struck me as appropriate, if quite unintended, that my first full-
length essay on Ramakrishna appeared as an invited essay in a book on homosexuality and religion, José Cabezón and Michael Stemmler's *Religion,
Homosexuality, and Literature* (Kripal 1992), that my work has been positively received, both in private and in print, among the American gay community, and that it has been showcased in *Trikone*, a magazine dedicated to
the South Asian–American gay, lesbian, bisexual, and transgendered community (July 1996). Within this same socially liberatory space we might place
the fact that the first major piece to appear on the saint after the book, Parama
Roy's brilliant "As the Master Saw Her: Western Women and Hindu Nationalism," both powerfully confirmed the homoerotic hermeneutic of *Kali's Child*
and took it, with queer theory (and more than a little psychoanalysis), in some
strikingly new postcolonial directions (Roy 1998).

   This implicit political dimension of scholarship also showed itself in the
correspondence. For example, I have communicated at considerable length
with a number of individuals who are interested in changing Indian and
American attitudes toward sexuality, and particularly toward homosexuali-
ties. Here I am thinking in particular of the remarkable Indian social activist
Ashok Row Kavi, who has pioneered and done so much for raising public
consciousness about sexual minorities in India; the Indian lesbian activist and
writer Giti Thadani, whose fascinating *Sakhiyani: Lesbian Desire in Ancient*

and Modern India (Thadani 1996) stands as the only extant full-length study of Indian lesbian cultures that we have; and Ginu Kamani, a talented American writer and eroticist interested in exploring the complexities of Indian sexualities through her sexually transgressive short stories (Kamani 1995) and provocative literary essays. Each of these figures reads *Kali's Child* from his or her own unique sociopolitical situation in India or America. Certainly, each has shared with me her or his own agreements, reservations, and criticisms— and these I do not want to deny—but for each the act of psychoanalytic scholarship can be quite consonant with the work of cultural change and sociosexual liberation. Speaking personally, I certainly do not see myself as "belonging" in India as these individuals do, nor do I understand my work as explicitly reformist. As I have asserted from the very beginning (Kripal 1995, xiii–xv), my intentions have always been and remain primarily religious and intellectual. I have always understood my "place" as an American academic writing to make comparative and sexual sense of my own postmodern, plural soul in the mirror of the Other. Still, I am quite proud of the fact that those who do belong in India and do understand their work in activist terms can use my work in their own ways and on their own terms. Such writing can, in the words of Ginu Kamani, help us all break what Ramakrishna called, in true Tantric fashion, the "bonds of shame, disgust and fear," wherever they are found or felt. Such a breaking is an act at once scholarly, mystical, transgressive . . . and ultimately liberating. If then, we are to apply to *Kali's Child* Linda Alcoff's fundamental challenge to postcolonial writers and ask what King calls "the crucial question"—"Does your narrative enable the empowerment of oppressed groups?" (King 1999, 214)—the answer, if the history of the book's reception means anything, appears to be a yes.

Psychoanalysis as Sympathetic Recovery

Others emphasize the ability of psychoanalysis to humanize or make more real the subjects it studies. Ramakrishna, like all great saints, has been the object of a long history of canonization, hagiography, and image making. The feeling many readers get, and especially Western readers, is that there is precious little of his humanity left at the end, that there is more hidden than revealed in the traditional portraits, and that the traditional image of the saint, in its absolute insistence on his transcendence of sexuality and his teachings on a nondual abstract *brahman*, is more alienating than helpful. How often have I heard about how the Ramakrishna of *Kali's Child* is "more human," "more loveable," or "more endearing" than the Ramakrishna of the tradition. Psychoanalysis, it seems, gives us access to what all human beings share, and in this it humanizes (and unites) us all.

Numerous correspondents and reviews commented on this phenomenon of sympathetic recovery. David Haberman, for example, described how the book's effective rescue of Ramakrishna from the stiff, stilted lens of neo-Vedanta increased his appreciation of Ramakrishna "immeasurably" (Haberman 1997). Unfortunately, this academic response, which sees the book as appreciative, nonreductive, and as deeply sympathetic, stands in stark contrast to many of the devotional responses and raises important questions about what exactly is going on in the "devotional read." Much of this, of course, could be explained by a rather simple fact: in the vast majority of cases, there simply is no devotional read—that is, they have not actually read the book (a number of people have actually admitted this to me).

Very much related to this humanizing function of a psychoanalytic method is the issue of humor and light-heartedness—that is, the ability to transcend not only one's social world but also oneself in a moment of emotional and intellectual freedom (which is also a kind of mild transgression). Strikingly, the Bengali texts are filled with such humor. Ramakrishna is always smiling or laughing out loud, telling jokes (some of them quite bawdy), and making fun of a visitor (who has often just left) or of himself. Phrases like "all laugh" or "with a smile" or "laughter" pepper the text in parentheses. I tried to capture something of this internal humor in my own text. Indeed, the book ends with Ramakrishna laughing at me, the book, and my "touchstone." Appropriately, many readers— American and Indian alike—responded accordingly, with their own laughter, smiles, and good humor. One South Asian literary critic shared with me her joy that the book obviously took itself no more seriously than its subjects, Ramakrishna and Kali, did. Many of them, not surprisingly, turned to psychoanalytic or sexual language to tell their jokes (none of which I am brave enough to repeat here). It was almost as if the psychoanalytic categories gave them a linguistic way to transgress beyond their normal public or religious selves. The release of repressed material thus had the effect that it often does—a mixture of fear, hearty laughter, and intoxicating freedom.

Psychoanalysis as Personal Therapy

Other readers responded to the book in ways that can only be called therapeutic. One reader now understood a history of parental abuse and neglect tied to trance states and religion. The book helped initiate a long healing process that would include seeing a therapist, ending a long dysfunctional marriage, and dealing more honestly and effectively with the abusive parent. Another person, this one a devout Christian with considerable theological training and unusual psychological sophistication, used the book to help explain his own troubling experiences of Kali. Such visions, devotional moods, and altered states of consciousness, which often spontaneously overwhelmed him, had terrified and baffled him for years. Through a long correspondence, he came to the conclusion that they could also be positive, that they had a definite mystical quality to them, and that they were most likely linked to an adolescent use of hallucinogens.

Psychoanalysis as Mystical Technique

Finally, I come to a realm of pedagogical experience for which I can claim much experience (that is, a thick file of letters) but little, if any, understanding or intellectual clarity: the phenomenon of an explicitly mystical response to psychoanalytic scholarship. It is at this point, I think, where all the usual pedagogical wisdom (about bracketing one's worldview, about objectivity, about the limits of cross-cultural understanding, etc.) breaks down and one is left in an existential situation for which there is little precedent and even less professional training. Which is another way of saying that I am lost. I may be lost, but I know that I am not alone here, for I have heard anecdotal stories similar to my own from a number of colleagues who work with mystical texts and traditions. I also know, again from such anecdotal material, that scholars sometimes respond to these responses by dismissing them as unimportant, tangential, or simply strange. I certainly understand this, and perhaps such a response is appropriate in some contexts. Still, I cannot help thinking that it is precisely at this point—when one's scholarship is religiously and positively engaged—that things can become the most pedagogically exciting, personally rewarding, and theoretically fruitful. Again, I claim no theoretical clarity or advance no thesis here—I am quite serious about being lost—but I am quite certain that such responses serendipitously hide within themselves important pedagogical, theoretical, and hermeneutical truths that deserve to be explored.

Consider, for example, the following. In the spring of 1996, I received in the mail an imaginatively written and quite insightful book review of *Kali's Child* published in *The Trident*, a journal sponsored by an American Tantric community (Sahajananda 1996). Quite unlike many of my academic reviewers, who did not seem to understand the ontological subtext of the book and so collapsed my dialectical psychoanalytic method into a naive and solely regressive reductionism, Sahajananda understood the dialectic perfectly well, read Ramakrishna's ambivalent sexual tendencies with me as catalyzing his mystical identification with the goddess, and, most important, engaged the book on its own sympathetic terms: "That is perhaps the most delightful aspect of Kripal's book: its ability to open a window onto the Marvelous, manifested in so many places in one's reading where one must pause, and, amazed, exclaim, 'So that's why _____!'" (Sahajananda 1996, 7). Here in Sahajananda's text the hermeneutical experience of reading a psychoanalytically informed book has become a religious experience, a place of psychological understanding, and a moment of delight. Few reviewers, I should add, have understood me better than this Tantrika.

Or consider my correspondance with "William," an American male Kali-mystic in his late thirties, who first contacted me in June 1996 to tell me that reading the book was "one of the most confirming spiritual experiences Mother [the goddess] has blessed me with." As he told me his story over the years, I began to understand why. William is a veteran of the American spirituality and guru cultures and has been graced with numerous powerful religious, visionary, and ecstatic experiences, including a number of early psychedelic shatterings of his categories ("I had no context for bliss") and a nondual enlightenment event that dramatically and permanently altered his psychological functioning and worldview.

Operating with a sophisticated developmental model of the psyche, William postulates that infants experience the Self as a thick cottony "nothing," a sensation so dense and undiluted that it can be compared to a kind of substance-sensation. "Infants experience themselves as Self-mother-environment all-at-once," he writes. As the personality develops through human maturation and the learning process, this experience of the Self becomes diffused and cloudy. William thus speaks of the "diffusion of the personality" as a kind of foggy or dirty glass sheet that must be wiped away to catch a glimpse of the pinpoint that is the Self; alternatively, ego development constitutes the building of a psychic false "floor" of identity, a "me" that must be dissolved in the direct and immediate perception that is the foundational event of realization. Such a process involved real psychological work, in his case years of therapy and analysis with an initiated Sufi and trained Jungian therapist who was open to—indeed knew—his mystical experiences but could also help him interpret his dreams and work through his psychosexual problems, or in William's own metaphorical language, help him dissolve the floor. William was particularly bothered by his transsexual tendencies and his deep desires to experience the goddess Kali through a ritualized cross-dressing practice. Traditional ascetic language about suppressing or rejecting active sexuality only played into this dilemma and produced in him a deep sense of horror and guilt over his sexual desires. What the psychoanalytic method of *Kali's Child* did for William is give him back an exemplary saint he had always deeply loved, but this time as a human being like him, with a sexuality that did not "fit" the culture but could nevertheless be acted out and enjoyed in and through the various *bhava*s ("states") of the goddess. William wrote:

> I'm not sure where to begin, but I can tell you with absolute clarity that I've lost what Ramakrishna refers to as "the idea of me." I watched it dissolve in front of my very "eyes" a few months ago. . . . So please let me know what you think of all this. I'm dying to talk about it but really cannot simply because nobody will believe it. I certainly don't look like a realized being to most folk. It is one's expectations about realization that are the biggest hindrance to one's being blessed by the event, and as I don't fit most people's expectations about what a realized person would be like they just aren't going to believe it. . . . *Kali's Child* made this all possible in this life. Before I read your book I was in a state of self-loathing over my transvestism (which is simply an enactment of Shakti [the "energy" or "power" of the goddess]). After reading the truth about Ramakrishna, I allowed myself to have a degree of acceptance about myself and my practice. . . . In order for the Self to perceive Itself in the context of an individual life there *must* be at least a minimum of self acceptance. I am indebted to you for mine.

Here in William's life we find psychoanalysis in its full pedagogical force: as an act of social liberation of a culturally suppressed sexuality, as a humanizing factor, as a therapeutic force or catalyst, and as a mystical technique—taken together, a powerful and ultimately effective way to travel back along the developmental arc and see the Self in its cottony silence. For William, such an accomplishment cannot be had through magical means (mantras and

the like), through the cult of saints, or through the false and constructed dilemmas of celibacy (the dysfunctional mechanics of semen retention, for
example). All such practices are built on dualistic assumptions, which the event
of enlightenment—the realization that one has always been enlightened, that
there is nowhere to go—exposes as misguided and futile. Nor can such an
enlightenment event be identified with the bliss of mystical or visionary experience. Indeed, the latter forms of experience are "infantile" and clearly
regressive for William. "That is what babies get—the ooey-gooey stuff [of
erotic bliss]." Quite conscious of why he originally sought such experiences
out (his own mother was cold and distant and treated him as an inconvenience,
hence "I've been looking for it ever since"), William is equally clear that such
mysticism is not realization, and that, indeed, mysticism (as maternal merger)
inevitably ends with the realization of the Self. The excesses of mystico-erotic
experience may be useful or even necessary to pull one out of the "consen-
sus-trance" of society or to help dissolve the ego, but the Self is in no way
dependent upon the retention of semen, the presence of mystical ecstasy, or
any other form of phenomenal experience.

It has occurred to me many times in my exchanges with William that I had
ceased being the teacher and had become the taught. True, I was quite familiar intellectually with traditional Vedantic discourse about the Self (*atman*)
and the nature of enlightenment, but never had I actually encountered these
experiences so clearly and convincingly in a living human being. Nor had I
ever met a being as happy, as free, as delightfully light-hearted, and as
ontologically gifted as William. That my work on Ramakrishna helped him
in some small way work through his psychosexual struggles—that is, helped
him de-diffuse his personality and clear away the "floor of me"—and into
this decidedly profound present is cause for more than a little joy in me.
Moreover, I am continually moved by his utter lack of self-consciousness
or sense of superiority: "The moment of realization is a fence, a portal,"
William explained to me, "I'm standing on the other side—that's the only
difference between us." I had no doubts, no doubts at all, that he was right—
there was just something in his voice. And in his actions. One of the last
times I spoke to him he showed absolutely no desire to be profiled and hung
up the phone to put on his Rollerblades and be pulled through the park by
an eager sheepdog.

My third example involves the positive "inside" reception the book received from the prolific contemporary Siddha guru Adi Da and his community.[9] To understand the full force of this example a bit of background is
necessary, particularly in regard to Hindu incarnational theology. In one traditional Indic model, the *avatara,* or "descent" of God, descends into the
human plane whenever the *dharma* or socioreligious order wanes. Hence the
Gita's classic description of Krishna descending into a human form whenever the *dharma* wanes: "Whenever, O son of Bharata, the dharma begins to
dissolve, I emit my Self in order to restore the *dharma*."[10] Within such a cy-
clical model of divine descent (which, of course, mirrors the doctrine of the
transmigrating soul), present *avatara*s can be seen as "re-incarnations" of

previous *avataras*. The Bengali texts on Ramakrishna employ this model at some length, as the Ramakrishna of these texts suggests repeatedly that he is in fact a reincarnation of the sixteenth-century Bengali saint Caitanya, who was in Ramakrishna's time an already divinized and recognized *avatara*. Ramakrishna, moreover, would take such a notion even further and argue that his disciples were actually reincarnations of Caitanya's own disciples, and that they had all reincarnated again in the present *together*.

Adi Da performs the same theological move in his own self-understanding and theologizing, this time with respect to Vivekananda and Ramakrishna himself. Hence *The Knee of Listening*, the guru's authorized biography, explains how Adi Da, starting in the 1970s, claimed that the subtle vehicle of Swami Vivekananda, who could not complete his mission to the West in his own lifetime, spontaneously conjoined with the physical vehicle of "Franklin Jones" (Adi Da's birthname) to fulfill his divine purpose. More recently (since 1993), Adi Da, pointing out that since Ramakrishna poured his own being into Vivekananda in an act of *sakti-pata* (lit. "descent of power") before his own death, has begun to claim that both Vivekananda and Ramakrishna came together to help produce his present incarnation. It was this same subtle vehicle of Ramakrishna-Vivekananda, the tradition suggests, that prepared Adi Da for his mission through his "Great Husbanding" of the goddess in the Vedanta Temple of Hollywood in 1970, a powerfully Tantric experience of mystico-erotic union with the goddess in the numinous spaces of what is probably the most important and well-known Ramakrishna center in the country (Adi Da, 1995, 554–57).[11]

It is in these theological, biographical, and Tantric contexts that Adi Da read my work in its 1993 dissertation form. A scholar, without my knowledge, had provided the guru's disciples with a copy, which they then flew out to Adi Da on his Fiji island community. After reading *Kali's Child* in its dissertation form, the guru put the work in his forthcoming *The Basket of Tolerance*, a select bibliography of books arranged according to his seven-stage model of spiritual development; indeed, the book merited an entire mini-essay, entitled "The 'Secret' Biography of Ramakrishna and the Universally Necessary Foundation Struggle with the Emotional-Sexual Character." Although respectfully critical of the reductive tendencies of my psychoanalytic methods—that is, the regressive side of the dialectic—Adi Da's reading of *Kali's Child* is hardly dismissive and deserves a careful reading for its deconstruction of any simplistic scholarship/religion or outsider/insider dichotomy:

> In his book . . . Jeffrey J. Kripal has done a useful service to all by presenting a very frank, open, and well-researched discussion of the emotional-sexual (and basically, homosexual, or homoerotic) aspects of Ramakrishna's life, sadhana, and visionary (or mind-based) mysticism. No doubt, [his] "disclosures" (or scholarly arguments) will shock some, for whom Ramakrishna *must* be associated only with puritanical, and especially non-sexual, interpretations. But it is time that it be understood, and openly and positively accepted, that religious and Spiritual life, even in the case of its greatest exemplars and Realizers (of whom Ramakrishna was, certainly, one), requires a foundation struggle with

the emotional-sexual character, and, in many cases, even an always ongoing association with one or another form of emotional-sexual practice or Yoga. . . . Jeffrey J. Kripal's book . . . serves the generally right purposes of a basic, and sufficiently revealing, "secret" biography of Ramakrishna. . . . Indeed, generally speaking, Jeffrey J. Kripal has, in *Kali's Child*, only dared to state openly what must have been already somehow obvious to even all those who have perceptively and sympathetically studied (and felt) Ramakrishna. (Adi Da forthcoming, 337–39)

Here again we see all three of the patterns discussed above: psychoanalysis as social criticism, sympathetic recovery, and personal therapy (here reconceived as religious reform). More dramatically, we confront a man who esoterically understands himself in some profound sense to *be* both Vivekananda and Ramakrishna and, as this dual being, endorses the secret biography of his past incarnation(s) by including it in a list of important texts for his devotees and by writing an appreciative and warmly supportive essay on its theses. Whatever one thinks of Adi Da's theological self-understanding—and certainly it is quite traditional within the parameters of Indian religious thought—its relationship to his reading of *Kali's Child* makes one thing unmistakably clear: any reading of the book's reception as a dichotomous battle between an "outside" scholarly acceptance and an "inside" religious rejection does not do justice to the immeasurably more fascinating facts. Certainly it would be difficult to imagine a more "inside" reception than this.

But what does one do with such a response? What should one do? I do not have any easy answers here. In my own case, I must confess that it took me years to feel comfortable with such an engagement, and only recently have I been able to actively participate in a personal correspondence with Adi Da and a number of his devotees. The result, as with William, has been especially rewarding: the book, far from shutting the door to this religious community, in fact opened it quite wide and allowed us to discuss the relationship between sexuality and spirituality in a manner that is especially rare in the history of North American guru traditions. Awe is not an inappropriate term to capture something of my own reaction to this almost surreal response. Once again, the psychoanalytic telling of secrets opened up the possibility of personal communication and scholarly analysis on the most satisfying and human of discursive levels. Secrets beckon secrets, many of which, it seems apparent now, need to be spoken for the sanity and health of both our religious and academic communities.

Concluding Reflections: Closing the Files with Bakan, Kirschner, and Parsons

As I close my files and shuffle away the letters for another day, what do I make of all of this, of the political, humanizing, therapeutic, and even mystical powers of a psychoanalytic method? I personally do not wish to draw any normative conclusions from the accounts discussed above, as if my hermeneutical experiences with a type of psychoanalytic Indology and its readers carry some universally applicable truth. Classroom and reader responses to psychoanalysis are usually highly personal, idiosyncratic affairs, and when one adds the intimacies of mystical experience (which is often also sexual experience) to the mix, the reactions become even more personal and more idiosyncratic. What does a teacher do when one's lecture on Freud elicits powerful memories of sexual abuse from a student? Or what does one say when a professional colleague hints at mystical experiences induced by one's writing? Or how does one handle the reality of a contemporary *avatara* engaging one's own work through his past lives? Or what does one say when told that one's book is being confiscated at the Indian borders? All of this, I would suggest, far from being irrelevant or simply unusual, is in fact very important—this, after all, is precisely how religion works, what it *is*, "on the ground." To ignore such fascinating details for safer, more traditional, or more temporally distant data may be understandable, but I cannot help feeling that such a refusal to gaze into and through these things is also something of a theoretical tragedy.

I have not ignored these facts of my pedagogical and professional experience. Indeed, I have thought about and struggled with them almost every day of my life for the last ten years. I have written about some of my conclusions elsewhere, particularly those concerning the reality and experience of censorship (1998a, 1998b) and the postmodern dialectic of cross-cultural psychoanalysis (1998c). Here I want to emphasize, if not quite develop, a third theme: the potentially mystical nature of psychoanalysis. The few stories I have recounted above are in reality only the tip of a very large iceberg, and no "gut feeling" is stronger in me than that which gurgles that there is something strangely analogous or uncannily similar about mystical traditions and psychoanalytic thought. Others have eloquently explored this possibility in some detail. Here I am reminded of David Bakan's early and still fascinating thesis that Freud's psychoanalysis—with its oral initiatory ritual structure, its emphasis on esotericism, its understanding of sexual symbolism, its antinomian engagement with the "lower" or "infernal" powers of instinct, and its rabbinic-like exegetical style—functions as a kind of secularized Kabbalah (Bakan 1958); of Suzanne Kirschner's study of the religious structure and romantic "naturalized supernaturalism" of psychoanalytic thought, seen again as a type of secularized mysticism (Kirschner 1996); and of William Parsons's most recent work on the Freud-Rolland correspondence and its implications for the psychoanalytic study of mysticism, with which I began this essay (Parsons 1999).

For now, I have nothing further to offer this discussion in terms of historical influence, intellectual history, or psychohistorical case study. All I can assert is that, taken as a whole, my personal experience of censorship (the mystical returns to its etymological roots as "the secret" [*to mustikon*]) and my correspondence with the readers of *Kali's Child* seem to confirm these theoretical insights. This in turn suggests to me that we need to revisit Bakan's thesis and approach those of Kirschner and Parsons with the utmost seriousness and interest. I realize that there is no linear argument here, and that nothing I have said above constitutes a proper demonstration of this final thesis. But I was asked to reflect on my pedagogical experiences teaching Hinduism with Freud, and these are my reflections. They are what they are.

To sum up, then, I might say that the discursive practice that is the psychoanalytic study of the Hindu Tantra possesses the potential to awaken powerful forces—both negative and positive—within the psyches and bodies of its practitioners, readers, and listeners. Once awakened, these forces are sometimes difficult to deal with, especially when they manifest themselves across cultures and times, but they are always there nonetheless, waiting for a language with which to speak, an opportunity to gush forth, as Romain Rolland might say. Psychoanalysis, for all its well-known limitations and faults, provides such a language and such an opportunity. Certainly the transgression and freedom it offers is not for everyone, but for those who want to go beyond the still essential acts of description and indigenous understanding to the near core of erotic forms of mysticism like the Hindu Tantra, there are few, if any, paths that are more exhilarating, more hermeneutically fruitful, and more rewarding. Like the Tantric traditions themselves, psychoanalysis is a powerful and dangerous path of secret rituals and sexual revelations. Any who choose to enter this hermeneutical *cakra* must be ready to struggle with the demons and deities and human beings who appear there in such colorful forms. Anything else is surface talk outside the ritual circle—comfortable, safe, and necessary perhaps, but not terribly revealing. To tell a secret—and that in the end is what both psychoanalysis and mysticism are about in their respective discourses—is to enact a transgression. That is what a secret is, what it must be—something that should not be told, *which must be told*. Transgression is thus built into the very heart of the mystical as the secret (*mustikon*). Any study of such a secret that claims more than superficial access must be willing to similarly transgress and consequently win both the denunciations and the gratitude of those who are listening. What other way is there to speak a secret?

Notes

This essay is dedicated to Bill Parsons, who taught me what it is I do and how it historically flows out of a friendship with Sigmund Freud. I would also like to thank Diane Jonte-Pace for encouraging me "to think again" about the transgressive natures of scholarship and pedagogy. The essay was finished in the summer of 1999 and so does not reflect any events or issues raised after that date. Small portions of it, moreover, have appeared in Kripal 2000 since then. I thank *Harvard Divinity Bulletin* for permission to reuse these.

1. I borrow the expression from the French Islamicist Louis Massignon, who used it to describe his own creative method of plumbing the life and teachings of the tenth-century Sufi al-Hallaj through the mystical experiences and spiritual intuitions of his own (Kripal 1999).

2. Rolland, of course, was thinking of Freud's *The Future of an Illusion* (*SE* 21), which had just appeared.

3. See also *SE* 22: 80.

4. See Narasingha Sil's review, "The Question of Ramakrishna's Homosexuality," in *The Statesman* (31 January 1997), the thirty-eight ensuing letters to the editors (7, 11, 13, 18 February 1997), and the editors' final decision to close off all correspondence on the issue, "Now Let It Rest" (18 February 1997). See also "Ramakrishna's Impulses Spark Row," in *The Times of India* (10 April 1997); interestingly, this last headline assumes the truth of my thesis.

5. It is important here to note that I have never claimed that Ramakrishna was gay. Nor have I ever even written that he was a homosexual, at least in any clear-cut conscious sense. (I studiously avoided the noun, opting instead for the adjectives "homosexual" and "homoerotic.") Ramakrishna, after all, would have had no access to any kind of homosexual social identity as we do in late-twentieth-century America or India—that is, there were no "gays" in nineteenth-century Bengal, although there were no doubt homosexually oriented human beings. Such human beings can express themselves (and, more radically, experience themselves) only within the idioms and symbolic systems that their historical cultures provide them. Ramakrishna was no exception. He experienced and so expressed his own energies (rather marvelously, I might add) through the languages of his culture and then transformed them through ritual, symbol, and vision into mystical experiences. Hence one will look in vain for any explicit references to "a homosexual" in these Bengali texts, and consequently in my work on these texts. What we have here is not a socially constructed identity stabilized in language, ideological category, and institutionalized practice, but a fluid, polymorphous movement of desire and energy and ecstasy, most of which is moving in a clear homoerotic direction.

6. One helpful way to begin a more nuanced discussion is to separate discourse and intention (King 1999, 89, 131). The question then becomes, not what the motivation or personal intention of such-and-such a scholar is, but how we are to understand the largely hidden or unconscious hegemonic powers of such binary thought systems as orientalism, whose historical legacy and present political and religious influence all contemporary Indologists must struggle with reflexively and openly.

7. But this, of course, implies that pedagogy should be about such location and challenge—that is, that pedagogy should be transgressive in nature. This, I recognize, is problematic for some. My only response to this is a faith statement—namely, that it is better to know than to not know. Put differently, knowledge, even when it is deconstructive (and especially when it is deconstructive of unjust or oppressive social practices), is good precisely to the extent that it carries its own argument, its own power, its own justification. There are, of course, issues of "timing" and context here, for not everyone in a classroom or bookstore is emotionally, cognitively, sexually, and/or religiously ready for something like a psychoanalytic method, especially one applied to religious phenomena, but this—unless we are willing to grant infallibility to a teacher-scholar—is a risk implicit in any public pedagogical setting.

8. I am indebted to Diane Jonte-Pace for the substance of this paragraph.

9. Adi Da wrote early about his own understanding of the Tantric Traditions as Bubba Free John in his *Love of the Two-Armed Form* (John 1978). The guru's disciples have told me that Adi Da had been critical of Ramakrishna's understanding of sexuality before reading my work.

10. *Bhagavad-Gita* 4.8; my translation.

11. The tradition has continued to develop this mystical hermeneutic in its literature. For the most recent statement, see Lee 1998.

References

Adi Da. Forthcoming. *The basket of tolerance*. Middletown, Calif.: Dawn Horse Press.
———. 1995. *The knee of listening*. Middletown, Calif: Dawn Horse Press.
Bakan, David. 1958. *Sigmund Freud and the Jewish mystical tradition*. Boston: Beacon Press.
Clooney, Francis. 1993. *Theology after Vedanta*. Albany: State University of New York Press.
Freud, Sigmund. 1953–74. *The standard edition of the complete psychological works of Sigmund Freud (SE)*, Volume 1–24, Translated and edited by James Strachey. London: Hogarth Press.
   1933. *New introductory lectures on psycho-analysis. SE* 22. 3–182.
   1930. *Civilization and its discontents. SE* 21. 59–145.
   1927. *The future of an illusion. SE* 21. 3–56.
Haberman, David. 1997. Review of *Kali's Child. Journal of Asian Studies* 56 no. 2 531–32.
John, Bubba Free. 1978. *Love of the two-armed form*. Clearlake, Calif.: Dawn Horse Press.
King, Richard. 1999. *Orientalism and religion: Postcolonial theory, India, and the "mystic East."* London: Routledge.
Kamani, Ginu. 1995. *Junglee girl*. San Francisco: Aunt Lute Books.
Kinsley, David. 1997. *Tantric visions of the divine feminine: The ten Mahavidyas*. Berkeley: University of California Press.
Kirschner, Suzanne. 1996. *The religious and romantic origins of psychoanalysis: Individuation and integration in post-Freudian theory*. Cambridge: Cambridge University Press.
Kripal, Jeffrey. 1991. Revealing and concealing the secret: A textual history of Mahendranath Gupta's *Srisriramakrsnakathamrta*. In *Calcutta, Bangladesh, and Bengal studies*, edited by Clinton B. Seely. Lansing: Michigan State University Press.
———. 1992. Ramakrishna's foot: Mystical homoeroticism in the *Kathamrta*. In *Religion, homosexuality and literature*, edited by Michael L. Stemmeler and José Cabezón. Las Colinas: Monument Press.
———. 1995. *Kali's child: The mystical and the erotic in the life and teachings of Ramakrishna*. Chicago: University of Chicago Press.
———. 1998a. Mystical homoeroticism, reductionism and the reality of censorship: A response to Gerald Larson. *Journal of the American Academy of Religion* 66, no. 3. 627–35.
———. 1998b. Pale plausibilities. Preface to *Kali's child: The mystical and the erotic in the life and teachings of Ramakrishna*, 2nd ed. Chicago: University of Chicago Press.
———. 1998c. Hinduism and psychoanalysis: Thinking through each other. In *Vishnu on Freud's desk: A reader in psychoanalysis and Hinduism*, edited by T. G. Vaidyanathan and Jeffrey J. Kripal. New Delhi: Oxford University Press.
———. 1999. The visitation of the stranger: On some mystical dimensions of the history of religions. *Cross Currents* 49, no. 3 367–86.
———. 2000. Secret talk: Sexual identity and the politics of the study of Hindu Tantrism. *Harvard Divinity Bulletin* 30, no. 1.
———. 2001. *Roads of excess, palaces of wisdom: Eroticism and reflexivity in the study of mysticism*. Chicago: University of Chicago Press.

Kris, Ernst. 1952. *Psychoanalytic explorations in art.* New York: Schocken Books.

Lee, Carolyn. 1998. *The promised god-man is here: Ruchira Avatar Adi Da Samraj.* Middletown, Calif.: Dawn Horse Press.

Mitra, Satyacharan. 1897. *Sri Sri Ramakrsna Paramahamsa—Jivana O Upadesa.* Calcutta: Great Indian Press.

Obeyesekere, Gananath. 1990. *The work of culture: Symbolic transformations in psychoanalysis and anthropology.* Chicago: University of Chicago Press.

Parsons, William. 1999. *The enigma of the oceanic feeling: Revisioning the psychoanalytic study of mysticism.* New York: Oxford University Press.

Ricouer, Paul. 1970. *Freud and philosophy.* New Haven, Conn.: Yale University Press.

Roy, Parama. 1998. *Indian traffic.* Berkeley: University of California Press.

Sahajananda. 1996. Review of *Kali's child. The Trident* 2, no. 4 6–9.

Stemmeler, Michael L., and Jose Ignacio Cabezón, eds. 1992. *Religion, homosexuality, and literature.* Las Colinas, Tex.: Monument Press.

Thadani, Giti. 1996. *Sakhiyani: Lesbian desire in ancient and modern India.* New York: Casell.

Vaidyanathan, T. G. 1997. Kripal and *Kali's child. The Hindu,* 4 May, xiv.

———. and Jeffrey J. Kripal, eds. 1998. *Vishnu on Freud's desk: A reader in psychoanalysis and hinduism.* New Delhi: Oxford University Press.

13

The Challenge of Teaching Freud: Depth Psychology and Religious Ethics

Ernest Wallwork

When we teach psychoanalysis, what exactly do we hope students will learn? Is it satisfactory to follow the usual scholarly route and teach psychoanalytic ideas in the abstract, apart from analytic practice and experience? If, as I believe, something more than mere intellectual comprehension is necessary to avoid misconstruing psychoanalytic theories and practices, what should our pedagogical aims be and how should we go about trying to achieve them? For example, should we seek to convey how psychoanalytic ideas are used in practice? And if we do aim for something more than mere intellectual knowledge of psychoanalysis, should we also aim for some change in the way students think and feel about themselves and others? If so, is it really possible to change the lives of students within the constraining context of a graded course in a contemporary college or university? And how do we relate the study of psychoanalysis to that of religion and morality? If religion and morality also require something more than mere intellectual comprehension, how do we invite experiential knowing in an academic context without moving beyond generally accepted scholarly goals? These are some of the disquieting questions that I want to pursue in this paper, by way of clarifying issues with which I struggle every year as I approach the task of teaching a course on psychoanalysis and religious ethics to undergraduates.

Introducing undergraduates to the kind of psychological mindedness entailed by psychoanalysis is analogous to teaching about religion to the "religiously unmusical" (Weber 1963). The closest many sophomores have gotten to a therapist is their high school guidance counselor! Of course, adolescents spend a lot of time thinking about themselves, but not often with an eye to typical intrapsychic defenses and self-deceptive practices. This inexperience with critical self-reflection presents the teacher of Freud with both a formidable challenge and an opportunity, insofar as undergraduates are not as resistant to self-examination as they are likely to become, and are often willing to acknowledge that they do not yet know themselves very well. However, deeply entrenched cultural misperceptions of Freud make tapping this reservoir of potential interest difficult. Students commonly approach Freud as a flawed scientist of a completely discredited psychological theory. When asked to "associate" to Freud, they think of beliefs and dogmas they thoroughly dislike, such as psychic determinism, systematic reductionism, psychological egoism, penis envy in women, the Oedipus complex, and the sexual etiology of all human behavior. Insofar as Freud's unmasking strategies are accurately understood, they evoke powerful resistance and defensive maneuvers that generate caricatures. Freud makes students think of "fool," "cocaine addict," "sexual pervert," "dogmatist" or "sadistically silent," as in *New Yorker* cartoons. The cumulative effect of these obstacles makes teaching Freud as "impossible" a profession as psychoanalysis. The teacher who aims at changing students psychologically must address the difficulty of breaking through the defensive armor that students use to protect themselves from taking seriously what Freud's work might plausibly imply for understanding their own lives. As Freud first observed, his work is disturbing to one's peace of mind, and this disturbance is rarely welcomed by the typical undergraduate.

Although I am still struggling with how to introduce students to Freud, I think I have learned some things about how *not* to teach him during the past thirty years of constantly reinventing an undergraduate course on depth psychology, religion, and ethics that I first introduced at Wellesley College in 1969. For instance, I believe it is a huge mistake to start, as my own teachers did, with either "Freudian" theory or a historical account of how Freud developed his distinctive ideas. These approaches focus on content, and on what is on the teacher's mind, rather than on the process of meeting and challenging student preconceptions about Freud and analytic self-reflection. What Freud says about the most propitious approach to dream interpretation applies also to teaching his work—focus on the *dreamer,* rather than on the *interpreter's* theory-driven speculations about the dream's meaning (*SE* 4: 98.n1.). The teacher of Freud needs to focus on the students in the classroom, and only later and secondarily on the syllabus and the teacher's instructional goals. It does little good to teach Freudian theory if students end up with little appreciation of what Freud's concepts and theories mean when used, as intended, to explore unknown and disavowed aspects of human behavior.

My approach focuses on student impressions of Freud, which are more often than not widespread cultural misinterpretations, and on Freud's clinical efforts to understand seemingly irrational conduct, like anxiety attacks, obsessional rituals, eating disorders, depression, and bizarre self-destructive actions. Students can identify with Freud the clinician and become open to how free association, dream interpretation, and defense analysis might help them grasp something they do not yet understand about themselves and others. This is especially the case if the pace is fast, humor is plentiful, and the issues discussed challenge students to think critically about issues of importance in their lives.

Currently, I begin the course by asking students to free-associate on paper for a few minutes about what Freud brings to mind. I do this before I say anything about the course requirements—the syllabus, educational objectives, texts, papers, and examinations. My intention is partly to learn something about specific misinterpretations we will need to address in order to make any real headway, but also to convey implicitly that psychoanalysis is about what people have on their minds—what they think they understand and what they do not. Additionally, the exercise invites them to try their hand with the free-association method that is so central to the practice of psychoanalysis.

Most students disregard entirely my request to free-associate and assume that I am looking for the usual academic written assignment: a well-crafted, logically organized, and cogently supported statement about what they know. Only a few students interpret my instructions as an invitation to freely express whatever involuntary, emotionally connected thoughts come spontaneously to mind about Freud and his work. One who did wrote, "Freud: father of us all, sexual desire, perverse but okay, buried needs and fantasies, my mother, my dad, why was he always so formal and aloof, cathartic venting, letting go of my stagnant brewing emotions." Later, I make use of the difficulty students experience following my instructions to highlight how free association in psychoanalysis differs from the logical organization of ideas.

I have been pleasantly surprised by the critical stance toward their own thoughts about Freud that a sizable minority of my students take in this assignment. Despite cultural indoctrination, many step back from some claim about Freud to interrogate what they think they know and how they know it. After mentioning Freudian slips, one student observed, "I can honestly say I know nothing about Freud, although I took a psychology course that covered his theories briefly and I use terms like 'Freudian slip.' Now I wonder if I actually know what it means." Another student expressed similar sentiments: "I have the same stereotypes of Freud as the average schooled American. I am vaguely familiar with his theories, like the id, ego, and superego, but I have not read much of what he wrote and I'm not sure I should trust what I've heard." Statements of this kind, indicative of student self-consciousness about the cultural lenses through which they view Freud, provide legitimation for the course's attempt to deconstruct the many powerful misreadings that adhere like barnacles to Freud's name and corpus. However, I have taught Freud long enough to know that familiar stereotypes resist the most persuasive evidence to the contrary from Freud's own pen and will reappear on some final examinations months after I had hoped they had been permanently put to rest.

The ambivalent tone of most of the student responses to what I call the "Freud association test" is reassuring, partly because it indicates that unfocused hostility is less of a problem than one might expect from the many negative notions conjured by Freud's name, recent Freud-bashing literature, and the controversy over the Library of Congress Freud exhibit. Students by and large are genuinely puzzled about issues such as how to interpret a dream or symptom and whether Freud really did overdo the role of sexuality and unconscious motivation in human affairs. They wonder whether classical psychoanalysis has been superseded by something better and whether a classical analysis is still worth the time and expense. Fortunately, most students associate Freud's name not only with beliefs they dislike but also with a beneficial therapy—which is why beginning with Freud's therapeutic strategies helps overcome some initial resistance. One student wrote that "Freud founded psychoanalysis, which helped my mother enormously with severe depression"; another said that "a psychoanalyst literally saved my life when I was ready to pack it in." After reading the students' Freud-association papers, I explain that ambivalence about Freud is as good a place as any from which to begin the course, and that contemporary "Freudian analysts," including their teacher, are also ambivalent about Freud's seminal work. The aim of the course is not to eliminate ambivalence but to shift it from standard cultural biases to informed reasons.

I justify my approach to Freud's corpus through his experience-based practices, as contrasted with his abstract theories, by citing several striking passages in which Freud marks his own preference for what he calls the "evergreen" or brilliant "blue-green" of clinical practice over the gray tones of abstract theories. On one occasion in 1926, Freud is reported to have reacted to one systematization of psychoanalytic theory by observing that "he felt like someone who had hugged the coast all his life and . . . now watched others sailing out into the open ocean. He wished them well but could not take part in their ventures: 'I am an old hand in the coastal run [of interpretative work] and I will keep faith with my blue inlets,'" he stated (Waelder 1964, 56 n.8). Similarly, contrasting his own approach with that of theoreticians, he wrote Lou Andreas-Salome: "You have observed how I work, step by step, without the inner need for completion, continually under the pressure of the problems immediately on hand and taking infinite pains not to be diverted from the path" (E. Freud 1975, 319). In this context, I distribute Freud's famous definition of psychoanalysis, in which the emphasis falls squarely on analysis as a process rather than as a set of distinctive theories or doctrines about, for example, the libido, cathexes, drives and their derivatives, psychosexual development, or the Oedipus complex. "Psychoanalysis is the name (1) of a *procedure* for the investigation of mental processes which are almost inaccessible in any other way, (2) of a *method* (based upon that investigation) for the treatment of neurotic disorders and (3) of a *collection of psychological information* obtained along those lines, which is gradually being accumulated into a new scientific discipline" (*SE* 18: 235, italics added).

I tell the class that I harbor an audacious ambition that goes beyond standard academic goals—to change them internally, if they are willing. I point out that there are two very different ways of engaging the course material: one is intellectual, the other existential. Both call for engagement and effort, but of different kinds. I urge them to respond in both ways because they cannot really know what psychoanalysis, religion, or morality are about without both. I empathize that I do not grade personal growth, but the course provides repeated opportunities for them to develop and practice critical self-observation skills. One of these is a dream paper in which they are asked to interpret one of their own dreams as fully as possible under a guarantee of confidentiality.

To defuse the unconscious resistance I expect my invitation to encounter, I tell the story of a clergyman who was sent to me by his superiors for psychotherapy after he embarrassed himself and his community by conducting himself "improperly." During the first year of therapy, he resisted "taking in" anything we learned about his difficulties as a way both of defending his autonomy against the authority figures who had sent him and as a thinly veiled expression of his rage at them and, in the transference, at me. Unfortunately, he suffered more from his prolonged resistance than anyone. It was not until therapy was no longer a requirement and he decided to continue it voluntarily that he allowed himself really to "own" what we had learned and to try to change the deeply entrenched behavioral patterns that had gotten him into trouble in the first place. The story helps clarify the bind the students and I are in. After all, the invitation to engage personally or on a deep level comes from an authority figure. I tell them that adoption of the additional, second-level goal is entirely voluntary, and I offer alternative, more theoretical options to the dream paper and other exercises. I hope that by acknowledging their resistance they will be less controlled by it, and at least consider seizing the opportunity to expand their psychological mindedness in ways that could prove invaluable to them for the rest of their lives. This presentation of the course goals acknowledges the powerful role of the unconscious in the classroom, even as it introduces the specific concepts of resistance and defense we study later.

Psychoanalytic Technique

Beginning the course proper, I introduce psychoanalytic technique by asking students to tell me how they would convince a skeptical friend or roommate that unconscious mental processes influence conscious behavior. "What evidence would you cite in making the case for the unconscious?" I ask. The question usually elicits a wide range of eager responses about dreams and various psychoneuroses, whereupon I assume the role of the devil's advocate and challenge their "evidence" with alternative accounts that deny any role to unconscious mentation. For example, I argue against the supposition that dreams are empirical evidence for the unconscious by proposing that dreams are neurological happenings only, quoting one eminent dream researcher to the effect that manifest dreams are no more than "the garbage the brain spews out at night." I adopt a similarly skeptical stance toward various behaviors the students cite, contending that they can be explained without positing an unconscious. Invariably, some student eventually observes that hypnosis enables subjects to recall memories stored unconsciously that cannot be retrieved consciously. In response to my rejoinder that this fails to show that unconscious motives *influence behavior*, another student will usually point out that posthypnotic suggestion provides particularly convincing evidence of unconscious motives at work, since the hypnotic subject acts without knowing why. These points about hypnotism lead naturally into a mini-lecture I have prepared on the discoveries of Bernheim and Charcot, which use posthypnotic suggestion with hysterical patients, and how this led Freud to break with the Helmholtzian school's exclusively neurological explanation of hysterical symptoms and try Breuer's innovative therapeutic use of hypnosis. I briefly recount the story of how Breuer and Anna O jointly discovered the "talking cure," which I credit as the foundation of virtually all contemporary schools of psychotherapy. Then, I provide a summary of the enormous and growing body of current neuroscientific research on mental and brain functioning that supports the psychodynamic model of the mind over the older cognitive and behavioral models with which these same researchers worked only a few years ago (see Wallwork 2000). I conclude by discussing some of the reasons for Freud's dissatisfaction with hypnosis (e.g., some patients could not be hypnotized, cures were only temporary, and he was not good at it) and his experimentation with free association, which I take to be one of Freud's greatest discoveries, since it lies at the core of the method by which he arrived at his other findings.

I assign Freud's short article on "wild" analysis (*SE*, 11: 221–27; *CP* 2: 297–304) as the first reading in the opening section on psychoanalytic technique, primarily because it argues so persuasively against the very method students associate with Freudian analysis. In "'Wild' Psycho-Analysis," Freud repudiates the kind of "Freudian interpretations" with which we are all too familiar—namely, "wild," speculative, one-upsmanship claims people make when they presume to know what someone else is "really" thinking unconsciously from a "slip of the tongue," dream, or behavioral "problem." "'Wild' Psycho-Analysis" begins with the story of a young physician's attempt to treat a neurotic middle-aged woman for anxiety. The physician erroneously believes he is following Freud's technique when he tells the patient her anxieties are due to repressed sexual desire. Freud writes that the physician fails to understand that psychoanalysis requires the therapist to deal with the whole person, including her "moral and religious" feelings, not just her unconscious desires, and that psychoanalytic interpretations require the patient's active cooperation and free associations. Otherwise, the therapist's interpretations are apt to be wrong and in any case, cannot be verified. The young physician's lack of analytic training leads him to mistakenly assume that for Freud sex refers to actual sexual acts, like masturbation and intercourse, whereas psychoanalysis is primarily interested in *psycho*-sexuality, which embraces all the emotions, desires, and fantasies involved in loving another person. Freud writes:

> In psycho-analysis the term "sexuality" . . . goes lower and also higher than
> the popular sense of the word. . . . We [include] all expressions of tender feel-
> ing. . . . For this reason we prefer to speak of *psychosexuality*, . . . laying stress
> on the point that the mental factor should not be overlooked or underestimated.
> We use the word sexuality in the same comprehensive sense as . . . the word
> *lieben* (to love). And we have long known that a mental lack of satisfaction
> with all its consequences can exist where there is no lack of normal sexual
> intercourse. (*CP* 2: 299)

Contrary to popular opinion, in Freud's time and ours, psychoanalysis does
not have as its goal simply informing people about their unconscious affects
and motivations. The patient who comes for help does not suffer from ignorance, Freud contends, but from powerful intrapsychic emotional conflicts
that need to be identified, understood emotionally as well as cognitively, and
"worked through" before relief can be obtained. Again, in Freud's words,

> If *knowledge about his unconscious* were as important for the patient as the
> inexperienced in psycho-analysis imagine, it would be sufficient to cure him
> for him to go to lectures or read books. Such measures, however, have as little
> effect on the symptoms of nervous disease as distributing menu-cards in time
> of famine has on people's hunger. (*CP* 2: 302; italics added)

Freud also points out that "wild" interpretations tend to harm the patient
by triggering anger against the interpreter and kindling resistance and internal defensiveness against continuing therapy. "Attempts to bully the patient,"
Freud writes, "by brusquely telling him the hidden things one infers behind
his story are technically reprehensible; they mostly lead to their own doom,
too, by inspiring a hearty dislike for the physician . . . and putting an end to
any further influence" (*CP* 2: 302–303).

I find that students are intrigued by this remarkable little essay because it
poses the implicit question: If psychoanalytic treatment is not what they
thought it was, what is it? The essay works as a superb introduction to Freud's
later "technical papers," since it stimulates curiosity about how psychoanalysts and patients work together to arrive at close-grained interpretations of
the patient's difficulties in living.

To help students develop a feel for how analysis actually works, I employ
several "live demonstrations" in the classroom. For example, I demonstrate
"free association" by lying down on the desk in front of the lecture room and
associating as unselfconsciously as I can under the circumstances to whatever I am experiencing at the time. Admittedly, this is a contrived demonstration, since I know I am not going to delve more deeply into the recesses
of my psyche than I wish to go. Nonetheless, I go to the edge of what I can
stand to tell students about precisely what I am feeling, in what Merton Gill
aptly calls the "here and now" of associating. Starting from my feelings of
discomfort, loneliness, embarrassment, and potential humiliation lying exposed and vulnerable to the class's critical scrutiny before I have gotten to
know any of them as individuals, I try to follow the trains of thought that occur
to me, as one emotional thought stimulates another, which triggers a third,

and so on. These feelings usually elicit memories of when I experienced similar feelings recently—yesterday, last week, or last month—as well as older feelings as the son of a narcissistic mother and distant, obsessional father who behaved in ways that lent a peculiar texture to my feeling states. Exposing my inner world in front of the class announces loudly that we are working in a very different and more personally risky realm than when we are teaching and learning about abstract ideas. After the demonstration, students seem freer and more comfortable sharing experiences and asking questions about topics, like bulimia, that their classmates might interpret as revealing personal problems. The "demonstration" also elicits e-mails and office visits from students who need to talk with someone about a personal crisis, such as a recurring traumatic dream, confused sexual identity, or suicidal thoughts. Sometimes I learn something new about myself while associating that is valuable in its own right, but whether I do or not, the exercise helps keep me in touch with the practices I am trying to teach, in the alien atmosphere of a university classroom.

Discussion of the demonstration, together with readings on technique, seems to help students understand some of the distinguishing features of free association. My meanderings illustrate how the tolerant "self-observation" that occurs in free association differs from what Freud calls "critical reflection." Freud writes:

> In reflection, there is one more psychical activity at work than in the most attentive self-observation, and this is shown amongst other things by the tense looks and wrinkled forehead of a person pursuing his reflections, as compared with the restful expression of a self-observer. In both cases, attention must be concentrated, but the man who is reflecting is also exercising his *critical* faculty; this leads him to reject some of the ideas that occur to him after perceiving them, to cut short others without following the trains of thought which they would open up to him, and to behave in such a way towards still others that they never become conscious at all and are accordingly suppressed before being perceived. The self-observer, on the other hand, need only take the trouble to suppress his critical faculty. If he succeeds in doing that, innumerable ideas come into his consciousness, of which he would otherwise never have got hold. (*SE* 4: 101–2)

Students are often struck by how much is revealed by allowing one's thoughts to wander undirected, and this helps them appreciate what Freud says about the "fundamental rule," which directs the analysand to communicate every idea or thought that comes to mind no matter how seemingly trivial, stupid, or ridiculous. I point out that this is much easier said than done and that it takes years of analysis before most people can allow their thoughts to run without the conscious or unconscious interruptions we all use to sift our thoughts as they occur. The concept of a "rule" that one is expected to follow often itself becomes an obstacle to free association, by eliciting pseudo-compliance and/or unconscious resistance.

The live experiment also shows how current affective experiences are shaped by our unique past. My embarrassment is refracted through a personality that has been molded by earlier experiences with shame and doubt that now color my present experiences, no matter how minor or seemingly insignificant. Students typically prove unusually adept at ferreting out my defensive moves when I am avoiding something too embarrassing to discuss. Their delight in turning the tables on a professor by playing the role of analyst is almost palpable and facilitates their readiness to learn more about the variety of intrapsychic defenses that Freud eventually unearthed. Most initially equate defense with repression. I illustrate additional defensive behaviors with clinical examples, such as the expressively flirtatious behavior that hid a coed's sexual fears and the macho male undergraduate's homophobic reaction formation against latent homosexual feelings.

Students are primed for transference interpretations showing the continuing significance of persons in one's past by reading assignments in Freud's "The Dynamics of Transference" (*SE* 12: 99–108), "Remembering, Repeating and Working-Through" (*SE* 12:147–56), and "Observations on Transference Love" (*SE* 12: 159–171). My expression of concern about the critical thoughts of the students while I am associating helps show how the void created by the abstinent analyst stimulates the analysand's fantasies. I illustrate the powerful effect of transference misperceptions by telling the true story of a former graduate student who wasted many years trying to write a dissertation that would please both Professor David Miller and me. The transferential nature of his difficulties was obscured by the usual scholarly issues until the day he expressed astonishment that Professor Miller and I were planning on teaching a seminar on Freud and Jung together. He said he thought we were bitter enemies, since Professor Miller is a well-known Jungian scholar and I work within the Freudian tradition. Although he had studied with both of us, he had managed to overlook the favorable comments we made about each other's work, the obviously complementarity of our views on a number of issues, and evidence of our friendship. Projecting conflict between his parents onto his teachers, the student created enormous problems for himself that delayed his progress for years because he falsely believed that he had to be careful not to alienate either of us as he worked his way gingerly through comprehensive Ph.D. examinations and a dissertation supervised by us both. It was not until I discussed his misperceptions with him that the student realized that his own psyche was the source of conflicts that he was convinced existed in the external world.

In the class session devoted to Freud's technical writings on transference, I bring in examples from working with very different patients, representing the main personality types—hysterical, narcissistic, psychotic, borderline, obsessional. With one female, borderline patient, I intermittently became in the transference the patient's long-dead mother, with whom she had felt a blissful symbiotic bond. In these moments, my patient and I both felt as if we were resonating wordlessly with one another. These maternal moments were punctuated by sudden shifts when she experienced me as an "evil witch," "dogmatic Freudian," or "sadistic researcher" and hated me intensely, at which time the patient would scream at me about my numerous shortcomings as a therapist. Yelling loudly enough for anyone in the waiting room to hear, she would accuse me of giving "textbook interpretations," of a total lack of empathy and a mean, hostile manner. Vignettes from several dramatic sessions with this patient, in which she shifted from symbiotic at-oneness to fury and then back to symbiosis, enrich the student's understanding of transference derived from the assigned articles. Needless to say, undergraduates are always intrigued by how it feels for a male analyst to play the role of mother to a young woman, and what happens to sexual feelings in such a transference.

A very different example of transference comes from the analysis of a middle-aged executive, for whom I was often the good father he never had. However, I was also occasionally this man's unreliable mother and the critical, punishing father he wished to defeat. Clinical excerpts show that when this patient viewed me unconsciously in the good father role, he felt confident and powerful. We were an unbeatable team who, in his fantasy life, won great victories together in business and sports. But when I was experienced as his critical father, he hid his anger by pretending to be my humble, subservient patient-slave, with dreams full of masochistic scenes in which he was defeated and punished by someone like his father or me. This man's case material highlights peculiarly well how analysis works, not by brainwashing patients, as Adolf Grunbaum (1984) contends, but by continuously interrogating the transference, including compliance with the analyst, for evidence of latent motives (see my discussion of Grunbaum, in Wallwork 1991, 293–98).

These vignettes also bring out aspects of transference phenomena that Freud failed to see, particularly how the analysand can subtly pressure the analyst to play an assigned role. For example, with the female patient, I acted out the uncaring parental role by "accidentally" locking her out of the office. I point out that self-analysis of countertransference enactments like this enable contemporary analysts to use their own affective reactions to interpret what their patients are experiencing unconsciously. By contrast, Freud saw countertransference mainly as an interference from the analyst's unresolved transference, not as a vital resource for understanding the patient through attention to how the patient can induce the analyst unconsciously to play out archaic dramas.

Clinical material is invaluable, not just to illustrate theoretical points but also to get close to the emotional truth that psychoanalysis explores and unearths. From my private psychoanalytic practice, as well as from my continuing self-analysis, I have a wealth of in-depth experience from which to draw in explicating the process of probing one's deepest affects in the face of powerful inner defenses. Fortunately, a number of my patients have given informed consent to use their case material, carefully disguised to conceal their identity, for educational purposes. I also draw stories from my own life and that of my children at different stages of development. I find that the short stories I tell not only facilitate the intellectual goal of educating students about psychoanalysis but also help stimulate by example the kind of inner struggle involved in understanding oneself in depth.

Dream Interpretation

After technique, a second section on dream interpretation offers careful *explication de texte* of Freud's Irma dream in *The Interpretation of Dreams*, and explores the meaning of typical dream images and the "dream work" of condensation, displacement, representation, and secondary revision. I avoid the heavily theoretical chapters one and seven of *The Interpretation of Dreams* because this material tends to be misunderstood by undergraduates unless they come to it with a firm grasp of how Freud went about interpreting the dreams upon which his theoretical "speculations" were based. Students typically need help identifying how Freud distinguished the psychoanalytic approach to dream interpretation from what he calls (1) the scientific approach, (2) the symbolic approach, and (3) decoding. Primed to see Freud as a scientist, students have difficulty understanding his rejection of the scientific approach, until they see that the scientific approach in his time referred to somatic accounts, and that Freud aligned psychoanalysis with traditional popular opinion and religious teachings on the meaningfulness of dreams. Nevertheless, they usually have difficulty understanding his rejection of "symbolic dream interpretation," which relies on intuiting an entire dream's meaning, and the "decoding method," which translates each dream symbol by a fixed meaning. Isn't decoding precisely what Freud himself does in *Interpretation of Dreams,* chapter 6, section E? they ask. In section E, Freud proposes that elongated objects (knives, sticks, tree trunks, umbrellas) in dreams represent the penis and that containers (boxes, cases, chests, ovens) and hollow objects (ships, vessels, and rooms), among others, represent the vagina and womb. With careful textual work, my undergraduates see that in section E, Freud explicitly is offering only some frequently found meanings for certain symbols, not universal fixed meanings Otherwise, Freud would have written a dream-book with fixed meanings like those in Antiquity. Against the fixed-meaning approach, Freud insists that dreams have meaning only in the context of the dreamer's life, personality, and current experiences. While symbols have a range of generally accepted meanings, they are sufficiently plastic to be shaped by the individual's unique past experience and personality. Thus, Freud writes: "The same piece of [dream] content may conceal a different meaning when it occurs in various people or in various contexts" (*SE* 4: 105). Typical latent symbolic meanings *may* be useful in orienting the interpreter to meanings that might be otherwise missed, but Freud warns that

> the peculiar plasticity of the psychical material [in dreams] must never be forgotten. Often enough a symbol has to be interpreted in its proper meaning and not symbolically. . . . A dreamer may derive from his private memories the power to employ as . . . symbols all kinds of things which are not ordinarily employed as such . . . that is to say, [the interpreter has to to have] individual grounds for . . . acceptance [of an interpretation] in addition to the typical ones. (*SE*, 5: 352–53)

The Freudian interpreter is "thus obliged, in dealing with those elements of the dream-content which must be recognized as symbolic, to adopt a combined technique, which on the one hand rests on the dreamer's associations and on the other hand fills the gaps from the interpreter's knowledge of symbols" (*SE* 5: 353).

I use Freud's Irma dream, as well as dreams of former students and patients, to explicate the "dream work" of condensation, symbolization, dramatization, displacement, secondary revision, and additional defensive strategies. The Irma dream is especially effective for this because it persuasively conveys the power of such disavowed affects as guilt, shame, worry, envy, jealousy, anger, humiliation, hatred, and revenge, and their displacement in the various images and narrative lines of Freud's dream. Condensation is evident insofar as Freud associates Irma with several patients, his wife, his daughter Mathilda, a patient also named Mathilda who died under his care from sulphonal, and his friend Fleischl von Marrxow, who died of a cocaine overdose after Freud recommended the drug to him. I use Max Schur's account of the Irma dream (Schur 1966; 45–85) to show that Irma also apparently represents both the patient Emma and Freud himself, upon whose noses Wilhelm Fliess operated. Students are struck by how seemingly "un-Freudian" the Irma dreams seems to be, since sex is hardly mentioned at all. I exploit this observation to emphasize that psychoanalysis is about disavowed affects of all kinds—some good, some bad—not just about sexuality, even in Freud's broad sense.

I present the class with several short dreams to practice what they have learned, even if "wildly." In the first, a male pre-med senior sees a bull on a small hill at a slight distance. The bull charges him, his horns aimed at the dreamer's genitals. The dreamer's only comment about the dream's meaning is that Freud could not be right that he is worried about castration because "I have no problems with my fiancée in that area." My students are very creative in imagining all the various things this simple dream could mean. I let them associate for awhile before mentioning the associations I shared with the dreamer: the Merrill Lynch bull, the similarity of "fiancée" with "finance" and "bullshit" in reference to the sexual meaning of dreams. When I shared these associations with the dreamer, who took the course a few years ago, they triggered in him thoughts about his precarious financial situation and his extreme discomfort with the prospect of his fiancée, a nurse, working to pay his way through medical school. It turned out that he did feel that his masculinity was threatened by these arrangements. Although he had no problems with sexual potency, he and his girlfriend were experiencing inexplicable tensions in their relationship that seemed related to their plans for him to be totally financially dependent on her after graduation. By thinking of dream interpretation as "bullshit" and countering his doubts with the narcissistic assertion that "I have no problems . . . in that area," he managed to keep himself from exploring and understanding the sources of tensions in his relationship with his fiancée.

In the second dream, I ask the class to interpret a young mother's dream that she is driving her car while a serial murderer is attacking her young daughter in the back seat. The murderer has a knife; her daughter's thigh is bleeding from an open wound. Typically, students first think the dreamer feels threatened in some way in her external life, until I tell them that houses and cars often represent the self. This makes the murderer in the dream the abusive part of herself. And she does, in fact, feel profoundly guilty about her severe, "out-of-control" abuse of her youngest child. She fears that she has permanently harmed her beloved daughter. But the murderer also represents the dreamer's own abusive mother. In this reading, she is the daughter who is bleeding. She associates the blood with her first menses, which she believes was a traumatic experience because her mother failed to prepare her adequately, and has left her with feelings of being permanently damaged, like her mother.

In a third dream, a thirty-year-old male patient is moving into a new apartment on the top floor of a mile-high apartment building in Rio de Janeiro. He is delighted when a dark-haired older neighbor appears to welcome him, and imagines that they will become good friends. Students are quick to suggest that a mile-high erection might represent a bit of narcissistic phallic grandiosity. Usually, some student will wonder if the location indicates that the dreamer is gay, which he is. But narcissistic grandiosity represents more than the dreamer's sexual fantasies about himself. In my work with this patient, we came to see that the mile-high apartment building also implies a desire for autonomy and emotional distance far from areas of current distress in his life, such as his deteriorating relationship with his lover. The neighbor represents the dreamer's wish for a fresh start with a new boyfriend, who reminds him of the analyst, with whom he is in treatment for deep depression and self-destructive, unprotected sexual behavior.

Psychic Determinism/Moral Responsibility

By this point, students are prepared to tackle the third topic on the syllabus: psychic determinism and moral responsibility. For this, I provide them with passages on psychic determinism from Freud's *The Psychopathology of Everyday Life* and quotations from Freud's technical papers on autonomy and psychoanalysis' freedom-enhancing goals. I assign Freud's remarkable essay, "Moral Responsibility for the Content of Dreams" (*SE* 19: 131–34), along with the chapters on determinism and moral responsibility in Wallwork, *Psychoanalysis and Ethics* (1991), chapters 3 and 4. Beginning with the standard view that Freud is a determinist, I pose the paradox: How can Freud be a determinist if he views analysis as enhancing freedom of choice?

"Psycho-analysts are marked by a particularly strict belief in the determination of mental life," Freud writes (*SE* 11: 38). Yet "analysis . . . sets[s] out . . . to give the patient's ego *freedom* to decide one way or the other" (*SE* 19: 50 n1). This paradox stimulates interest in the various forms of soft and hard determinism, leading to the conclusion that what Freud says about "psychic determinism" is not at all equivalent to hard metaphysical determinism—that is, the doctrine that human action could not be other than it is. Freud is primarily interested in arguing that seemingly arbitrary, meaningless actions, such as slips of the tongue and pen, are not random happenings but motivated behaviors. Motives are causes of behavior for Freud, but not the sorts of causes that determine results, in the sense of hard determinism modeled on the natural sciences. True, unconscious motives may compel behavior, but the person who knows his own motives by "owning" previously unconscious motivations is capable of choosing among a limited range of reasons for action. In his mature theory, Freud ascribes choice to the mature ego.

If psychoanalysis is compatible with moral responsibility, I then ask, how do we know when someone is in fact responsible? In this connection, we read and discuss a *New York Times* article, "Mother Who Killed: Loss, Betrayal and a Search for a Fairy Tale Life," which addresses whether Susan Smith was responsible for murdering her two sons when she released the brake on her car and allowed it to roll into a lake, apparently with the hope of marrying her wealthy boyfriend, who had broken off their affair on the grounds that he did not want a ready-made family. The article points out that Mrs. Smith was sexually abused as a child by her stepfather, a pillar in the local Christian Coalition, and suffered what the defense called a "split personality." But it also quotes neighbors to the effect that she was simply trying to get what she wanted—a rich husband. Murdering her kids was a despicable means to that end. Was she mentally ill at the time of the murder or, as one neighbor suggested, only a manipulative narcissist? I ask the class to imagine that they are the jurors. After extensive debate, they usually conclude that Mrs. Smith should be deemed morally responsible in the sense that she could have acted otherwise than she did when she strapped her boys into their car seats and pulled the handbrake, even though she seems to have been under severe emotional stress at the time. In the words of a student this year, "she had an alternative, not to pull the handbrake." They also hold her responsible for going on TV subsequently and accusing a phantom black man of kidnapping her children. It takes awhile to arrive at this point, however, and the arguments pertaining to her mental state show how ambivalent we are about how we decide cases like this.

At this point in the course, students write their dream papers, which provide a more personally meaningful opportunity for them to engage in the kind of self-observation and self-scrutiny that psychoanalysis commends. I instruct students to divide the paper into three sections, as Freud does in presenting the Irma dream: the first describes the raw dream, the second summarizes their associations to the dream, the third provides their interpretation of what they believe the dream is about. The dream papers typically discuss anxieties about separation from parents and former friends and struggles with intimate relationships, with roommates as well as romantic and sexual partners. Some papers focus poignantly on guilt feelings—about betraying a loved one, lying or failing at a job; some deal with deep psychopathologies, such as gender dysphoria, suicidal depression, and unassimilated traumatic experiences due to rape or violent attack. A common weakness lies in the difficulty students, like everyone else, have spotting their own defensive operations. I typically invite students whose papers indicate a potentially severe psychological problem to come to my office to talk. Most take me up on it, and almost every year I end up making several referrals for psychotherapy.

The Problem of Reading Freud

It is only after familiarizing students with psychoanalytic technique, dream interpretation, and the autonomy and responsibility-enhancing aims of treatment that I approach Freudian theory by raising the question, How does one read Freud? By this point (the beginning of the fourth week), students have read enough Freud to appreciate that his interpretative work is far more complex than the usual readings of the metapsychology would lead one to believe. Familiarity with Freud's interpretative work prepares students for the argument I present in my discussion of reading Freud in *Psychoanalysis and Ethics*, chapter 2. Contending that Freudian metatheory is no less important than his interpretative work, I propose that Freud should be read dialectically, by moving back and forth between what he says at the levels of the metapsychology and clinical interpretations.

In class, we study several texts in which Freud writes against the grain of his own metatheoretical speculations, and I identify some of the ways Freud fiddles with his metapsychology in order to reach views compatible with what he knows at the level of ordinary experience and clinical practice. This approach to the hermeneutical problem of reading Freud differs from Paul Ricoeur's, who in my view takes the metapsychology far too seriously. Freud himself expresses great caution with respect to his metapsychological enterprise, and repeatedly describes the metapsychology as "tentative," "speculative," and "hypothetical" (see *SE* 14: 77; 14: 234; 18: 59; 20: 32–33, 59; 23: 225), even going so far as to call it a "myth," a "phantasy," a product of wish fulfillment on his part (*SE* 22: 95, 212; 23: 225). Although Freud never abandons his commitment to the metapsychology's scientific aims, he cautions readers to treat it as a scaffolding that will need to be dismantled.

I stress Freud's treatment of the human mind as an unfathomable mystery, in part because it underscores the acknowledged limitations of his theory, but also because it expresses a certain religious sensibility. In a now well-known footnote in *The Interpretation of Dreams*, Freud states: "There is at least one spot in every dream at which it is unplumbable—a navel, as it were, that is its point of contact with the unknown" (*SE*, 4: 111, n.1). Elsewhere, Freud keenly recognizes that psychoanalysts work all the time with a large unknown factor: "We know [only] two kinds of things about . . . our psyche (or mental life): firstly, its bodily organ and scene of action, the brain . . . And . . . [secondly], our acts of consciousness, which are immediate data and cannot be further explained. . . . Everything that lies between is unknown to us, and the data do not include any direct relation between these two terminal points of our knowledge" (*SE* 23: 144). Thus, despite his this-worldly naturalism, Freud remained profoundly aware of the degree to which we live in the world darkly. Our insights are always partial, our knowledge incomplete. Freud's stance here is close to Wilfred Cantwell Smith's description of "positive secularism," which acknowledges a sense of mystery-yet-to-be-explored as a part of secularism, as opposed to "negative secularism," which denies the existence of any such mystery (see Wallwork and Wallwork 1989, 168).

Ethics, Religion, and Morality

I conclude the Freud part of the course with several weeks on the deep ethic that informs Freud's interpretation of religion and morals. One aim here is to help students appreciate the special moral stance toward oneself and others that has evolved within the psychoanalytic tradition, which involves being simultaneously completely present emotionally and also sufficiently removed to explore the psychodynamics of what is going on and think critically about various interpretations, options, moral principles, and values. The psychoanalytic stance simultaneously involves both passion and reflection and calls for a special kind of tolerance toward oneself and others that avoids harsh judgments and cultivates nonjudgmental openness, curiosity and a willingness to restrain the inclination to retaliate in kind when attacked. I find that some students typically fear that if you experience morally unacceptable fantasies, motives, and emotions, you will inevitably act on them, while others imagine that *thinking* about feelings inevitably entails distancing oneself so that one does not *feel* when one thinks morally. Considerable discussion is necessary for them to appreciate the psychoanalytic view of these issues.

I find that reading Freud's critique of religion and superego moralism through his ethic provides the best angle from which to understand his critical positions (see *Psychoanalysis and Ethics*, chapters 9–14). This approach, based on Freud as proponent of an alternative ethic, also makes Freud's famous critiques more interesting and accurate than more familiar readings aimed at Freud as determinist, reductionist, or egoist. I enhance the material by staging classroom debates in which students are asked to argue that "Freud's critique of religion is right on target" versus "Freud misses what is most essential about religious faith."

I start the search for Freud's own ethic with his discussion of the meaning of life in *Civilization and Its Discontents*, chapter 2, where he aligns psychoanalysis with the classical goal of happiness in life, not pleasure in the narrow, hedonistic sense too often ascribed to him. Freud proceeds to identify eleven different "paths" or "strategies" for achieving happiness, as recommended by various "schools of ancient wisdom" and practiced by ordinary people (*SE* 21: 77). Students usually read Freud as if these eleven paths are simply different "means" to the same end of happiness, but a close reading of the text reveals that Freud carefully distinguishes "negative" paths of coping defensively with un-pleasure from "positive" paths that aim at qualitatively distinct, robust pleasurable mental states. Freud, it turns out, disapproves of the "negative" paths, which include isolation from others, intoxication, asceticism, illusion, and delusion. He writes against isolating oneself from others, stating that "there is, indeed, another and better path: that of becoming a member of the human community," and against "intoxicants," declaring that they are dangerous and "injurious." By contrast, Freud endorses the remaining five paths to happiness: participation in the human community, sublimation (such as the pursuit of knowledge and artistic creativity), mutual love, aesthetic enjoyment, and freedom, as each embodies a qualitatively distinct enjoyment that is valuable both for itself and for the very special contribution it makes to the inclusive end of happiness in life as a whole.

To get the class to struggle with whether pleasure is the sole intrinsic good, as some interpreters of Freud contend, I borrow from Robert Nozick and instruct them to imagine an "experience machine" at the front of the room that is capable of creating the illusion of any experience by artificially stimulating the brain (Nozick 1974, 42–45). An individual in the machine would fully experience whatever desirable scenarios he or she wanted, such as writing a great novel or having great sex, while plugged into the machine and doing nothing at all. He or she would not be conscious of being connected to a machine, since that would alter the experience. I ask students if, after selecting the most desirable experiences they can imagine over a lifetime, they would choose to be plugged into a virtual machine for the rest of their lives, never again to become conscious of where they are. Some initially respond, "Why not?" But as the discussion proceeds, even these students begin to realize that they value not just pleasurable, subjective mental states, but actually doing what they value and being in contact with reality and other persons. The value of love is not only in the subjective emotion but also in actually loving someone. As the realization dawns that entering the machine is a form of suicide, most students usually decide that they would not choose to enter because they would have to sacrifice values and goods that are important to them, beyond subjective pleasurable sensations.

I then ask, "Would Freud attach himself to the machine or recommend it to others?" "Obviously, he would not," they tell me. Freud's main criticism of religious illusion is that it is untrue, even though, from a strictly hedonistic perspective, religious faith might be desirable: "It soothes the fears that men feel of the dangers and vicissitudes of life . . . assures them of a happy ending and offers them comfort in unhappiness" (SE 22: 161). Freud, it turns out, actually works with a concept of happiness that is closer to the Aristotelian ideal of functioning well than the utilitarian notion of feeling good. A psychoanalysis that ended with the patient becoming a happy alcoholic or drug addict would not be considered a success. The aim of psychoanalysis is to enable neurotics to play with a full psychic deck in meeting the difficulties of living head-on.

For Freud's critique of the love commandment, I assign selected rabbinic and Christian commentaries in conjunction with Freud's discussion of the love commandment in *Civilization and Its Discontents*, chapters 4–8. Students see that Freud's animus is directed not against a love ethic as such, but against a particularly naive, overly grandiose version that historically has been too often used to justify wanton aggression against outsiders, deemed inferior for ascribing to less heroic ideals. That established, we turn to the important issue of how analytic self-reflection might enhance one's ability to be moral. Although Freud is often held singularly responsible for the unabashed selfishness, privatism, and narcissism of our "psychological" era (see Rieff 1961; Bellah et al. 1985), I see the Freudian critique of the love commandment as posing a challenge to find a new and different way of understanding how to be moral (see Wallwork 1986, 1991). Suspicion of one's own moralistic motives is a crucial aspect of a psychodynamic reformulation of ethics.

I end the Freud part of the course by asking two questions: What did Freud ultimately trust? And what were his primary ethical commitments? The first question is addressed by having students read selections from *Future of an Illusion* and *Beyond the Pleasure Principles* (which is Freud's most metaphysical text). Certainly, Freud shows a certain "religious" sensibility when he writes movingly of the individual's "insignificance or impotence in the face of the universe." Whatever else one says about the Freudian self, the individual lives with an acute sense of vulnerability to the vicissitudes of forces and powers beyond the capacity of human beings to control. Freud is also acutely sensitive to the deep mysteries that surround human existence. We do not know ourselves or our environments very well. Most of our theories are temporary "scaffoldings," the products of "secondary elaboration," obsessionality, and wish fulfilment. Freud ultimately places his trust in what he calls "my God, *logos*," and it is clear that for him, as for the Stoics, Reason structures reality. Freud has faith that the human mind can know truths because he believes that the mind is constructed to discern structures that exist external to the mind itself. In *Beyond the Pleasure Principle*, Freud moves more daringly into the realm of metaphysics and names the twin forces at work in all matter, Eros and Thanatos.

The second question about Freud's ethic is partly answered by his treatment of the multiple intrinsic goods (knowledge, beauty, love, autonomy, community, creativity) that are appreciated by the comparatively well-functioning person. Love is a key norm for Freud, which is one reason he is so critical of alternative love ethics, such as the commandment to Love Thy Neighbor as Thyself, as traditionally interpreted. The two moral pathologies in intimate love are self-love, or narcissism, on the one hand, and excessive idealization and self-depreciation on the other. The golden mean is mutual love, "loving and being loved." Freud commends respect for others, but only insofar as the legitimate claims of the self are similarly respected. Individuals are better off when they contribute to their communities, but communal obligations are balanced by special duties to family members and friends. The key to success in living morally lies less in the normative guidelines themselves, which Freud takes for granted, than in how moral values and principles are held psychologically.

The post-Freudian half of my course changes from year to year. My goal is to highlight the main developments in the evolution of psychoanalytic theory and their implications for the study of religion and morality after Freud's death. To me, this means covering at least the rudiments of Jungian analytic psychology; the neo-Freudian "humanistic" movement represented by Erich Fromm and Karen Horney; psychoanalytic ego psychology (Anna Freud, Heinz Hartmann, Erik Erikson); object relations theory (Melanie Klein, Winnicott, Ana-Maria Rizzuto, W.W. Meissner), and self-psychology (Heinz Kohut, E. Wolf, Peter Homans). Because only some of these developments and figures can be studied with care in any one year, I select two or three for full exploration and give short synopses of the other developments. I also acquaint students with some developments in post-Freudian theology and ethics that respond to some of Freud's concerns—for example, Tillich's view of God beyond God, and the Other in postmodernism. Most recently, I have used Fromm and Erikson alongside Tillich and Levinas. I try to show how each figure calls for a revision of Freud's seminal work, and the implications of these revisions for the understanding of religion and morality/ethics, including especially reinterpretations of the love commandment.

When I first started teaching Freud I thought that his followers improved on his work, but I have felt for some years that Freud remains an important critic of his followers, and so I try to help my students think about how Freud would critique Fromm, Tillich, Erikson, and Levinas, as well as how they critique him.

References

Bellah, Robert N. et al. 1985. *Habits of the heart*. Berkeley: University of California Press.

Freud, Ernest, L., ed. 1975. *Letters of Sigmund Freud*. New York: Basic Books.

Freud, Sigmund. 1953–1974. *The standard edition of the complete psychological works of Sigmund Freud (SE)*, Volumes 1–24, Translated and edited by James Strachey. London: Hogarth Press.

1900. *Interpretations of dreams*. SE 4:1–338 and 5:339–621.

1910. *Five lectures on psycho-analysis*. SE 11:9–55.

1910. "Wild" psycho-analysis. *SE* 11:221–27.

1912. The dynamics of transference. *SE* 12:99–108.

1914. On narcisism: An introducion." *SE* 14:73–102.

1914. Remembering, repeating and working-through. *SE* 12:147–56.

1915. Observations on transference love. *SE* 12:159–71.

1917. A metapsychological supplement to the thery of dreams. *SE* 14:222–35.

1920. *Beyond the pleasure principle*. SE 18:7–64.

1923. Two encyclopaedia articles. *SE* 18: 235–59.

1923. *The ego and the id*. SE 19:10–59.

1925. Some additional notes on dream-interpretation as a whole. *SE* 19:127–38.

1925. *An autobiographical study*. SE 20:7–74.

1930. *Civilization and its discontents*. SE 21:64–145.

1933. *New introductory lectures on psycho-analysis*. SE 22:5–182.

1937. Analysis terminable and interminable. *SE* 23:216–53.

1940. *An outline of psycho-analysis. SE* 23:144–207.

———. 1959. *Collected Papers (CP)*, Vols. 1–5. New York: Basic Books.

Grunbaum, Adolf. 1984. *The foundations of psychoanalysis*. Berkeley: University of California Press.

Nozick, Robert. 1974. *Anarchy, state and utopia*. New York: Basic Books.

Parsons, Anne. 1969. *Belief, magic, and anomie: Essays on psychosocial anthropology*. New York: Free Press.

Rieff, Philip. 1961. *Freud: The mind of the moralist*. Garden City, N.Y.: Doubleday, Anchor Books.

Schur, Max. 1966. Some additional "day residues" of the "Specimen dream of psychoanalysis." In *Psychoanalysis—a general psychology*, edited by R. M. Loewenstein, L. M. Newman, M. Schur, and A. J. Solnit. New York: International Universities Press.

Waelder, Robert. 1964. *Basic theory of psychoanalysis*. New York: Schocken Books.

Wallwork, Ernest. 1986. A constructive Freudian alternative to psychotherapeutic egoism. *Soundings* 69: 145–64.

———. 1991. *Psychoanalysis and ethics*. New Haven, Conn.: Yale University Press.

———. 1995. Sexuality in society. 1. Social control of sexual behavior. In *Encyclopedia of Bioethics*, rev. ed. 5: 2386–92.

———. 2000. Psychodynamic contributions of religion ethics: Toward reconfiguring askesis. *The Annual of the Society of Christian Ethics, 1999*, Vol. 19: 167–89.

Wallwork, Ernest, and Anne Wallwork. 1989. A psychoanalytic perspective on religion. In *Religion and psychoanalysis*, edited by Joseph H. Smith. Psychoanalysis and the Humanities Series. Baltimore: Johns Hopkins University Press.

Weber, Max. 1963. *The sociology of religion*. Boston: Beacon Press.

14

Teaching Freud's Teachings

James E. Dittes

What do we want to teach when we set out to "teach Freud"? From the rich mélange of themes and texts and biographies and commentaries and cases, from the prodigal Freudian legacy, what does one choose to render "Freud"?

How do we decide? What criteria do we use for determining what material is "Freud"?

Do we try to choose what is most distinctive, what of his legacy most sets him apart from other figures, other thinkers?

Do we try to judge what has had the most impact on the contemporary mind and culture?

Do we favor what is most accessible and of most interest to contemporary undergraduates? Should we avoid what is either so concrete in psychological case study or so abstract in philosophizing as to become quickly too technical to sustain student interest?

Should we make the effort to judge what was of most interest—even what was of passionate concern—to Freud? What questions did he most persevere in addressing? What, finally, did he most care about?

As custodians of Freud's legacy, a century after Freud's manifesto, *The Interpretation of Dreams*, what do we highlight? What do we bring into focus and what do we let stay in the background?

I think there is a package of Freudian wisdom—strategies for maneuvering life—that most of us intend to teach when we "teach Freud" just because this package does meet all these criteria: distinctiveness, impact, accessibility, salience to students, highly cathected for Freud, of lifelong passionate concern to him. It is this set of insights that sustained, gripped his attention, surmounting pain and other torture in his final years. These appear especially to be the wisdom that animates his final books, the legacy he wanted to transmit. These are Freud's "teachings."

This wisdom is at a middle level of abstraction—"metapsychology" perhaps, not the technical psychological analysis, not the relatively unreflective broad metaphysical preferences. These are the tools and premises, the theorems and the strategies with which one negotiates the daily adventures and risks of life. The Freudian legacy we transmit—whether in a consulting room or a classroom—is a homily on how to live. How to tolerate reality. How to survive and, yes, even how to aspire to an abundant life.

This wisdom is the testimony of Freud the passionate participant in life, not the cool analysis by Freud the detached observer.

Theorems and Strategies: The Teachings of Freud

Here are some of the theorems and strategies that Freud recommended for negotiating life, some of the piecemeal verities, the working hypotheses, the analytic tools and convictions, the recipes that, hard-won, are essential and reliable not just for the practitioner of psychoanalytic therapy but also for the practitioner of life. These are the stepping stones by which you can make your way through the eddies of reality.

(1) Vulnerability is fundamental to the human condition, but is a threat to human survival. It can be contained and limited by vigilance and resourcefulness. Indeed, it *must* be controlled and managed, at least disguised. Dependence on others must be avoided, for safety's sake. So Freud insisted almost all his life until perhaps at the end he would come to trust vulnerability not only as inevitable (part of the Creation, so to speak) but also as containing its own gifts and resources (part of the Redemption, so to speak).

(2) Whatever is of significance occasions enigma and mystery, so that, conversely, enigma and mystery signal and locate significance.

(3) Mystery is to be solved, not savored. There *are* answers to our existential and intellectual dilemmas, and these answers can be discerned and expressed in human terms. If God talks to us, it is in our language, not God's.

(4) Expect multiple, layered meanings. Truth comes in layers, which can be analyzed, so that different levels of truth can be perceived simultaneously. Outer layers are not untruth, just not the whole truth. Outer layers both reveal and conceal the truth of inner layers. They encode and give metaphor to what *can* be stated more plainly, but usually is not. The outer layers function to provide protection and comfort. Therefore access to inner layers is governed largely by fear and safety but requires finally a commitment of will.

(5) Whatever is of significance occasions ambivalence and inconsistency, blending strong reactions of attraction and avoidance, love and hate, trust and fear. The most adaptive responses are those that simultaneously express both the attraction and the avoidance. Conversely, ambivalence and inconsistency signal and locate significance.

(6) Continuities are profound and demand recognition. Conventional boundaries and dualisms—such as unconscious / conscious, child / adult—convenient as they are, mislead us. In fact, the irrational shapes the rational; the rational manages the irrational; children face dilemmas once thought reserved to adults; childhood trauma persists into adulthood.

(7) Yet maturity requires interrupting these continuities and acknowledging distinctions. For example, the rational can be (virtually) autonomous and can withstand and contain the irrational; events traumatic to the child need not be so for the adult.

(8) All utterance is autobiography. Our most earnest and rigorous efforts at "objective" accounting—whether of the animate or the inanimate, ideologies and epochs, credos and their predicates, the grand or the trivial—every accounting we make is not nearly so self-contained and autonomous as we pretend, but is contingent; it is, in some significant measure, an accounting of our selves. The motifs and themes, the patterns and contours I claim I detect in the history are unwitting metaphors for my own story, or even unwitting agents in its own unfolding. This is as true for utterances deemed systematic theories as for dream reports, as true for accounts rendered around a seminar table as for stories told around a campfire. Though we all (including Freud) want to claim immunity from such internally imposed spin, the autobiography permeates (including the autobiographical overtones to be found in Freud's writing). Communication is more futile than necessary, relationships more sterile, when we fail to hear the autobiography. (Freud thought he knew which motifs, which dramatic plots would emerge as our stories. At least he had his favorite metaphors, the dramas of the unsolvable dilemmas and insufferable traumas of infancy, especially the sexual dilemmas and traumas. But he respected the individual's own variation on the theme.)

(9) All autobiography is constructed. It is given "spin"—as we can say now that modern journalistic idiom has caught up with the traditional awareness that the teller of tales is spinning them. As honestly as I may aspire to tell my "real" story it comes out artfully rendered—a self-portrait—as I *want* to be seen.

(10) Yet, as essential as it is to recognize that the account of reality is shaped by desire and wish, it is urgent to try to disentangle the two. Murderous wishes, for example, must have different status from murderous deeds.

It is in such cadences as these, I think, that we express the teachable Freud, and, I contend, the essential Freud. Some such constellation of principles as these is what constitutes psychoanalysis. Whether that analysis is turned to the therapy of an individual, the interpretation of a text, the representation of a culture, or is left (for awhile) in the classroom as one more unselected option on the menu of liberal education, to venture such habits of the mind is to venture Freudian psychoanalysis.

To approach any problem of living or problem of the intellect with perspectives like these is to psychoanalyze. To psychoanalyze—to assemble the principles just inventoried—is to probe relentlessly every utterance and activity for intention, for the passion, the hunger that fuels and drives behavior and words. To psychoanalyze is to decode the utterance and the behavior, to allow them to reveal intention and passion and hunger, to interpret their meaning. To psychoanalyze is to recognize how the utterance and the behavior obscure and hide the meaning; more than that, psychoanalysis is the art of exploiting this covering to discover the meaning. To psychoanalyze is to discover, by exploring the daily routines and trivial pursuits, how a person addresses the universal, fundamental questions of existence.

This is not the place to argue that these brief formulations provide an accurate and complete restatement of Freud's legacy. I am quite ready to accept the judgment that they do not. (For the present purposes, I would be quite content to have my inventory of "theorems and strategies" be replaced, for example, by Philip Rieff's (1959) inventory of assumptions and implications and to have my assertion of "pastoral" intent be replaced by his exegesis of Freud's "moral" intent.) But even if my inventory of "theorems and strategies" may not define psychoanalysis, they do sample it. They illustrate a class of formulations that take Freud at a level of abstraction and generalization and at a degree of practical, even existential—even pastoral—concern that he welcomed and that students welcome and which, therefore, cry out to be taught.

Topics Bypassed

There are other elements of Freud's writing and thought that are candidates for our syllabi, often because they may seem more socially relevant or because they fit more easily into existing courses or because they set up a politically correct critique. But they are distractions, red herrings; they blur the focus on Freud.

Two favorites are, Was Freud religious? And, Was Freud Jewish? People persist in needing to make a case (inevitably oversimplified) that Freud was inside or was outside of some such identifying boundary.

Favorite targets frequently set up for classroom target practice are the unexamined cultural prejudices, such as those about gender roles and sexual identities, which were Freud's because they were part of the culture that he was part of.

If we determine to teach Freud's psychology, we find ourselves enmeshed in the constantly rearranged quaint metaphors and neologisms with which he—or his translators—attempted to portray psychological processes and regimens. Our blackboard diagrams soon pall.

It is sometimes tempting to teach "Freud the man"—to uncover the distinctive character and history of this enigmatic and often distraught personality—as the essential Freud. It is easy, for example, in this age of gender studies, to focus on the habitual cycle of high rapture and hostile rupture that he imposed on relationships with men colleagues.(substitute fathers, brothers, and sons). It is tempting to examine his preoccupation with "father issues," to the determined neglect of "mother issues"—even while his own forceful mother was part of his household almost all of his adult life. Some even find it still tempting to pursue the possibility of a romantic affair with his wife's sister.

But these are distractions, sometimes titillating but not of great importance. If we would "teach Freud" what is important and essential about him is not what was peculiar or particular about his personal history, nor what was deepest in his unconscious. What *is* most essential and teachable about Freud is to be found in his human experience, to be sure, but in that human experience which he shares with all of us, that which is inevitable, that which is relatively universal, that which is relatively conscious—for example, Freud's encounter with the accumulating fragilities of aging.

To be sure, Freud—and Freudians and anti-Freudians—have spent many words on these issues. Yet we know that to do that in the classroom soon becomes tedious, a cultish exercise in reciting (or refuting) a text. We are missing or blunting the message within the text, the metapsychology, the modes of thinking that are to be employed if we are to try to think like Freud, to practice psychoanalysis.

Implications for Teaching

If teaching "Freud" aims to focus on the cluster of Freud's "wisdom" as proposed here, there are several implications for the teaching.

Locating Freud's Own Religious Legacy

Why teach Freud in religious studies? Why should members of this guild feel sufficiently commissioned as custodians of Freud's legacy to construct a volume pondering how to teach Freud? There are many good answers to that question. The reflections in this chapter provide one of them. Freud's metapsychical wisdom, his theorems and stratagems, can be regarded as his religion. He would not have done so, and perhaps you prefer not to. But it can be so regarded.

In approaching this Freud, we approach a man struggling to form and to share a working life philosophy, to learn the arts of meaning-making, to encounter the world in manageable terms and proportions, to honor the limits and demands of Creation, yet to survive, even flourish. He has wrestled with reality (not with God; that was for Jacob—his father's namesake and nemesis) for what meager blessing it can yield. If the contest has left him limping a bit, that is better than crawling. The fruits of that lifelong wrestling, limps and scars and all, become his credo, his teaching, as to how things are and how one best fits into how things are.

Freud codified the rules for relating to reality. They demand fierce and thorough compliance, or one suffers. This is how the individual encounters the universal, the fundamental, the inevitable. Freud displayed and demanded skills in the arts of pursuing the questions behind the questions, the answers beyond the answers, the rigors of wrestling a blessing from the mysteries of life. He made the desperate demand, this intemperate archeologist of the living soul, that the unfathomable give up its secrets. The legacy of Freud is not the vocabulary he invented, the entities he posited, the processes he theorized, the histories he tracked. These were temporarily convenient vehicles and mechanisms and hypotheses. But they were disposable. As Freud wrote more and more from his heart, particularly in his final books, he wrote less and less about things like Oedipus and obsession and more and more about things like survival and purpose, the fundamental questions.

It is over such issues as these that Freud stubbornly proselytized, displayed, and demanded from adherents unrelenting often unreflective commitment, fought sectarian battles, and encouraged cultish routines.

Why let a class get overinvolved in reciting (or attacking) Freud's rather dreary, unoriginal, often uninformed, and adolescent critiques of conventional religion when he poses such vibrant and robust, if unsystematic, alternatives?

The Issues Worth Fighting About

These theorems identify major issues with which to make connection, comparison, and contrast with other thinkers. The debates carried on between Freud and others (especially perhaps Jungians), and the development of Freudian ways of thinking (especially perhaps those of the postmodern flavor), tend to be about just these metapsychological issues and are most easily interpreted with these issues made explicit. The early defections (e.g., Adler, Horney, Jung) tended to be based—so we have conventionally been told—on more concrete psychological issues (e.g., *which* drive can be identified as the major force in human development?). But later debates, even with these early defectors, seem to be about these metapsychological theorems and strategies, so that understanding *them* clearly helps to understand the debates more clearly.

Accessing Freud's Teachings as He Did—
Through Experience

Freud did not garner this set of wisdom by deriving it from systematic thinking, his own or others'. He derived it from piecemeal accumulating observations and his reflections on what he observed. He observed the actual experience of people, himself foremost, then codified, as unblinkingly as he could, what he observed. Why should we not, even in the classroom, take the same route when it is available, accessing his ideas through the experience that generated them and shaped them?

This strategy is most easily illustrated in teaching two books of Freud's maturity, *Civilization and Its Discontents,* Freud's most taught book; and *Moses and Monotheism*, his most baffling book. Freud professed to find both books unsatisfactory, perhaps for the same reasons students often do: when taken as books—as autonomous documents out of biographical context—they are enigmatic, impossible to parse or paraphrase or render into preces.

They make the most sense when understood as metapsychical homilies struggling to convey Freud's best wisdom about the strategies and theorems of living. They make the most sense when understood in the context of Freud's own encounter with some of the painful verities of life. The continuities and the differences between the two books can be most sharply discerned when they are read for the metapsychology and when the drastic changes in Freud's circumstances over the intervening ten years is kept in the forefront.

If *Civilization and Its Discontents* has a theme, I think it is the desperate warning that vulnerability leads to pain, suffering, and death; vulnerability is to be avoided at all costs. As attractive a guise and as official a sanction as vulnerability may bear, it is a trap. If *Moses and Monotheism* has a theme, I think it is the search to affirm vulnerability as a path to life and fulfillment. I think the difference is in the relentless and overwhelming and undeniable vulnerability that Freud has come to experience; even this robust old Stoic, this mocker of wishful thinking, has come to discover vulnerability as a fact of life, a harbinger of life.

Civilization and Its Discontents

What is the gist, the message, the intention of *Civilization and Its Discontents*? I ask students to find out by approaching the book this way.

You are visiting Sigmund Freud at his summer retreat, at a location called Snow Corner in the Bavarian resort area of Berchtesgaden. It is 1929. Freud has moved his household to these mountains every summer for decades. He receives you with all courtesy and invites you to sit by him in the white wicker chairs in the garden. Bourgeois that he is, he is impeccably dressed in a three-piece suit, and his manners are equally exemplary. His chow Lin Yug lies at his feet. His daughter Anna hovers nearby, attentive to a fault. There is no sign of his wife, and he doesn't mention her.

He graciously evades your inquiry about his health. But you know that at seventy-three—as for the last dozen years—he is in constant pain from cancer of the jaw, and severely inconvenienced by the prosthesis which is supposed to replace the roof of his mouth but that never fits right. With his speech and eating thus handicapped and his hearing and vision fading, he shuns company. He seems subdued. When he refers to Anna as "my Antigone" he is casting himself as the blinded, lamed, and doomed Oedipus.

He is willing to chat about the ominous times, on the verge of severe economic depression and political mayhem. Adolf Hitler, on the verge of power, is spending the summer nearby in the same Berchtesgaden mountain area. Already Freud knows there is serious reason to fear for his legacy, still largely identified with German-speaking Jews. Psychoanalysts are having difficulty getting patients. Psychoanalytic publications are waning, and the organization of psychoanalysts is dissolving. Most alarming—Freud reveals his chauvinism—there is emerging a hint that psychoanalysts will emigrate to America! Freud himself is financially dependent on the largesse of wealthy women disciples and admirers. If you commit the faux pas of asking about some of the men who have been close disciples, you elicit a bitter remark about their "betrayal." It's a bleak world for him.

He has been writing, but disparages his own work as "banal" and "dilettantish" and a time-filler. "One cannot smoke the whole day long and play cards; I no longer have staying power for walking, and most of what one can read no longer interests me. I wrote, and I passed the time with it quite agreeably."

He has just finished the slim book we will come to know as *Civilization and Its Discontents*, and his bleak disparaging tone about the writing project is the message of the book. Life is bleak, unfriendly, and unrewarding, and don't count on being rescued. He warms to share this lifetime of wisdom with you.

If you came to discuss psychology, topics like ego and neurosis and repression, you may be disappointed. Now in his late years Freud is grappling— as perhaps he was less explicitly when he addressed the psychological questions—with questions about the survival and significance of human life. What is most real, and what illusion? What can and cannot be counted on, trusted? How do we know these things? Which will finally prevail—love and life, or death? How can an individual thrive or even survive in a world not friendly to individual needs and desires? How can the finest of human achievement be protected? Freud is confessing to urgent existential questions not very different from those that the student visitor may confess to, and not much more decisively formulated or convincingly answered than the student visitor has achieved. But he shares with the visitor the urgency and earnestness of the questions. And he desperately wants to convey his testimony. He wants to pass on his wisdom as a gift.

Most especially he wants us to benefit from his painful experience and not make the excruciating mistake of trusting what is untrustworthy, the mistake of letting ourselves be enfeebled by becoming dependent on what will not abide and what cannot sustain us. There is bad news: What we are often induced to trust is not trustworthy. But there is good news, which too often gets muffled in the shocked reaction to the bad news; the good news is that we *can*—not just that we should—survive without these unreliable props. Honesty is the key. Dr. Freud is a cool Stoic—one suspects his soul armored by huge scars—when he disdains illusory daydreams and wishes, postures of dependence, all vulnerabilities. But he is passionate when he warms up to celebrate the efficacy of honesty. Discard pretense and wishing. "Get real." Honesty may provide cold comfort, but it is not intended to comfort; it is intended to energize and to harness energies, to put energies to work. Honesty may seem feeble match for the distress and dreams of the human soul, but it is all we have, and it is enough. Dr. Freud almost loses his cool and becomes a preacher, so urgently does he want us to hear and heed this wisdom.

It has been a hard-won wisdom. Freud's life can be told as a sequence of episodes of unrequited and disappointed trust. He was the first-born and favorite of a young and beautiful Jewish mother who doted on her "golden" boy yet who seemed to abandon him at decisive moments, as when her absences for pregnancy and illness sent the toddler storming about the house tearing open closets and cabinets searching for her. Then his beloved nanny was sent packing overnight without warning or explanation. The playmate he should have dominated because the playmate was his nephew was in fact older, bigger, stronger, and quite unwilling to play his proper role as a subordinate.

But if mother, nanny, and nephew could not be relied on to play the roles he was led to expect, neither could his father, remote, unforgiving, unheroic. His most memorable conversation with his father provoked only chagrin and disdain: his father reported that a gentile had knocked his hat off into the street; what had the father done about that, the boy asked, hoping for a hero. The father had bent down in the gutter and retrieved his hat.

Over and over again, throughout his life, men on whom he enthusiastically relied as heros, partners, mentors, or disciples repudiated the assignment and became adversaries. (Jung, whom Freud dubbed "crown prince" and whom he cast as Joshua to his own Moses, repaid this trust, as Freud experienced it, with betrayal, only one of many to do so.)

After a long engagement during which he gave vent to passionate love letters full of longing and promise, Freud found the actuality of marriage dull and confining, and by the age of forty had, apparently, relinquished sex.

The professional career, launched so auspiciously by the Jewish mother who organized the household to support it (her son, the medical student, got the only private room, the best lamp, and the quiet provided when his sisters were denied their piano playing) foundered in the real world of anti-Semitism and entrenched medical theories. The Jewish heritage in which he was raised teased him with the affirmation that he was one of the Chosen People, but being so "chosen" worked out in Freud's experience and in Freud's time to be something quite other than unmitigated blessing.

All these roller coasters of fundamental hopes raised and dashed are part of the reference when Freud warns so vehemently, in *Civilization and Its Discontents*, against making the self vulnerable by trusting in the advertised verities, such as love and God. We treat the book with irresponsible shallowness if we try to abstract it from these still throbbing heartbreaks, and we deprive our students of the points of access with which they can most naturally and fruitfully connect with Freud.

Moses and Monotheism

The same is true for *Moses and Monotheism*, which, taken at face value apart from the life experiences and anxieties, is but a silly and patently wrongheaded, perverse revision of biblical narrative. In approaching this book, too, we owe Freud the courtesy of venturing his own clinical approach: the less sense the account makes rationally, the more we are permitted and required to explore its nonrational referents. We are to respond to the curious with curiosity.

In this case it is a decade of overwhelmingly manifest vulnerability and fragility that is the context, that is the signal of the subtext. When the students pay their hypothetical visit this time, he is wrapped in a blanket, passive, virtually mute, with a near-vacant stare, constantly and solicitously attended. Freud is now totally dependent—for his survival and for what relief from pain and distress that he can muster—on the goodwill and loyalty and resourcefulness of others, on the readiness of others to take chances and make themselves vulnerable. The exodus from Nazi-occupied Vienna to London, which occurs literally in the midst of the book's publication, is totally engineered by others, women being key among them. Even so, death is imminent and Freud is helpless to ward it off. His only remaining control is to hasten it. Any blessing must be found within this reality, not around it.

On the verge of losing his personal battle for survival, watching his people face extermination, the most devastating threat Freud is facing is his fear for the survival of his legacy. What will become of his discoveries and wisdom and disciples? He broods, as he writes the ending pages of *Moses and Monotheism* in London, that Charles Darwin is buried in honor in Westminster Abbey, and Freud probably anticipates what turns out to be the case—that he will not be buried in Westminster Abbey, not even in the nearby cemetery at Hampstead (where Karl Marx's grave has become something of a shrine), but in an inaccessible cemetery much more remote from the center of London. Darwin's teachings have been honored. What will become of Freud's?

In the context of this overwhelming preoccupation with survival, it seems plausible to suppose that this desperate motif of Freud's life would be a dominant motif of this last, highly cathected book. What became of Moses' teachings? Moses, too, offered a set of solid, liberating teachings to his people, to be met with uncertain fate. But they did survive and prevail—the message of the book—survived and prevailed precisely because of Moses' vulnerability and sacrifice.

As the book is usually read in classrooms, without regard to the context here portrayed, the most irritating and irresponsible piece of the story Freud spins is the surmise that Moses was assassinated by his Jewish followers. The only evidence Freud can produce is a fatuous guess by Ernst Sellin that some verses in Hosea imply such an event. But even Sellin had repudiated the idea by the time Freud wrote, and Freud knew that. What do teachers of Freud do with this embarrassment, that the central event in Freud's story is fabricated of such flimsy stuff? Taking the text out of context, we can scold Freud or apologize for him or hurry past.

But in context, the context of Freud's utter vulnerability and of Freud's desperate concern about survival of his teaching, we can discern something momentous in Freud's story: In Freud's account, the assassination is essential for Moses' legacy to survive and prevail. As every father comes to prevail in the life of his son just as a consequence of the son's murderous wishes, so the once disloyal people eventually atoned for their guilt by conceding adherence to Moses' teachings. This, the motif of Freud's last years, is the motif of his last book. Once this motif is identified, other puzzling or annoying or distracting sections of the book fall into line (see Dittes 1991). Taken in context, the most distressing part of the text proves to be the keystone the builders rejected.

We may also be better prepared to notice Freud's shift from suspicion of vulnerability/dependence to a regard for its efficacy by noticing one other change in Freud's life circumstances during the decade that separates the two books. In that decade, Freud's mother has died, this strong and dominant and beautiful woman. Freud now had much less need to protect himself against the traps of dependence and much less need to insist on his own (masculine) independence.

Freud could freely turn his attention to the dynamics of aging. Oedipus, Freud's constant yet ephemeral role model, identified in the Sphinx's riddle a three-stage typology of human life: the four-legged (crawling) stage, the two-legged (upright and striding) stage, and the three-legged (assisted living) stage. Earlier in life and career, Freud was preoccupied with the first two stages. What are the events of infancy that establish, develop, and distort the growth of self, which still tinge the adult stage? How define and encourage that bold upright striding of adulthood, making its way through the morass which surrounds? Now he becomes, by the nagging accumulating enfeeblements of aging and approaching death, able to recognize the stage of the aged as its own legitimate arena of life, with its own rules. Must aging and death be perceived as defects to be avoided and wrestled with and corrected? Or are they defining of life as given and demanding of its own claims? Does one adjust to these verities or adjust them, as the good two-legged ego should? This personal existential question became a question for systematic theorizing.

A different personal theme is sometimes said to pervade and illuminate *Moses and Monotheism*. This is Freud's alleged struggle to discern his own Jewish identity (e.g., Rice 1990; Yerushalmi 1991). This would be excellent illustration of my methodological point if I could agree that this was a burning issue for Freud in his later years. But I am persuaded by Peter Gay's (1987, 1988) judgment that Freud early became comfortable with his secular Jewishness. So the search for this theme in this text tends to run fallow.

Situating Freud's Teaching in Its Existential Context

The first section of this book (at least in the proposed table of contents I have in hand as I write) is called "Institutional and Curricular Contexts." I am not surprised by this choice of keynote. In context is a natural way to "teach Freud." It is probably the most common way anything is taught in the humanities. Pick up this strange piece of the jigsaw puzzle, with its grotesque shape resembling nothing and bearing swaths of color and design that make no sense; twist it and locate it—connect it—fit its contours into their own niche, show how its patternless patterns are part of a larger pattern and thereby achieve a meaning. Historical and cultural patterns are relied on to provide the context that provides the meaning. This is how to teach, how to "teach Freud" or anyone else. The classic "compare and contrast" question: Show how his ideas resemble those who preceded and followed, and how they differ. (Did one directly influence the other, or are they common expressions of the Zeitgeist?—That's a harder question, more often reserved for dissertations than the classroom, a "research" question more than a "teaching" question.)

Balancing that opening section, identifying and illuminating Freud's thought by situating it in historical and intellectual context, this final chapter could be called "Situating Freud's Thinking in its Existential and (Perhaps) Theological Perspective." The ideas—the thinking, the theorizing—that Freud advances are part of an earnest and urgent, even passionate personal quest. What can be trusted? Is (my) human life and aspiration supported or ultimately condemned by what holds power? What promises will be kept? What promises must I keep? How do I find transcendent meaning in the ordinary? In the dialectic of discernment, how to identify what is primary and fundamental and what is secondary and derived, reflected, reactionary? The basic dilemmas of revelation and of salvation are Freud's dilemmas.

Just as "historical" and "cultural" are two terms with virtually overlapping reference, so too "existential" and "theological" may be virtually overlapping. These are the fundamental questions asked about the self in its ultimate context.

But these questions hardly overlap with the historical questions. They are virtually ahistorical. They are the same questions asked by Freud and by the students we teach, and by us the teachers. Historical questions are concerned with particularities and peculiarities; they connect but they also measure distance (between Freud and others, for example). The existential questions are concerned with what is universal, and they measure alliance.

This is a profoundly important reason for teaching Freud at all. His enduring personal passions, expressed in his enduring intellectual passions, coincide with ours and with those of our students.

There still exists a conspiracy of dishonesty in our religious studies classrooms, the pretense that students, and teachers, and authors are not provoked into the "study" of religion by their own personal religious questioning (or else that the personal questioning can be held irrelevant to the study). With supreme irony, we invoke the authority of the humanities to dehumanize ourselves, our students, our authors, and their authority by consigning personal religious quest to the closet or the corridors or the chapel.

We cannot faithfully teach Freud without confronting the restless depths of our own souls.

References

Dittes, James. 1991. Biographical / theological exegesis of psychological texts. *Religion and social order* 1: 37–51.

Gay, Peter. 1987. *A godless jew: Freud, atheism, and the making of psychoanalysis*. New Haven, Conn.: Yale University Press.

————. 1988. *Freud: A life for our time*. New York: W. W. Norton.

Rice, Emanuel. 1990. *Freud and Moses: The long journey home*. Albany: State University of New York Press.

Rieff, Philip. 1959. *Freud: The mind of the moralist*. Chicago: University of Chicago Press.

Yerushalmi, Yosef. 1991. Freud's Moses: Judaism terminable and interminable. New Haven, Conn.: Yale University Press.

Index